Academic Ethics Today

PRAISE FOR *ACADEMIC ETHICS TODAY*

"This is a valuable addition to the growing body of work on the ethical dimensions of higher education. As universities are subjected to moral scrutiny from all points on the political spectrum, its wide-ranging chapters offer models of deeply informed and ethically astute analysis from which we can all learn."

—Randall Curren, University of Rochester

"Professor Steven Cahn is a giant when it comes to academic ethics. This is a must-read for everyone in academe."

—David L. Levinson, Connecticut State Community College

"A timely and provocative anthology by leading philosophers, created by an editor with a lifelong interest in good teaching and ethical administration in higher education."

—Gregory E. Pence, University of Alabama at Birmingham

"Steven Cahn has done a masterful job bringing together diverse and insightful scholars to examine important moral considerations in higher education. From admissions and athletics to technology and tenure, no ethically controversial issue for colleges and universities is off limits. Too often analyses of higher education—and even ethics—are centered on perspectives from the social sciences to the exclusion of the humanities. This volume bucks that trend and importantly centers philosophical thinking; chapter authors lay out astute arguments and key implications for ethical decision-making by campus leaders. Each timely issue is considered in a nuanced way, accessible and relevant to students, professors, and academic leaders alike."

—Michele S. Moses, University of Colorado, Boulder

"*Academic Ethics Today* is an outstanding collection of thirty-one thought-provoking new essays by leading philosophers. The chapters address a broad range of moral questions concerning academic life, from the nature of academic freedom and professors' responsibilities to the role of administrators and the social mission of the university. The volume is arranged in fourteen topical sections, allowing readers to access multiple perspectives on each theme. This collection is essential for anyone working in academia."

—Robert B. Talisse, Vanderbilt University

"Kudos to Steven Cahn for assembling this important and timely collection. The essays, written by a first-rate set of authors, take on pressing moral issues facing universities and their students and faculties with clarity, insight, and a fair measure of audacity. The book is full of thoughtful and challenging arguments. It should be of interest to anyone involved in university life."

—Harvey Siegel, University of Miami

Academic Ethics Today

Problems, Policies, and Prospects for University Life

Edited by
Steven M. Cahn

ROWMAN & LITTLEFIELD
Lanham • Boulder • New York • London

Published by Rowman & Littlefield
An imprint of The Rowman & Littlefield Publishing Group, Inc.
4501 Forbes Boulevard, Suite 200, Lanham, Maryland 20706
www.rowman.com

86-90 Paul Street, London EC2A 4NE

Copyright © 2022 by The Rowman & Littlefield Publishing Group, Inc.

All rights reserved. No part of this book may be reproduced in any form or by any electronic or mechanical means, including information storage and retrieval systems, without written permission from the publisher, except by a reviewer who may quote passages in a review.

British Library Cataloguing in Publication Information Available

Library of Congress Cataloging-in-Publication Data

Names: Cahn, Steven M., editor.
Title: Academic ethics today : problems, policies, and prospects for university life / edited by Steven M. Cahn.
Description: Lanham, Maryland : Rowman & Littlefield Publishers, 2022. | Includes bibliographical references and index. |
Summary: "An all-star cast of philosophical thinkers about higher education, more than half women, offers new essays exploring major ethical problems facing American higher education today. Among the crucial topics discussed are free speech on campus, challenges to the tenure system, the proliferation of adjunct faculty, historical injustices, affirmative action, admission policies, opportunities for applicants from the working-class, faculty and administrative responsibilities, student life, threats to privacy, treatment of those with disabilities, the impact of technology on teaching and learning, curricular controversies, the impact of unions, philanthropy, sports and intercollegiate athletics, and the aims of liberal education. The authors are leading researchers and teachers, many with extensive administrative experience, and they are members of the faculties at public and private institutions throughout the country. The essays are jargon-free and address the most pressing problems for higher education, weigh alternative policies, and assess future prospects for overcoming present challenges. Philosopher, scholar, teacher, and novelist Rebecca Newberger Goldstein provides a foreword to this unique collection"— Provided by publisher.
Identifiers: LCCN 2022010208 (print) | LCCN 2022010209 (ebook) | ISBN 9781538160503 (cloth) | ISBN 9781538160510 (paperback) | ISBN 9781538160527 (epub)
Subjects: LCSH: Education, Higher—Moral and ethical aspects—United States. | Universities and colleges—Administration—Moral and ethical aspects—United States. | College teaching—Moral and ethical aspects—United States. | Academic freedom—United States.
Classification: LCC LA227.4 .A316 2022 (print) | LCC LA227.4 (ebook) | DDC 378.73—dc23/eng/20220419
LC record available at https://lccn.loc.gov/2022010208
LC ebook record available at https://lccn.loc.gov/2022010209

To the memory of
CHARLES FRANKEL
(1917–1979)

Old Dominion Professor of Philosophy and Public Affairs,
Columbia University
Assistant Secretary of State for Educational and Cultural Affairs
President and Director, National Humanities Center

Contents

Foreword   xiii
   Rebecca Newberger Goldstein

Preface   xix

PART I: ACADEMIC FREEDOM

1. Racism, Naming Racism, and Academic Freedom   3
   Elizabeth Harman

2. Free Speech Violations and Campus Politics   15
   Mary Kate McGowan

PART II: TENURE

3. In Defense of Academic Tenure   25
   Richard T. De George

4. What Should Count for Tenure and Promotion?   33
   David Shatz

5. Academic Career Success   43
   Keota Fields

PART III: PRIVACY

6. Confidentiality and Professional Practice   51
   Peter Markie

7. Big Data and Artificial Intelligence   59
   Christa Davis Acampora

PART IV: INJUSTICE

8 Misogyny, "Himpathy," and Sexual Harassment on Campus 71
Cynthia A. Stark

9 Institutional Inequality 81
Jennifer M. Morton

PART V: SEEKING JUSTICE

10 Reckoning with Past Injustice 89
Ann E. Cudd

11 Should Universities Pay Reparations? 99
Alan H. Goldman

12 Rethinking Affirmative Action 105
Steven M. Cahn

PART VI: DISABILITIES

13 Achieving Disability Inclusion 113
Leslie P. Francis

14 Discontent with Disability Accommodations 123
N. Ann Davis

PART VII: THE FORGOTTEN

15 Overlooking Community Colleges and the Working Class 135
James F. Keenan, SJ

16 The Cruelty of the Adjunct System 145
Alexandra Bradner

PART VIII: ADMINISTRATIVE RESPONSIBILITIES

17 Prudent Reserve in Academic Administration 159
Karen Hanson

18 The Discretion of Academic Administrators 167
Anita L. Allen

PART IX: TECHNOLOGY

19 Ethical Online University Instruction 179
Shelley Wilcox

20 Improving Fully Online Instruction 189
Laura M. Howard

PART X: ADMISSIONS

21 Merit, Wealth, and the Ethics of College Admissions 199
  Meira Levinson

22 The Ethics of Doctoral Admissions 209
  Bryan Warnick

PART XI: STUDENTS

23 The Goals of Campus Discipline 221
  David A. Hoekema

24 The Social Costs of a College Education 231
  Anthony Simon Laden

PART XII: THE CURRICULUM

25 Why College? An Education for Freedom 243
  Dan Edelstein and Debra Satz

26 Ethics Requirements in the Liberal Arts Curriculum 251
  Kyla Ebels-Duggan

PART XIII: THE UNIVERSITY'S MISSION

27 Taking Undergraduate Teaching and Learning Seriously 261
  Harry Brighouse

28 Assessing Faculty Unions 273
  Judith Wagner DeCew

29 Friendraising 281
  Deni Elliott

PART XIV: SPORTS

30 Intercollegiate Athletics as Entertainment 291
  Peter A. French

31 Intercollegiate Athletics and Educational Values 297
  Robert Simon

Notes 303

Index 325

About the Authors 337

Foreword

From Plato's Academy to Ours

Rebecca Newberger Goldstein

The concerns of philosophy have been at the center of the Western academic tradition from its inception. After all, it is Plato who is credited with creating the first iteration of the European university, utilizing for his purposes a sacred grove called *Akadēmeia* that was located outside the ancient walls of Athens. Associated with the mythological Attic hero Academos, *Akadēmeia* contained a gymnasium, sanctuaries, and walks wending their way through olive trees. These public grounds, as well as the private home and gardens that Plato purchased nearby, were the physical site of what came to be called Plato's Academy, a community which drew thinkers not only from Athens but from the many Greek-speaking city-states. They came not only to hear Plato pursue his own ideas and to pursue their own but also to engage in the kind of dialectic that for Plato constituted the soul of philosophy.

Given that many participants in the Academy were thinkers in their own right who were granted ample freedom to pursue their own special interests—Theaetetus of Athens and Eudoxus of Cnidus were mathematicians, and Philip of Opus was involved in astronomy—the distinction between teachers and students is somewhat misleading. A variety of Greek terms were applied to participants, including *sunēthēs* (associate or intimate), *hetairos* (companion), and *philos* (friend). In contrast to the practices of the sophists, and following the example of Socrates, no fees were charged, though those who participated in the Academy had to have the means to provide for their own sustenance. The majority were upper-class men, which is hardly a surprise. Rather the surprise is that Diogenes Laertius includes in his list of associates two women, Lastheneia of Mantinea and Axiothea of Philius.

The most prominent of those associated with Plato's Academy was, of course, Aristotle. Son of the personal physician to the king of Macedon, Aristotle traveled as a young man from remote Stagira in northern Greece to the Academy, where he remained for twenty years, only leaving to create his own school, the Lyceum, after the death of Plato in 347 BCE. The long residence of Aristotle is not the only evidence we have that Plato not only tolerated but encouraged the thinking of those highly critical of his own views. It is believed that Aristotle wrote many of his extant works while still at the Academy, while also embarking on the biological studies which led him to the hands-on empirical investigations that were removed from Plato's more rationalist approach to knowledge.

Although Plato was undeniably the animating force of the community, being a *philos* of the Academy did not require adherence to Platonic orthodoxy. In this way, perhaps above all others, Plato paid homage to the spirit of Socrates, whose enthusiasm for probing and prodding and palpating ideas meant that his discussions often ended not in the gratifying finality of a conclusion but rather the frustrating uncertainty of aporia. Though much about Plato's Academy remains obscured, one fact that emerges is the degree of its intellectual freedom. The Academy cultivated a diversity of perspectives that, far from entailing the kind of man-is-the-measure-of-all-things relativism espoused by such sophists as Protagoras, was rather intended to aid and abet the pursuit of truth: premises that might seem intuitively obvious from within one point of view could be revealed as questionable when contemplated from another's vantage.

The circumstances of Plato's founding the Academy are pertinent to the focus of the present anthology, which forcefully makes the case that universities are unavoidably steeped in ethical concerns. Plato would have approved, since his creation of the Academy was born of a profoundly personal ethical crisis. An aristocrat, it would have been natural for him to play a prominent role in the politics of Athens, and there is evidence that he had harbored such aspirations. But these ended when, in 399 BCE, soon after the routing of the Thirty Tyrants and the restoration of the democracy, the Athenians put Socrates on trial, charging and ultimately convicting him of the capital crimes of impiety and corrupting the youth.

Socrates had been a street philosopher, his main place of business the agora, where he indefatigably engaged others in the kind of discussion meant to compel them to question the presumptions that underlay their way of life, including many that were embedded in the ethos of imperial Athens. As befitted his line of work, his favored argumentative ploy was the reductio ad absurdum. Watching him execute it was good entertainment, and he regularly attracted an audience, many of them young, including Plato. The eccentric philosopher was indulged so long as Athens was riding high. Its humiliating defeat by the Spartans in the drawn-out Peloponnesian War brought out the vengeful side of a society that had prided itself on its *parrhesia*—literally, its freedom to speak anything. The account Plato gives in the *Apology* of Socrates' trial presents it as a travesty, culminating in the absurdity of a larger majority of his 501 jurors voting for his death than had voted for his guilt.

In what must have been a state of both personal grief and moral disgust, Plato turned his face on Athens for more than a decade, traveling widely. There is evidence that he went south and studied geometry, geography, astronomy, and religion in Egypt and that he went west to Italy, there to immerse himself in the otherworldly blend of mathematics and mysticism of the Pythagoreans. (The Pythagorean Archytas of Tarentum, reputed to be the founder of mathematical mechanics, would be associated with the Academy.) But eventually Plato ended his self-exile and returned to the Athens that, in betraying Socrates, had betrayed him. Soon after he established his community, putting into practice his belief that the *polis* can best be served by cultivating the rigorous pursuit of truth in an atmosphere of uncompromising intellectual freedom. And for Plato, the pursuit of truth always carries an ethical dimension.

Following in Plato's footsteps, the essays in the present volume collectively demonstrate that many of the concerns of the modern academy are intrinsically moral concerns. *Academic Ethics Today* presents thirty-one essays tackling a wide range of issues—including unionization, tenure, student discipline, adjunct professors, working-class students, donors, and college athletics—revealing and analyzing the specifically ethical dimensions entailed. Included are also essays addressing such overtly ethical issues as confidentiality of university records, disability policies, sexual harassment, and reparations for past academic injustices. Obligations of many kinds fall under the purview of the anthology: obligations of the university to students, to faculty, to society at large, as well as obligations of its community to the university itself. Collectively, the essays stake out in an unprecedented way the contours of a branch of applied ethics where the object of application is the academy itself. All the essays are written by philosophers, with quite a few of the authors being philosopher-administrators. In fact, one of the essays, written by Karen Hanson, turns the moral focus on the very decision to become an academic administrator.

Some of the issues addressed here—for example, the digitalization of education—might seem unconnected to any that Plato confronted as his Academy's philosopher-administrator. And yet I can imagine Plato, who expressed wariness regarding the newfangled technology of writing (*Phaedrus* 275a–277a), studying with interest the essays by Laura Howard on how digital technology affects student learning and by Shelley Wilcox on massive online open courses.

The essays that might more startle him are those by Steven Cahn, Ann Cudd, Alan Goldman, Elizabeth Harman and, jointly, by Dan Edelstein and Debra Satz. Each of these essays addresses, one way or another, the responsibilities of the university in confronting the injustices—most notably racism and sexism—that have systematically plagued society at large, not excluding academia. Cahn's essay explores the dense complications presented by preferential affirmative action. Cudd's essay argues that we must actively reckon with the past injustices of our universities through not only acknowledgment but actions, including changing the lingering false beliefs that led to them. Harman, very much in the spirit of the academic freedom that can be traced back to the first Academy, argues that racist research must be allowed to be pursued, the better for its falsity to emerge, while simultaneously being called out as racist. Edelstein and Satz address the worth of a general liberal arts education partly by way of considering the fascinating argument between W. E. B. Du Bois and Booker T. Washington concerning the kind of education appropriate for the newly free Black men of Georgia following the Civil War and the end of Reconstruction. Goldman addresses the question of whether universities—having been complicit with slavery, the stealthy acquisition of lands from Native Americans, and discrimination against women—should now pay reparations by directing resources such as scholarships, preference in admissions and hiring, and remedial programs to descendants of victims of past injustices.

I say that Plato would have been surprised by these essays, but not, of course, because he did not prioritize the nature of justice and seek mightily to define it so that society could be reconfigured in conformity with it. What else is the *Republic* about? But a thinker who came from a slave society, an institution which he never fundamentally questioned—arguing only that Greeks should not enslave other Greeks (*Republic* 5, 469b–c)—did not possess the concept of individual rights that later centuries would provide. It would take those centuries, and the clash of diverse perspectives rooted in diverse lived experiences, for the equal moral worth of each human to emerge into full consciousness—or at least to emerge sufficiently to reveal the unmitigated evil of such practices as slavery, colonization, and genocide.

Clearly, philosophy can't take credit for the moral progress. The vital blood, sweat, and tears has come, and continues to come, from the sufferers, not the theorizers. And yet philosophy did have its auxiliary part to play, fashioning new concepts and distinctions with which to articulate the emergent truths and provide them with grounds in reason.

And it still has this role to play, a point forcefully made in Kyla Ebels-Duggan's essay in which she argues that a course on ethics equipping students with the conceptual tools to think about normative questions—indeed to apprehend the crucial distinction between normative and descriptive propositions—ought to be an undergraduate requirement. Since all of us, whether philosophers or not, must make normative choices in pursuing our lives, such a requirement falls, she argues, under the category of obligations that the university owes to its students. It can also be argued to fall under the category of obligations that the university owes to society.

Which brings me back again to the founding of the first academy. It is not only one or two of the essays in this collection but virtually all of them that reaffirm the values that were crucial to the community that Plato established among the olive trees of *Akadēmeia*: an uncompromising commitment to intellectual freedom; the pursuit of truth as itself a moral endeavor; the advancements that can, and ought to, accrue from academia to benefit society at large.

—Rebecca Newberger Goldstein, research associate at Harvard University and visiting professor of philosophy and English at New College of the Humanities, London

Preface

Academic ethics explores moral issues arising in education, most often, higher education. Such investigation may discuss either the duties of professors or the institutional policies of colleges and universities. The former subject is examined in my book *Saints and Scamps: Ethics in Academia*, first published by Rowman & Littlefield in 1986 and twice revised. The latter subject is the focus of this collection of new essays.

Granted, academic ethics has not received the attention given to medical ethics, business ethics, or legal ethics. Why not? Perhaps some scholars believe that life in academia raises no moral problems (a dubious supposition), but the more likely possibility is that many are dissuaded from conducting such a study by concern that they may find fault with their colleagues or even themselves. Yet, as Socrates taught, no inquiry is more important than the search for self-understanding.

I am most grateful to the eminent philosophers who have contributed to this collection. Many have held administrative posts and draw on this experience in their discussions. Others are researchers in higher education who write in light of their scholarship. All, however, are concerned with ethical problems that arise in the world of academia.

No single collection of such size and scope has ever before been published, and I am grateful to Natalie Mandziuk, senior acquisitions editor at Rowman & Littlefield, for her support and guidance, as well as to manuscript editor Mary Ann McHugh for her elegant polishing of each of the essays. Finally, I am indebted to Rebecca Newberger Goldstein, philosopher, scholar, teacher, and novelist, for her insightful foreword.

The theme of this book is the critical role that moral considerations should play in university life. The distinguished contributors approach their topics from different perspectives, but all agree with one principle: A concern for ethics should be central to decision-making in higher education. I hope these essays illustrate and illuminate this central feature of the academic mission.

For those wishing to consult previous works in academic ethics, I would recommend the series of fifteen books titled *Issues in Academic Ethics,* general editor Steven M. Cahn, published between 1994 and 2006 by Rowman & Littlefield. I would also call attention to the articles found in the volume *Morality, Responsibility, and the University: Studies in Academic Ethics*, ed. Steven M. Cahn, Temple University Press, 1990, as well as the collection, intended for classroom use, titled *Moral Problems in Higher Education*, ed. Steven M. Cahn, Temple University Press, 2011, reprinted by Wipf and Stock Publishers, 2021.

This present volume is dedicated to my teacher Charles Frankel. He devoted his life to exercising practical influence on advancing the quality of education for American democracy. I am confident that he would have looked with favor on these contemporary explorations of academic ethics, a field in which he was a pioneer.

Part I

ACADEMIC FREEDOM

Chapter 1

Racism, Naming Racism, and Academic Freedom

Elizabeth Harman

In the fall of 2015, the main administration building at Princeton University, where I teach, was occupied by a student group called the Black Justice League. The peacefully protesting students made several demands, including that the Woodrow Wilson School of Public and International Affairs be renamed. To my disappointment, the university's response later that year was to keep the school's name in place, while adding a new outdoor sculpture that addressed Wilson's history of anti-Black racism. It was not until the summer of 2020, when Black Lives Matter protests gripped the nation, that Princeton finally stripped Wilson's name from the School of Public and International Affairs. That summer, hundreds of my faculty colleagues signed a long letter urging many different reforms, in an effort to address anti-Black racism. The letter called for more hiring of faculty of color, for more leadership positions to be offered to faculty of color, and for more recognition of the extra mentoring burdens that Black faculty face. I support all of these reforms. The letter also called for a committee to investigate and punish racist research.

Should a university have a committee to investigate and punish racist (or otherwise bigoted) research? I will argue that it should not. Some people may worry that such a committee might get the judgments of what is racist wrong; while this is a serious worry, I will set it aside. I will argue that we should not have a committee to investigate and punish racist research, even if the committee would only get the answers right. I will argue that the protections of academic freedom should be broad.

After the letter signed by hundreds of Princeton professors, another professor here published an essay criticizing the letter.[1] In his essay, he referred to the Black Justice League as a "terrorist organization." In the ensuing conversation, his comment was called "racist"—correctly, in my view. The University President, Christopher Eisgruber, weighed in,[2] voicing his commitment to academic freedom but saying that we should aim for civility and should avoid calling each other names such as "terrorist" and "racist." While President Eisgruber talked specifically about calling a *person* racist, many people think it is also a violation of civility to call what someone has said or done racist. Should people in university conversations refrain from calling what others are saying racist? No. I will argue that accusations of racism (and sexism, homophobia, transphobia, and ableism) play a valuable role in serious intellectual conversation. When a view is racist, we need to say so.

The two questions I address in this essay are both about what to do when racism (or another kind of bigotry) appears in academic conversation. Part of my view is that racist (and bigoted) academic work must often be protected by academic freedom. But the other part of my view is that, while we should allow this work, we should also name the racism (or other kind of bigotry) we see in it. In the next section, I'll explain how my work as a moral philosopher informs my thinking about academic freedom. Across the following four sections, I'll argue for my view. Then, I will explain how my view contrasts with two commonly held views, a "conservative" view which agrees with me about academic freedom but disagrees about naming racism, and a "woke" view which agrees with me about naming racism but disagrees about academic freedom. Finally, I'll consider and respond to some objections to my view.

WHAT MORAL PHILOSOPHERS DO

Something that I love about my work and my teaching in moral philosophy is that I regularly address questions that matter to all of us and that most people have thought about. My first published paper was about the ethics of abortion and the moral status of fetuses. I've written about whether we are all morally required to be vegetarians and about whether people who are caught in the grip of false moral views are blameworthy when they do terrible things that they think are morally good. My favorite undergraduate course is "The Ethics of Love and Sex." In this course, we talk about what it is to love someone, why we love another person, what we owe to someone we love, what counts as consensual sex, whether it's wrong to deceive another person into sex, whether it should be legal to pay for sex, whether there should be legal same-sex marriage, and whether there should be legal polyamorous marriage. The questions I write and teach about are controversial. My readers, my interlocutors, my students, the authors we read, and I all feel strongly about these questions. We recognize that there is a lot at stake, and we recognize that those who have the wrong answers are in a position to do a great deal of damage to other people and to our society. These questions matter. The right answers matter.

I believe in the power of argument, the importance of thinking slowly and carefully about difficult questions, the value of following a line of thought even when it leads in a surprising direction, the importance of listening to others, and the significance and beauty of a good objection. If I didn't believe in these things, philosophy wouldn't be right for me. But believing in these things is not special to philosophy. These are basic values in college education, and they are basic values in serious public debate in a democratic society.

If heinous views are not to be part of academic conversation, then it will be impossible to do serious moral philosophy about important topics. Consider two of the topics on which I teach: abortion and romantic relationships. I assign readings that argue that abortion is morally wrong and that abortion should be illegal. I assign readings that argue that gay and lesbian couples cannot share the special relationship that straight couples can share and that same-sex marriage should not be legal. It is my view that opposition to abortion rights is sexist; making abortion illegal oppresses women, and any argument for its illegality is thereby a sexist argument. It is also my view that opposition to same-sex marriage is bigoted, that it is homophobic. But we can't do serious philosophy about these two extremely important, and politically relevant, questions without engaging with arguments that are sexist and homophobic. We need to read and address bigoted arguments to deal with these questions, at this point in time in our society.[3]

Thus, it is at the very heart of my academic work as a moral philosopher that I am engaged with arguments for heinous views. When the stakes are high, when the questions matter, the wrong answers are heinous. But we must engage with those wrong answers. In a nutshell, that's my take on academic freedom for bigoted views. In the next two sections, I'll try to convince you that I'm right about this.

RESEARCH MISCONDUCT VERSUS IMMORAL RESEARCH

Universities already have procedures in place to deal with research misconduct. For example, researchers aren't allowed to plagiarize, fake data, or mistreat the subjects of their research. Some of what is already clearly disallowed is racist research, such as the Tuskegee Syphilis Study, in which the researchers lied to the Black men they were studying about whether they were providing medical treatment to them. Perhaps there is a quick and decisive argument that *all* racist research should be investigated and punished. Consider this:

All racist research is immoral research.
All immoral research is research misconduct.
All research misconduct should be investigated and punished.

Therefore:
All racist research should be investigated and punished.[4]

This argument is valid: if its three premises are true, then its conclusion is true. Are its three premises true?

In my view, the first premise is true: all racist research is immoral research. This is a premise that some people might deny. They might say that someone could argue for a racist conclusion while arguing in good faith (really trying to get the answer right) and thus would be doing racist research without behaving immorally. I disagree. If you are arguing for a racist conclusion, you are doing something morally wrong, though you may not know that you are doing something morally wrong.

The third premise is also true. By definition, research misconduct is all and only that research behavior that should be investigated and punished.

So, is the second premise true? It is a basic feature of morality that there are many cases in which someone acts morally wrongly without it being true that they should be punished for their actions. Some people are morally obligated to give more money to charity than they do give; they're acting morally wrongly, but it would not be right to punish them for their morally wrong choices. (We should tax the wealthy more heavily than we do, but that is not a way of punishing them.) There are myriad lies that people tell in their lives, both trivial ("I didn't get your phone message") and serious ("I haven't been having an affair") which, while morally wrong, are not things for which we should punish them. There can be a big gap between something's being morally wrong and it being right to punish someone for doing it.

The question of whether racist research is *research misconduct* is a different question than the question whether racist research is *morally wrong*. Not everything that is morally wrong constitutes a violation of professional responsibilities. Thus, we must address the question head on: should racist (or otherwise bigoted) research be permitted in academia?

SHOULD RACIST, SEXIST, AND OTHERWISE BIGOTED ARGUMENTS BE PERMITTED?

Suppose you are an undergraduate student at a university. While in college, you will be taking a variety of courses including some courses that take up important moral and political questions. The readings assigned in these courses will be written by academics. What should you want academic freedom to protect?

You already have some beliefs about moral and political questions. Let's suppose the beliefs you have so far are correct. Of course, there must also be some hard questions that you haven't answered yet. For some of the questions on which you already have settled beliefs—beliefs we are supposing you are correct in holding—you are aware of many people around you, including people in some of your peer groups, who disagree with you. Some of your fellow students, some of your coworkers at your part-time job, and some of your fellow citizens disagree with you on some of the important questions on which you already know the right answers. Some of what they believe is actually racist, sexist, homophobic, transphobic, ableist, or otherwise bigoted, though they probably don't understand that about these beliefs. In light of these facts about you and your peers, should you want specific views and arguments to be disallowed in academic conversation, because they are racist or otherwise bigoted? I will argue that you should not, for three reasons.

First, let's consider those questions on which you are unsure of the right answer. Your goal is to come to believe the right answer, and to understand why it is the right answer. To do this, you'll have to consider a number of different answers and what arguments can be made for and against them. So you want your professors to be able to assign a range of different views on these questions to you, and you want your fellow students to be allowed to offer and argue for a range of different views in class. In fact, only one of these views is correct. All the views that are incorrect may well turn out to be racist, sexist, homophobic, transphobic, ableist, or otherwise bigoted views, at the end of the day. But they need to be part of the conversation, if you are going to think these questions through and come to understand why the right answer is right.

Second, let's consider those questions on which you know the correct answers, but you are aware that others in your peer groups disagree with you. Should you want those who hold the incorrect views to be forbidden from doing academic work that offers and argues for their incorrect views? When such views and arguments are forbidden, we are saying to those who hold these views that they are not allowed to say what they really think, and that they just have to submit to the official view. When we refuse to allow them to speak honestly, we treat them disrespectfully and we lose an opportunity to engage in meaningful dialogue with them that might persuade them.

Third, let's consider those of your peers who are uncertain about questions for which you already know the right answers. Should you want those who disagree with you to be able to argue for their views *in speaking to those who are unsure*? When such views and arguments are forbidden, we make it harder for those who are unsure to come via open discussion and deliberation to the true view—they lack access to good speech and arguments on one side, and they see that they are being denied that access, so they don't know what to make of what they are allowed to hear.

For these three reasons, if you are an undergraduate student, then you should want wide academic freedoms to be in place. And what should others want, who are not undergraduates? Everyone should want there to be open debate on these topics within our society, for all three of these reasons. We need to figure out the answers that we don't already know. We need to be in dialogue with those who are in the grip of wrong answers (both in order to treat them respectfully and in order to have some chance of persuading them). And we need to be able to reach those who are unsure.

Thus, we should not want universities to have committees that investigate and punish bigoted research.

FALSE ANSWERS MAY TURN OUT TO BE RACIST OR OTHERWISE BIGOTED

In the previous section, part of my argument was that when we don't know the answers to important moral and political questions, we need to consider a range of answers, but the false answers may end up being racist, sexist, or otherwise bigoted. This supported the first reason I gave in favor of allowing bigoted research within academic discussion: we need such research to be allowed so that our deliberative processes can proceed.

Someone might question this. They might think that if we already have a lot of the answers right (as let's suppose we do), and we are arguing in good faith, then whatever answers we take seriously, even if they are not exactly right, couldn't possibly turn out to be racist, sexist, or otherwise bigoted. But that's just not true. Let me give two examples.

People who are aware of widespread racism in our society are working hard to take it seriously and address it. In the course of these efforts, they sometimes make mistakes that are in fact racist. For example, Robin DiAngelo's book *White Fragility*[5] complains that centering Jackie Robinson in stories of his breaking through the color barrier in baseball fails to acknowledge the way that Black players were kept out of the major league for so long. She says that we should tell the story by saying "white people finally allowed him to play." This analysis has been critiqued as follows.[6] The analysis leaves out the agency of Black people in the integration of baseball: the protests by Black players and fans and the hard work, amazing talent, and bravery of Jackie Robinson are all absent from a story that sees the main point as "white people finally allowed a Black person to play." While DiAngelo does good anti-racist work in her book by naming and analyzing the important concept of white fragility, the analysis she gives of Robinson's story is racist.

One of my heroes is the philosopher Sally Haslanger, who has done valuable work exposing the way that academic philosophy has been a hostile environment for women, and who has done important academic work on the way that categories of race and gender are socially constructed. In 2000, Haslanger published an article arguing for a new way of understanding what it is to be a woman that accommodated the idea that transgender women are women; this was groundbreaking and trans-affirming at the time.[7] But subsequent criticism pointed out that Haslanger's proposed view did not allow that a transgender woman who is openly transgender could count as a woman.[8] While Haslanger's paper was a step forward both for feminism and for trans recognition, anyone who affirmed that view today would be saying something transphobic, because it's transphobic to deny that an openly transgender woman can be a woman.

These two cases show that someone who has a lot of the answers right can nevertheless get something wrong in a way that is ultimately racist, transphobic, or otherwise bigoted. We should not think that our own deliberations are immune to this; yet we need to be able to deliberate.

RACISM AND BIGOTRY MUST BE NAMED

Let's turn now to naming racism and bigotry. Is it okay to say that someone is saying something racist, sexist, homophobic, transphobic, ableist, or otherwise bigoted? Within academic conversation, is it okay to say "what you're saying is racist" or "that's bigotry"? One might reason as follows:

> In serious academic conversation, we should avoid "name-calling" and we should treat each other with respect. For these reasons, we should not call what others have said racist, sexist, homophobic, transphobic, ableist, or otherwise bigoted.

Along these lines, my Princeton University colleague Robert George and two of his coauthors took time in a serious academic piece to express alarm that their anti-same-sex-marriage view is sometimes called "bigotry," an appellation they apparently take to be self-evidently false and unfair.[9]

In my view, accusations that views and actions are instances of bigotry belong within academic conversation for two reasons: such accusations are often true, and they are useful to making progress in discussing serious matters. Sometimes it is *correct* to say that an idea is racist, sexist, homophobic, transphobic, or ableist. But more importantly, descriptions of views, utterances, policies, or actions as bigoted can usefully illuminate what is happening and what should happen next.

There are a lot of debates within academia today in which one side can correctly be described as racist. Debate continues over whether any kind of affirmative action, in admissions and in hiring, is warranted, and if so, what forms it should take. Debate continues over whether reparations for slavery are warranted. During these debates, one side sometimes proceeds in a way that minimizes or denies the role of racism in the past and the present. False denials of racism are themselves racist, and it's important to see that, to understand what's happening in these debates. Similarly, in popular political conversation, when one side says "Black lives matter" and another side responds "No, all lives matter," the response denies there is any failure in our society to see the value of Black lives. The utterance "all lives matter" is a racist denial of racism; we have to be able to say this, as upsetting as it may be to those who make the utterance.

Similarly, when it comes to describing opposition to same-sex marriage as "bigotry," that description communicates the view that opposition to same-sex marriage is no better than opposition to interracial marriage. Perhaps George and his coauthors think that a view cannot be "bigotry" unless it amounts to unarticulated gut-feeling hostility to some group; on this understanding of bigotry, anyone who has thought carefully and seriously about a question cannot be guilty of bigotry. But so much bigotry throughout history has been carefully thought through and elaborately wrapped up in fancy arguments.[10] The mere fact that George writes long papers defending his view that gay and lesbian relationships are of less worth than heterosexual relationships doesn't make it incorrect to call his view "bigotry." Racists who opposed interracial marriage could speak at great length on the topic. That does not make it any less apt to call their opposition both "racist" and "bigoted."

Treating others with respect does require letting them talk, but it does not require shying away from honest critique of what they say. When what someone says is racist, we can and should point that out.

THREE VIEWS OF BIGOTRY AND ACADEMIC FREEDOM

Let's contrast the view I'm offering in this essay with two other views. This essay addresses two questions: *Should academic freedom protect bigoted research?* and *Do accusations of bigotry belong within academic conversation?* I answer "yes" to both questions. Here are two views that disagree with me:

> The conservative view: The protections of academic freedom should be broad, to cover much work that would today be called racist, sexist, or otherwise bigoted. Such accusations are typically false, since bigotry requires animus that is rarely present in sincerely held views. For example, serious academic work opposing the legalization of same-sex marriage is not bigoted. Accusations of bigotry have no place in academic conversation because they are almost always false.

> The woke view: Accusations of bigotry are important in academic conversation. Much actual academic work, such as work opposing the legalization of same-sex marriage, is bigoted and needs to be named as such. Academic freedom should not protect any bigotry.

The view I've argued for in this essay stands between these two views. I agree with the woke view about the truth and importance of many actual accusations of racism, sexism, homophobia, transphobia, and ableism; I agree that opposition to same-sex marriage is bigotry. But I agree with the conservative view that the views themselves must enjoy the protections of academic freedom.

My view:[11]

> When we discuss important moral and political questions, some of what gets said is racist, sexist, homophobic, transphobic, ableist, or otherwise bigoted. It is useful and important to name bigotry when it occurs. We must not prevent racist, sexist, homophobic, transphobic, ableist, or otherwise bigoted claims from being made within academic conversation, for three reasons: first, we need to be able to consider alternative views while we figure out the answers to some questions (and at that point we don't know which views are bigoted); second, on those questions on which we already know the right answers, we need to be able to converse with our peers who hold the wrong views; and third, also on those questions on which we already know the right answers, we need to be able to converse with our peers who are undecided.[12]

OBJECTIONS TO MY VIEW

I want to close this essay by considering some objections to what I've said so far. I'll discuss four objections to my claim about academic freedom and two objections to my claim about naming racism.

The Harm Objection: This discussion hasn't taken into account that racist, sexist, or otherwise bigoted speech is itself very harmful. The speech itself harms, and it also causes further things that are harmful.

The objector is right that speech is powerful, and that bigoted speech is harmful. But it's precisely because these issues and questions matter so much, for real people's lives, that we need robust academic freedoms. We need to get the answers to these questions right, and we need to convince as many people as possible of the right answers.

Here's a closely related objection:

The Climate Objection: This discussion hasn't taken into account how bad for university climate it is to have bigoted speech occurring in serious academic conversation. It's horrible for students from targeted groups (as well as for faculty from those groups) for bigotry to be allowed in serious academic conversation. That it's okay to debate their basic status as equal persons, or their basic legal rights, is gross and disrespectful of them.

The objector is right that robust academic freedom creates serious climate problems, that bigoted speech is disrespectful of members of the academic community, that it harms them, and that the university has a duty to take these climate problems seriously. But it doesn't follow that academic freedom should be restricted when it comes to bigoted speech.

There is a mistake that both sides of debates about academic freedom tend to make:

The "Defense" Mistake:
Thinking that defending some speech as *protected by academic freedom* means defending it as *speech that has not done anything bad or problematic*.

Those who seek to restrict academic freedom notice—correctly—that bigoted speech does great harm, both immediately and in its long-term effects. They make the "Defense" Mistake and think that because the speech cannot be defended as innocuous, it cannot be protected by academic freedom. Those who seek to preserve robust academic freedom observe—correctly—that bigoted speech should often be protected. They make the "Defense" Mistake and think that because the speech can be defended as involving no misconduct that should be investigated or punished, nothing bad has happened here.

We need university leaders to recognize both that their policies must protect robust academic freedom, and that serious climate problems result from these policies. We cannot pretend that nothing bad has happened when a famous Princeton University professor says that a gay or lesbian relationship is really, at root, a mere friendship, compared to a heterosexual relationship, which is something more.[13] This is a climate problem that has concerned me since the day I became a Princeton professor in 2006. The way I handle it is to talk a lot about the bigotry we have here on campus. I want my gay students and colleagues to know that I see it too, and that I see them.

What should university leaders do in the face of these climate problems? This is a hard question. I think they should start by voicing anti-racist, feminist, LGBTQ+-friendly, anti-ableist views in response to bigotry.

The Psychological Naïveté Objection: This discussion has presupposed the naïve view that open discussion leads people to the right answers, and that if we just talk fully about important matters, we'll all end up with the right view. But that's not true.

This objector claims that I assume that, with open discussion, "the truth will out"; but this is obviously false. We all know plenty of cases in which full open discussion failed to convince people. We all know people caught in the grip of false views who, it seems, will hold steadfastly to their views forever. But I'm not making this strong assumption. My assumptions are much weaker. One is that, when we don't know the right answers to important questions, we stand the best chance of making progress if we allow full open discussion for the purposes of our own thinking. Another is that, when confronted with people who hold false views, we stand a better chance of convincing them if we allow them to say what they think as we discuss with them. It's compatible with this claim that, overall, our chances of convincing them are low. Finally, we stand the best chance of convincing the undecided of the right views if they see that we're letting all sides speak.

But my argument hasn't just been pragmatic—that we need academic freedom to find out the truth and to bring others to the truth. Part of my argument has been about what it is to engage in serious conversation about important matters with peers who disagree with us. That means letting them say what they think. It would be nice to only have peers who lack bigoted views. None of us are so lucky. Sexism, racism, homophobia, transphobia, and ableism, in subtle and less subtle forms, are present in every community. That's the reality we confront; and that's one of the facts on which my argument relies.

The Third Person Objection: If what's really valuable is discussing the awful views and arguments that are out there, then academic work could just talk *about* those views and arguments, discussing them in the third person without ever endorsing them. But then no academic work need actually be racist or otherwise bigoted.

I agree with this objection that a lot of the good of a robust academic conversation can be had in conversation *about* claims and arguments, even if some of the claims and arguments being discussed are not actually endorsed or offered by anyone within the academic discussion. But if we systematically exclude a viewpoint that is in fact widely held from ever being offered or argued for within academic conversation, then we will not learn the best arguments for it, and in particular we will not learn what those who believe it take to be the best arguments for it. And we will not be able to convince those who are undecided that we're having a serious academic discussion, since one side will be known to be systematically silenced.

Finally, let's consider two objections to my claim that racism should be named.

The Ending Debate Objection: It's not true that naming racism is useful in academic conversation. Rather, calling something "racist" effectively shuts down the conversation.

The objector is right that sometimes a conversation can't proceed after something is called "racist." But why is this so? Sometimes it's so because the person being told that their view is racist finds it so uncomfortable and intolerable to be told it that they shut the conversation down. Or sometimes that person goes on to make the conversation all about them and their hurt feelings. Neither of these responses is okay. The fact that someone who says something racist might respond badly to having this racism pointed out should not be a decisive reason against truly naming their racism.

Sometimes it's the person who says that something is racist who thereby ends the conversation—they don't want to dignify what has been said with further engagement. That can be a perfectly reasonable stance in response to someone saying something racist. But not everyone who calls something racist takes this stance. Often, someone calls something racist and is ready to patiently explain why they said so, what they meant, and where to go from here.

The Moral Peril Objection: Incorrect accusations of racism can mess up the lives of those who are accused. It's so dangerous to get this wrong, that we should refrain from calling what others have said "racist" to be safe.

The objector is right that sometimes someone says that something was racist when it wasn't, and that it can be bad for the accused when this happens. People should not call something that isn't racist "racist." Getting this wrong is a serious matter. (That you thought you were correct isn't much of an excuse in this case, any more than it is in others.) But letting racism occur without naming it is also a serious matter. When stakes are high, no path is without peril. Avoiding the explicit accusation of racism is not a prudent, cautious move. It fails to honor those who are the victims of racism, by failing to name and acknowledge what is happening to them.[14]

Chapter 2

Free Speech Violations and Campus Politics

Mary Kate McGowan

There is mounting concern that institutions of higher education are too liberal politically and that campus conservatives are unfairly disadvantaged because of it. In particular, there is concern that the voices of conservative students are silenced in a way that violates their right to free speech. Could the climate on some campuses be so left leaning that it routinely stifles such an important liberty?

This is an important but also extremely complex question. Although we cannot satisfactorily settle it once and for all here, we can clarify some of the issues and offer relevant tools for exploring this question in a more fruitful and productive way.

So, let's jump right in and make this scenario concrete by considering a hypothetical case:

> *Politically Conservative Student:* Sarah is a politically conservative student at a university where the majority of students and faculty are liberal. In a political science class discussion of the pros and cons of public funding for Planned Parenthood, Sarah decides against expressing her views; she believes that no good will come of it.

Is Sarah's right to free speech being violated here? Before trying to answer this question, we first need to separate a few related but distinct issues. First, what is this right and how is it violated? The second section discusses different free speech rights; each such right primarily concerns communication and, accordingly, its violation involves some kind of harm to a person's communicative capacities.

Second, we need to know whether a decision against speaking can involve a free speech violation. After all, in *Politically Conservative Student*, this is precisely what happens. Sarah doesn't try to communicate only to have something get in her way. Instead, Sarah decides for herself that not speaking is what she wants to do. And this raises a second question, namely, can a decision to refrain from speaking involve a violation of the right to free speech? In the third section, we see that the answer is yes. It certainly cannot be a violation, however, every time a person decides against speaking (or decides against saying a particular thing). This raises our third question: under what circumstances might a decision against saying something involve a free speech violation? The fourth and fifth sections address this question.

One more caveat before we get started. Our case, *Politically Conservative Student,* lacks detail. Many different sorts of things could be going on here, some less troubling than others and only some concerning free speech at all. Further detail will be supplemented in the case to consider whether free speech concerns are warranted. But first, some background on the right to free speech is required.

ON FREE SPEECH AND ITS VIOLATION

In a nutshell, the legal right to free speech protects us from illegitimate governmental interference with our ability to communicate. If there were a law that criminalized saying anything critical of the government, for example, it would be a clear violation of this right. Countries that severely punish such political dissidents do not embrace a principle of free speech protected by law. In liberal democracies, by contrast, such political expression, as it is often called, is one of the most valued kinds of speech.[1] Understood in this way, free speech is a legal right, one enshrined in the First Amendment to the U.S. Constitution. As such and strictly speaking, the only entity that can violate this right is the government or an agent acting on behalf of the government.

That said, there are other, that is, nonlegal, rights to free speech. Consider, for example, a person jailed for criticizing a government in a country or jurisdiction that does not legally protect free speech. If you think that the jailed person's free speech is being violated, then the free speech right in question must be a nonlegal one. In a case like this, it's a moral or even a political right to free speech.

In general, though, a free speech right—whether legal, moral, or political—involves freedom of communication. Furthermore, this right is typically understood as a negative right, that is, a right not to be interfered with. So, going forward we shall operate on the assumption that having one's communicative capacities interfered with is a necessary condition for a violation of free speech. Communicative interference is necessary, but it's not enough.

To see this, consider the following case:

Noisy Truck: A noisy truck rumbles by and drowns out Tamron's comment to her sister.

In *Noisy Truck*, there is communicative interference. The noise of the truck prevents Tamron's comment from being heard by her sister. As a result, Tamron's comment is not successfully communicated. Despite the communicative interference, though, viewing the passing truck as a violator of Tamron's free speech right seems obviously wrong. This suggests that a free speech violation requires more than interference with communication.

What else is required, however, is both complex and contested.[2] First, whatever interferes with communication must be systematic rather than idiosyncratic or accidental. If the government deliberately and routinely sent noisy trucks to drown out the speech of protesters, then the protesters' free speech rights are violated. But the communicative interference with Tamron's comment in *Noisy Truck* does not seem to be such a case.

Another consideration is that a free speech violation is harmful. When the random truck drowns out Tamron's comment, she might be inconvenienced, frustrated, and even annoyed, but she is seemingly not harmed. Tamron did not lose anything of real significance in the process. When a person's right to free speech is violated, by contrast, that person is harmed, and this means roughly that that person is made worse off by being denied something valuable that person ought to have. When the government routinely drowns out the speech of dissidents, for instance, those dissidents are harmed. By being systematically prevented from communicating their political views, the dissidents are made worse off than they ought to be; the communicative interference in this case is genuinely harmful, and this is part of why it's a free speech violation.

In sum, going forward, we shall be interested in cases of communicative interference that are both harmful and brought about systematically. As we have seen, these three conditions appear necessary (but that does not establish that they are enough). With this working characterization of free speech violations in hand, let's now return to Sarah in *Politically Conservative Student*.

ON DECIDING AGAINST SPEAKING

In *Politically Conservative Student,* Sarah does not attempt to communicate only to have that attempted communication interfered with. Instead, she *decides against* trying to communicate in the first place; that is, Sarah decides to remain silent. Our first order of business is to determine whether a decision to remain silent can involve a free speech violation.

Now, a person might decide not to speak for all sorts of reasons, some of which are entirely unproblematic. A person might remain silent because it is someone else's turn to speak, because one has nothing relevant—or sufficiently supported—to say, or just because one is tired.

Of course, Sarah's reasons differ from any of these (not-so-worrying) reasons: she decides against speaking because of what she anticipates will happen if she does speak. But can doing that ever involve a free speech violation?

It can. To see this clearly, consider the following (thankfully fictional) case:

> *Unconstitutional Treason Law*: The U.S. government declares that any significant public criticism of government policy constitutes treason and is thus a criminal offense. Although Judy fervently disagrees with the current administration's spending policy, she nonetheless decides against voicing her opinion because she knows that, if she does, she will go to prison. To avoid this, Judy keeps her opinions to herself.

I think we can all agree that Judy's right to free speech is here being violated. I assume we can all also agree that this treason law would and should be struck down as a clear violation of the free speech clause of the First Amendment! However improbable, *Unconstitutional Treason Law* illuminates an important conceptual point: it is possible for a decision against speaking to involve a clear violation of the free speech right.

Judy's situation in *Unconstitutional Treason Law* also satisfies all three necessary conditions of our working characterization of a free speech violation. First, Judy experiences communicative interference. Although she does not say anything (and thus attempt to communicate), her potential communication is nevertheless interfered with by her knowledge of the treason law. After all, Judy knows full well that she risks imprisonment by speaking her mind, and so, in light of this, remaining silent is rational. Her knowledge of the treason law thus interferes with her communication by preventing her from attempting it. Second, this interference is also systematic. It's no accident; it's perfectly predictable and even codified in a law that is explicit about punishing certain sorts of communications. And, third, Judy is clearly harmed by the communicative interference; she is made worse off by this treason law that denies the important ability to communicate her political views free from threat of imprisonment. Since Judy's free speech right is here violated, this is enough to show that a decision against speaking *can* involve a free speech violation. In other words, it's possible.

Unconstitutional Treason Law involves what is sometimes called self-silencing, that is, where a person decides against speaking (or against saying a certain thing in a certain context) to avoid unjust harms that would result from speaking.[3] Self-silencing is an important phenomenon, and it will come up again in assessing Sarah's situation in *Politically Conservative Student*.

MERE DISAGREEMENT

Let's now return to *Politically Conservative Student* and look more closely at Sarah's reasons for not speaking. We know that Sarah is worried about how others will respond to her expressing a conservative point of view, but she might be worried about a variety of different things.

Here is one way to spell out what is happening:

> *Mere Disagreement.* Sarah knows that she is the only conservative in the room. Consequently, she knows that her classmates will disagree with her and just does not feel like dealing with that. Tired and stressed, she has to pick her battles. She's fairly sure she won't manage to change anyone's mind anyway. So, Sarah decides to remain silent even though she disagrees with some of what is being said in the class discussion.

This is worrying, especially if it is a widespread phenomenon across different classes and campuses. If conservative viewpoints are not being expressed and evaluated, then everyone loses. We really ought to be considering a variety of viewpoints, methods, starting points, and goals. To systematically skew discussions in this way harms the collective quest for truth and knowledge while undermining the integrity of higher education.

That said, it does not appear to be a free speech issue. After all, Sarah can successfully communicate her opinion, and she can do so without being harmed; she is perfectly able to exercise her free speech right. And others who disagree with Sarah are exercising their free speech right in turn. Being disagreed with is not a violation of one's right to free speech. Neither, it seems, is deciding not to speak in anticipation of being disagreed with. If this is what is happening in *Politically Conservative Student*, we may well have a problem, but it is not a free speech problem.

It's worth thinking about what would follow if the expression of disagreement were treated as a violation of free speech. In short, it would be a total disaster. Disagreement and the expression of disagreement play a crucial role in what makes speech so valuable. Theorists disagree about what justifies a commitment to free speech.[4] Some think it has to do with the search for truth. Others think it has to do with the communications necessary for a democracy to function well. Still others think it has to do with self-expression and the development of individual autonomy. But no matter which sort of justification one favors, successful communication and expressing disagreement—even forcefully—will play a required role in speech doing the valuable thing it does.

So, if anticipating being disagreed with by her liberal peers is the sole reason for Sarah's silence, *Politically Conservative Student* does not appear to raise free speech concerns.

ANTICIPATION OF HARM

That said, filling in the details differently might well raise free speech concerns. To see this, consider yet another version of Sarah's case:

Avoiding Unjust Harm: Sarah's classmates operate with ignorant and hateful negative stereotypes about conservatives, and Sarah knows this. Because of this, Sarah knows that her classmates will misunderstand what she is trying to say, discredit her claims, infer all sorts of false negative stuff about her, and socially shun her. In light of all this, Sarah decides to keep her opinions to herself.

If this is why Sarah decides to remain silent, it's a very different story. There is much to say here, but we will focus on the possibility that Sarah is self-silencing here, that is, deciding against speaking to avoid unjust harms that would result from her saying what she otherwise would say. In what follows, we will identify three potential unjust harms that Sarah believes would result from her speaking, the avoidance of which contributes to her decision to refrain from speaking.

The first potential harm concerns being misunderstood. Sarah is concerned that others' caricature of conservatism will cause them to misunderstand what she means by what she says.[5] If that's true, then there are impediments to Sarah's successful communication. In other words, factors in Sarah's environment (i.e., the false beliefs held by her audience) will systematically prevent her from being properly understood and thus communicating successfully. Arguably, this means that Sarah's communicative capabilities are impaired and that seems harmful. So, if Sarah decides against speaking to avoid this harm, Sarah self-silences.

A second potential harm concerns damaged credibility. Sarah might also be concerned that what she has to say (assuming some of it is properly understood) will be met with more skepticism than is warranted; in other words, Sarah will be given less credibility than she deserves exactly because she is a conservative surrounded by liberals. So, even if her classmates understand some of what she is saying, Sarah realizes that they are seriously disinclined to believe her. Since sharing knowledge is a huge part of what makes speech valuable, this is also arguably a speech-related harm, and it is different from being misunderstood. So, if Sarah chooses to remain silent to avoid this kind of credibility harm, she is self-silencing for a different reason.

The third harm concerns being punished for expressing unpopular views.[6] In particular, Sarah is concerned that students will socially shun her for expressing her politically conservative opinion. Since she remains silent to avoid that harm, Sarah is self-silencing in yet another way.

We have here identified three different unjust harms whose anticipation give rise to Sarah's decision to remain silent. We have considered, that is, three different potential forms of self-silencing. I leave it to the reader to think through whether Sarah's free speech right is thereby violated. It might be helpful to consider similarities and differences between Sarah's case in *Politically Conservative Student* and Judy's in *Unconstitutional Treason Law*. Finally, even if one does not think that Sarah's free speech right is violated, there is nevertheless reason to be concerned about her case and with the possibility (or even probability) that cases like it occur on our college campuses.

CONCLUSION

As noted at the outset, the issues are complex, and we have not settled them here. That said, here are a few takeaway messages. First, free speech violations involve cases of communicative interference that are both harmful and systematic. Second, being disagreed with, and deciding to remain silent to avoid being disagreed with, does not violate the right to free speech; instead, it exercises it. Third, deciding to remain silent to avoid unjust speech-related harms, by contrast, is potentially a violation of free speech, and we have seen several ways in which politically conservative students might self-silence on left-leaning college campuses. Fourth and finally, it is worth stressing that other groups face all these sorts of challenges on our campuses, and some of those groups face various kinds of disadvantage in just about every other aspect of social life too. And, in thinking through what's unjust for some conservatives on campus, it is important to keep this in mind.

Part II

TENURE

Chapter 3

In Defense of Academic Tenure

Richard T. De George

Faculty tenure is under attack in many colleges and universities in the United States. Wittingly or unwittingly, these critics, in denouncing tenure, are also undermining academic freedom, weakening the U.S. system of higher education that has been a magnet for students from around the globe for many years, and threatening the benefits that vibrant universities bring to civil society.

The justification of academic tenure lies in the institutional and social good that it promotes and protects. Academic tenure in private and publicly supported colleges and universities alike provides the necessary underpinning of the freedom of the faculties in those institutions to pursue knowledge wherever it leads without regard to partisan political or other parochial interests. It is a public good. Colleges and universities can and do exist without academic freedom and tenure, but the societies of which they are a part are poorer for their absence.

The AAUP (American Association of University Professors) 1940 Statement of Principles on Academic Freedom and Tenure defines academic tenure as follows: "After the expiration of a probationary period, teachers or investigators should have permanent or continuous tenure, and their service should be terminated only for adequate cause, except in the case of retirement for age, or under extraordinary circumstances because of financial exigencies" (4). The probationary period is usually a maximum of six years, after which a faculty member is either awarded tenure or dismissed. Generally included under adequate cause are academic incompetence and failure to meet one's professional obligations. Academic tenure provides guaranteed continuous employment, a good for the individual receiving it. But that good—with which it is often equated by its critics—is not its main purpose. Equating academic freedom with guaranteed employment fails to appreciate the fact that the guarantee is a means, not the end or purpose of the tenure system.

Academic tenure is justified as the best means our society has devised to protect academic freedom, which is the freedom to pursue one's research independent of political powers and pressures and without fear of dismissal. Guaranteed academic freedom allows the university, through its faculty, to develop new knowledge, make discoveries, develop innovative approaches to problems, advance science, medicine, and technology, and educate—not just train—a dynamic workforce, and produce citizens who are trained in critical thinking. The leaders of society or any other group that dictates what it sees as truth to the university and that wants a docile citizenry has no interest in academic freedom. A free society needs universities that, while maintaining accountability, exercise their autonomy to pursue and develop knowledge free from inimical outside political, corporate, and popular pressure; and this means a faculty that pursues new knowledge wherever it leads. The society that academic tenure is established to support believes that not all truth is known and that society benefits from the development of new knowledge. Academic tenure provides a guarantee that faculty will be allowed to pursue knowledge in their areas of competence freely and objectively without fear of being penalized if they break with tradition, try new approaches, or turn up unpopular results. It is awarded to those who have served a sufficient period of time to demonstrate their competence and their ability to pursue and advance knowledge and to communicate it to students and pertinent others (colleagues, other specialists, industries, and the general public, as the case may be).

Tenure has been misperceived and misrepresented both within and outside the university. If understood as I have suggested, which is its original and long-held purpose, it is both defensible and of such benefit to society that it deserves to be continued and defended against its opponents.

The attacks on tenure that have received the most public attention rarely mention academic freedom and the social benefits of the tenure system. The primary arguments are economic.

The most frequently heard argument is the "deadwood argument." There are various versions. The most extreme is that faculty members may work hard during their first six years in order to get tenure. But once they have attained tenure, they have little incentive to continue to work hard, and consequently do not. They tend to do as little as possible. They may teach, but they do not publish. They do not keep up in their fields. They spend as little time as possible in their offices or working with students. This is the claim. The basis for it is primarily imaginary, the result of the imaginations of those who are not in academe and assume that this is what must take place. There is no evidence that those who achieve tenure suddenly and en masse stop acting as they did before they got tenure. Any such broad claim is without substance. But a variation is that over the years after receiving tenure, some faculty members, perhaps a considerable number, find that they have little new to say and stop publishing, that they lose some of their energy and interest in teaching, that they perform at an adequate level but not more. And then they cannot be replaced because they have tenure.

Even this more modest charge is routinely made without any evidence. But it would be equally unreasonable to claim this never happens. It happens in every profession and every area of work. And it is typical for burned-out employees to be kept on as long as they perform adequately. Those with civil service positions or union contracts usually cannot be fired. And even in areas where people can be fired, they often are not. In cases of true incompetence, a college or university can fire a tenured faculty member. But in all these circumstances, whether at a university or in business, the proper first recourse is not termination but counseling and attention to rekindle the flame that once burned. Moreover, in the case of college and university faculty, they have undergone longer periods of both training and probation than people in most other areas, and the chance of their becoming deadwood is correspondingly less than in other areas. Nonetheless, institutions do make mistakes, especially if they do not exercise the care they should in granting tenure. In such cases, the institution suffers the result of its mistake, just as in other cases.

These bad effects are not a result of tenure. In fact, the tenure process, with its requirement that one either get tenure or leave, is more likely than otherwise to help institutions terminate those who are not likely to be productive. Without such a system, marginal people would likely be kept on, perhaps indefinitely, one more year at a time. They become friends whom one does not want to hurt or who have been around so long that dismissing them for behaving as they have been behaving for years seems unethical.

The deadwood argument is exaggerated, and true deadwood can be terminated for incompetence or for failure to perform adequately. The problem, to the extent that it exists, is not with tenure but with the failure of institutions to counsel and help, and if necessary, ultimately dismiss those deserving of dismissal.

The next charge is one of inefficiency. Corporations downsize and, in the process, get rid of excess workers—executives as well as those in the ranks. The rationale is that the firms become more competitive by becoming lean and mean. By contrast, it is claimed, universities are saddled with tenured faculty—perhaps too many or in the wrong areas as needs have changed. They cannot become lean and mean. These institutions cannot become efficient. Because they are overwhelmingly not-for-profit organizations, they face no competition and have no incentive to cut costs or change with the times. Even if they wanted to, tenure makes doing so impossible for them.

This charge is really multiple. The general charge of inefficiency is a difficult one to evaluate, because it is not entirely clear what inefficiency means when applied to an institution of higher learning. "Efficiency" should not be equated simply with the number of degrees awarded or the number of courses or students taught. And in fact, competition exists among colleges and universities.

The costs of running a research institution exceed those of running a primarily teaching institution. Tuition at a prestigious institution of higher education is typically much higher than tuition at a state-supported institution. Yet it is not evident that a school with a lower student/faculty ratio is more efficient than the inverse. Attracting students from around the globe, American colleges and universities are still the envy of most countries and remain highly competitive in the worldwide educational arena.

The salient point, however, is that the criterion of efficiency is not the appropriate one to apply. Universities should not be compared to factories, nor should the education of their students be compared to the products turned out by factories. This does not mean that colleges and universities cannot be held accountable for what they do and how they use their funds. But the criteria should be suited to their mission, which is not the production of goods but the preservation, transmission, and development of knowledge.

The claim is rarely made that tenure makes it impossible or difficult or unlikely for universities and colleges to be run in such a way that they cannot or do not measure up when evaluated by the proper criteria.

If it were made, then the difficulty would be to prove that tenure is the culprit. But this is unlikely. Tenure in part helps keep the salaries of faculty members low in comparison to the training required. The economic value of tenure is factored into the salary structure. Since a faculty member cannot opt out of tenure, all faculty members pay in lower salaries for the job protection tenure provides. Moreover, tenure provides a relatively stable faculty for an institution. It cuts down on the costs of constant recruiting and the training that takes place at the initial period on a new job.

Finally, unlike many other positions, faculty members may grow in insight in their discipline as they grow older, ideally gaining wisdom with maturity.

Wisdom differs from knowledge. Although it involves a great deal of knowledge, it also understands how such knowledge fits within a broader perspective. Wisdom also involves appreciating the value of what is known and its place in a grander order of things, as well the ability to make sound judgments that do not depend only on knowledge. It involves knowing not only what to do and how to do it but knowing what is worth doing. In a business whose end is profit and whose means are fairly well circumscribed, wisdom may play no important role. In a college or university setting whose purpose is to train young minds, prepare them for the fruitful functioning of a society, and counsel them in how to live well, wisdom is an essential ingredient in the faculty. Older faculty are not the same drag on an institution they might be considered in a business environment.

There are many other differences between a university and a business. A business arguably exists to make a profit. It downsizes in part to make it more likely to do so, and usually with an eye toward raising the value of its stock. Not only is a university usually a not-for-profit organization, but it has no unique end or bottom line by which it can be evaluated. It is multifaceted: it exists to educate students, to increase knowledge, to preserve and interpret that knowledge, and to serve a number of varied and complex needs of the state or society in which it exists. Downsizing does not necessarily make the university more efficient (the same is true of corporations), nor does downsizing raise its value. On the contrary, downsizing faculty tends to diminish the university.

Corporations tend to be managed hierarchically. The CEO with or without the board of directors and with or without other senior managers can decide what or who is to go and what restructuring should occur. A university is not typically structured in this way. Faculty members are not told what to do but help decide what to do. They are the authorities in their own area, and they usually and appropriately have a strong voice in what the institution does and how. The president or board is not competent to direct the university as a CEO can, at least in theory, direct the corporation. In fact, many companies are moving to a structure of shared responsibility and empowerment of lower-level managers and employees in order to improve morale, efficiency, and productivity. Such a structure is already present in the university and does not need to be achieved by downsizing. Without faculty consultation, downsizing is more likely to have precisely the opposite effect—lower morale, less efficiency, and decreased productivity. Loyalty to any institution on the part of those who work there is not automatically deserved or given but is rightly the result of reciprocal consideration.

Finally, although some fields fall out of favor and new ones emerge, such transitions take many years, and a well-managed institution will not find itself with faculty whose expertise is no longer needed. Before that happens, faculty can be retrained and moved to more relevant fields to teach.

A third argument deals more with supposed inequity than economics per se, prompted perhaps by a veiled sense of envy. Because many ordinary citizens live and work in an environment where people are laid off through no fault of their own—due to downsizing or technological changes, for example—they ask why faculty at colleges and universities should be treated differently from the mass of workers. When university budgets become tight, employees who are not faculty or civil service or union-protected often raise the same question. Because these people are not necessary to guarantee academic freedom, they are vulnerable in a way that tenured faculty are not. Once again, the justification for academic tenure is not the good of the individual faculty member or even of the individual institution but the good of society as a whole. Those who attack tenure for its supposed inequality ignore the fact that others, such as federal judges, also have tenure and that civil servants enjoy greater job security than employees in the private sector. They also ignore the fact that faculty face a crucial period in which they either get tenure or are terminated, unlike those in other areas. The issue is not whether faculty with tenure are treated differently from other workers but whether such differential treatment is justified—an issue that the argument ignores.

Although the economic arguments receive the most attention, they are far from decisive, especially since I have argued that academic tenure is best justified as being beneficial to society rather than as being primarily beneficial to individual faculty members, even though tenure guarantees their continuous employment. I have argued that the rationale for academic tenure is academic freedom. Viewed this way, academic tenure is not simply gifted to faculty members, it is conferred for certain reasons and carries with it certain obligations. When the obligations are not met, then the point of continuing the practice is correctly open to question.

Since academic tenure exists to allow faculty members to pursue the truth in their disciplines wherever it leads them, those who have tenure have the concomitant obligation in fact to pursue the truth in their areas to the best of their ability. They have the obligation to be as objective as they can be, to be as critical as appropriate in their field, and to follow arguments and their data wherever they may take them. This is not a right they have because of their tenure but an obligation that goes with tenure.

Accordingly, since the point of academic tenure is to preserve academic freedom, a second obligation of the tenured faculty is to protect academic freedom throughout the university. This means that they have the obligation to protect and promote academic freedom for their untenured faculty as well as for their students. Academic freedom solely for tenured faculty makes little sense. All members of the college or university must have academic freedom if the institution is to fulfill its mission. Since not all faculty are tenured, those who have tenure and hence cannot be fired except for cause—understood as incompetence or moral turpitude—are in a strong position to defend the academic freedom of those without tenure. This is another consequence of seeing tenure as not exclusively or even primarily for the benefit of the tenured but for the institution as a whole and ultimately for society. This perspective allows us to develop the ethics of tenure—that is, not the ethical justification for tenure but the ethical conditions that tenure imposes on institutions and on those members to whom it is awarded.

Academic tenure so understood allows us to evaluate and rebut some noneconomic critiques of tenure. We shall look at four of the more prominent of these: (1) the deadwood argument, again; (2) the six-year conformity-training argument; (3) the postmodern attack; and (4) the politicization attack.

1. The deadwood argument, again. This version is noneconomic but also claims that some who get tenure use it as an excuse to do little, and eventually turn into deadwood. While certainly an abuse of tenure, there is little evidence that this is widespread. Academic tenure protects faculty in their pursuit of

truth. The guarantee of continuous employment is circumscribed and is not absolute. We have already noted that the failure to perform required academic tasks is grounds for dismissal. Tenure does not prohibit regular review for purposes of promotion and of salary increases. It does not relieve departmental chairpersons, deans, and other university administrators from evaluating tenured faculty or from encouraging, counseling, and helping those who are not as productive as they once were or as the institution feels they should be. Tenure should not be an excuse for tolerating incompetence, laziness, or failure to perform at an acceptable level. In these cases, then both the faculty member who abuses tenure and the institution that allows the abuse are at fault. But such failures do not reveal any intrinsic failure or weakness in the practice of awarding academic tenure.

2. The six-year conformity-training argument. The second charge claims the system encourages young faculty to play it safe rather than take risks during their six or so years as faculty members without tenure. They spend six years conforming to the desires and views of their senior colleagues, who hold the tenure decision in their hands. These senior colleagues are unlikely to vote tenure for new faculty who will challenge their views or undermine their authority with students. Hence young faculty members conform, perhaps thinking that after six years they will be free to be creative and really express individual views. But six years of repressed or constrained thought yield a habit of thinking, and the practice of routine research takes over and typically supplants more creative impulses. The result is a habit of safe research. Those who do not conform are weeded out prior to or in their sixth year.

This argument describes not the result of the tenure system but an abuse of the tenure system. Understood as I have portrayed it, tenure confers the obligation to protect the academic freedom of those without tenure. If their academic freedom is protected, then untenured faculty members will have little reason not to pursue truth and to follow their pursuit wherever it leads them. A university should in fact expect this of its new faculty members, and unless they do pursue their research in this way, they may not be deserving of tenure. Hence tenure does not deter the pursuit of truth, but just the opposite. To the extent that this is not the case, the tenured can be faulted for not promoting the proper atmosphere of academic freedom in their institutions and for not demanding such pursuit of their new faculty.

3. The postmodern attack. According to postmodernists and some others within the university, there is no such thing as objective truth, only opinions, points of view, and different stories. I have argued that the rationale for academic tenure is academic freedom and that this presupposes there is knowledge and truth yet to be developed and pursued. If there is no such knowledge and if there is only opinion, then the basis for academic tenure and academic freedom seems to disappear. This would indeed be the case if all one had

was opinion with no objective criteria for deciding that one opinion is better than another. A complete answer to this objection is a long story. The short answer is that in some fields—most clearly in the sciences—ample evidence indicates that some theories are better than others because of the impressive results possible as a consequence of accepting those theories. Even in the humanities, which are more prone to the attack, sophisticated versions of the attack on objectivity redefine it and redefine truth so that not everything within the various disciplines is equally defensible or acceptable. But if there were in fact no way to discern valid from invalid or true from false or better from worse claims, then it is not clear why those subjects are pursued at the university. The claim is not damaging so much to tenure as it is to the disciplines themselves. And if these disciplines were removed from the university, then those who teach them would have little claim to tenure. But even postmodernists are reluctant to draw this conclusion. What they wish is not the abolition of the university or certain departments but a dominant voice within them.

4. The politicization attack. The fourth attack is somewhat similar to the third. If universities are not institutions that search for truth but are the repositories of power that impose certain political views on students, then academic freedom loses its rationale. And if academic freedom loses its rationale, so does academic tenure. Political correctness, some claim, is nothing new but simply a new name given to behavior that characterizes the university, which is and always has been politicized. The politicization of the university is inimical to academic freedom whether the politicization comes from without or from within—whether it is the tool of politicians or the tool of politicized faculty members.

The proper answer is that if the universities are politicized, they should be depoliticized. But if they cannot be, then the rationale for academic tenure dissolves, academic freedom loses its meaning, and the very existence of a university as it has been known for centuries is undermined.

In all these cases I have conceded that if the attacks are justified, then academic freedom is not justified. But in each case I have maintained that pointing out abuses is not a legitimate attack on the principle of academic tenure per se. Faculties and institutions invested in academic tenure are obliged to use it properly and to police abuses. But abuses, unless they cannot be corrected, are not sufficient justification for eliminating tenure.

The major cost of the loss of tenure would not be to faculty members, who would for the most part learn to protect themselves, to conform, and to secure their positions. The greater loss would be to the fabric and quality of society as a whole.

Chapter 4

What Should Count for Tenure and Promotion?

David Shatz

Why couldn't God get tenure? Because He wrote only one book, and it wasn't refereed.

—Academic jokelore

Anyone who labors at academic scholarship knows vividly—perhaps even painfully—how much that enterprise depends on the process known as peer review. Peer-reviewed articles and books are the gold standard in decisions about hiring, tenure, and promotion. This is as it ought to be: the process provides quality control in scholarly communication. It doesn't just filter out inferior work; it provides incentive for scholars to do their best work. Moreover, the criticisms and suggestions of referees improve submissions dramatically.

Even so, assessments of candidates for tenure and promotion (T&P) can go awry by adopting a narrow paradigm for what should count as a meritorious contribution, deviation from which can destroy careers. This system is based on an exclusionary way of thinking that I deem unjustified and unfair, as well as unwise. In this essay I explain why.

JEAN'S PLIGHT

Jean, a freshly minted Harvard PhD in philosophy, has just landed a position as an assistant professor at Dumont University. Although not in the same league as Harvard or Princeton, Dumont is a respected school that expects scholarly productivity of its faculty. Jean's position is of that increasingly rare breed—a tenure-track job. She is eager to begin compiling a record of publications that down the road will earn her tenure and promotion.

Her mentors ranked Jean highly as a graduate student. She published an article in grad school, and her name had been circulating in the publishing grapevine. No sooner did she earn her doctorate than she received an email from her Harvard professor, whom a university press had contacted to edit an anthology in philosophy of language—her specialty. With his own plate already full of commitments, he decided to turn this one down while recommending Jean as a promising scholar who is on top of the literature, reliable, and judicious. Highly flattered by this opportunity, Jean undertakes work on the collection.

A few days later, a top journal invites Jean to review a new book by a giant in her field, a philosopher whose work she grappled with in her dissertation. The thought of publishing in such a fine venue on such a prominent author excites her. She gets to work immediately.

Not long afterward, a well-known philosopher who has heard wonderful things about Jean's work asks her to contribute to *New Essays in the Philosophy of Language*. Jean jumps at the chance.

Her apparent good fortune continues. Jean's paper is accepted for a highly prestigious conference. Then a well-known publisher recruits her as the sole author of a text introducing students to the philosophy of language. A nice royalty offer sweetens the publishing pot.

In total, in the first few weeks of her job at Dumont, Jean has landed editorship of an anthology, a contribution to an anthology sure to be read and respected, a presentation spot on a conference program, and authorship of a textbook.

After this rousing start, more invitations follow for articles and book reviews, as do offers to do a second text and other attractive options. Jean is riding high. The run continues: she publishes part of her dissertation and a well-placed article coauthored with a colleague. Then she posts a lot of her work in progress online.

Highly knowledgeable on social issues, Jean also assumes the role of public intellectual. Widely read highbrow magazines carry her political writings; newspapers of distinction publish numerous op-ed pieces by her. Space in these venues is at a premium, but Jean is good and gains the coveted spots.

Six years later, Jean's tenure committee convenes. And the bubble bursts as her evaluators question most of the projects that had so excited her.

> Anthologies don't count.
> Reviews don't count.
> Conference presentations don't count.
> Textbooks don't count.
> Invited contributions don't count.
> Coauthored pieces do not count.
> Online postings do not count.
> Work as a "public intellectual" does not count.

Ultimately, Jean is turned down for tenure.

Variants of Jean's seemingly outrageous narrative occur in real life. Junior faculty who accept offers like those that came her way can in certain schools find themselves in precarious positions. Indeed, they would be well-advised to turn down such work. Other conditions may even be imposed: some schools count only books published by a major university press toward tenure or promotion. Favorable external book reviews from highly regarded scholars are not enough; the publisher must be prestigious.

The consequences of junior faculty living under Dumont's policies would be decidedly negative for their profession. Scholars and students would feel the impact. In some areas, there wouldn't be enough textbooks, or enough high-quality textbooks, without the Jeans of the world writing them. There also wouldn't be enough articles to fill certain anthologies, conferences would be understocked, and so forth. Alternatively, there would be such books and articles, but people as talented as Jean would not be writing them. Applying Dumont University's standards would harm the dissemination of knowledge to scholars and students—in other words, education.

Certain jobs need to get done in a well-functioning profession; certain types of scholarly work needs to be produced; certain settings need to exist (such as symposia). Arguing that people who do these jobs or who join these settings are jeopardizing their chances of professional success seems anomalous. Prima facie there is something fundamentally wrong with a system that prevents much work from helping professional advancement even if it is (1) of quality and (2) beneficial to professors, students, and society. You might retort that, by my logic, a candidate's regularly taking out the garbage or making coffee (tasks beneficial to the profession) should count toward tenure. But obviously these tasks are not professional activities that call upon philosophical skills or whatever skills an academic's field requires. Someone needs to write the textbooks; someone needs to do oral presentations. And these, unlike garbage-dumping and coffee-making, require expertise in one's discipline.

SHOULD INVITED WORK COUNT?

Jean's situation, while obviously a caricature, nevertheless raises serious questions about how T&P committees assess the work of faculty. I want to address one question in particular posed by Jean's dossier: How should these committees weigh invited articles that appear in collections?

Some years ago, I invited an assistant professor at a major research university to contribute to an anthology of new essays I was editing. I did not know this individual personally, but his published work convinced me that he would be the best person to write on a particular area that needed coverage. Before extending the invitation, I consulted my colleagues and friends in the field to confirm my assessment. Thus my invitation was based on an evaluation of his previous work and in no way betokened a friendship with the invitee.

Two days after his initial acceptance, much to my surprise and chagrin, this young assistant professor turned my invitation down. He explained that senior colleagues had cautioned him that in tenure review, articles in books of essays would count far less than those in refereed journals, if at all. So the time needed to write the anthologized article would be better spent on an article (on the same or a different subject) that would undergo competitive peer review. Accepting invitations, he was told in effect, should be the luxury of the secure and famous.

Disappointed over losing what I expected to be a splendid contribution, I lamented the senior colleagues' general attitude (or the attitude they were ascribing to *others*). For one thing, publishers often send proposed essays to reviewers, albeit they comment less expansively than when judging journal submissions. Moreover, when candidates come up for tenure or promotion, their work is sent out for review by outside specialists anyway, regardless of where the writings were published, in addition to being reviewed by colleagues. The T&P committee could have a dozen or so evaluations in hand for an anthologized article—far more than a journal editor has—and some are likely to be from experts of greater renown and experience than referees the invitee would have had for a refereed submission. If these evaluators are superior in number and quality to the potential referees, why should it matter that the piece was not refereed? Also, if a refereed journal rejected the articles, one wouldn't know who the referees were or even perhaps their reasons for rejection; how, therefore, could one judge the quality of their particular reviews? By contrast, the personnel letters would be signed and could serve as a check on a referee's recommendations. By soliciting further evaluations of refereed published material, universities seem to be accepting a higher court than that of the original referees, one with still higher standards for assessing the quality of an invited published work. Further complicating the picture, some articles in peer-reviewed journals are in truth invited articles. If an article thought to be peer reviewed received a fine reaction and was influential, are we supposed to retract our favorable view when we learn that an editor invited it?

Any assumption that an invited piece signals nothing more than a friendship is unfounded and unfair without hard evidence. Indeed, in the particular instance I cited, I had formed my opinion of this individual by conducting my own "peer-review" process when I assessed his articles and solicited opinions of others. Besides, academics often form "friendships" like this: X has heard of an article Y wrote. X finds it online, likes the article, and writes a nice note to Y. Y finds material by X and likes it. Each asks the other to send work in progress. Out of this mutual appreciation and respect for each other's work, a friendship grows. The two scholars may meet personally only rarely, perhaps at conventions, or they may never meet. But they become friends, via correspondence, because they value each other's scholarly abilities. The assumption that an invitation from a "friend" is unrelated to the invitee's competence is gratuitous, indeed false in many cases.

This is not to say that a T&P committee member can be expected to differentiate cases in which people become friends out of mutual respect for each other's work from cases in which an editor invites a schoolmate, cousin, or lover. Furthermore, an invitation does not usually entail a positive evaluation of a particular piece already written but rather of the author's *previous* work. Acceptance to a journal, by contrast, testifies to a particular piece's quality. But once again, scholars will evaluate that work when the time comes for a decision about tenure or promotion, and it may even be assessed in print before then. Remember, too, that editors want to protect their own reputations and to that end will want papers that meet a high standard. For that reason, they are unlikely to invite a paper only as a favor.

Speakers are invited to forums without prior knowledge and review of the particular speech they will deliver. Yet (1) one would not normally infer that the invitation came from friendship alone; and (2) if someone rates the speech highly and hears others praise it as well, it would be absurd to moderate that assessment just because the speech was not subject to prior review. As with good invited speeches, so too with good invited articles. And let us not forget that a policy of disparaging unrefereed pieces would diminish the works of Plato, Aristotle, Descartes, Hume, Kant, and, of course, God.

I am not denying that the fact a piece was peer reviewed creates a presumption of quality via a reasonable inductive argument. But even if peer review were truly sufficient to guarantee high quality (which it is not—peer-reviewed published work is often later discovered to be seriously flawed), it is not a necessary condition, as non-peer-reviewed works can also be excellent. And, of course, some peer-reviewed articles are accepted with minimal revisions, suggesting they might be of high quality even before the review process. Invited works are often presumed to be in this category. Granted, without a peer-review system, committees would have a tough time sorting the wheat from the chaff. But it would be doable.

It might be replied that outside evaluators for a tenure and promotion case are likely not as demanding as referees and editors for a competitive journal or press. Personnel evaluators who decide to recommend X are not normally forced to choose between X and someone else, to compare X to other candidates. Journals and presses are competitive, however. So a positive recommendation from a referee carries more heft than a positive recommendation in a personnel evaluation.

This rebuttal is specious. The referee's original reports were not made in the context of a competition. As a rule, referees are not comparing one article to others submitted to the journal. With a vast literature out there, referees may have missed some relevant recent work and thus cannot even do a good job of comparing an article to other published ones. An editor perhaps makes a competitive decision, but an editor will not always have read submitted papers carefully and will instead adjudicate the competition based on referee reports. Since an individual referee's report is usually not based on a straightforward competitive evaluation, the editor may not have a direct way of ranking two "competing" submissions.

Personnel committees, by contrast, are often asked to offer comparisons—not only about where candidates rank relative to others in the field but also where particular works rank and what those works have contributed. Evaluators often say things like "this is the best piece I know of on the subject . . ." or "it's one of the two or three best." Why not count such praise of an invited article if one counts it for a refereed article? Can it in good conscience be ignored?

A personnel evaluator has one advantage that the original referees lack: hindsight. By the time the evaluation is written, the reviewer will be aware of something the referees could not know—namely, how well the article or book has been received and has withstood *public* scrutiny. Needless to say, the personnel referee's evaluation should not slavishly follow others' reactions, but an awareness of those reactions will help the evaluator form a more meaningful assessment. Nobel laureate Rosalyn Yalow originally had her prizewinning work rejected, and J. R. Mayer's 1842 paper reporting the first law of thermodynamics was rejected by a leading journal and accepted by a relatively obscure one. The value of ideas is better judged after publication than before.

There are additional considerations in favor of counting invited articles heavily. First, many scholars are more familiar with key anthologies in their fields than with journals (in part because anthologies are used in courses). If more scholars would read a paper in certain anthologies than would read it in a journal, surely this ought to be significant in assessing the publication's value to the field. Second, an exclusionary approach has a most untoward consequence. Departments must advise anyone planning to apply for tenure and promotion (like the young scholar I mentioned earlier) not to contribute any invited paper, nor even to deliver an invited lecture, when doing so is accompanied by the expectation that the paper will be published in conference proceedings. The cost of not heeding this advice could be a career. Whatever benefits there are to gaining exposure and name recognition are not likely to outweigh this drastic outcome of joblessness.

Forcing young faculty to decline invitations seems unfair. A young scholar may have a better chance of earning a reputation by publishing in a well-placed anthology than by publishing in a journal. Any good publication leads to expanded contacts and further opportunities. Several volumes of mostly invited essays have had great impact on the philosophical profession. I know of no one who disparages the quality of those books just because the essays were invited. Similar arguments apply to another criterion often used—the prestige of the journal or press that published the article. Were great works of philosophy judged by "who published it?" Merit is merit, and post-publication reviews, published or unpublished, can detect and reflect it.

OBJECTIONS

At this point someone might object that I have been too generous to outside evaluators for hiring, tenure, and promotion. Letters of recommendation can be exaggerated and written irresponsibly. Often the letter writers include some whom the candidate requested. Evaluations may be to some degree dishonest or inflated. Further, an evaluator called upon to offer an opinion of a candidate's oeuvre perforce does not examine each thesis and point with the same care as a referee. The evaluator will form an overall opinion of each work and cast it in the form of a few sentences. A truly conscientious evaluator will probe as deeply as a referee, and that happens, but it is not the rule.

If, however, we fear irresponsible external evaluations, would this not call into question the wisdom of relying on those letters altogether? If outside evaluations are the core of personnel decisions, we have to assume a basically honest and dependable system. As for the claim that an evaluator will not probe an article as a referee would, it doesn't matter if this is the case. Awarding people tenure or promotion is not tantamount to proclaiming their positions correct and their arguments unassailable. If it were, then published criticism of a tenured professor's article should be grounds for claiming tenure was a mistake, which needless to say it is not. Doing high quality work and being correct are not equivalent. Great philosophers often have views that most people reject, but this does not diminish the quality and significance of their work. Personnel evaluators can spot quality and importance.

A remaining argument for more heavily weighing certain organs of publications is status. Every department in a research university wants members of stature in the field, which top journals and presses create. Also, the impact of a work emanating from certain journals or presses is greater. Although not to be dismissed lightly, this argument gives an imprimatur to bias and snobbery that ought to be remedied. The perception of what constitutes status should itself change once publication in those journals or by those presses is seen not to *necessarily* spell higher quality. Letters to potential evaluators could emphasize that they are to comment on quality and not be influenced by provenance. Quality is quality and can be judged so by personnel evaluators; it cannot be discarded in the interests of prestige. Additionally, an invitation from certain editors might carry its own prestige.

Two concessions must be made. First, in hiring decisions, looking for candidates with peer-reviewed works in prestige journals or presses is a good mode of operating. It is much more efficient and cost-effective to pare down a large initial pool, with hundreds of candidates, by identifying applicants who have published in peer-reviewed journals, unless the invited articles listed are known to the search committee. And members of the search committee are not necessarily expert enough in the applicant's field to assess those works. Second, the distinction between prestigious and nonprestigious journals is relevant when evaluators decide whether to be impressed by the *quantity* of a candidate's publications. Ten papers in relatively undemanding journals may be less impressive than five in exacting ones. Hence, I am ready to countenance an adjustment of quantity requirements based on the journals' rejection rates. Still, quality is quality no matter where it appears.

SHOULD UNPUBLISHED WORKS COUNT?

My analysis confronts a number of challenges of the *reductio ad absurdum* variety. Wouldn't my arguments on behalf of invited pieces apply to unsolicited papers in unrefereed electronic journals? Wouldn't they support counting unpublished, privately circulated works as well as invited pieces? Why not just rely on outside evaluators in these cases too? In fact, why insist on candidates *publishing* their work at all?

Is the conclusion of these *reductio ad absurdum*s really absurd? Publication is thought to be essential for disseminating knowledge. But what if someone frequently presents work in oral form to a large audience over Zoom? What if Fred emails or snail mails his unpublished work—good work—to every member of a professional association and pays them to actually read it? Won't more people then read it than if it were in a print journal or digital venue? Some important papers (for example, David Kaplan's "D-That" back in the 1970s) were originally circulated widely but not published immediately, achieving a degree of status and fame in the process. With so many scholars now posting work online in advance of print, this can happen more often. In short, content, not medium, is crucial.

A key advantage to the practice of publication is that it provides an access point for the scholarly community; by means of indexes, library records, citations, and so on, scholars both in and out of one's field can locate the work for generations to come. Unpublished work cannot be as readily accessed this way. In other words, publication enables authors to share their work with the larger community—and with future generations.

At the same time, as others have pointed out, ideas can be perpetuated in forms other than traditional publication. Why would we not want *all* that we think to be passed on to future generations? Referees and editors shape their disciplines according to concerns and trends of their own time. But the interests, methods, and standards of the next generation may differ from ours, and work overlooked in our period may become vibrant and show new merit in another. We need to think about how scholars will think in later times, as well as how rapidly tides may turn in our own. Taking the long view leaves us wondering whether, by being as selective as we are and by privileging some modes of dissemination over others, we are neglecting future generations. Admittedly, there is a countervailing consideration: inundation. We serve future generations by preventing this consequence. I do not know how to strike the right balance here, but both lines of thought should be considered.

Let me emphasize that a candidate for tenure or promotion would be wise to submit material to prepublication peer review. Doing so prevents committees from judging that individual adversely and maximizes quality, since the author's work would profit from peer review and from the extra incentive to do one's best for referees. But after the fact, that is, if the person has, say, published work in response to an invitation, the work should be judged by postpublication review.

SUMMATION

I have argued, first, that the practice of discounting certain sorts of publications and presentations in tenure and promotion decisions sits uneasily with the fact that those sorts of work contribute significantly to the profession. The scholarly community may have unfairly belittled quality work of capable scholars and discouraged some from placing their work in forums more likely to reach a large audience than refereed journals. My main point, however, is that in certain ways—notably by its ability to speak from hindsight—postpublication peer review is a more reliable guide to quality and of course impact than the refereeing process. Committees no doubt want their departments to have "status," but if they would cease to view status as dependent on where something appeared and view it instead as dependent on postpublication reception, the objection to ignoring where the work appeared would fall away.

Peer review creates a highly competitive environment and therefore a higher quality set of submissions; it also improves work, making it likely that the published version of a manuscript will be better than what came over the transom. However, this does not settle the question of how to weigh items that were not subjected to competitive refereeing when we have other instruments by which to evaluate them.

To return to the misfortunes of Jean, let us hope that her next university will give Jean's invited publications their due and accord greater weight to other publications and presentations that are the lifeblood of the profession and indispensable to its members.

Chapter 5

Academic Career Success

Keota Fields

The academy's efforts to recruit and retain faculty, and to support academic careers, are challenged by what I shall call "externalities." These are events, activities, obligations, or restrictions that affect career success without being fully reflected or acknowledged in a candidate's dossier (e.g., they don't appear on a curriculum vitae). Externalities often have a negative impact on career success. To a reviewer unaware of outside influences on their work, candidates might appear less productive, qualified, or effective than they actually are. Conversely, of course, externalities can have a positive impact on career success, making candidates appear more productive, qualified, or effective than they actually are. Setting consideration of such positive externalities aside, this essay is concerned with negative externalities—those that adversely affect career success. I argue that academics have a "Minimally Decent Samaritan" moral obligation to develop routines that help blunt the impacts of negative externalities on academic career success, a task that is not supererogatory. After considering some objections, I offer two suggestions—one for identifying negative externalities and another for ensuring fair and effective routines to mitigate their impacts.

Faculty should be familiar with some instances of negative externalities, those recognized with sufficient regularity that routines have already been developed to mitigate their influence. Suppose, for example, an assistant professor unexpectedly becomes a new parent. That event and its attendant obligations are likely to negatively impact the candidate's publication record. So, when evaluating a tenure dossier, external reviewers unaware of this situation may rate the candidate somewhat lower than would have otherwise been the case. Many campuses have developed routines that blunt much of the negative impact of unexpected parenthood on academic career success, such as the candidate's colleagues intervening during the tenure review process. Indeed, such routines are so widespread that some campuses have moved to formalize them.

Unfortunately, these interventions are inconsistently deployed and often met with resistance. Suppose, for example, that the faculty vote to weight a quantification such as the number of publications during the period of tenure review to account for any candidate's unexpected parenthood. Although a hopeful change, such developments are commonly met with counterarguments about weakening academic standards or about giving some candidates an unfair advantage. These rejoinders, however, either misunderstand or fail to recognize the moral obligations of faculty to help thwart the impacts of negative externalities. They are also debatable.

Let's assume that academic standards are direct measures of competitiveness; and because competitiveness is a direct measure of academic quality, let's assume that academic standards are indirect measures of academic quality. In that case, the concern may be understood as follows: weakening academic standards directly weakens competitiveness and indirectly weakens academic quality. But in general, only *absolute* measures weaken competitiveness, while *conditional* measures can and often do maintain a target level of competitiveness. Consider various conditional rules in competitive sports. These include rules for tiebreaking, overtime, tournament ranking, and so forth. In a typical competition, the team that scores the most points wins. But if there is a tie, then certain tie-breaking rules come into effect to determine the winner. This conditional tie-breaking rule doesn't weaken competitiveness. On the contrary, it promotes competitiveness by allowing a fair determination of the winner if certain conditions obtain. In particular, the standard that whichever team scores the most points wins remains unchanged in normal circumstances. Presumably, a truly weakened standard would allow a team to win in *any* circumstance without scoring the most points.

Something similar may be said of routines designed to mitigate the negative impacts of unexpected parenthood on academic career success. Those routines are conditional: if the externality had not occurred, then the candidate would be held to the normal standard. Similarly, if a tie had not occurred, then the team with the most points would win. In both cases, the standards are implicitly understood to obtain ceteris paribus. But when negative externalities are present, all things are not equal. In such cases, conditional routines allow for a fair determination of a candidate's productivity, quality, and effectiveness in light of a negative externality. That is, conditional routines permit fair evaluations of competitiveness and, therefore, indirectly permit fair evaluations of academic quality. Presumably, similar to the earlier example, a weakened standard would permit *any* candidate to be awarded tenure with fewer publications, whether or not negative externalities were a factor.

But even supposing conditional routines that blunt the impact of negative externalities do weaken competitiveness, it's clear that maximal competitiveness is not morally important. Suppose that not requiring protective gear for players can maximize competitiveness in sport Q. With lighter gear or none at all, Q-players can run faster and farther and jump higher. But without the heavier gear, they are at significantly higher risk of sustaining lifelong debilitating injuries. (American football is such a sport.) It's uncontroversial that maximal competitiveness is not morally important in this scenario. Needlessly risking severe injury to players just to have a maximally competitive contest (consider ancient Roman gladiator fights) would be morally abhorrent. But even if one gives some moral status to maximal competitiveness, it is vastly outweighed by the moral imperative to prevent or reduce needless injuries where possible.

A similar principle applies to the moral status of maximal competitiveness in the name of academic quality. If an externality has the potential to harm an academic's career, then the moral imperative to prevent or reduce that harm vastly outweighs any possible moral status of maximal competitiveness, assuming it has any moral status at all. Why should harm to an academic's career have any moral weight? Because success, in any career, is an indispensable component of one's overall well-being, and a person's overall well-being presumably has intrinsic moral value.

It might be objected that even if preventing or reducing harm to an academic's career is a moral imperative, it obligates only the academic whose career is in danger, not other academics. In that case, any conditional routines put in place to blunt the impact of negative externalities is supererogatory. One academic is not morally obligated to help prevent, or to help mitigate, harm to another academic's career. This objection overlooks what are often called, in their strongest form, "Good Samaritan" moral obligations to help those in peril, which are sometimes construed in supererogatory ways. For instance, whether one has a Good Samaritan obligation to help those in peril even when doing so would cause significant harm to oneself remains a matter of debate.

A weaker principle says that we are morally obligated to minimally help those in peril when doing so causes no harm to oneself. Following Judith Jarvis Thompson,[1] let's call this the "Minimally Decent Samaritan" obligation. A Good Samaritan would risk injury to herself to prevent a stranger from being assaulted. A Minimally Decent Samaritan would call the police from her cell phone. Even if we do not have Good Samaritan moral obligations, it seems that we have Minimally Decent Samaritan obligations to help others. It would surely be morally repugnant of you to do nothing to help prevent the assault of a stranger when calling the police from your cell phone would do you no harm.

To borrow an example from Peter Singer,[2] it would surely be morally repugnant of you to do nothing to help a child drowning in a river when jumping in would do you no harm. We might say (on Singer's behalf) that you have a Minimally Decent Samaritan obligation to help the child. Singer's example addresses a potential objection to the case for helping faculty whose careers are threatened. Why are faculty morally responsible for externalities they didn't cause? In reply, being morally obligated does not entail being morally responsible in a causal way. As you didn't cause the child to be in the river drowning, you are not morally responsible for that state of affairs. Nevertheless, you *are* morally obligated to help save the child from drowning.

I do not mean to suggest that negative externalities pose threats equivalent to drowning or assault. Nor do I mean to suggest that academic career success has the same moral status as life itself. Academics have a Minimally Decent Samaritan obligation, however, to help prevent negative externalities from needlessly harming the careers of other academics. Doing so poses no risk of harm to the career of the Minimally Decent Samaritan, largely because those in a position to help typically have tenure and thus a career largely inoculated from harm. One could even argue that the inoculation from harm to one's career gives academics with tenure stronger Minimally Decent Samaritan obligations than academics without tenure. And since maximal competitiveness is not morally comparable to the imperative to prevent or reduce unnecessary harm to another academic's career, there is no moral basis for weighing the obligation to help against concerns about weakening academic standards.

As noted earlier, most academics are familiar with the example of unexpected parenthood and its potentially negative impact on academic career success. The widespread agreement that faculty *should* develop routines to help tenure candidates who unexpectedly become new parents is evidence that faculty recognize their own Minimally Decent Samaritan obligations. Often, the question for faculty in such cases isn't whether they should help, but what kinds of interventions would be fair and effective.

But there are many other negative externalities whose impacts on academic career success are not routinely blunted, often because they go unnoticed or unacknowledged. As a result, otherwise promising academic careers are hobbled. Sadly, negative externalities can and often do impact recruitment of high-achieving undergraduates into graduate programs, retention of graduate students, and navigating the academic job market. In such cases, negative externalities threaten to end promising academic careers before they even begin.

Consider the following example. You are an advanced graduate student in the midwestern United States hoping to submit a paper for publication prior to going on the job market. You have been advised to have your paper vetted prior to journal submission by presenting its main findings at an international conference. The next such conference where you're likely to receive helpful feedback happens to be in Helsinki, Finland. Airfare from your local airport to Helsinki is over $2,000. When added to the cost of meals and lodging, even at a hostel, the trip would be prohibitively expensive. Your institution offers a $500 travel stipend for graduate students, but you simply cannot afford to cover the remainder of the cost. You are forced to skip the conference, not even bothering to submit your abstract for review. A similar story might be told for an assistant professor gearing up for tenure. If the resources to cover the remaining costs out of pocket after the reimbursement are lacking, that professor may not be able to attend the conference.

I do not mean to suggest that conference presentations are the primary means of vetting works in progress in every discipline. But they are a way for academics to advertise their work to potential reviewers—often the only way. (How often does a busy faculty member read email from strangers? How often do they read a paper someone randomly sends them and reply with detailed comments?) Thus, although peer-reviewed articles are the gold standard for academic success, conference presentations are vital to the career advancement of many academics.

The consequences of being forced to forgo vetting works in progress have negative impacts on an academic's career. Without sufficient scrutiny prior to submission, the already-slim chances that your work will be published in a top journal diminish considerably. Without the feedback, networking, and interactions that come from presenting at a major conference, your prospects for participation in other practices in the system of academic vetting also worsen. You're less likely to be invited to contribute chapters to edited volumes, to blind referee journal submissions, or to give talks at department colloquia or other professional meetings.

There's also the straightforward issue of practice. The more academics work, the better their work gets. Preparing for conference presentations, writing referee reports for journals, and writing chapters for edited volumes are all opportunities for academics to practice their craft. Negative externalities thwart those opportunities, hobbling the careers of academics who endure them.

Many academics may manage to publish and their careers may flourish despite the presence of negative externalities. It's at best unclear that these threaten to harm academic careers in any significant way. And without the threat of significant harm, other academics do not have Minimally Decent Samaritan obligations to help. But this objection is based on too restricted a data set. Considering only successful academics doesn't account for, say, academics who are struggling professionally as "permanent adjuncts" or are otherwise underemployed precisely because they cannot establish a strong publication record. It certainly doesn't account for aspiring academics who gave up as advanced graduate students or after many years of failed job searches due to negative externalities.

Other externalities can have similarly negative impacts on academic career success: a parent's immigration status, a disability, homelessness, a gender transition. All these strain an academic's cognitive and financial resources in ways likely to result in being forced to skip such-and-such conference, to delay work on such-and-such publication, or to set aside such-and-such research project until a particular storm has passed. Unlike the case of a tenure candidate who unexpectedly becomes a new parent, academics have yet to develop routines that diminish the negative impacts of these and other externalities on academic career success. My sense is that this is partly due to failure to identify some of those externalities and partly due to lack of consensus about what routines are most effective when such externalities have been identified.

Nevertheless, faculty have Minimally Decent Samaritan obligations to help blunt the impacts of negative externalities, and this can only happen if they identify those externalities in the first place. Some recognition of financial burdens imposed on faculty and graduate students, and the risks they pose to career success, is already happening. The COVID-19 pandemic forced many conferences to be held fully remotely. Spared the costs of international or transcontinental travel, academics may have participated in virtual events that they could not have otherwise attended (although data is not yet available). By forcing everyone to stay home, the pandemic made venues for vetting academic work more accessible. I suspect that options for remote participation, and consequent accessibility for more academics, will continue long after the pandemic ebbs.

Note that practical challenges remain, however, even when faculty recognize negative externalities and are motivated to help mitigate their impacts. A strategy that works for a department with thirty faculty, a bustling PhD program, and hundreds of undergraduate majors may be unworkable for a department with four faculty who mainly teach "service" courses, no graduate students, and few undergraduate majors. Similarly, a strategy that works for elite institutions might not work for non-elite institutions (and vice versa). Given the decentralized nature of the academy, with its variety of departments, programs, and institutions, it may be impractical to offer armchair solutions to the challenge of negative externalities. Predicting what externalities will emerge, when, under what circumstances, and at what type of department, program, or institution is simply too difficult. The best approach is to promote awareness of negative externalities while encouraging academics to develop local strategies to confront these challenges and share information about what works and why.

Although specific strategies to combat specific externalities might be impractical, it's worth offering two general suggestions for identifying negative externalities and ensuring fair and effective routines to mitigate their impacts. First, faculty should be consistently receptive to a variety of reasons to believe that a negative externality is occurrent and to help a colleague or graduate student confronting a career obstacle. Such receptivity might, for instance, alert faculty to the professional risks associated with financially burdensome conference travel. Second, for routines that thwart negative externalities to be fair and effective, they should be transparent, consistently applied, and reflectively endorsed by the faculty deploying them. If faculty understand why they are obligated to help, how a particular routine satisfies that obligation, and how this routine promotes rather than weakens academic quality, they are more likely to be motivated to help by means of that routine.

Part III

PRIVACY

Chapter 6

Confidentiality and Professional Practice

Peter Markie

A physician who violates patient confidentiality isn't very good at doctoring; an attorney who violates client confidentiality isn't very good at lawyering. For these and many professionals, being good at what they do includes honoring ethical duties of confidentiality. Academics—professors, advisors, and university administrators—are no exception. Professional duties of confidentiality help define the quality of our practice. Legal rules, such as the Family Educational Rights and Privacy Act ("FERPA"), support some of our ethical duties. Yet the duties exist independently of the law and often exceed its requirements, and they give rise to important questions: What aspect of our professional practice supports them? What are they? How weighty are they? What factors enhance/lessen our ability to honor them, and how are these factors best developed/eliminated?

These questions are notable for being ignored. Books and essays on academic ethics seldom consider them. Where other professions make confidentiality duties a central part of professional education, we, for the most part, do not. We attend to them in programs on research ethics but not in discussions of teaching, advising, or program administration. An internet scan reveals several university training initiatives on FERPA and other legal confidentiality requirements, but these programs seldom consider the related ethical factors.

Nonetheless, duties of confidentiality are central to our professional lives. After making some general points, I'll give these duties some of the attention they deserve and consider some of their related challenges.

CONFIDENTIALITY IN GENERAL

Ethical duties of confidentiality are prima facie in nature. They can conflict with other ones, such as our duty not to harm, and, when they do, they sometimes prevail and sometimes do not.

We have both professional and nonprofessional duties of confidentiality, distinguished by whether the relevant information is learned or used as part of our professional practice. If we learned the information in the course of our professional practice, our duty is a professional one. It doesn't matter if the occasion for our revealing it is nonprofessional, a passing conversation with a neighbor perhaps. If we gained the information outside our professional practice but our revealing it would be integral to our professional practice, our duty is again professional. If, for example, we are on an award selection committee and our sharing some negative information about a colleague will violate someone's trust, we have a professional duty to keep the information to ourselves.

We gain duties of confidentiality in two different ways. They often piggyback on other ethical duties. When divulging information will cause someone harm, our standing ethical duty not to harm requires not disclosing it. Similarly, if keeping some information confidential will promote justice, our standing duty to promote moral goods gives us a duty of confidentiality. I'll refer to duties of confidentiality gained in this way as implied duties. The content and weight of an implied duty are determined by the duty or duties on which it rides. Since they reduce in this way to other ethical duties, I don't focus on our implied duties of confidentiality here.

I'm concerned instead with our trust-based duties of confidentiality. Others, exercising their right to privacy, often grant us access to personal information with an understanding about how we will use it. In accepting the information, we commit to honoring their trust and thereby gain a duty of confidentiality. The understanding that informs both their trust and our commitment specifies the duty's content. The ethically relevant consequences of our violating our commitment determine its weight. Since it arises from a commitment to the person providing information, a trust-based duty of confidentiality is an ethical duty to them. We owe it to them to keep the information confidential. They have a right to our doing so.

PROFESSIONAL TRUST-BASED DUTIES OF CONFIDENTIALITY

Many relationships within the university community support trust-based duties of confidentiality. Professors and academic advisors make a commitment to their students: they will use their skills to promote the students' knowledge and academic success. Students, in turn, disclose private information needed to honor that commitment, such as their intellectual strengths and weaknesses, academic achievements and failures, career plans, and personal problems. In peer reviews, faculty members look to their colleagues for a fair and objective evaluation of and constructive advice on how to improve their efforts. To support this review, they provide colleagues with assessments of their performance, including external referee reports, peer teaching reviews, and student teaching evaluations. Administrators have access to a wide variety of information about students, faculty, and staff, ranging from performance evaluations to salary and health records. In every case, access carries a duty of confidentiality. Those sharing information trust that it will be used only as required to advance the purpose for which it is given. Those accepting it commit to honoring that trust.

Our duties are not without challenges. An initial one is to distinguish between professional and nonprofessional duties. We need to be sensitive to context in our professional practice. I once asked a student why he had chosen to write on a particular topic and learned that his father had been charged with embezzlement. Given the context of our exchange, I clearly had a professional duty to keep the information to myself. I once asked a student if she had enjoyed spring break and found out about her abortion. Neither my question nor her response had anything to do with our professional relationship, but her response was likely informed by it, as I was someone with whom she regularly shared otherwise private information. That was enough to give me a professional duty of confidentiality.

The understanding that defines a trust-based confidentiality duty is often tacit, and its details are frequently unclear, posing another challenge. Moreover, there is generally an imbalance between those requesting information and those providing it. The former know what information they seek, how they intend to use it, and with whom they intend to share it. The latter often do not. Students seldom consider how much information about themselves they are sharing with their professors and advisors. Faculty members undergoing a tenure review are sometimes surprised to learn that external referee reports of their work are not readily available to them, even with the referees' identities removed. Faculty and staff at public universities may be shocked to learn that the administration has given their salary information to the local newspaper. The imbalance supports an important duty to ensure that those providing us with information understand what content is involved and how it will be used; otherwise, we haven't obtained the information through informed consent.

We often rely on reasonable expectations in this regard, but there are important limits. It is reasonable to expect that students understand that their grades will appear in their academic record and be shared with those with an educational need to know. It is not reasonable, however, to expect them to understand that failing a course due to academic dishonesty will also be noted on their academic transcript. It is reasonable to expect that students will consent to our singing their praises to their parents but not to telling mom and dad that they failed our course with the lowest grade in its history. It is reasonable to expect that external referees in a tenure and promotion case will understand that their identities and reports will be shared with the relevant evaluation committees. It is not reasonable to expect them to understand that a legal subpoena can pierce the confidentiality of their reports. It is reasonable to expect that a member of the university who files a sexual harassment complaint with the Title IX officer understands that an investigation will ensue and consents to it. It is not reasonable to expect that students who experience harassment understand that if they share that information with a trusted academic advisor or instructor, an investigation will follow with or without their consent, because the university has designated every such employee a mandated reporter.

Consider the routine task of writing a letter of recommendation. Students generally make the request with the expectation that our letter will be complimentary, if not laudatory. It is a letter of recommendation, after all. They assume we will accentuate the positive and eliminate the negative. We, however, see our task as messing with Mister In-Between. We support the student's application but owe our readers a useful account of strengths and weaknesses. When the student's expectation doesn't mesh with ours, a discussion is required to ensure their request is based on informed consent. A colleague once wrestled with how to write a medical school recommendation for a student who had always performed admirably in his class. An instructor had told him of the student's academic dishonesty in another class, information the student, quite reasonably, didn't expect him to have for inclusion in the letter. Whether it belonged in the letter is a matter for debate, but what's not is whether, if he had decided to include it, my colleague should have informed the student, who may have then wanted to withdraw his request.

We often look to university rules to define the understanding central to a trust-based duty of confidentiality. Universities, for example, create rules on how student information will be used and shared. Because the rules are public, students who provide information are assumed to have done so with an understanding of them, and faculty, staff, and administrators who use the information have a duty to operate within that understanding. We proceed in the same way in other areas, such as faculty reviews and many HR matters. The source of our duty of confidentiality is the trust of those providing the information and our commitment in receiving it; the rules specify the content of that trust and commitment.

A reliance on university rules also has its limitations. For starters, our professional duties often surpass university requirements. With the arrival of FERPA, universities tightened their rules on the confidentiality of student information, but the newly prohibited practices, such as returning tests and term papers by leaving them in a box outside one's office door, had violated ethical duties of confidentiality long before. If a student complains to us about a colleague's teaching in an advising session, no university rule prohibits our sharing the student's complaint and identity with the colleague, but we've a professional duty not to do so.

Moreover, the rules are often just vague enough to create, rather than eliminate, problems of confidentiality. Rules guiding promotion and tenure reviews, for example, will frequently require that the proceedings be confidential, without indicating just what confidentiality demands. Departments are left to their own devices to provide the content. As a result, faculty under review often find that they are prohibited from knowing details about their case, even though such information is readily available to colleagues under review in another department. The resulting insecurity and frustration serve no one well.

In addition, department rules often slide by obvious problems. Many a department's rules prohibit members of the review committee from revealing the comments and votes of other members to the candidate while allowing them to reveal their own position. Yet revealing one's own position can involve revealing someone else's. Suppose a candidate consults the three members likely to have been supportive in a negative 5 to 3 decision. If sharing their positive votes will inform the candidate of the other members' votes, should they be barred from doing so? That seems too much to demand, as it limits their ability to support the candidate's appeal to the next decision level. One solution is to require that committee members reveal their vote, but no one else's, to the candidate. In this way, they sacrifice their confidentiality while protecting that of other committee members. Yet very few departments take this approach.[1]

Even when university rules are uniform and appropriately detailed to anticipate problems, yet another challenge remains. Just about every member of a university—student, faculty, staff, or administrator—knows so little of the regulations that it is hard to see how they support trust-based confidentiality duties. Consider the rules that universities develop to honor FERPA. Many students are unaware of these and even of FERPA itself. How then can these policies support the mutual understanding required for a duty of confidentiality? We might argue that students need not know the particular rules. When they share their private information, they consent to the university using their information as specified by its protocol, whatever it is. The university's corresponding commitment is to follow its rules. Yet even if this is the case, the university has a twofold educational obligation. First, it must ensure that those providing information have an appropriate opportunity to learn the regulations so that their consent is informed. Second, it must ensure that those receiving the information know the rules well enough to honor them.

Universities have made certain efforts in this last regard. Some have developed online educational resources about FERPA for employees. My university requires student employees in the registrar's office to sign an agreement detailing their FERPA duties. By emphasizing to employees the importance of their responsibilities, providing managers with a stronger basis for dismissal in case of violations, and strengthening the university's claim to take its legal obligations seriously, such endeavors serve a practical purpose. But they also serve an ethical one by reinforcing individuals' understanding of their trust-based duties.

Much more needs to be done, however. Universities generally concentrate on rules backed by legal requirements and potential sanctions, with a focus on educating those entrusted with information rather than on those providing it. This tendency toward self-protection is understandable but regrettable. Universities need to extend their educational efforts to cover other confidentiality rules and those providing information. Students are generally unaware of the FERPA requirements on the information they provide. Those who experience sexual harassment are often uninformed of the extent to which various faculty, staff, and administrators are required to report what they tell them. Consider too the faculty peer-review process. Those serving on promotion and tenure review committees are generally provided with copies of the rules defining the review process and their duties, including their duties of confidentiality. However, the faculty members under review are often left to their own devices to gain an understanding of the rules and their rights under them.

Even as we turn to university rules to understand many of our trust-based duties of confidentiality, it is important that we not give them more deference than they deserve. They at best define the content of a duty of confidentiality; they don't determine whether that prima facie duty overrides other ethical considerations in cases of conflict. Consider here the case of David Shick, who died in 2000 as a result of a fight with another student at Georgetown University. When his parents requested information from the university about the discipline imposed on the other student, the university asked them to sign a nondisclosure agreement. The Shicks refused, as the agreement would have prohibited them from sharing the information with their children. The administrators stood their ground, with the Assistant Vice President for Communications citing university confidentiality rules formulated to support its educational mission: "We continue to believe that maintaining the confidentiality of student code of conduct proceedings and outcomes best serves our educational mission."[2]

The university's position, at least as represented by this reported statement, misses the point. The university and its administrators clearly have a trust-based duty of confidentiality to those involved in the disciplinary process, including the disciplined student, and that duty, with its content defined by the university's rules, includes one to require a nondisclosure agreement with the Shicks. Yet the challenge presented by the Shicks' claim is not whether that duty exists or whether the rules defining it best serve the university's educational mission. It's whether that duty, as a prima facie duty, is overridden by their right to know the student's punishment and to share that knowledge with their children. The university and its administrators seem to overlook this fact by focusing narrowly on what their rules require and whether their rules fit their mission.

A final challenge concerning our trust-based duties of confidentiality is rooted in the fact that universities, as well as their colleges and departments, are fairly insular communities, where information about members is a major coin of the realm. It is easy to fall into thinking that any information we have is ours to share. Moreover, the virtue of collegiality is often misunderstood to include a readiness to do so. Declining to answer a colleague's inappropriate question about how a student is performing in our class can seem downright rude, especially when it requires explaining that sharing such information would be unethical. Consider too a case from a department I know in which a faculty member, whose promotion had just been unofficially approved, asked to sit in on the annual review of a soon-to-be junior colleague. Once officially promoted, this faculty member would be a member of the review committee, but that wouldn't be for another month. Every committee member, including the department chair, approved the request. After all, it was their committee, the information was theirs to share as they saw fit, and to insist that the colleague's promotion actually be official wouldn't have been collegial. The one person who wasn't consulted was the person under review; the person to whom the committee owed their duty of confidentiality.

To effectively honor our duties of confidentiality, we need to alter our understanding of our professional practice. The information we receive is not ours to share in whatever way we will. In this area, and others, the ethical dimensions of our profession confine us. We need to attend to them, in both our practice and our training of those who will follow us. It is part of being good at what we do.

Chapter 7

Big Data and Artificial Intelligence

Christa Davis Acampora

College and university leaders have access to an extraordinary array of data they routinely collect for current and prospective students and employees. Increasingly, they are asked to make use of those data for a variety of purposes—many of them linked with core mission functions and responsibilities. Using data to support better outcomes would seem to be an uncontroversial good, though much turns on what constitutes better, which outcomes are given priority, and what trade-offs are required to attain them. Increased pressure to achieve certain performance metrics combined with technological advances that increase efficiency in obtaining, using, and sharing data presents higher education leaders and other stakeholders with distinctive challenges and opportunities in both the near and longer term. This essay scouts just some of that terrain and makes modest proposals for immediate and longer-term actions.

In the context of higher education, at least three general types of data are concerns: (1) those generated in the course of conducting routine campus operations and activities; (2) those generated outside the institution about the institution and any and all of its members (i.e., students, staff, and faculty); and (3) those generated in the course of analyzing and using the data from either or both sets 1 and 2. Artificial intelligence and machine learning increasingly enable institutions to access, generate, and utilize data of this third type.

Massive amounts of data are generated for nearly every activity on campus and many activities that take place remotely. The university identification card (or digital equivalent through network credentials) tracks holders' campus locations, vehicles driven, buildings entered, meals and other purchases made, materials browsed or accessed, classes and events attended, and more. University-sponsored apps may track precise locations of users within a geofence, on or off campus. IP addresses may disclose where university affiliates are around the world. Learning management systems (LMS) identify users' courses viewed, locations accessed, documents opened, assignments completed, and lengths of time engaged with materials. Faculty collaborations are tracked; their funding sources, expenses, and travel monitored; and their social media followed. Recent threats to health and safety, especially perceived threats to economic and national security interests and those arising from the pandemic global health crisis, have accelerated efforts to collect more data and, importantly, to use it, that is, to do more with it.

Applications of artificial intelligence and machine learning can draw on data from the student information system, campus chatbots, learning management systems, website analytics, social media analytics, financial aid records, and the campus ID management system with capabilities of combining those data to identify regular and *irregular* patterns in student activities and behaviors. These can identify levels of student engagement and risks to student success, including student retention. Profiles generated from those data can inform specific interventions to increase likelihood of success, a seemingly benevolent act, and inform admissions algorithms, which could identify which *types* of student are less likely to succeed and therefore present greater risks to institutional success measures or more significant drains on academic support resources.

Increasingly, faculty data relating to research productivity can predict future academic impact relative to peers and its contribution to the reputation of one's department or academic unit as a whole. While data use agreements might prohibit the use of predictive analytics in actual individual performance evaluations, these data may, nevertheless, influence judgments about competitive compensation as well as major career decisions, including hiring, tenure, and retention, which are prospective judgments about future performance and likely contributions.

As universities outsource various administrative functions and services, as many needed to do when colleges and universities shifted to remote operations during the COVID-19 pandemic, data aggregated and derived from the use of health, wellness, financial, and mental health services became available, accessible, analyzable, and potentially *sharable*. The higher purposes to which these data may be put can be positive. They can provide insights to improve teaching and learning and possibly enhance students' sense of well-being. The use of multiple data sources enables university administrators to draw greater connections and, arguably, refine their understanding of specific student needs to support targeted, just-in-time assistance to help students achieve their goals. Chatbots may serve as effective way-finders and improve the student experience more than passive forms of communication such as kiosks, directories, and web pages. Additionally, data collected from chatbots—student queries and requests—can also inform needed improvements in communication or services, for example, ultimately enhancing the campus stakeholder experience and even opening the possibility of creating a more curated, student-centric experience. These data also augment the demographic data concerning staff, faculty, and students, potentially enhancing diversity on campus. Finally, data that track faculty activity can indicate the returns on investment in research infrastructure and support as well as community impact.

Achieving these gains entails not only the collection and analyses of discrete or combined datasets. The application of artificial intelligence and machine learning (AI/ML) is necessary to achieve predictive insights, determine points of intervention, and make the sorts of assessments of whole fields of inquiry on the order that is required in predicting student performance and faculty impact. Nearly all institutions rely, to varying degrees, on external vendors and equipment in order to make use of big data on their campuses. And nearly all of these data management and analytic platforms require extensive data sharing. This raises significant concerns about the security of these data and the institutional risk and vulnerability institutions face when reliant on them.

The costs of collecting, analyzing, and interpreting these data are high. In addition to the cost of the software platform and any specialized servers it may require, the more data collected, stored, and shared, the greater the need for compliance management, legal services to support analysis and finalization of licensing agreements, and technical services to assess and refine service contracts. Others have examined the broader costs of the big data era in terms of the vast amounts of energy and human resources required to develop and maintain them.[1] Such costs might include other forms of social and moral capital, including conceptions of our *privacy, personhood*, and, at perhaps the extreme limit, *humanity*. In what follows, I explore several of these dimensions before offering concrete recommendations for university leaders.

PRIVACY

The topic of privacy is developed elsewhere in this volume and in the rich literature devoted to the theme, including in specialized contexts of education, human resources, and healthcare. Thus, I will highlight only a few key dimensions and offer some cautionary guidance.

A robust legal and regulatory infrastructure guards against breaches of privacy arising from disclosure of personal information, including the Family Educational Rights and Privacy Act (FERPA), which provides for parental access to educational records of their children and limits disclosures to others; the Individuals with Disabilities Education Act (IDEA), which extends greater privacy to the educational records of those it covers; the Health Insurance Portability and Accountability Act (HIPAA), which safeguards health information with emphases on disclosure and consent; and, most recently, the General Data Protection Regulation (GDPR) in the European Union, which has impacted activity globally insofar as it protects its citizens wherever they may interact virtually. Safeguarding personal information is enshrined not only in case law and relevant domains of social life. Most professional associations for university administrators also affirm and integrate professional ethics concerning personal information, and some specifically highlight duties to ensure data integrity and the importance of protecting personal information. These measures are all oriented to protect individual rights and reasonable expectations of privacy. They do not generally take up protection against the effects of pernicious algorithms, although the GDPR treads into that territory. Nevertheless, it is helpful to briefly examine the conception of privacy that the legal system protects, particularly given that it looms so large.

The conception of privacy that generally informs the legislative protections and professional practices most closely associated with higher education is drawn from ideas developed as extensions of European common law traditions, made more urgent at the dawn of the twentieth century by social and technological advances of an active press and the then newfound ease and speed of photographic technology. Fundamental to this sense of privacy is a right to be left alone.[2] Most modern conceptions of privacy arise from or are linked with our conceptions of autonomy (control over oneself, presentations and representations of aspects of one's life, and control over one's likenesses). The GDPR includes "a right to be forgotten," a right to erasure about information previously collected but which no longer enjoys consent for use or representation. Privacy is also relevant to (if not essential for) other dimensions of a good life and key to achieving what we might describe as personhood.

PRIVACY AND PERSONHOOD

These conceptions of privacy affirm the right to develop and enjoy one's individual personality, free of any unnecessary intervention on the part of the state. They also recognize that development of personhood is not simply cumulative—the piling up of one experience after another—but also iterative, such that it includes taking away information that one might have previously shared but which one no longer wishes to have publicly available. Some argue that control over information about oneself is important for the development of one's life, as privacy affects one's relationships with others and even defines and limits the *types* of relationships that one can have.[3] This is because our senses of intimacy and closeness are measured and meted, at least in part, by our ability to disclose, withhold, or share information about ourselves. Following this line of thought, breaches of privacy might well inhibit or impair our ability to have certain types of relationships, degrees of separation or closeness. For example, this is one of the bases of rape shield laws and, consequently, some elements of Title IX proceedings, which prohibit evidence of intimate details about the sexual life of the alleged victim and protect against public disclosure of the victim's identity. In this sense, then, we can see that privacy is connected with our ability to have a say over what is and is *not* shared (by others) about us, to have a measure of control over what representations are permitted about oneself, and to retain certain crucial human possibilities such as initiating, maintaining, and distinguishing a wide range of relationships, including friendship and love. What we share with others and the extent to which we entrust others with deeply personal and detailed information amounts to a form of *moral capital*, the accumulation and expenditure of which are essential aspects of what makes us human.

AI.HUMANITY[4]

Much of the legislation devised to protect privacy, as well as popular and academic discussions of it, focuses on protecting individuals. Broader social impacts are relevant, however, and, given the stakes of decision-making in higher education, should be considered in development, adoption, and deployment of AI/ML systems. Social sustainability, an emergent assessment criterion, might be integrated in future design processes. Concerns for sustainability, generally, include consideration of the management and conservation of resources so that they remain available and accessible for future generations. A broader domain of social goods and their environmental conditions and dependencies are at risk of being overlooked if limited to considerations of the privacy of individuals.[5] Rapid changes in technological capabilities and developments in artificial intelligence only underscore the need to articulate priorities of social sustainability in the interest of humanity.

The application and integration of artificial intelligence within human social systems is evidence of what some have described as the fourth industrial revolution with an accompanying shift in understanding the place of humans in relation to the rest of the world. This change is characterized by transformations of "systems of production, management, and governance," driven largely by advances in technologies, particularly those derived from applications of artificial intelligence and machine learning. While some imagine this as a doomsday scenario that radically disrupts the workforce preparation to which higher education contributes, others envision a future of work that enhances and even potentially perfects positive and pro-social human capabilities.[6]

Regardless of the ultimate outcome, there is clear agreement that data—its collection, analysis, and utilization—is already driving fundamental changes in virtually every aspect of human life, including how we think about preparation for the world of work, what we think of as research and discovery, and how we think about teaching and learning.[7] This is evident in the "Internet of Things"

(IoT) in which physical objects with imbedded sensors share, access, and process information among and with other objects and systems via the internet or some other communication system. The objects connected in these ways can also be human bodies on campus.

A company marketing itself as providing "data-as-a-service" has developed stickers called "BioButtons" that adhere to the human body for up to ninety days. Their embedded sensors continuously measure and monitor temperature, respiration, heart rate, gait, activity levels, sleep patterns, and bodily positions. The sensors connect with "conversational AI" for remote care. During the pandemic, the company struck a deal with a university seeking community health surveillance and a way to track students on campus, monitor their health for symptoms of COVID-19, and support contact tracing. Insofar as BioButtons would provide early alerts for infection and enable tracking even among persons otherwise unknown to each other, the system would have more information about certain important features of the lives of all campus constituents than even the individuals themselves could know.[8]

The Internet of Things allows us not only to do more things via connected devices, for example, pay for a cafeteria meal using a smart phone or open the door to one's home from a remote site, it also collects large amounts of data. Even when such data are entirely depersonalized, they are still collected, aggregated, and potentially indexed to other activities among other devices, and all of this has a value; it can be monetized. These large datasets, rendered intelligible and actionable by artificial intelligence, can be used to develop profiles, providing information about the interests and inclinations of large groups of people, who may have dozens, even hundreds of distinctive similarities and distinguishable traits that had been unrecognizable by ordinary human intelligence in the past.

Data generated by and among entities in the IoT potentially shed light on users' interests, behaviors, and states. Machine learning can be used not only to identify otherwise indiscernible patterns of similarity but also to devise predictive insights and uses intended to influence behaviors. This has led some to suggest that it is not the IoT that matters so much as the "Internet of Behaviors" (IoB). The IoT connects physical objects with embedded sensors to exchange information, whereas the IoB extrapolates from those data to understand behaviors and to *influence* them in the future. In a now infamous "experiment," Facebook programmers sought to influence and measure "emotional contagion" in which they manipulated the content of user feeds to test the hypothesis that users could be emotionally directed—both positively or negatively—relative to the emotional content in the newsfeeds of their social networks. This research was conducted entirely without the consent or awareness of the participants.[9]

As a way, in part, to address the widely acknowledged mental health crisis among college-age persons in the United States, Ellipsis Health developed a machine-learning app to identify people with speech patterns matching those with depression. The app, piloted by a college in late 2020, detects changes in tone, pitch, and voice modulation that match the behaviors of those with anxiety and depression. The app is supposed to be driven by an AI/ML engine that enables the program to learn from large data sets rather than rely on specific, predetermined characteristics. In addition to the partner in higher education, the company is working with a healthcare system to create an app-based visualization of mental health wellness for its clients. While an application like this might be seen as valuable for connecting students with mental health resources before they reach a point of crisis, there is also a risk of pathologizing ordinary human emotions and cultural differences.

Data in the IoB come from a range of sources, including commercial data from transactional purchases, social media and data derived from facial recognition in the vast libraries of personal photos amassed through Instagram and Snapchat, and images captured unwittingly through surveillance technologies.[10] At the current stage of development of AI/ML, personal and personally identifiable information is becoming increasingly less important except insofar as it provides an index connecting other data bits in a profile that can become *actionable*, that is, a profile that can be used for nudging or, more aggressively, determining the behavior of so-called subjects. Instead of personalized data, there are intersections or arrays of datapoints. These may be entirely depersonalized, stripped of all personally identifiable information and perhaps even utterly unrecognizable by the subjects in question, denuded of their agency, so to speak, such that one can refer to *behaviors without subjects*.

This should be worrisome for higher education as one of its higher aims is to enable the development of human capabilities and respect diversity. An Internet of Behaviors could foster homogenization and polarization. If measured, in a primary way, by behaviors, human diversity could be diminished by an IoB that nudges or directs toward specific targets. In this respect, the concern may be less about what data we are selecting to store and share and more about the ways in which those data neural networks fuel the creation of virtual environments that are, essentially, *selecting us*.

Without thoughtful deliberation, not just about protection of personally identifiable information, uses of artificial intelligence on campus could significantly impact the expression of human intelligence in teaching, learning, and discovery.[11] Personalized learning environments could limit academic choices, constrain exploration of new ideas, and diminish the powers of selection and discernment of learners who might not fit the profiles of those who had succeeded in those fields in the past. In that case, areas of human inquiry could very well stagnate. Chatbots, while optimizing student experiences and interactions on campus, could end up directing behaviors (e.g., funneling some students to certain opportunities and not others) and ultimately shaping their relationships.

Not only are these tools intrusive and subject to malicious tampering, they are also potentially misleading as in a 2021 case of Dartmouth medical school students who were charged with cheating after a large number of students had accessed the learning management system (LMS) during an examination. It was later discovered that the LMS generates usage data even when users are not actively using the system. Students protesting the action underscored the ways in which the incident undermined *trust* on campus, a key component for creating a learning environment that encourages students to *take risks*. Remote proctoring services require scanning of surroundings (in most cases during the pandemic, this was students' bedrooms) and monitoring eye and head movements. Persons with cultural backgrounds that differ from those of the subjects used to train the system and persons with learning differences and disabilities could be flagged as cheating even when they are not.[12]

There are similar concerns about automated decision-making in college and university enrollment management practices, including how and where institutions recruit, whom they admit, and what aid they award.[13] AI applications enable institutions to predict student persistence based on a variety of indicators that have nothing to do with readiness, preparation, or academic achievement and aptitude. Misuse of these tools could adversely affect efforts to enhance student access. For example, colleges and universities can now track prospective student behaviors in their interactions with the institutions' websites, other behaviors on the internet more broadly, as well as interests suggested by their uses of social media. Artificial intelligence and machine learning tools allow institutions to develop profiles comparing prospective students with successful graduates. In a recent university business journal, an admissions officer describes using AI in the applicant selection process, implementing a scoring system that integrates internet behaviors and social media interactions along with data collected from the application itself. In this particular case, accessing the college's library website contributed fewer points to a prospective student's admissions score than pulling up the admissions requirement page because the latter shows greater specific interest in the institution.[14] When interest in the institution itself, an indicator of likely yield (an institutional metric referring to the percentage of students who accept an offer of admission and enroll at the institution) is more valuable than a perceived interest in academics (presumably a core mission of the institution), then these data are not serving students themselves but rather the institutions recruiting them.

Typical student success indicators, such as first-year retention rates, are not attributes of *students* but rather *institutions*. If an institution applies the metric to the student, then the institutional mission or accomplishment appears to be just being good at picking winners, not actually helping students to succeed. Colleges and universities that recruit and select in this way reproduce a particular type of student rather than identify those most likely to benefit from the educational opportunities the institution can provide. Risks to diversity and institutional development are clearly evident as well. Furthermore, this is also potentially not a winning enrollment strategy in the long run because demographic shifts suggest that, in order to thrive, institutions will need to reach new students and adapt their academic offerings to reflect new fields of knowledge as well as new workforce demands and opportunities.

RECOMMENDATIONS

The potential for bias in the algorithms used in and derived from artificial intelligence is significant,[15] and there is a growing body of research and advocacy for the development of design principles and professional standards that pursue what is sometimes referred to as FATE: Fairness, Accountability, Transparency, and Explainability. Indeed, a growing number of entities are beginning to regulate development and uses of AI, not only with concern for more individual privacy protections but also to minimize or reduce known biases that can arise from the machine-learning and transfer processes,[16] and to protect from discriminatory exercise of automated decisions (e.g., in borrowing and housing) as well as predictive reach, such as in policing and, as illustrated earlier, in college and university admissions.[17] Leaders in higher education should be supporting the development of FATE standards and accountability measures, integrating them in curricula, and applying them within the campus administrative context, including:

1. Adding literacy standards to include learning objectives related to practices of *obtaining* information (data acquisition literacy) and standards for learning about how personal information is collected, shared, extrapolated, and applied in other contexts; learning standards should also include understanding how machine-learning works and its potential applications.[18]
2. Charging custodians of data with developing data use agreements that ensure standards for ethical use and supporting their integration in statements of professional association ethics. (Various professional organizations affirm privacy values but have not yet integrated value statements connected with responsible uses of data beyond privacy.) Accrediting bodies should expect these to be adopted at the institutional level. These should be specific to heighten awareness and support full community literacy.
3. Ensuring that institutional licenses and service agreements expressly prohibit *data brokerage and data retention* by third parties, including the creation of datasets and secondary analytical data.
4. Disclosing—in plain language—what data the institution collects and allowing students and employees to opt out of nonessential data collection activities (including a right to be free from nudging).

5. Developing data collection, retention, *and destruction* policies and practices, much like those that many institutions have for document collection, retention, and destruction.
6. Nurturing a culture of questioning that can support trust rather than suspicion. Just because we *can* collect data and develop extrapolations does not mean that we *should*. Does *want-to-know* among campus administrators license *should-know*?

CONCLUSION

This chapter has focused on some significant risks associated with the use of artificial intelligence and machine learning in higher education, highlighting specific ways it is currently implemented. Another risk, however, is that of *not* using it. This risk arises from what would be missed opportunities to reap the benefits of AI to develop novel solutions to large and complex problems (e.g., addressing and mitigating the impacts of systemic and institutionalized racism on generations of students). It is possible that AI could allow us to realize forms of agency and problem-solving on scales that are nearly impossible today. To do this, however, and to avoid the pitfalls that were the focus of much of this essay requires more than simply *raising* concerns about ethics. In that domain, too, we are far from a set of agreed-upon principles or settled systematic ways of making hard choices that we could build into algorithmic structures. Fears of uses and abuses of AI could result in holding its applications at arm's length, which could also mean that higher education institutions do not contribute the intellectual resources and commitments to develop best practices identified in the previous recommendations.[19] Thus, efforts to define AI.Humanity should be welcomed, since such a task pushes us to articulate the values that are important in humanity-preserving design principles and critical frameworks.

Part IV

INJUSTICE

Chapter 8

Misogyny, "Himpathy," and Sexual Harassment on Campus

Cynthia A. Stark

Sexual harassment in education is a pressing problem. It consists of such things as suggestive comments, lewd gestures, demands for sex, name-calling, groping, physical and verbal abuse, sexual assault, and rape. It is perpetrated by peers, coaches, teachers, and other superiors.[1] According to a 2015 survey of college campuses, 23.1% of women undergraduates experienced sexual harassment in the form of sexual assault, sexual misconduct due to physical force, and incapacitation. Among seniors, 26.1% of women and 29.5% of trans, gender-queer, or gender non-identifying students reported nonconsensual sexual contact. Verbal or visual forms of sexual harassment were reported by 61.9% of undergraduate women and 44.1% of graduate and professional women.[2]

This essay addresses the issue of sexual harassment in education on two fronts. First, I outline and defend an account of sexual harassment. Second, I present a critique of the deliberate indifference standard—the liability standard applied in Title IX lawsuits. The argument I advance treats sexual harassment as a form of misogyny understood as a set of hostile social forces frequently experienced by women.[3] Its advantage is that it explains, unlike a well-known alternative view, both sexualized and nonsexualized sexual harassment and sexual harassment in both work and educational settings.

The deliberate indifference standard states that an educational institution receiving federal funds is liable for sexual harassment only if an official with the authority to take corrective measures was given actual notice of the harassment and acted with deliberate indifference. My objection to this standard is that it institutionalizes a cultural phenomenon called "himpathy," a close relative of misogyny. Where misogyny consists of hostility directed toward guiltless women, himpathy consists of sympathy directed toward guilty men—specifically, men who are guilty of violence against women. The deliberate indifference standard codifies himpathy insofar as it embodies two of its main features: the downplaying of perpetrators' accountability and the erasure of victims' pain.

I begin with a summary of the evolution of sexual harassment law, especially as it pertains to educational settings. Second, I outline the theoretical shifts in scholars' conceptions of sexual harassment that both prompted and arose from this evolution. Third, I explain how the notion of misogyny can aid in refining our current understanding of sexual harassment. Fourth, I provide the details of the deliberate indifference liability rule, and fifth, I argue that the rule amounts to a codified version of himpathy. Finally, I make some brief remarks about eradicating sexual harassment at colleges and universities.

SEXUAL HARASSMENT AS SEX DISCRIMINATION[4]

Title VII of the Civil Rights Act of 1964 prohibits sex discrimination in employment. Title IX of the Education Amendments, passed in 1972, prohibits sex discrimination in educational settings that receive federal funding. In the 1970s, courts, influenced by the work of Catharine MacKinnon,[5] established that sexual harassment is a form of sex discrimination, and in the 1980s, the U.S. Supreme Court expanded Title VII liability to include two types of sexual harassment: quid pro quo and hostile environment. The former occurs when a supervisor makes submission to sexual activity a condition of an employment consequence, such as not being fired or getting a raise. The latter occurs when an employee is subjected to unwelcome conduct of a sexual nature that creates a hostile, offensive, or abusive work environment. By 1992 courts had established that Title IX also prohibits both types of sexual harassment.

Initially, the only recourse available to a person sexually harassed at a federally funded educational institution was to file a complaint with the Department of Education's Office of Civil Rights (OCR) charged with enforcing Title IX. To comply with Title IX, funding recipients must follow the OCR's evolving guidelines, which require schools to prevent sexual harassment, protect victims, investigate reports, remedy harassment that has already occurred, and prevent its recurrence. The OCR is authorized to terminate federal funding if it finds a violation of Title IX only after the institution is given a written notice of violation and an opportunity to rectify the situation. However, the OCR has never exercised its power to revoke an institution's federal funding.[6]

Three Supreme Court decisions in the 1990s significantly changed Title IX's enforcement. The first, *Franklin v. Gwinnett County Public Schools*, allowed plaintiffs to sue funding recipients (school districts, universities, etc.) for money damages in cases of intentional discrimination, including teacher-student sexual harassment. The second, *Gebser v. Lago Vista Independent School District*, ruled that, in cases of teacher-student harassment, funding recipients are liable if an official with the authority to remedy the situation has actual notice of the harassment and is deliberately indifferent to it.

The third case, *Davis v. Monroe County Board of Education*, established that funding recipients are liable for peer harassment when they have substantial control over the alleged harasser and when the harassment takes place under the operations of the recipient—that is, on campus, in the classroom, on a field trip, and so on. Endorsing the liability standard adopted in *Gebser*, the *Davis* decision also stated that for a claim of peer sexual harassment to be successful, plaintiffs must demonstrate harassment so severe, pervasive, and objectively offensive that it deprived them of access to educational opportunities or benefits. Recently, hostile environment harassment has been interpreted under Title IX to encompass not only instances of a sexual nature, but all campus sex- and gender-based harassment, including that of gender nonconforming people.[7]

TWO CONCEPTIONS OF SEXUAL HARASSMENT[8]

Sexual harassment was originally recognized as a problem women face in the workplace and was conceptualized in terms of unwanted sexual conduct motivated by an eroticized desire for power over women and constituting a form of sexual violation. Following Vicki Schultz, I will call this the "desire-dominance approach." This approach arose from the radical feminist view that heterosexuality, as an institution, is a major contributor to women's oppression and that male supremacy is largely perpetuated by the eroticization of male dominance and female submission enacted through the norms and practices of heterosexuality. This view, focused as it is on (hetero)sexual arousal, does not explain the frequent nonsexual, derogatory, and abusive behaviors (now termed "gender-based harassment") directed at women that clearly create a hostile work environment.

In order to address this explanatory defect, some have proposed conceptualizing hostile environment sexual harassment as a means of making favored lines of work, and the competencies required to occupy them, a masculine domain. On this "competence-centered approach,"[9] men tend to see women's participation in traditionally male jobs as a sort of anti-masculine[10] incursion. Hostile and abusive acts, such as calling women stupid or weak, assigning them impossible tasks, sabotaging their projects, and requiring them to do service-oriented duties outside their job description, are designed to brand women as incompetent and hence not entitled to their jobs. This, in turn, allows men to reserve favored occupations, and their attendant status and perks, for themselves.

Three phenomena that are difficult to explain through the competence-centered framework are sexualized hostile environment harassment, quid pro quo sexual harassment, and many instances of sexual harassment in educational settings. Consider, first, sexualized hostile environment harassment, which is easily explained by the desire-dominance view: men who rub up against or proposition women coworkers or subordinates are exerting power through the norms of heterosexual interaction. Proponents of the competence-centered view attempt to explain this type of behavior along two lines. First, they claim that it aims to portray women workers as incompetent by sexualizing them, thus positioning them as unprofessional, physically weak, or intellectually deficient—traits that are, by cultural standards, incompatible with competence in various job settings.[11] Second, they argue that this behavior enables men to maintain a sense of masculine entitlement by reminding women of their proper place within a gender hierarchy.[12]

There is a problem with both these explanations. The first cannot account for the sexualized harassment of women occupying traditionally feminine jobs, such as nurses or secretaries. Those women are typically seen as rightfully subordinated to men on the job. Because they are doing feminized work, they are not perceived to be encroaching upon masculine prerogative. When bosses grope or sexually tease their secretaries, then, they must be doing something other than undermining their perceived competence as a secretary. The second explanation is flawed because it abandons the competence-centered framework altogether, describing sexualized harassment not as an attack on women's competence, but rather as a means of reinforcing patriarchal values.

Now consider quid pro quo sexual harassment, which is also readily explained by the desire-dominance conception: men who make sexual favors a condition of an employment or educational consequence are deploying heterosexual desire as a way of exercising power over subordinate women—either workers or students. The competence-centered view falters here because it is not clear how making sex a condition of receiving a benefit attacks women's competence. Providing sex for one's professor seems compatible with being, and being perceived as, a capable student. Further, it seems plausible that these tactics are indeed sexualized exercises of power, as the desire-dominance view maintains, or that they are attempts to signal to women their place in a gender hierarchy. Moreover, the competence-centered view may not be intended to explain quid pro quo sexual harassment but only hostile environment harassment. So, the competence-centered view either cannot adequately explain, or was not intended to explain, quid pro quo sexual harassment, in which case it is inferior to accounts that unify the two types of sexual harassment under one explanation.

Finally, consider sexual harassment that takes place in secondary schools and higher education. As discussed earlier, the competence-centered view was created to theorize workplace harassment proscribed by Title VII, although its proponents claim that it can be applied to harassment on college and school campuses.[13] Central to this view is the idea that the workplace is conceived as an essentially masculine territory where women who are not employed specifically to assist men or to engage in traditionally feminine tasks, such as caregiving, are seen as trespassers who must be positioned as incompetent. This approach, which applies to some instances of sexual harassment in education, can be expanded to others. First, it applies explicitly to instances of professors or teachers harassing their colleagues or staff in a way that creates a hostile environment, as such conduct constitutes workplace harassment. Second, it might explain the sexual harassment of college students by professors: as the academy was not long ago a primarily masculine institution, the proponent of the competence-centered approach might argue that those male professors dissatisfied with the increased presence of women at colleges and universities engage in hostile environment harassment to position their female students as incompetent—as incapable of handling the rigors of college-level instruction.

What the competence-centered view seems unable to explain is, first, teacher to student sexual harassment in secondary schools and, second, student to student sexual harassment in both secondary schools and higher education. Because secondary school has not been traditionally a masculine domain in the United States, it seems implausible that male teachers and students regard the presence of female students as an incursion into territory rightfully occupied only by men. Likewise, it seems implausible that present-day male college students regard campuses to be exclusively their domain. Hence, male students and secondary school teachers are unlikely to harass female students to label them incompetent interlopers.

A THIRD CONCEPTION: THE MISOGYNY APPROACH

I propose that sexual harassment is an expression of misogyny. Following Kate Manne, I treat misogyny as a dispositional property of social environments that functions to enforce a patriarchal ideal of women as willing supporters of others, including, and especially, men. This conception holds that misogyny is not (merely or primarily) a hostile attitude toward women held by some individuals but rather a systemic political phenomenon. It comprises *acts that enforce* (as opposed to *arguments that justify*) women's subordination to men.[14] Individuals are misogynists derivatively—they are persons who consistently exhibit deeply misogynist attitudes.[15] Social environments can be misogynist, then, even if devoid of misogynists, for misogyny commonly manifests itself through the negative reactions of well-intentioned people to women who fail to fulfill the central obligations assigned to them under patriarchy,[16] namely the duty to provide such goods as care and support, without asking for any in return, and the duty to forgo such goods as authority and influence, to which men alone are perceived as entitled.[17] Misogyny is conveyed nonviolently through shaming, belittling, vilifying, demonizing, mocking, and so on, and violently through anything from hitting to homicide.[18]

As an expression of misogyny, sexual harassment is not (only) an attempt on the part of men to keep women *out of* a masculine-coded domain, but (also), I maintain, an attempt to keep women *in* a feminine-coded domain. This feminine domain is not a physical space, such as the workplace or the university, but rather a sphere of knowledge and activity wherein willingly giving to others is the dominant value. According to patriarchal ideals, it is *the* place where women belong whether they are (also) politicians, educators, workers, artists, students, homemakers, or athletes.

The misogyny approach described earlier can explain sexual harassment in virtually all its actionable manifestations: quid pro quo and hostile environment harassment, sexualized and nonsexualized harassment, and harassment both at work and at school. All these instances of sexual harassment, according to the misogyny view, function to place women in their perceived rightful role of givers. Start with quid pro quo. A male professor or employer who demands sexual favors from female subordinates in exchange for a grade or promotion implies that, as women, they owe him a service for receipt of a benefit that his male subordinates are given based just on their performance. He thus (re)positions them as givers despite their official designation as workers or students, thereby putting them (back) in their place.

Consider, second, sexualized hostile environment harassment such as teasing, propositioning, leering, forcible kissing, and sexual assault. Arguably, these actions, like demands for sexual favors, are designed to thrust women into the role of giver; the less violent conduct signals to women that they owe men sexual service or titillation, and the more violent conduct forces them to provide it. Note that this explanation, unlike the competence-centered approach, applies to women in traditionally masculine and feminine occupations. Both the male stockbroker who gropes his female coworker and the boss who sexually teases his secretary are forcing their targets into the position of sexual giver.

The misogyny approach to sexualized hostile environment harassment works for both employment and educational environments: male supervisors, coworkers, teachers, and students alike use sexualized harassment to force women into the feminine domain, where they are seen as obligated to provide, among other things, sexual gratification. This maneuver can occur when those women are present in not only a masculine territory, such as the shop floor, but also in what might be deemed a neutral territory, such as a university. In either case, this is the message: your job is to be sexually available for men.

Last, consider nonsexualized hostile environment harassment such as name-calling, threats, and physical attacks. The misogyny approach treats these actions as punishments delivered to those women who are seen as abandoning their alleged duties of nurturing others and shunning power. In other words, this approach treats such harassment as a hostile reaction to women's refusals of the giver designation. The misogyny view's explanation of nonsexualized harassment, like that of sexualized harassment, applies to both employment and educational settings. Slurring, shoving, or striking women is plausibly seen as punitive whether those acts take place in the workplace, on a university campus, or in a secondary school. Such conduct might be directed at a woman who exhibits career ambition or a woman who demonstrates academic prowess. In these instances, this is the message: do not desert your caregiving position for a position of status or authority.

ACTUAL NOTICE AND DELIBERATE INDIFFERENCE[19]

As noted earlier, a funding recipient is liable for sexual harassment only if it had actual notice of the harassment and acted with deliberate indifference to it. Clearly, the ability of a complainant to prove liability under this standard depends heavily upon how courts have interpreted "actual notice" and "deliberate indifference." Consider, first, actual notice. The precise boundaries of this idea have not been fully established, but typically an appropriate official is said to have actual notice if they knew about the specific incident of misconduct at issue. It is not sufficient that they *should* have known about the misconduct, nor is it sufficient to have known about the risk of the misconduct, except in cases of *substantial* risk, defined as risk so great that it is almost certain to materialize if nothing is done. So, for example, if an appropriate official knows, based on prior complaints, that a professor is a serial harasser, then they are said to have actual notice because they have been made aware of a substantial risk of harassment.

Now consider deliberate indifference. A funding recipient is said to be deliberately indifferent to what it knows if its response is clearly unreasonable given the known circumstances. In general, a recipient responds unreasonably when it either turns a blind eye or when it responds in a plainly apathetic fashion—for instance, by merely recommending counseling for a harassing teacher and then not following up. Consequently, responses that are concededly incompetent or callous do not qualify as deliberately indifferent. For example, in one case, a university was found to have not been deliberately indifferent when it sanctioned a professor with a one-week paid suspension for propositioning a student in a closet while blocking her exit.

The deliberate indifference standard is therefore, in practice, hard to meet. But, in fact, it was designed that way. Courts have explicitly stated that, especially with respect to peer-to-peer sexual harassment, deliberate indifference is intended to be "an extremely high standard to meet in and of itself." This intention reflects the courts' desire to prevent funding recipients from being saddled with large damage awards. As a result of this stringency, vastly more cases have lost on deliberate indifference than have won. Further, deliberate indifference is arguably the main issue used to dismiss cases on preliminary motions under Title IX and the main issue used by litigators to decide whether to bring cases for victims at all.

HIMPATHY AND DELIBERATE INDIFFERENCE

In what follows, I argue that the intentional stringency of the deliberate indifference standard[20] institutionalizes the attitude of himpathy, thereby undermining Title IX's aim of establishing sex equality in education. First, in making it difficult for complainants to hold funding recipients liable, the deliberate indifference rule sends the message that educational institutions are generally not accountable for sexual harassment occurring under their operation. This message conflicts with the mandate, implicit in Title IX's objective, that schools act to curtail sexual harassment on their campuses.[21] Himpathy, as we will see, similarly downplays the accountability of wrongdoers.

Second, in focusing on the consequences of sexual harassment for schools rather than the consequences for victims, the deliberate indifference rule disregards the suffering of victims and reinforces an existing societal tendency toward such disregard. This focus, then, conflicts with the recognition, implicit in Title IX's objective, of the detrimental impact of sexual harassment on women's educational experience. Similarly, himpathy—again, as we will see—focuses on perpetrators rather than victims and thus enacts and reinforces a propensity to ignore victims' suffering.

We can see how himpathy diminishes the accountability of perpetrators and institutes a lack of concern for victims by considering an example provided by Manne.[22] She relates the case of Brock Turner, a college athlete at Stanford who, in 2016, sexually assaulted an unconscious woman behind a dumpster after a party. Turner's father lamented the extent to which his conviction had ruined his son's appetite and deprived him of his happy-go-lucky demeanor. A friend of Turner's blamed the verdict on "political correctness." Moreover, the judge in the case, concerned about the "severe impact" of the conviction on Turner's future, gave him a lenient sentence, which Turner's father, nevertheless, condemned, maintaining that his son should do no jail time because his crime was a mere "twenty minutes of action."

The excessive sympathy for Turner detracted from his accountability by positioning *him* as a victim due to his distress from being rightfully convicted, his loss of an apparently promising future, and the fact that his crime did not take very long. These factors were regarded as grounds for partial exoneration. Deliberations, official or otherwise, about his sentence—about how he should be held accountable—concerned *his* tribulations and the difficult road ahead of *him*. They made little mention of the victim's tribulations and the difficult road ahead of *her*. Turner should be held accountable for a mistake, his allies seemed to think, but not for a crime.

Not only does himpathy's focus on the pain of perpetrators diminish their accountability, it also enacts and fosters apathy toward their victims. Himpathy turns the camera toward the culprit, bathes him in soft light, and places the victim completely outside the frame. Neglecting victims is itself an act of indifference toward them. But it also encourages indifference, as it is difficult to sympathize with those who have been made invisible to us.

Let us look now at the similarities between himpathy and the deliberate indifference standard. First, note that the deliberate indifference standard, like the attitude of himpathy, is directed at perpetrators known to be guilty. Men granted himpathy are known to have committed rape or sexual assault; likewise, schools held to the deliberate indifference standard are known to have failed to protect students from sexual harassment. The issue in both instances is not whether a woman was in fact harmed. Rather, it is whether the person who harmed her, in the case of himpathy, or the entity obligated to protect her, in the case of the deliberate indifference standard, is culpable.

Second, by the lights of both himpathy and the deliberate indifference standard, multiple factors are seen as militating against accountability, many of them involving the perceived need to protect the guilty party from harsh consequences, despite the severity of their misconduct. Himpathy, as we saw, manufactures reasons, often preposterous, to minimize the perpetrator's culpability. Similarly, the deliberate indifference standard goes to great lengths to exempt schools from liability. It excuses those that are heedless of harassment about which they should have known and those that ignore risks of harassment, unless those risks are substantial. Further, it excludes delays, bungling, leniency, obtuseness, gaslighting, callousness, cynicism, victim-blaming, and the like as grounds for liability.

Third, both himpathy and the deliberate indifference rule overlook victims and encourage apathy toward them. Where himpathy—again, as we saw—overlooks the victim by foregrounding the perpetrator's hardships, the deliberate indifference rule overlooks the victim by foregrounding the funding recipient's knowledge and handling of sexual misconduct. These three similarities suggest that the deliberate indifference standard amounts to a codification of the cultural phenomenon of himpathy.

SOLUTIONS

Sexual harassment, as I have theorized it, is but one manifestation of misogyny and hence one aspect of the sexism that misogyny enforces. The deliberate indifference standard, as I have analyzed it, is but one instance where sexist norms have been baked into our legal system. Eliminating sexual harassment on campuses, then, ultimately requires eradicating sexism from our society altogether. In the meantime, two reforms present themselves. The first is for the OCR to exercise its power to revoke the federal funding of institutions that do not comply with its guidelines regarding Title IX. Institutions will have more incentive to be in full compliance if the threat of sanction is not idle. This might require significantly increasing the OCR's capacity for enforcement.

A second reform, proposed by Catharine MacKinnon, would be to replace the deliberate indifference standard with a due diligence standard.[23] This would hold federally funded institutions liable for neglecting to do due diligence, including active interventions to prevent sexual harassment, thorough and effective investigations of sexual harassment that has occurred, transformative measures to prevent it from recurring, appropriate punishment for perpetrators, and adequate compensation for victims. Further, this standard applies to sexual harassment that the funding recipient either knew about or should have known about. It essentially enjoins funding recipients to create an environment of sex equality and hence to fulfill the objective of Title IX. Institutions are liable, then, when they fail to establish sex equality, not merely when they are deliberately indifferent to sex inequality.

CONCLUSION

I have argued that it is fruitful to theorize sexual harassment as a manifestation of misogyny and Title IX's deliberate indifference liability standard as a codification of himpathy. Seen through the lens of misogyny, sexual harassment functions to place women in the position of giver and punish them if they refuse that position. Seen through the lens of himpathy, the deliberate indifference rule functions to protect educational institutions from liability for sexual harassment and to expunge the suffering of victims from the recounting of that harassment. I offered two proposals for mitigating sexual harassment in education: actually denying federal funding to institutions that violate Title IX (rather than merely threatening to do so) and replacing the deliberate indifference standard with a due diligence standard.

Chapter 9

Institutional Inequality

Jennifer M. Morton

Discussions of inequality in higher education tend to focus on access, affordability, and, to a lesser extent, completion. These three aspects of inequality are no doubt important. Too often, accidents of birth, such as whether students' parents went to college and the zip code in which they grew up, determine access to higher education. This sector reflects and compounds injustices that pervade education from preschool to high school.[1] Affordability is also a barrier for many students from low-income families and increasingly for those from middle-class families.[2] Attending college requires that students be able to afford not only tuition and living costs but also the related opportunity costs. Furthermore, many college students have family members that depend on them to earn an income. This situation puts students from low-income families and so-called "nontraditional" students in a difficult position—pitting their educational ambitions against their desire to support their families.[3] Finally, completion is one of the most significant issues for low-income students, who might take years to finish an associate degree or, worse, not finish at all. For students who go deeply into debt to pursue college, not completing a degree can be even worse than never having attended.[4] These students often end up mired in debt with no commensurate increase in their earnings potential to compensate. Access, affordability, and completion are undoubtedly critical to understanding how inequality manifests itself in higher education.

Another crucial kind of inequality, however, too often gets ignored—the massive disparities in resources between institutions. A tiny number of higher education institutions have amassed a gargantuan share of resources in the form of massive endowments, grants, and real estate holdings. While at the same time, many public colleges and universities have seen state appropriations per student decrease as enrollments have increased. I will argue that inequality between institutions of higher education should concern us just as much as these other forms of inequality. By focusing solely on access, affordability, and completion, well-resourced higher education institutions tend to ignore their critical ethical obligations due to their position within the higher education system. If this argument is correct, then there is room for policy that redistributes resources within the higher education sector. And there is an ethical argument to be made that well-resourced universities and colleges have an obligation to use their resources to benefit those institutions that have a legitimate claim to serving the neediest students.

INSTITUTIONAL INEQUALITY

According to a report by the Education Trust, as of 2013, 3.6% of all colleges and universities held 75% of all postsecondary endowment wealth.[5] These institutions educate a fraction of all college students and even fewer low-income students. Furthermore, the wealthiest colleges and universities spend around 4% of their endowments while they usually see returns closer to 8%, thus significantly increasing the size of their endowments year after year. Until recently, all of this was tax-free: from donations to earnings on the endowment. President Trump, however, signed a law in 2018 that taxed net endowment income on higher education institutions with assets worth more than $500,000 per student. Those institutions had to pay 1.4% on income earned from their endowment.[6] Though controversial, this increase in taxation has barely chipped away at the wealth of the most affluent colleges and universities. An institution like Harvard, for example, has an endowment worth about $1.6 million per student. This much wealth is astronomical compared to the resources available to many public community colleges or universities that depend on state appropriations and tuition to pay the bills.

This disparity in resources, unfortunately, tracks the student populations these institutions serve. According to the National Center for Education Statistics, students from low-income backgrounds are much less likely to go to college than their better-off counterparts. For example, 60% of higher-income students earn a bachelor's degree compared to just 14% of lower-income students.[7] When low-income students do pursue higher education they are much more likely to pursue an associate degree. As is often the case in the United States, these disparities are also seen in the numbers of Latinx and Black students going to college and the kinds of institutions they attend.[8] Well-resourced universities serve a disproportionate number of students from wealthier families; these institutions also tend to have higher graduation rates and expenditures per student. Community colleges and less-selective public colleges, typically under-resourced institutions, mainly serve students from lower-income families; these institutions tend to have lower graduation rates and expenditures per student. So, students from less affluent backgrounds and minority students are less likely to attend college. If they do attend, they attend less-selective, under-resourced institutions. This affects their educational attainment.

John Bound and colleagues make the case that the decrease in completion rates is at least partly explained by a decline in spending on students. They find that since the 1970s, student-to-teacher ratios increased in non-top public and two-year institutions (by 14% in non-top publics and by 40% in community colleges), while they decreased in highly selective, private institutions:

> while "access" or initial college enrollment has increased dramatically over the past three decades, many of the new students drawn to higher education (likely to take advantage of the increased returns to a BA) are attending institutions with fewer resources and are not graduating . . . That decreases in college completion rates are concentrated among students attending public colleges and universities outside the most selective few suggests a need for more attention to the budgets of these institutions from state appropriations and tuition revenues. These institutions may face tradeoffs between fulfilling an open access mission by increasing enrollment at low tuition with reduced resources per student and either raising tuition, which may reduce "access," or limiting enrollment in order to increase resources per student.[9]

In effect, what we are seeing, then, is a decrease in investment in non-elite public sector institutions of higher education, which affects the education received by students who attend such institutions—low-income students from under-resourced backgrounds. This segregation of students from less well-resourced backgrounds into less wealthy institutions is even evident within the same public system of higher education. For example, the California system, which invests heavily in its highly selective campuses, siphons students from lower-income backgrounds and minority racial groups into the less-selective campuses in the system, which also happen to be less well-resourced.[10]

RECONSIDERING THE SANCTITY OF THE HIGHER EDUCATION SECTOR

If we were to use the same equity considerations for evaluating the K–12 system, the fact that the higher education system allows such substantial disparities in spending per student that track socioeconomic class and race so closely would be plainly unjust. Still, significant differences exist between these two educational systems. Thus, one might argue that considerations of equality do not apply in the same way to the higher education sector.

First, primary and secondary education is compulsory and aimed at children. Powerful civic and equity considerations justify this. The state must ensure that children can be fully participating citizens irrespective of the family into which they were born. Providing a sufficiently good primary and secondary education helps all children achieve this standard. A college education does not meet this justification for compulsory provision.[11] Adults choose to attend college because they want to enrich their lives, pursue career paths that require it, or because their families expect it. The state might see a public good argument that leads them to encourage these pursuits, but this would not justify guaranteeing that everyone has access to an equally good college and university education.

The challenge to this argument is that a college degree is becoming increasingly necessary to access many forms of stable, well-paid employment. College graduates are much more likely to be employed and make more money than those without a college degree.[12] College is becoming a precondition to the freedom to pursue a good life. Consequently, the argument that providing access to higher education is not the responsibility of the state is losing its force.

Second, institutions of higher education play an essential role in a civic society—one that requires them to be at arm's length from the government. Colleges and universities seek to advance our knowledge and understanding of the world. Research is central to the mission of universities and colleges. As Amy Gutman writes in the classic *Democratic Education*:

> Control of the creation of ideas—whether by a majority or a minority—subverts the ideal of *conscious* social reproduction at the heart of democratic education and democratic politics. As institutional sanctuaries for free scholarly inquiry, universities can help prevent such subversion. They can provide a realm where new and unorthodox ideas are judged on their intellectual merits; where the men and women who defend such ideas, provided they defend them well, are not strangers but valuable members of a community. Universities thereby serve democracy as sanctuaries of nonrepression.[13]

This argument is often taken to justify the tax exemptions these institutions enjoy. Such incentives support the creation, maintenance, and expansion of institutions devoted to unfettered research. Furthermore, if we accept that the research mission of universities serves an important political role in a democracy by being free from interference, then there is a strong argument against governmental control. Interference risks dampening the freedom critical to the pursuit of knowledge. Of course, this does not mean that universities and colleges are exempt from interference but rather that the bar needs to be set high to justify state interference.

The problem with this argument is that the state does interfere in ways that aggravate institutional inequality. For instance, wealthy research institutions not only have massive endowments protected from taxes, they also tend to attract federal money through research grants and tuition loans for students. Federal policy enables the privileged standing of these universities. The question is not whether interference is justified but whether current policy advances all of the state's aims. The research aim is undoubtedly essential. And though cutting-edge research occurs at many universities, those with vast resources to invest tend to attract high-level researchers and produce the kind of research breakthroughs that are the crown jewels of American higher education. However, when this mission comes at the expense of an equitable distribution of educational resources, we need to consider how much we are willing to trade other educational aims, such as equity, for the sake of the research aim. Would the research mission of the universities and colleges with the highest endowment per student suffer if they were to pay higher taxes on their wealth? And if it did, would the benefits outweigh those costs? I suggest that some resource inequality is justified based on this critical mission, but the current staggering inequality is not. In any case, there should either be a limit on the level of inequality or a guaranteed minimum. Currently, we do not have either.

The final argument one might make in defense of safeguarding the resources amassed by wealthy colleges and universities is that they play a critical role in educating the elite and perform a gatekeeping function. Their graduates populate think tanks, universities, political offices, the judiciary, and other high-status professions. Consider, for example, that every member of the U.S. Supreme Court has a degree from at least one highly selective, well-endowed research university. Educating "the best and brightest" might justify highly selective universities claiming a larger share of resources. It is in our collective interest, one might argue, that elites receive the best education. The productivity of our society depends on such expertise.

The problem with this argument is that it is not clear that a truly democratic and representative elite should be educated at colleges and universities dominated by students from the wealthiest families. Even if these schools admit an increasing number of students from low-income families, the social world of such campuses and the cultural capital that prevails there continues to reflect the dominance of the wealthy and well-connected. As a result, elites who emerge from such educational institutions are not well-positioned to represent the interests of the diversity of communities in our society.[14] If this argument is correct, we should not be concerned with maintaining the wealth of elite institutions but rather investing in higher education institutions that are genuinely well-situated to provide us with a representative and democratic elite. This democratic consideration would have us turn to the public colleges and universities that enroll a large number of students from low-income backgrounds as well as middle- and upper-middle-class students.

CONCLUSION

In sum, I have suggested that the argument in favor of treating inequality between universities and colleges differently than that in the K–12 sector is weak. The reasons offered in favor of that distinction do not support the levels of resource inequality that we see in the higher education sector today. The university's research mission, although undoubtedly essential, should not be indulged at any price. Students born into under-resourced neighborhoods and families have a legitimate claim to access to good quality higher education. These students rarely attend the sort of universities that amass the bulk of the resources in higher education. The universities and colleges they do attend are underfunded. This affects their educational attainment. They are more likely to be taught by overworked adjuncts, enjoy fewer student support services, attend overcrowded classes, and find it difficult to pay for college. The effects of this disinvestment can be seen in the lower graduation rates and longer time to degree. These students have a genuine complaint about how higher education policy enables and reifies a dramatic institutional inequality that does a disservice to their educational prospects.

If this argument is correct, then at least two critical points follow. First, from a policy perspective, we should consider how to redistribute resources within the higher education sector to ensure that the institutions that serve the majority of low-income students have the resources they need to do this job well. We should be aiming to reduce the current massive inequalities in resources, whether by taxing those institutions or incentivizing them to share their resources with those colleges and universities that serve students from under-resourced backgrounds. Second, higher education institutions sitting on enormous endowments should recognize their ethical obligation not only to admit more low-income and first-generation college students but also to share their resources with those colleges and universities that educate large numbers of those students. The most considerable impact they could make in the lives of students from under-resourced communities is to meet those students where they attend college. In doing so, elite institutions would better live up to their civic mission.

Part V

SEEKING JUSTICE

Chapter 10

Reckoning with Past Injustice

Ann E. Cudd

INTRODUCTION

Academic institutions are purpose driven, not profit driven, and heavily subsidized by government funding. As such, they are committed to seeking and exemplifying truth and justice in their mission and operations. In a democratic society, one principal purpose of higher education is democratic equality, the idea that all persons are worthy of equal dignity and respect, that their status is not inborn or tied to their nonvoluntary social identity in race, class, ethnicity, gender, or sexual orientation. To live up to this ideal or purpose, academic institutions must treat persons fairly, without prejudice or bias. Moreover, in their academic activities, institutions should pursue truth, and their functional operations need to exemplify justice and fairness.

Academic institutions are, however, products of their times. Our society has committed atrocities and injustices in and through the central institutions of society, including colleges and universities. The longer their history, the more time they have had to accumulate and embody historical injustices in various ways. Thus, we find that many, perhaps all, institutions of higher education in existence for any length of time are implicated in injustices of the past as well as the present. To honor the ideals of democratic equality, institutions must reckon with the ways that they have participated in or been complicit with injustice.

This essay explores the ethical questions that institutions and their leaders ask when they consider how this reckoning is to be done. "Reckoning with" in the sense that I am using it means coming to understand, acknowledge, and attempt to repair the accumulated harms done to individuals and groups. What are institutions' duties and responsibilities to uncover and make transparent their past actions that contribute to current inequities, and what must be done about these?

HISTORIC INJUSTICES OF ACADEMIC INSTITUTIONS

Many kinds of wrongs and injustices have occurred in and through academic institutions. It will help the discussion to consider some examples and draw some distinctions to narrow the topic. This essay will not consider those wrongs resulting from individual actions that are neither authorized by the institution's leaders and bylaws nor supported by processes and practices that normalize them in the institution. These include unlawful violations of individual rights through fraud or lies committed by employees or trustees, such as the sexual assaults by Jerry Sandusky at Penn State or Larry Nasser at Michigan State. While their institutions' leaders were negligent in not discovering and stopping the assaults sooner, this is not historic injustice of institutional process so much as individual crime.[1] Similarly, the so-called "Varsity Blues" admissions scandals resulting from the bribery of athletics coaches and fraudulent test takers violated institutional rules, and these crimes were duly prosecuted when uncovered.

This essay considers lawful injustices from the past that resulted from intentional institutional decision-making carried out by administrative leaders, trustees, and faculty members acting within the institutions' rules and established practices. Although neither unlawful nor socially forbidden when they occurred, these practices were immoral and unjust. These actions or events, authorized by the bylaws, policies, and practices of the institution, can be said to be performed by the institution. By speaking of an institution's responsibility for injustice, I do not mean to let individuals off the hook but rather to implicate the material, legal, and intellectual fabric of the institution in the injustice to explore how its responsibility carries forward in history through that fabric.

The most infamous historic injustices highlighted by recent research are academic institutions that owned and dealt in chattel slavery.[2] The most well-known example is Georgetown University's sale of 272 enslaved persons to save the financially strapped institution in 1838.[3] Another kind of injustice that this essay considers is the unjust taking of land on which the institution sits, or lands taken and then sold for its benefit, including institutions located on lands stolen from Native peoples or lands[4] acquired through processes of redlining and gentrification[5] that moved out minorities in exploitative but not illegal ways.

Another set of historic injustices were accepted forms of violence perpetrated on members of the institution themselves, including enslaved[6] or exploited[7] workers. In other cases, students were forced to attend and mistreated through violent punishments. Such was the fate of students at institutions designed to assimilate Native children into Euro-American culture. Haskell Indian Nations University, now run by the Bureau of Indian Affairs as a pan-tribal college, is one example.[8]

We should also consider other kinds of historical injustice that were legal and normal but now recognized as unjust. Such is the categorical exclusion of certain identities, such as women and Blacks, who were simply outright excluded from many universities until the mid-twentieth century. Harvard College first accepted women in 1946, and Yale College, not until 1969. Blacks were excluded from state universities in the South during the Jim Crow era. James Meredith was the first Black student to enroll at the University of Mississippi in 1962, and in 1963 President Kennedy had to federalize the National Guard to enforce desegregation at the University of Alabama. Although Jews were admitted in restricted numbers, selective quotas excluded many of the deserving and qualified from being educated at or being hired by the nation's most prestigious colleges and universities. Yale's College of Arts and Science, for example, did not have a Jewish member of the faculty until Paul Weiss in the mid-1940s. Because these institutions were (and are) the source of opportunity for building wealth and social power, the categorical exclusion of certain groups effectively denied them a fair chance at cultural and economic equality, not to mention leadership, while stigmatizing the group and thereby harming its individual members.

Another kind of injustice, both historic and continuing in many cases, is the symbolic and cultural injustice done when universities memorialize in a positive light unjust institutions and events or persons who committed injustices. Such is the case with memorials to the Confederacy and buildings named after notorious racists or misogynists. As well, honorary degrees have been presented to persons who have committed crimes or heinous actions against women and racial and ethnic minorities. The memorials and honors have in some cases been bestowed despite knowledge at the time of the injustice.[9] Allowing these memorials or honors to stand in the face of such awareness, without due consideration of the reasons for and against removing them, will rightly be seen as continuing to endorse the honor.

Finally, I also include in this category of injustices what I call curricular exclusion, by which I mean the intentional or unintentional exclusion from the curriculum of the history, norms, and expressions of certain groups and individual authors from those groups. This includes non-White or non-Western minorities and women. Not only does curricular exclusion present history in biased ways that distort truth or perpetuate falsehoods, thereby violating a primary purpose of universities, it also unjustly treats those whose cultural and social identity is excluded. Excluding women from the history of science, for example, perpetuates the notion that women cannot be (or are constitutionally less able) scientists, which reinforces stereotypes about women's roles and mental capacity.

This introduction illustrates a range of historic injustices that academic institutions have committed, and from which the majority students and culture have benefited, at least in the short to medium term and in the past. I focus on the past because it seems well accepted by all that universities and their administrators and trustees must intervene to stop current injustices. Less clear is why and how these historic injustices must also be addressed.

THE IMPORTANCE OF RECKONING WITH PAST INJUSTICE

Those responsible for current injustice must obviously end and repair it. But why is reckoning with past injustice so important when the perpetrators and the victims are dead, perhaps long dead? In as far as there are no living victims, digging up the past seems like a mere historical, academic exercise. As institutions that seek truth, such academic exercises have value in themselves for pursuing an accurate, complete, and meaningful historical record. But in many instances, past injustice transmits benefits and harms through the ways that those injustices shape current social institutions and norms to affect currently living persons. This implies an ethical answer to the question of why it is important to understand, acknowledge, and repair past injustice. The ethical answer gets to the heart of what it is for injustice to be built into social institutions, a point summarized ironically by William Faulkner: "The past is never dead. It's not even past."[10]

The first reason to reckon with past injustice is because it may be passed directly on to descendants of the initial victims. Deprivation of wealth, status, and opportunity is the primary means by which injustice directly affects subsequent generations. Unjustly denied the ability to accumulate wealth or gain status, the initial victims could not then pass on opportunities that come with wealth and status to their children and henceforward to their children's children. Let's call this direct (historic) injustice. When a historic injustice directly causes current injustice, the only way to end the current injustice is to repair the historic injustice, and since injustice demands action, the case for reckoning with direct historic injustice, through direct payment and other forms of repair, is clear.

The second reason to reckon with past injustice is because it may harm current individuals, not (or not only) through a direct causal chain stemming from the initial injustice but from the memory or consciousness of the injustice in the minds of living persons. Some past injustices cause painful or humiliating reminders that traumatize living persons even if they did not witness the events or have any causal connection to the victims. This trauma may cause affected persons to be unable to interact or engage fully with the world, depriving them of an equal opportunity to benefit from current opportunities or causing mental anguish and physical harm. Persons who identify with or share some social identity with the long-ago victims suffer from this harm when they are forced regularly to confront the knowledge or memory of the past injustices. Let's call this memorial (historic) injustice. As with direct historic injustice, memorial injustice is currently occurring and thus demands to be reckoned with—understood, acknowledged, and stopped.

The third reason to reckon with historic injustices is because they may perpetuate norms and beliefs that harm currently living persons. Some past injustice is really not past in the sense that it is not universally recognized as injustice. For instance, the past injustices done to women by excluding them from equal opportunity to participate in the full range of public life and education is not generally acknowledged to be injustice but rather thought to be quaint traditions of a different time or perhaps natural consequences of the lack of birth control. Some other past injustices are acknowledged to have been unjust, but the victims are considered in some sense partially blameworthy, and the descendants of the victims are tainted by their shared identity. The enslavement of Blacks or the genocide of Native Americans are acknowledged as unjust, but stereotypes of both groups remain: they were easily preyed upon because they came from "primitive" cultures.[11] Let's call this systemic epistemic injustice.

The case for reckoning with systemic epistemic injustice is also compelling, if not as straightforward to enact. Systemic epistemic injustice makes it difficult for individuals who belong to the wronged group to be taken as sources of evidence or knowledge. Not only is their testimony questioned but also their trustworthiness in making promises, contracts, or commitments. Such injustice makes it harder to cooperate or bargain with strangers, making economic and legal interactions more difficult and expensive. Systemic epistemic injustice persists in society's norms and beliefs, and these cannot be reformed as readily as making cash payments to repair lost wealth or removing statues or memorials to reduce current psychological trauma. As a trusted, knowledge-making institution, academia is well placed to understand and repair this kind of injustice by making curricula more inclusive of marginalized voices and subjecting mainstream ones to critique from alternative perspectives.

RESPONSIBILITY OF INDIVIDUAL INSTITUTIONS FOR HISTORIC INJUSTICE

With this list of historic institutional injustices and the moral case for action, we can now distinguish two ways in which academic institutions bear responsibility for past injustice. The point in examining the form responsibility takes in these instances is not to assign blame but to establish what justice demands of the institutions today and going forward. One kind of responsibility is for past harms caused by institutional actions or inactions that directly harm individuals. Backward-looking responsibility arises from and whenever a causal chain connects past injustice to current victims. As I argued, direct historic injustices are sometimes passed on to descendants of victims. This is the case for descendants of enslaved persons bought and sold by institutions or descendants of the owners of land taken to locate an academic institution. This is backward-looking responsibility of the sort that tort claims impose, and such harms need to be directly engaged by addressing the harmed individual and repairing through the financial, intellectual, and educational resources of the institution.

A second kind of responsibility is forward-looking, to change the course of the future. Institutional actions or inactions that directly harm individuals qua members of groups, as is the case with memorial injustice and systemic epistemic injustice, place a responsibility on the institution to repair by changing the way we understand and view the historic event in question and its perpetrators and victims. Memorial injustice harms by shining a positive light on a historic injustice or unjust actor and disrespects persons who share a social identity with the victims. For instance, an academic building named for Thomas Parran, the surgeon general who oversaw the Tuskegee syphilis experiments, harms Black persons by honoring someone who intentionally inflicted a terrible injustice on them, sending the message that their dignity and well-being was unimportant because of their race.[12] One crucial way to change the way we view Parran and his experiment is to publicly acknowledge his actions and, after public discussion, remove his name from the building. This changes the future by teaching a new set of norms that acknowledge the wrongness of the actions and beliefs of the past.

Systemic epistemic injustice instills a forward-looking responsibility to change the narrative through which we understand the historic injustice. This responsibility is in the first instance to those who identify with the victims of the historic injustice, but also to others, since believing a falsehood or distortion of the past is not good for anyone in the long run. By understanding slavery as the serious moral failure of slaveholders and enslaved persons as resistant and courageous, we come to view White and Black Americans differently. In viewing each other differently in ways that correct past distortions and lies, we can achieve a greater level of mutual respect and ultimately justice and peace.

Similarly, institutional complicity with background norms and social conditions that harm individuals qua members of groups through harmful stereotypes and social stigma is another form of systemic epistemic injustice. The (now ended) categorical exclusion of Blacks and women by academic institutions harms members of these groups by supporting continuing beliefs and norms that suggest they are less intelligent or less worthy of education. Although women now comprise the majority in academia, they have not achieved equality in STEM fields in large part due to those lingering stereotypes. Blacks remain significantly underrepresented in academia as a whole. This underrepresentation and the beliefs and norms it supports signal complicity with those harmful prejudices, which bestows a forward-looking responsibility on academic institutions to play a role in changing the false beliefs and harmful norms the earlier injustices created.

PRINCIPLES FOR ACADEMIC INSTITUTIONS FOR RECKONING WITH PAST INJUSTICE

This essay provides some principles for academic leaders and trustees to guide their thinking about historical injustice. As we have seen, many kinds of injustice harm in different ways and impose different responsibilities on institutions. My analysis points to three principles for considering these varied kinds of injustice.

First, wherever an institution directly harms living persons by its past actions or inactions, it must do what it can to apologize for and repair this historic injustice. One way to repair is a backward-looking responsibility to repay lost wealth. The example of Georgetown University's ownership and sale of enslaved persons long ago, which prevented them from accumulating wealth at the time and for generations, resulted in their descendants having less wealth and opportunity than they would have had otherwise. Georgetown has continued to exist and thrive financially because of this past action and therefore should repay those persons. Georgetown may fulfill its responsibility in more forward-looking ways as well. In other cases, universities may have a direct responsibility to a neighborhood whose home values were destroyed by unjust uses of rezoning laws and financial power. An institution can also help replace lost opportunity by offering scholarships and academic outreach and enrichment programs that prepare descendants to succeed in college in the future. This may well change the face of the future not only for the descendants but for society at large.

Second, wherever the institution harms living individuals qua members of marginalized or disadvantaged groups by unacknowledged unjust actions or inactions, or through its symbols, it must do what it can to listen, recognize, acknowledge, and correct the situation. This is the primary form of responsibility for memorial injustice, though it stems from direct injustice as well. Institutions should consider renaming buildings or programs named for, or honorary degrees bestowed upon, individuals who have committed injustices. Institutions should consider removing statues and memorials to slaveholders, war criminals, and other perpetrators of injustice. This should be done in a way that acknowledges and names the harm, apologizes to the affected persons, and moves toward changing false beliefs and social norms those honors supported.

This second principle will be seen as much broader and more radical than the first. Most of the powerful and famous people who founded this nation were slaveholders or complicit with and benefited from the institution of slavery. Our economy was built on the unpaid labor of slavery, and social stratification by race was constructed for and because of it. The land on which this nation sits comprises large portions of stolen lands whose theft came through genocidal acts by many of our founders. Academic institutions founded before the Civil

War all owe their existence to the endowments they gained through funds and land amassed through slaveholding and land theft. Should academic institutions remove all honorary references to these past powerful figures? What about George Washington, the father of our nation and a slaveholder?

These questions need to be surfaced and debated as part of the forward-looking responsibility of academic institutions implicated in injustice. This essay cannot dive deeply into these questions, but I offer a set of distinctions to consider. In considering what to do and which injustices to prioritize, distinguishing among the reasons the honor was bestowed is important. Those persons honored for the injustices they committed most obviously warrant revocation. Civil War generals celebrated for their leading role in that war should clearly have that honor revoked, their names and statues removed, and a clear statement of repair issued. Public revocation should state clearly that these past deeds were unjust and unworthy of glory. It allows opportunity to reflect on the harm that continued from the point at which the honor was bestowed and continues into the present. And it acknowledges pain and injury to those affected by personal or group-based identity with the victims of injustice.

Honors bestowed on persons for good deeds who have also committed injustices fall into two different groups: those whose power and ability enabling the good deeds came from the injustices they committed and those who were complicit with but did not actively participate in injustice. The first group includes wealthy persons recognized for their donations to an institution whose wealth came from slaveholding, and the surgeon general honored for his public service yet used that role to commit injustice by approving and conducting immoral research on vulnerable groups. With this group, clearly, the honor must be revoked even if that person also did many good things. The second group includes persons honored for good deeds not directly enabled by any injustice they personally committed, yet they benefited from the injustices and social inequalities that privileged members of their social group at that time. Examples in this group include virtually every honored White male, which also reveals the absurdity of revoking honors for everyone in this group. There can be mitigating reasons to acknowledge their unearned social privileges while continuing to honor them. "They were products of their time" is not a defense, however, if they actively upheld status quo injustices through their words and deeds.

The third principle I propose addresses systemic epistemic injustice and implies additional responsibilities to reckon with direct and memorial injustice. An institution must support academic investigation, understanding, and deconstruction of the norms and social conditions with which it is complicit and promote in particular marginalized voices. As I argued earlier, categorical exclusion of groups from academia continues to cast a shadow of stereotypes and stigma on living members of those formerly excluded groups. Memorial injustices likewise harm living members of victimized groups through symbols and cultural beliefs and norms supported by honoring the memory of those who committed the injustices. Curricular exclusion hinders the ability of marginalized groups to create and promulgate widely held norms and beliefs that would correct false narratives, stereotypes, and stigma that continue to harm them.

Academia is well placed, however, to repair these harms. Universities have a forward-looking obligation from their complicity with these past systemic epistemic injustices to offer scholarships and programs for underrepresented minorities and women in STEM fields. Institutions have a forward-looking responsibility as well to expand the representation of faculty from previously excluded groups and embrace their interests in previously overlooked questions and methods of research. Likewise, academic institutions have a responsibility to engage in reform that expands the curriculum to include cultural and historical knowledge of previously excluded, ignored, and mistreated groups.

CONCLUSION

Academic leaders and trustees are entrusted with guiding their institutions to achieve their particular missions with integrity and to ensure their ongoing continuity. Reckoning with injustice is clearly an important value that academic institutions must pursue. But as any academic administrator will immediately interject, other values and principles compete for attention and sometimes conflict with the project of repairing historic injustice. Among the competing principles are such weighty values as academic freedom and freedom of speech, norms of faculty governance and autonomy, religious freedom, property rights, and institutional continuity and financial viability. When reckoning with past injustice, how much and whose attention should institutions focus on, and what weight should that project have against these other important values? Should institutions have standing committees or commissions to seek and discover injustice or merely a process for assessing claims of stakeholders or others? Further questions arise in choosing how to prioritize among historic injustices to address. Examining how these principles and values are to be weighed against reckoning with historical injustice will involve institution-specific conditions and an in-depth investigation of the particular historic injustices and how they affect currently living persons.

The purpose of this essay has been to expand the scope of historical injustice in which academic institutions are implicated and to argue for principles that pose backward- and forward-looking responsibilities to address them. I endorse a growing conviction that academic institutions must reckon with the direct historic injustices of slaveholding that many of our most prestigious institutions were built upon. I expanded on that argument to include other direct historic injustices that implicate many more institutions. I also discussed how academic institutions commit other forms of injustice, namely memorial injustice and systemic epistemic injustice, and the responsibilities to repair them. Academic institutions have been complicit in the creation of beliefs and norms that continue past injustices into the present. But we can make material changes in our institutions and discuss these issues in ways that affect our cultural understanding and social norms. We have a forward-looking responsibility to do so.

Chapter 11

Should Universities Pay Reparations?
Alan H. Goldman

Universities have been built by slaves or founded by those who directly profited from slavery, have been built on land stolen from Native Americans, and have denied women admissions and faculty positions. Should they now pay reparations by directing resources such as scholarships, preference in admissions and hiring, and remedial programs to descendants of victims of such distant past injustices? As a prelude to answering this question, consider the following pairs of cases.

Duane is an African American descended from slaves. His parents many generations later have, however, prospered, his father holding an executive position in a large corporation. He grew up in an upper-middle-class environment and attended a prestigious private high school. Jimmy is an African American not descended from slaves: his paternal grandparents came from Nigeria, and his mother is from Trinidad. His father left the family shortly after his birth, and his single mother has struggled to keep a job and raise the children. He lives in a poverty-stricken inner city, has tried to attend school regularly when not in charge of younger siblings, and has achieved fairly good grades when able to attend.

Enola is a Native American woman descended from a tribe whose land was taken in part to build a university in the nineteenth century. Her parents left their reservation and have done quite well economically. She too qualifies as upper middle class. Winona is a Native American whose tribe was not exploited by any university. But she grew up on a chronically deprived reservation with inferior schools. She aspires to life outside the reservation and has worked hard to achieve that goal, hoping to receive a scholarship from the University of New Mexico.

Mary lives on Park Avenue in New York City. She has done very well in a private city high school and expects to be admitted to the University of Pennsylvania or a comparable college. Her grandmother was unable to attend any Ivy League university, and, having earned a PhD with high honors at an excellent graduate school, was passed over for faculty positions in favor of males with lesser paper credentials. Jane has had to work part time while in high school to contribute economically to her family that struggles to pay rent and buy decent food. Immigration authorities have persecuted her parents, who are Latin American immigrants and have had trouble finding jobs because of their heavy Spanish accents. Jane has managed to get good, but not outstanding, grades in school despite her brutal schedule, and she aspires to be the first in her family to attend college.

Given limited resources, to whom among these pairs should a university direct extra support and preference for a scholarship? To me it seems obvious that preference should be given to the second in each of these pairs. Each of them has suffered greater hardship and social and economic injustice despite not having descended from ancestors who themselves were victims of injustice perpetrated by universities or by those who benefited universities with their endowments. Duane, Enola, and Mary do not need extra support from a university to gain admission and succeed once admitted. They have already benefited from their parents' hard work and success and their places in the social and economic ladder, and further preference would only exacerbate their unearned advantages over the likes of Jimmy, Winona, and Jane. The latter three could not be paid reparations for injustices to their ancestors involving universities. There were no injustices of that type. But clearly, they themselves are victims of social and economic injustice, and, given their ages and aspirations, universities are especially well positioned to partially compensate for these injustices that have resulted from the workings of the American free market.

Are there arguments that should convince us to reverse this initial judgment that at best places reparations on the back burner? One might question first why universities could not do both: make reparations to descendants of those they previously treated unjustly and also help those in greater need of support because of injustices in which the universities were not involved. But I am assuming limited scholarship funds and other resources that could be used for compensatory purposes. Aside from Yale and Harvard, which might have virtually unlimited funds (although you would never know it from their appeals), this assumption seems reasonable. Given limited funds and virtually unlimited potentially needy applicants, priorities must be established. If the priority is as I have judged it, reparations will not be paid.

One might also object to my priorities that in focusing only on economic inequality, I am ignoring the psychological harms to descendants, perhaps felt as continuing stigmatization, resulting from the history of slavery, discrimination against women, and stolen lands along with negative images of Native Americans. In this context, reparations do not simply help correct economic inequality but also represent an important symbolic gesture to help ease these psychological burdens. Admitting a wrong and offering reparations alleviate to some degree the psychological harm caused. Yet I maintain that a choice must still be made between correcting for the real material disadvantages of potential applicants from severely deprived backgrounds, amounting to insurmountable obstacles in the absence of scholarships, and adding to material advantages of those more fortunate but with possible psychological burdens deriving from past injustices to ancestors. My priority remains the same.

The objection might continue ad hominem, not always fallacious when focused on empathy or appreciation of the psychological states of others. Who am I, a privileged white male, to estimate the psychological burdens of those whose race, gender, or ethnic group was for so long stigmatized and victimized? Perhaps I can begin a reply on personal grounds regarding not myself, but my wife. Her grandparents, who had prospered in Eastern Europe, what is now the Czech Republic and Hungary, had their property stolen and were then murdered in concentration camps. Certainly, no ethnic group was victimized more than European Jews in the Second World War, only two generations away. Yet I do not see that the resources of the German government would be better spent compensating my wife and others like her than on poor immigrants to that country or in reducing unjust economic inequality there.

The German government did pay reparations to actual surviving victims of the Holocaust and gave substantial foreign aid to Israel. But it is instructive how this case differs significantly from present proposals for reparations based on such distant wrongs as slavery on the part of universities that benefited from it.[1] Foreign aid to other countries is a different matter that we can leave aside. The crucial difference is between direct victims of serious injustice and distant descendants of those victims. The difference lies not only in that many members of the latter group do not suffer substantial harm limiting opportunities in the present deriving from that history, but also in the very application of the fundamental principle of compensation. Reparations, as a form of compensation, fall under that principle.

This principle requires victims of wrongdoing be restored to the positions they would have occupied had the wrongdoing not occurred. Although involving counterfactual reasoning, the principle can be plausibly applied to immediate victims of injustice who have suffered measurable harms, especially material harms. But when we are attempting to apply it to distant descendants of injustice whose harms are mainly psychological if they exist to any great extent at all, the results will be highly variable and of questionable accuracy. This contrast clearly emerges in relation to the pairs of examples with which we began. The second members themselves suffer extreme material disadvantage through no fault of their own, while the first members might or might not be psychologically harmed by the unjust history of their ancestors. As members of previously discriminated against groups, those applying to universities might even be more highly motivated.

Two aspects of the principle of compensation might be argued by the other side. First, that such a principle exists at all suggests that we cannot simply leave wrongdoing uncorrected or unpunished. While the primary purpose of compensation or reparations is to restore the victims of injustice to their rightful positions, a secondary purpose is to hold wrongdoers accountable and publicly demonstrate that they will be held accountable. Present administrators in universities may have had nothing to do with distant past injustices, but the institutions themselves can and should be held responsible for correcting injustices which they caused, in which they were implicated, or from which they benefited. Second, and seemingly most relevant here, a debt owed must be repaid before those resources can be used for other benefits, no matter how much utility those other uses may provide. Reparations can be considered payment of a debt owed and so fall under that corollary of the principle of compensation.

As for the first point of holding universities accountable for the wrongs in which they were implicated, they can accept and demonstrate such accountability through means other than directing reparations to distant descendants. First, they can publicly announce and ensure that all discrimination based on race, ethnicity, and gender is scrupulously avoided. Second, they can remove all symbols and vestiges of past discrimination such as statues and names from buildings of those who engaged in racist practices. Third, but more controversial, they can aim for racial and gender diversity in admissions and curricula, although I will not take a stand on the extent to which such policy is justified, a topic beyond the scope of this essay. Finally, special programs for and admissions of those low on the social and economic scale itself will disproportionately benefit minorities presently overrepresented in the lower classes, including descendants of slaves, while not selecting those minority applicants who least need special help. Duane, Enola, and Mary will not be among the recipients of preference in such a program despite being descendants of victims of past injustices.

As for paying debts before providing benefits to others, our question is precisely whether universities do owe prioritized debts to all descendants of past victims of injustice in which the universities were involved. To assume that such debts must be paid before addressing problems of extreme economic inequality is to beg the question. Again, the contrast here is with debts owed to direct victims of injustice or their immediate families. Such direct debts must indeed be paid, but the question is whether distant descendants of injustice not presently materially harmed by that injustice have equal claims. I don't see that Germany owes a debt to my wife, despite the horrendous annihilation of her near ancestors by a now disavowed government. And I don't see how a debt to more distant descendants of slavery is more plausibly alleged. As horrible as slavery was, it was no worse than slave labor followed by mass murder. The debt to descendants of slaves may seem more plausible when we think of such descendants as presently economically deprived, as opposed to my wife and me, who have fared very well, thank you, without help from Germany. But if the deprived economic status of applicants suffices for special treatment, then the claim to reparations is superfluous for them. And, as I have argued, that claim is much more difficult to establish for well-to-do descendants of past injustice.

A final counterargument is that universities owe compensation in the form of reparations only if they were involved in some way in the previous injustice. Arguably, while some or many universities benefited from the practice of slavery and injustice toward Native Americans, they were not primarily responsible for the economic inequalities that so greatly handicap present applicants in the lower classes. Hence, it might be concluded, they are responsible for paying reparations but not for correcting inequalities caused by other sectors of society.

Again, two responses. First, elitist private universities, such as those in the Ivy League, have helped perpetuate and exacerbate economic inequality by preferring legatees (children of alumni, especially of those who have donated to the university) and applicants from expensive private and prep schools. If graduation from these universities is a ticket to higher paying careers, this practice tends to make the rich richer. And if such practice is unjust in violating equality of opportunity, then these universities do have some responsibility for addressing economic inequality in the present and future. Second, state universities, as public institutions funded by government, must contribute what they can to fulfilling the state's obligations to its citizens. If the state is obligated to address the extreme inequalities caused by the operation of its economic system, then its universities have a role to play in fulfilling this obligation. Thus, both private and public universities have a more immediate obligation to address present unjust inequalities than distant past injustices. And, as noted, they are in an especially good position to equalize opportunities for good careers.

I have considered several arguments designed to alter my initial intuitions about who should receive special help or resources such as scholarships, presumably the main form of reparations universities would offer. None of these arguments persuaded me that my initial reactions to the examples were morally off base. Of course, universities must choose between paying reparations and addressing current economic inequalities only if scholarship funds are limited and potential lower-class applicants exceed available scholarships. If conditions were different, unjust, severe economic inequality might be irrelevant to the question of reparations. Their remediation might simply be given separate consideration. But the question of reparations by universities must be answered in the real world as it is now and likely to remain in the foreseeable future. In this world, any claim to reparations on the part of descendants of past victims must compete for relatively scarce resources.

A final possibility, one that might seem to evade the force of my argument, is that reparations are due to all members of previously harmed groups such as African Americans and Native Americans, but that preference will be given to members of those groups presently most in need of special help. This might seem to play out the same in practice as that which I advocate. But again, if social and economic deprivation suffices for special treatment, the appeal to reparations in this context seems not only superfluous but disingenuous. And it is also questionable why those not even descended from people who were earlier harmed should be thought to be proper recipients of reparations for those harms, as opposed to legitimate claimants to equal opportunity.

Chapter 12

Rethinking Affirmative Action

Steven M. Cahn

In March 1961, less than two months after assuming office, President John F. Kennedy issued Executive Order 10925, which established the President's Committee on Equal Employment Opportunity. Its mission was to end discrimination in employment by the government and its contractors. The order required every federal contract to include the pledge that

> (1) The contractor will not discriminate against any employe[e] or applicant for employment because of race, creed, color, or national origin. The contractor will take affirmative action to ensure that applicants are employed, and that employe[e]s are treated during employment, without regard to their race, creed, color, or national origin. (Executive Order 10925, part III, subpart A)

Here for the first time in the context of civil rights, the government called for affirmative action. The term meant taking appropriate steps to eradicate the then-widespread practices of racial, religious, and ethnic discrimination. The goal, as the President stated, was "equal opportunity in employment." In other words, procedural affirmative action, as I shall call it, was instituted to ensure that applicants for positions would be judged without any consideration of their race, religion, or national origin. These criteria were declared irrelevant. Taking them into account was forbidden.

The Civil Rights Act of 1964 restated and broadened the application of this principle. Title VI declared that "No person in the United States shall, on the grounds of race, color, or national origin, be excluded from participation in, be denied the benefits of, or be subjected to discrimination under any program or activity receiving Federal financial assistance."

But before one year had passed, President Lyndon B. Johnson argued that fairness required more than a commitment to such procedural affirmative action. In his 1965 commencement address at Howard University, he said:

You do not take a person who for years has been hobbled by chains and liberate him, bring him up to the starting line of a race and then say, "You're free to compete with all the others," and still justly believe that you have been completely fair. Thus it is not enough just to open the gates of opportunity. All our citizens must have the ability to walk through those gates . . . We seek not . . . just equality as a right and a theory but equality as a fact and equality as a result.

Several months later President Johnson issued Executive Order 11246, which stated: "It is the policy of the Government of the United States to provide equal opportunity in Federal employment for all qualified persons, to prohibit discrimination in employment because of race, creed, color or national origin, and to promote the full realization of equal employment opportunity through a positive, continuing program in each department and agency." Two years later the Order was amended to prohibit discrimination on the basis of sex.

While the aim of President Johnson's order was stated in language similar to that of President Kennedy's, President Johnson's abolished the Committee on Equal Employment Opportunity, transferred its responsibilities to the Secretary of Labor, and authorized the Secretary to "adopt such rules and regulations and issue such orders as he deems necessary and appropriate to achieve the purposes thereof."

Acting on the basis of this mandate, the Department of Labor issued in December 1971, during the administration of President Richard M. Nixon, Revised Order No. 4, requiring all contractors to develop "an acceptable affirmative action program," including "an analysis of areas within which the contractor is deficient in the utilization of minority groups and women, and further, goals and timetables to which the contractor's good faith efforts must be directed to correct the deficiencies." Contractors were instructed to take the term "minority groups" to refer to "Negroes, American Indians, Orientals, and Spanish Surnamed Americans." The concept of "underutilization" means "having fewer minorities or women in a particular job classification than would reasonably be expected by their availability." "Goals" were not to be "rigid and inflexible quotas" but "targets reasonably attainable by means of applying every good faith effort to make all aspects of the entire affirmative action program work."

Such preferential affirmative action, as I shall call it, requires that attention be paid to the same criteria of race, sex, and ethnicity that procedural affirmative action deems irrelevant. Is the use of these criteria morally justifiable? That is the key question that has remained a divisive issue in the United States for a half-century. Indeed, during that time opinion polls have remained remarkably stable, indicating that approximately half the population supports affirmative action, the other half opposing it.

Yet procedural affirmative action is not controversial. Few oppose announcing positions openly, banning any racial, religious, or ethnic tests for candidates, and eliminating from all procedures any policies that harbor prejudice, however vestigial. The source of the debate, however, is preferential affirmative action, which calls for making special efforts to recruit individuals who meet institutional goals related to racial, gender, or ethnic identity. Announce any program of this sort, and the subsequent debate will generate more heat than light.

Part of the problem is that advocates of preferential affirmative action, which I shall henceforth refer to simply as "affirmative action," do not share one rationale. Is the aim to offset past discrimination, to counteract present unfairness, or to achieve future equality? The first is often referred to as "compensation," the second as "a level playing field," and the third as "diversity."

Note that each of these can be defended independently of the others. Compensation for past wrongs may be owed, although at present the playing field is level and diversity is not sought. Or the playing field at present may not be level, although compensation for past wrongs is not owed and future diversity is not sought. Or future diversity may be sought, although compensation for past wrongs is not owed and presently the playing field is level.

Of course, all three factors might be relevant, but each requires a different justification and calls for a different remedy. For example, past wrongs would be offset if suitable compensation were made, but once provided to the appropriate recipients, no other steps would be needed. Present wrongs would be corrected if actions were taken that would level the playing field, but doing so would be consistent with unequal outcomes. Future equality would require continuing attention to ensure that an appropriate balance, once achieved, would never be lost. Thus defenders of affirmative action would likely favor at least one of these policies but not necessarily more than one.

Nowadays, the most frequently cited defense of affirmative action is an appeal to diversity. The term first gained currency when Justice Lewis Powell, in his pivotal opinion in the Supreme Court's 1978 *Bakke d*ecision, found "the attainment of a diverse student body" to be a goal that might justify the use of race in student admissions. The term "diversity," however, while frequently cited approvingly, requires a modifier, such as racial diversity, gender diversity, religious diversity, and so on. Without this clarification, diversity fails to be a useful concept.

Consider, for example, a sample of the innumerable respects in which people can differ: age, religion, nationality, regional background, economic resources, military experience, bodily appearance, physical soundness, sexual orientation, marital status, ethical standards, political commitments, or cultural values. The crucial question is: which sorts of diversity should be sought?

Imagine a ten-person philosophy department that has no African American, no woman, no non-American, no person under fifty, no non-Christian, no registered Republican, none whose doctoral degree is from other than an Ivy League University, none who served in a war, none who is gay or lesbian, none who has ever been on welfare, none who is physically challenged, none whose work is outside the analytic tradition, none who specializes in aesthetics, and none who is widely heralded for success as a teacher. When the next appointment is made, which characteristics should be stressed so as to render this department more diverse? I know of no compelling answer.

To put the matter more vividly, suppose that the ten finalists for a position in that department include an African American, a woman, an Argentinian, a thirty-year-old, a Buddhist, a Republican, someone whose doctoral degree is from a midwestern university, a veteran, a lesbian, someone who was once on welfare, someone who uses a wheelchair, a specialist in continental philosophy, an aesthetician, and a widely acclaimed teacher. Which one should be favored purely on grounds of enhancing diversity? The question is unanswerable.

Suppose the suggestion is made that the sorts of diversity to be sought are those of groups that have suffered discrimination. The problem with this approach is clearly put by John Kekes:

> It is true that American blacks, Native Americans, Hispanics, and women have suffered injustices as a group. But so have homosexuals, epileptics, the urban and the rural poor, the physically ugly, those whose careers were ruined by McCarthyism, prostitutes, the obese, and so forth . . . There have been some attempts to deny that there is an analogy between these two classes of victims. It has been said that the first were unjustly discriminated against due to racial or sexual prejudice and that this is not true of the second. This is indeed so. But should we accept the suggestion . . . that the only form of injustice relevant to preferential treatment is that which is due to racial or sexual prejudice? Injustice occurs in many forms, and those who value justice will surely object to all of them.[1]

Kekes' reasoning is cogent. In addition, another difficulty looms for the proposal to seek diversity only of groups that have suffered discrimination. Consider, for instance, a department in which most of the faculty members are women. In certain fields, for example, nursing, dental hygiene, and elementary education, such departments are common. If diversity by gender is of value, then such a department, when making its next appointment, should prefer a man. Yet men as a group have not been victims of discrimination. On the other hand, Jews and Asians have been victims of discrimination but do not presently suffer from minimal representation. Thus the question of which groups need enhancement to achieve diversity cannot be answered satisfactorily by an appeal to history.

Nor is the situation clarified by arguing that the appeal to diversity favors those from a group who experience the world from a distinctive standpoint. Celia Wolf-Devine has aptly described this claim as a form of "stereotyping" that is demeaning." As she puts it, "A Hispanic who is a Republican is no less a Hispanic, and a woman who is not a feminist is no less a woman."[2] Furthermore, are Hispanic men and women supposed to have the same point of view by virtue of their common ethnicity, or are they supposed to have different points of view by virtue of their different genders? And why suppose only race, gender, or ethnicity determine one's point of view? Why not also the numerous other significant respects in which people differ, such as age, religion, political outlook, and so on?

Another problematic aspect of affirmative action is its call for giving preference to members of certain groups. But what sort of preference is urged? For example, imagine a search for an assistant professor in which one hundred persons apply, and among them are some who are members of a group designated for affirmative action. Let us refer to them as AA candidates. Suppose the dean has permitted five applicants to be invited for campus interviews. After studying all the vitae and sets of recommendations, the department ranks ten candidates as outstanding, twenty as good, fifty as merely qualified, and twenty as unqualified. Let us suppose that four applicants are AA candidates, and among them one is ranked as outstanding, one as good, one as merely qualified, and one as unqualified.

The key question remains: Assuming AA candidates are to be preferred, what forms of preference are called for? One possibility is to interview any AA candidate who is outstanding, regardless of the merits of any other outstanding candidates. Another possibility is to agree to interview any AA candidate who is good, even though many other candidates are stronger. Yet another possibility is to agree to interview any AA candidate who is qualified, even though again most candidates are stronger. A theoretical possibility is to interview even unqualified AA candidates, although I know of no one who would support that policy, so let us set it aside. What remains are three different models of preference, any of which might be defended.

Next assume two AA candidates are chosen for interviews, one ranked outstanding and another good. Afterward, the department places the outstanding candidate second and the other fifth. Does giving preference to AA candidates require that the second candidate be offered the position? And if the candidate ranked second receives a more attractive offer and withdraws from consideration, need the candidate now ranked fifth be preferred?

Of course, an AA candidate may be ranked the highest, thus avoiding any problems. Otherwise, the call for giving preference requires an interpretation that is rarely, if ever, provided ahead of time.

Furthermore, even assuming that the department has explicitly agreed to a policy regarding preference, the question remains whether that policy will be made public. Suppose, for instance, that the administration has told the department that its next appointment needs to be an AA candidate. Shouldn't that information be publicized, so that those who are members of the groups in question and those who are not can plan accordingly? Surely those who have instituted a policy of preference believe that their action is within moral and legal bounds. No one should object, therefore, to stating that policy without equivocation. Yet the usual approach is to keep such information under wraps.

Such secrecy, however, leads to difficulties. For instance, during my years as an administrator, I once met with a candidate who was considering our school's offer of a faculty position and sought my assurance that he would have been chosen regardless of affirmative action. I responded truthfully that he was held in high regard but that I didn't know the answer to his concern. Yet I believe he was entitled to raise the matter, for whatever the steps required by a school's affirmative action policy, surely they should not be hidden.

Thus far my discussion has centered on faculty appointments, but different considerations may arise in justifying affirmative action in student admissions. After all, colleges traditionally take account of a high school applicant's athletic prowess, community service, personal relationships to alumni, and geographic home. Such criteria, however, are not considered in a faculty search. No wonder defenders of affirmative action are most comfortable supporting it in the context of a complex admissions decision involving many nonacademic factors, while opponents most often think of the policy in relation to assessing the research and teaching of applicants for faculty positions. The two decisions are different in kind, and the same arguments may not apply to both.

In addition, circumstances matter. Consider a department that has never appointed a woman and, when given a promising opportunity, refuses even to interview one. Suppose the dean insists that in the next search process some women should be interviewed, and if a woman with a superlative record is found, she should be appointed. Would opponents of affirmative action object? I think not.

On the other hand, consider a department that announces its intention to achieve a goal of fifty percent women, and in its next search prefers a minimally qualified woman to a man who is far more promising as a researcher, teacher, and contributor to the life of the department. If the dean insists that the man be appointed, would proponents of affirmative action be upset? Again, I think not.

Both these cases are admittedly extreme, although not entirely unrealistic, but the lesson is that presuming affirmative action to be at odds with merit, as its opponents do, or to be a means of obtaining justice, as its defenders do, are oversimplifications. The context matters.

In conclusion, I recognize that I have neither supported nor opposed affirmative action. As it turns out, however, that decision depends on whether the goal is compensation, a level playing field, or diversity; what sorts of diversity are sought; what sorts of preference are proposed; whether the policy will be made public; whether the focus is faculty appointments or student admissions; and whether any special circumstances are part of the context. Without that information, taking an unconditional position for or against affirmative action suggests a failure to appreciate the matter's complexities.

Part VI

DISABILITIES

Chapter 13

Achieving Disability Inclusion

Leslie P. Francis

Debates about laptops in the classroom are intense. On the one side are faculty concerned that students will use their laptops in class to play games, surf the net, or communicate with each other over email or social media. Sometimes these arguments seem sanctimonious, antediluvian, and downright paternalistic. Sometimes they seem self-interested or self-aggrandizing: a professor thinking that a student cannot be listening to important gems of wisdom if a laptop is open. Sometimes they express genuine concern for student learning and especially for other students who might be distracted by their compatriots' laptop use. Studies of laptops in the classroom increasingly address nuanced questions about which uses may be harmful and which may be beneficial.[1]

The voices of students with disabilities are largely unheard in these debates. Yet one of the primary concerns of students with a variety of disabilities—from visual impairments to difficulties with coordination to attention disorders—is the critical importance of laptops or similar electronic devices to their educational success. Disability "accommodation" is a standard answer to this concern: students with a disability documented to meet the standards of the Americans with Disabilities Act (ADA) may request to use a laptop as a reasonable accommodation. In a classroom where laptop use is generally forbidden, however, such an accommodation has significant disadvantages. It reveals students as in some way disabled, thus potentially newly stigmatizing or exposing them to implicit bias if their disability has been otherwise hidden. Even worse, peers who perceive this as an unfair privilege or competitive advantage may resent them. Laptop prohibitions combined with exceptional accommodations are ethically problematic for these students who face the choice of being targeted or being educationally compromised by foregoing an educational tool that is essential for them. Such prohibitions, therefore, cannot simply be assumed to be acceptable; they must be fortified by an overriding moral reason. Faculty distaste for technology or their belief that laptops will disrupt their classrooms does not justify prohibitions, putting the burden on students to request accommodations to fill educational gaps for themselves.

In this essay, I use laptops in classrooms as a case study in what disability nondiscrimination requires—and does not require—in higher education. I begin by explaining an important distinction between accommodations and modifications. I then describe how the law of disability nondiscrimination in education got off in the wrong direction from the outset by confusing accommodations and modifications. Finally, I explain what disability nondiscrimination requires and why it is not in any way "special" privileging.

ACCOMMODATIONS AND MODIFICATIONS

Curb cuts, with which we are all familiar, are an example of a modification. Required by the ADA for pedestrian crossings on public streets,[2] they have transformed the built environment for everyone. Anyone may use curb cuts; no one has to ask for them (at least once they are installed), no one reveals their disabilities by using them, and no one is resented as receiving an unfair privilege by rolling or strolling down them. Bicyclists taking to the sidewalks, travelers pulling suitcases, parents pushing strollers, and students dragging roller backpacks all benefit from the change in sidewalk design. Parenthetically, the one disadvantage of curb cuts was for the visually impaired, who no longer had the level change of the curb to alert them that they were moving from the sidewalk to the street. The solution was to install curb cuts with tactile warnings such as little bumps in the surface.

Policies, as well as the built environment, can be modified too. Consider a parking problem in a lot near a university housing complex. The lot requires a university sticker but is open to both housing residents and others coming to campus. Students living in the residence hall constantly complain that they cannot find parking near their units and may have to park farther away. This problem is especially acute for students with mobility impairments during inclement weather. To solve this problem, the university might accommodate students with disabilities by allowing them to sign up for designated parking places. Or it might adopt a narrow policy of designating several spots available only to people who qualify for a disabled parking permit. These changes, targeted either to particular individuals or to people with disabilities as a group, might be viewed as disability accommodations. But policy modifications that benefit everyone—at least everyone in the residence halls—might be available too, for example, a policy allowing residents in each unit to sign up for a numbered parking place nearby. The modification gives everyone in the residence halls something, although it raises more general questions about how to make transit to campus convenient for everyone; the accommodation responds to the situation of particular individuals making a claim tailored to their disability. Changing the focus from accommodations to modifications removes the burden from people with disabilities, who must reveal their conditions to receive a special parking place or license plate, and raises more general questions about how to design transit to and from campus. Many other university policy modifications also shift the focus to how to increase accessibility more generally rather than singling out people with disabilities as special cases: asynchronous online classes, hybrid classes that students may attend either in person or virtually, regular use of closed captioning with PowerPoint slide presentations, instructor use of microphones in classes, and websites that meet accessibility design standards are just a few examples.

Accommodations, by contrast, are adjustments that enable individuals to participate in activities, perform successfully, or benefit from services. Individuals with documented disabilities may be accommodated by text readers, sign language interpretation, ergonomic equipment, or extra time on exams, among other common examples. Or they may be able to use disabled parking spaces or purchase accessible seats at sporting events. These accommodations require individuals to apply for them based on their disability and are particular to the individual receiving them.

Rest rooms are an interesting hybrid example. Disabled stalls are expected to be set aside for people with disabilities who need them. On the other hand, abled people may find disabled stalls more convenient because of their design or location, or because they might be just another open stall when there's a line of people waiting. Using disabled stalls, however, when they do not see disabled people waiting for them is problematic: people with invisible disabilities may not be apparent to others, people with disabilities may arrive and be unable to access open stalls, and people may be unaware that the time they thought would be "just a minute" really is far longer. Still, when restrooms are infrequently used, or when there is a single room with universal design, everyone benefits from the design change.

And so too for laptops in the classroom. They could be accommodations, tailored to the known disabilities of individuals requesting them and only available upon qualification. Or policy modifications could allow laptops for all but try to use them in a way that is educationally beneficial. Which should it be, and why? And how should we think about answering this question from the perspective of disability nondiscrimination? In what follows, my goal is to tease out some of the important differences between viewing inclusion as a problem of accommodation and viewing inclusion as a problem of modification, before bringing the discussion back to whether classroom laptops should be viewed through the lens of accommodation or through the lens of modification.

CONFUSING ACCOMMODATIONS AND MODIFICATIONS IN HIGHER EDUCATION: *SOUTHEASTERN COMMUNITY COLLEGE V. DAVIS*

In 1973 Congress passed the Rehabilitation Act. Section 504 of the Act provides, "No otherwise qualified individual with a disability in the United States . . . shall, solely by reason of his or her disability, be excluded from the participation in, be denied the benefits of, or be subjected to discrimination under any program or activity receiving Federal financial assistance." Soon thereafter the U.S. Supreme Court heard a case[3] interpreting this statute. Unfortunately, it confused accommodations and modifications in a manner that continues to resonate today.[4] Most basically, the case failed to consider how accommodations might function to achieve inclusion.

Here are the facts of the case. Frances Davis had enrolled in the "College Parallel" program at Southeastern Community College (the College), an institution that received federal funds, for the academic year 1973–1974. She had been assured that good performance in the program was a pathway to the College's associate degree nursing program, which would enable her to become a registered nurse. Davis then sought admission for an associate degree based on her success in the College Parallel program. But during the admission process, her hearing impairment became apparent, and the College deemed her unqualified for admission to a nursing program. Davis challenged this rejection, and her case went all the way to the U.S. Supreme Court, where it was argued and resolved in a way that first sowed the confusion of accommodations and modifications. Davis argued that her qualifications for admission should be assessed on only her academic success—without consideration of her disability. The College argued it should also consider her disability—whether she was qualified in spite of her disability rather than apart from it. When the issue was posed in this way, there seemed to be only two alternatives: admit Davis to the program based only on her academic qualifications or reject her. The College said that the former would require an unreasonable modification to the nursing program: eliminating her from participation in the clinical portion of the program. Her being unable to hear adequately in clinical settings could pose a danger to others. The Court saw the College's position as entirely reasonable: how could someone graduate as a nurse, and then be licensed to practice as a nurse, without any clinical experience? Indeed, had Davis proposed this as a modification, it is easy to see how it is unlike curb cuts or parking policy modifications that may be more generally beneficial.

But Davis's contention was not that the program should be modified to allow her to graduate without any clinical training. It was instead that *if* she was academically qualified for admission, *then* the College should consider whether reasonable accommodations could allow her to participate successfully in most, if not all, of the clinical experiences. Davis was an accomplished lip-reader who could understand adequately when people turned their faces toward her so that she could see them speaking. Sound augmentation such as microphones might be available in some settings. In others, where masks needed to be worn, Davis claimed that she might participate successfully with either sign interpretation or the help of a mentor. Yet the College and the Court entertained only the option of excluding Davis from any clinical training. Here, the analysis confused modification—a full-on change in the program—with an analysis of whether accommodations might enable Davis's success in the program. Now, there may have been problems with accommodations—their inconvenience or their expense, for example—but these problems raise entirely different questions from the problems raised by whether allowing someone to graduate without clinical training is a reasonable modification or a fundamental alteration of a nursing program.

Davis had not sought the modification of the program that the College would have imposed on her, graduating as a nurse without clinical training. Instead, she contended that she could rely on her hearing aid, lip reading, close clinical supervision, and sign interpretation in clinical situations where surgical masks needed to be worn and lips could not be read. These were suggested *accommodations* for Davis's disability that would enable her to participate in the clinical program in almost the same way that other students could. The College had flatly refused to consider what her performance could be like with these accommodations. Instead of asking whether Davis's request for accommodation could have enabled her to participate capably in the program, the Court instead regarded her as asking for "services of a personal nature." Legally, the proper inquiry about accommodations would be whether the adjustments she sought would enable her to perform in the program. In employment discrimination, the employer would have an "undue hardship" defense if the accommodations sought in the individual case would cause significant difficulty or expense. For public services, like education at a public institution, the consideration would be whether the burdens of the accommodation would fundamentally alter the program.[5] Would, for example, having instructors speak in a way that would enable Davis to lipread fundamentally alter their teaching? Would sign interpretation when necessary in clinical settings fundamentally change the clinical experience for Davis? Would it have been possible to arrange for such interpretation in settings where masks are worn sufficient to allow Davis to engage in the clinical program? Would her accommodations be disruptive to other students or so expensive that the educational program for all would have been compromised? While not asked in the *Davis* decision, these were precisely the questions that should have been asked in an analysis of whether reasonable accommodations were available for her. Consequently, the sole alternative considered was a modified nursing program in which Davis had no clinical experiences. It was easy, then, for the Court to conclude that she was not qualified for the program and her rejection was not disability discrimination. It was instead a reasonable refusal by the College to graduate an unqualified nurse.

Sometimes, students with disabilities require auxiliary aids and services or other alterations to succeed in a program. These aren't bending the requirements or allowing the unqualified to acquire a credential inappropriately. Changes allowing someone to graduate as a nurse without any clinical experience from a program aimed to train nurses for clinical settings does fundamentally alter the program. The mistake in the *Davis* decision, however, was failing to see whether individualized aids could have enabled Davis to participate in the program in a way that did not change fundamentally. The College and the Court in *Davis* failed to see that accommodations were a possible alternative to modifications.

UNDERSTANDING ACCOMMODATIONS AND MODIFICATIONS FOR INCLUSION

Davis was a legal case and wrong about the law.[6] But the confusions it introduced matter ethically too. The failure to see a difference between approaching questions of disability inclusion through the lens of accommodation and through the lens of modification is also ethically important. There are at least three kinds of ethical problems that require further examination here: the standard of inclusion, the judgment of unfairness, and the idea that accommodations necessarily burden others.

A first problem illustrated by *Davis* is the failure even to consider accommodations as an alternative to modifications as a way of achieving inclusion. In the case, Davis was not seen as an individual whose capabilities needed to be examined with accommodations. People with physical or mental impairments should be considered for what they can do, albeit in different ways, not for whether they perform in standard ways or in the same ways that other people do. Inclusion requires no less.

This is not to say that assessing what people can do is an easy matter, however. Examination accommodations are notoriously problematic cases. Consider the frequent accommodation of extra time on a test. For people whose vision, attention deficits, or other disabilities mean that questions take longer to read, an accommodation of extra time would enable them to demonstrate what they can do, albeit in a way different from others taking the same test. If speed is the skill being measured, on the other hand, the accommodation would change the expectations for performance rather than the manner of performance. On most tests, speed is not essential to the performance, except for administrative reasons such as the time period the instructor or the classroom is available. For other tasks, speed really does matter, such as the split-second decision-making required to avert an emergency. Another frequent objection to extra time as a testing accommodation is fairness to other students. If extra time unlevels the playing field, enabling some to perform better than they otherwise would have done is arguably unfair. For this reason, accommodations are tailored to try to adjust for the speed deficit associated with the disability on an individualized basis.

Or consider the accommodation of changing the format of questions. In one litigated case, a physician who had performed with continuing success in a newborn intensive care unit was required to become board certified in pediatrics to continue in his position.[7] He had prior surgery for a brain tumor that made memory retrieval out of context difficult and requested an essay rather than a multiple-choice format for the board exam. His request was denied on the basis that the format change would fundamentally alter the exam. He lost the case, as the court determined that he had failed to show that the exam format measured his disability rather than his aptitude for and understanding of clinical material in pediatrics. Leaving aside whether they were right on the facts, the court asked the right question: whether the exam format was necessary to assess clinical understanding.

A second problem that might be raised by accommodations is that of unfairness to others. In some circumstances, educational evaluation is competitive, but in other circumstances, it is not. Grading on the curve limits the number of high grades. If percentile ranks on tests such as the SAT or the LSAT matter for admission to selective programs, comparative position matters. For many years when the LSAT was taken with accommodations, test scores were flagged. The U.S. Department of Justice sued the Law School Admission Council (LSAC) for disability discrimination because this practice stigmatized anyone taking the test under accommodations. LSAC settled the suit, despite continuing to contend professional standards supported its practice.[8] Yet it is difficult to see what these standards could be. One possibility is doubt about the validity of accommodation standards and whether any accommodated test measures what it is expected to reflect. This concern raises deeper questions about the validity of the test itself, whether, for example, the LSAT measures likely success in law school or some other factor such as test-taking savvy.

A third, related problem is that accommodations might burden other students. In employment law, accommodations are considered not to be reasonable if they require impositions on other employees, such as taking on extra responsibilities or covering shifts at unpopular times. Some accommodations could present this possibility. For example, someone might request the presence of a service animal trained to detect and warn of an oncoming seizure. Yet other students might have serious allergies triggered by the presence of the animal, a clear burden. In such circumstances, it would be important to work out how the accommodation can be honored without burdening the allergic student, perhaps by providing a separate testing room for the student with the service animal.

Problems of potential unfairness or burdens do not occur in a vacuum. They emerge against backgrounds of imperfect justice. Consider the fairness of tests such as the LSAT, for example. While the LSAC makes extensive efforts to implement fairness in test-taking procedures,[9] it cannot fully factor out the effects of backgrounds such as the quality of prior education, the ability to pay for expensive test-preparation programs, or the comparative affluence of the testing center's location and its related ability to provide separate rooms, for example. What LSAC does is caution against placing too much weight on the test itself, cautions that may ring hollow in the face of pressures on law schools to increase the test score profile of their entering class to ascend in the competitive rankings of law schools.

Accommodations are experienced in such contexts of imperfect justice. As the U.S. Department of Justice contended against the flagging of LSAT scores, the identification of someone as having received disability accommodations may stigmatize. Many people with disabilities are reluctant to disclose their conditions because of these concerns. Disabilities such as mental illness, relapsing/remitting multiple sclerosis, or a history of substance use may be readily hidden. Accommodations may be required for continued monitoring or treatment, but students may be disadvantaged by revealing their disability. In higher education, these disadvantages may include not only how faculty evaluate these students in grading or in allocating scholarships and other honors but also how their peers judge them.

When accommodations seem to present students with no good alternatives—when the choices appear to be either go without and be disadvantaged or request accommodations and be disadvantaged—remembering that modifications are an alternative to accommodations is important. The confusion in *Davis* was analyzing a request for an accommodation as a request for a wholesale modification of the nursing associate program. But the reverse can also occur when the response perhaps should not be an individual accommodation but an assessment of the need for policy change. Issues like extra time on tests press the question of whether it would be preferable to modify the structure of testing. It may be possible to achieve the same educational goals by changing practices for everyone, just as it was possible to continue to achieve ambulation with curb cuts. Perhaps the current practices have been accepted without validation and without consideration of the many ways in which they may disadvantage all students, not just students with disabilities. Many educational practices, from summative rather than formative assessments to whether lectures are recorded for later review by students, may fall into this category. Instead of placing the burden of requesting accommodations on students with disabilities, modifications of potential benefit to all should be a favored alternative.

LAPTOPS?

Now, let's return to laptops. How should they be viewed? Seeing them solely as accommodations for individual students may place burdens on the students who need them to perform as they are capable. Students must recognize their need for an accommodation and request it. This will require revealing their disabilities. They may bear considerable expenses for evaluation to substantiate their disability claims. Their disability will be obvious not only to student services and perhaps the faculty member for the class but also to their fellow students who see them use laptops forbidden to most.

On the other hand, laptops may offer many modifications that benefit all, even those who could not or do not wish to qualify for disability accommodations. Technologies are available to block internet access during class time, thus eliminating the possibility that students will distract themselves or others by surfing the net or using social media. Instructors can consider how to incorporate educational use of laptops into class sessions, for example, by signaling when it may be beneficial to try to paraphrase what is being said in notes, and when it might be beneficial just to stop and listen. Laptops may enable students to view slides as instructors present them, or to see closed captioning when they might miss what is said by a soft-spoken faculty member. Rejecting laptops without consideration of these alternatives fails not only to create an inclusive environment for students with disabilities but may also forestall potential educational benefits for many others.

CONCLUSION

Sometimes law evolves in ways that yield important moral insights. This has been true with disability antidiscrimination law that recognizes doing the same thing for everyone may be discriminatory when there are significant underlying differences.[10] Sometimes the law sets off in problematic directions, as the Court did in *Davis* by ignoring the possibility of accommodations. Inclusion in higher education requires considering both accommodations and modifications and the need for one or even both in many different circumstances, not only when disabilities are in question. Pregnant women (who are not legally entitled to accommodations under the Pregnancy Discrimination Act, but who may be entitled to accommodations if their pregnancy is disabling), people with different religious obligations (who may be legally entitled to accommodations), students with small children or other caregiving responsibilities, and students who need to work to stay in school present just a few types of cases where the difference between accommodations and modifications matters.

Some of these cases of difference may present the need for particularized adjustments: the student whose sudden family emergency made attendance at a test impossible, for example. But others should challenge colleges and universities to ask whether an accepted practice no longer serves its purpose (or perhaps never did), presents a barrier when reasonable alternatives are available, or bears more heavily on some differences than on others. Curbs, after all, once prevented sewage running down gutters from flooding sidewalks, but the sanitation practices that necessitated them have long passed. Accommodations and modifications are importantly different approaches, and both are critical to inclusive higher education.

Chapter 14

Discontent with Disability Accommodations

N. Ann Davis

I have been engaged in discussions about academic institutions' disability policies for some time and have grappled with theoretical and logistical problems that have arisen as the institution I worked for has assessed and emended its disability policies.[1] Conversations about accommodations for students with disabilities have become decidedly more uncomfortable in the last few years. Why is this? The explanation is complicated. We may be able to get closer to an answer, though, if we pay attention to some of the ways that current disagreements about disability accommodation echo prior disputes. Looking more closely at disagreements prior to the 1990 Americans with Disabilities Act (ADA) may help us attain useful perspective: some older disagreements seem to have been sensibly resolved, and some have not. Before describing the earlier disputes or attempting to draw lines from those to current ones, I will sketch one of the sorts of uncomfortable recent conversations I am referring to.

In the past few years, I have been contacted more often by students who, though they certainly appeared to be compassionate and fair-minded, were nevertheless dismayed by the way they believed that their institution handled disability accommodation. More specifically, these students thought that a number of classmates who represented themselves as having disabilities were essentially cheating to obtain academic advantages like extra time on exams and longer deadlines, advantages that were neither needed nor warranted. The complaining students thus came to think that their institutions awarded certifications of learning disability (in particular) in a way that was careless and morally unsound. A familiar complaint was that these certifications have often been effectively for sale: students whose parents had money and connections could use them to procure unwarranted accommodations for their children. They could—and did—seek out the services of less-than-scrupulous professionals who were then less than honest in their assessments. A quite general distrust of institutions' disability policies has been the result.

In an atmosphere of increasingly intense competition for good grades, the complaining students' displeasure and resentment seem understandable. After all, the objections have often come from hardworking students who believe that they are being unfairly disadvantaged. Especially pointed are complaints from students with less affluent backgrounds and from first-generation college students—students whose families are more likely to lack the financial means (or the knowledge and connections) to effectively "game the system" to procure academic advantages for their children.

These student reactions also suggest that the colleges' disability policies are, in some ways, quixotic and potentially self-defeating. A number of the complainants have been members of the very demographic groups that liberal arts colleges like mine have actively recruited in hopes of increasing the economic and social diversity of their student body and more widely and fairly distributing the benefits of higher education. The fact that so many of these students believed that their more affluent or better-connected peers were exercising privilege to—dishonestly—avail themselves of unnecessary options and resources likely widens their perception of the size of the gaps between them and their more affluent, well-connected classmates. However unintentionally, this substantiates worries that even hard-earned admission to a good college may not do much to alleviate the disadvantages these students still have to face and the unevenness of the playing field on which they must compete. The institutions' current disability certification practices thus seem to have had two important (related) deficiencies. First, the policies and practices appear not to have been founded on reliable, accurate, honest input. Second, because of this, the institutions' continued reliance upon professionals' disability certifications has run the risk of increasing enmity toward students who receive disability certifications.

I am calling attention to this source of friction not because I think it presents the clearest or most formidable difficulty for colleges' attempts to formulate workable disability policies. But I have spent enough time reading about earlier eras' disputes about disability accommodation and enough time talking with students to conclude that a solution to the problem I have identified here is not likely to be simple or painlessly implementable. I am calling attention to the problem here because I hope that further reflection on why it is hard to resolve can help us gain some insight into how to make college disability policies better. The problem is also one with a long history of antecedents: the suspicions, resentments, and mistrust that underlie students' views of their colleges' proposed disability accommodations recapitulate aspects of some pre-ADA era complaints and objections to policies of disability accommodation. Thinking more about why it continues to be difficult to resolve those complaints and objections may help us unearth, and dig out, the roots of the rancor that underlies students' dissatisfaction with their colleges' approach to providing accommodations for students with "invisible disabilities," viz, cognitive, emotional, and more broadly affective disabilities such as anxiety disorders and phobias.

My decidedly modest hope is that if we step back and look more closely at two of the larger social forces that have framed colleges' discussions of disability policies, we may understand better how to move forward constructively. To that end, I suggest that we look first at political and philosophical disagreements about disability and disability policy just after WWII, and that we then consider some of the wider consequences of the increasing medicalization of physical and behavioral anomalies and discomforts that began in earnest in the 1990s. The embrace of drug-focused treatment as a paradigm has impacted people's views about health and illness across the board, and also shaped their more specific views about disability and disability accommodation. I will say a bit more later about how earlier discussions of disability and the rise of medicalization have influenced colleges' current disability policies (and their discontents). After looking more closely at how these elements have shaped colleges' disability policies, I will append a coda with some tentative suggestions for improvement.

Some of the enmity that characterizes current discussions about colleges' accommodations for people with invisible disabilities is residue, if not simply a recapitulation, of political and philosophical disagreements that shaped post-WWII challenges to the expansion of disability benefits and accommodations. As Keith Wailoo reminds us, medical advances—notably the availability of antibiotics—and technological improvements to the instruments of warfare made it possible for WWII combatants to survive what had previously been fatal or untreatable injuries and illnesses.[2] In consequence, there were many veterans who returned from the war with debilitating injuries and long-term disabilities, as well as emergent disabilities, compromised or fragile health, pain that became persistently worse, and life restrictions that would present themselves as the veterans aged.[3]

What was to be done with—and for—all these disabled veterans? Conservatives and liberals responded differently to these questions and championed different policies.[4] There was general acceptance of the proposition that the nation (and the current government) had an obligation to provide medical and financial support to people who had sustained serious injuries in the course of defending it. But conservatives and liberals diverged in their understanding of the scope and ground of this obligation. Conservatives saw the obligation narrowly as one of recompense to the veterans for their service and sacrifices. While not rejecting the view that disabled veterans deserved compensation, liberals saw support for government assistance to disabled veterans also as the instantiation of a more general obligation of the state to meet citizens' needs and promote their welfare.

Conservatives viewed proposals to provide benefits for nonveterans with disabilities who had not served their country or sacrificed for it as a slippery slope. Since people in the mid-twentieth century were living longer, there would predictably come to be many individuals with disabilities that caused significant pain and reduced life prospects. Their needs would thus be ostensibly as great as the veterans'—and their claims as powerful. Conservatives thus viewed the proposal to extend benefits to nonveterans as an unwelcome, undemocratically inflicted expansion of New Deal policies, and railed against what they feared would be increased and potentially uncontainable growth of the welfare state. Physicians, in particular, were vocal in their contempt for policies they perceived as steps on the path toward "socialized medicine." Both physicians and conservatives decried what they viewed as an impending, unconscionably large fiscal burden: an increase in the size of tax obligations facing large swaths of people and the looming redistribution of resources from "hard-working taxpayers" to people with disabilities. These ideologically colored complaints, or ones quite similar to them, still shape many people's opposition to expanding health care and government assistance programs.

Resentment at the prospect of having to provide benefits to people who they believed were unworthy was clearly one of the principal drivers of conservatives' opposition to proposals to provide benefits to disabled nonveterans. In addition to the belief that nonveterans had not done anything to deserve this favored treatment, then, as now, there was considerable doubt about whether people who professed to be disabled were being altogether truthful about their need for the assistance they sought. Conservatives believed many claimants would lie, dissemble, or exaggerate. The foreshadowing of students' current complaints about colleges' disability accommodations seems quite clear here. Students resent classmates who receive extra time on exams, for example, not because they think that people who truly have disabilities do not need or deserve assistance but rather because they suspect that a number of these classmates are being dishonest in claiming to need that assistance. It is not sympathy the disgruntled students lack but trust. When colleges think about how to formulate and implement their disability policies, they need to bear this in mind and do more to address this distrust.

As Wailoo pointed out, it was, specifically, skepticism about the truthfulness of claims to be in *pain* that was a significant impediment to forging broader agreement on policies to assist disabled returning veterans. There was no sound, agreed-upon way to dissolve that skepticism. Since there was substantial disagreement about whether it was even possible to formulate objective, verifiable standards of pain, and about who (if anyone) was qualified to formulate and apply such standards, there was no way to allay the conservatives' worries about being taken advantage of by what they saw as "malingering social parasites." The conservatives' "distrust in subjective complaints" and worries that "rewarding pain complaints encouraged deceit" and "skewed social incentives" could not be laid to rest.[5] These objections and worries are ones that were articulated seventy years ago, but elements of them linger and affect current students' views about the defensibility of colleges' accommodations for people with invisible—that is, not easily verifiable—disabilities. The idioms have changed over the course of the past several decades, but the character of the skepticism is quite familiar.

It is still true that people who profess to have disabilities—especially invisible disabilities—face unwelcome interrogation about whether they "really" are unable to engage in the activities or complete the tasks that they profess to be unable to do (or do without significant pain or compromising their health or well-being). And it is still true that such people get asked whether they could do anything more to transcend their invisible limitations. Exhorted to "just try harder," they are suspected of seeking unneeded assistance and special accommodations. Seventy years ago, conservative critics could voice the view that a veteran should "be a man" and thus make a strenuous effort to show grit and personal fortitude—and so eschew government handouts. The wounded (and now disabled) veteran was expected either to transcend his pain or to soldier on in spite of it.[6] While expectations about how veterans should show valor have changed, suspicions like this linger, even if they are no longer directed specifically at veterans (or at men). Especially in the case of avowed pain or other invisible disability, a person's appearance of "normality" can feed the distrust. Improvements in prosthetics and in reconstructive and cosmetic surgical techniques and outcomes have enabled more disabilities to become effectively invisible. But this is in some ways equivocal progress. People whose disabilities are not obvious continue to encounter challenges and accusations, as those who have both an invisible disability and a disabled parking permit can attest. Though many people with nonobvious disabilities face this burden, the voicing of such suspicions in the academic context can appreciably exacerbate the difficulties for college students with disabilities. Famously, young adults are already exquisitely sensitive to their peers' opinions of them. Having to contend with classmates' doubt and resentment adds to the students' challenges in living with and managing their disabilities.

The second thing that I think merits a closer look in this context is the lingering effect of the aggressive, cynical, and often deceptive marketing practices of Big Pharma. Amplified by the expansion of permissible forms of direct-to-consumer (DTC) advertising in the late 1990s, the ubiquitous marketing and hawking of drugs has wrought an interlocking web of society-wide changes.

Changes in our understanding of disability and our beliefs about reasonable responses to it have seldom been a principal focus of discussions about the effects of medicalization.[7] That is unfortunate. The acceptance of pharmacological intervention as the preferred mode of treatment for an ever-expanding list of ills and ails has changed both global perceptions of health and illness and people's understanding of the nature and meaning of disability. People have come to embrace the view that medical, often pharmacological, treatment of disabilities is generally appropriate. Forty years ago, those struggling with the symptoms of (what is now seen as) depression were often harangued to try to overcome it by trying harder: by pulling themselves up by their own bootstraps, by ceasing to be "self-indulgent," by drinking less (or more), by taking up a new hobby, and so forth. The echo of conservatives' postwar framing was loud and clear. In more recent decades, the advice to people who are similarly sad, insomniac, worried (etc.) has been to visit the doctor and get a prescription for antidepressants. Both approaches—the "suck it up" and the "suck it down" strategies—have problems. But the now virtually ubiquitous directive to seek out antidepressants as a cure is seen as unproblematic.

Advertising, famously, exploits anxieties to sell products. The goal of much pharmaceutical advertising is to instill fear at the prospect of living with a body that is "broken, dysfunctional, deficient, and decaying" or of being the helpless victim of one's own uncontrollable, uncomfortable emotional responses.[8] Even minor discomforts and anomalies are painted as potentially health-compromising and dangerous, and thus as things that should be treated, generally by consuming one of the latest entries in the steady stream of "new and improved" chemical offerings. Pharmaceutical companies' incessant braying about the wonders of their wares has ingrained the belief that there is—or soon will be—"a pill for every ill." Thus even normal grief has sometimes been recast as depression, a pathological state that can and should be medicated with SSRIs or their patented progeny. And the representation of a child's boredom, inattention, or acting out in the classroom as a disorder or deficit (ADHD) has meant that the appropriate response has been thought to be treatment of the individual child, and that the appropriate treatment has been thought to be medical. The cure lies in a prescription for Ritalin (or more likely one of the newer stimulants whose patent has not yet expired) rather than in trying to change the child's environment by providing more stimulating, less-crowded classrooms. Interpreting shyness and introversion as the popular and rather recently formulated "social anxiety disorder" (characterized by a clever advertising campaign as an "allergy to people") comes with a recommendation for Paxil or one of its still-under-patent descendants.

Unsurprisingly, both the general acceptance of drugs as the preferred mode of treatment for a panoply of ills, and the specific endorsement of drugs as the appropriate management strategy for difficulties like depression, anxiety, and attentional problems—which of course are common in young adults—have influenced colleges' understanding of disability and its appropriate accommodation. Aggressive medicalization frames many disabilities as, essentially, medical problems. As such, they are viewed as (caused by) diseases that should be treated, and can be cured by consuming the right medications. This overarching medicalized perspective has undoubtedly also contributed heavily to shaping students' perceptions of what sorts of disability accommodations are possible and appropriate.

Because the FDA's approval of a prescription drug must be predicated on it being demonstrably effective as a treatment of disease, not simply as a general untargeted tonic, pharmaceutical companies have had to frame the ailments, discomforts, and abnormalities they have identified as treatable diseases. Since the expansion of DTC advertising in the 1990s, a torrent of new diseases, both physical and behavioral, have been "discovered" even as Americans have ostensibly gotten healthier. But it is not merely the increase in putative diseases that should concern us, however, or even the vast increase in "new" drugs. Also important is the fact that the standard of efficacy for new drugs is very weak. Pharmaceutical companies do not need to demonstrate that their new products are more effective than other available drugs and treatments but only that they are more effective than a placebo. To put it somewhat tendentiously, the need to meet only this weak standard has enabled pharmaceutical companies to represent new drugs (that are often just "me too" variants of older drugs) as effective merely if they are better than nothing at treating largely fabricated diseases. These new diseases could well be relatively inconsequential and—what is perhaps most relevant to the current discussion— instances of the virtually universal experience of transient episodes of sadness, uneasiness, confusion, and discontent that result from quotidian social pressures and expectations rather than from any structural or chemical anomaly. More and more of the expectable vicissitudes of normal life have been pathologized.

Immersion in the stew of ubiquitous, misleading, and fear-inducing advertising and promotion has encouraged people to see themselves as unhealthy, not as merely transiently uncomfortable, unhappy, or anxious because of, for example, social pressures that could potentially be eased or surmounted by changing jobs. And so they have been encouraged to turn to medical practitioners for access to prescription drugs that promise relief, if not a definitive cure. A drug's physical effects may be truly minimal—recall that FDA approval is predicated merely on the drug being better than a placebo. But the narratives that accompany pharmaceutical companies' introduction of their newest wonder drugs can effectively prime nervous drug-takers to see results (whether there really were any) and to view them as real medical amelioration.

Since expanded medicalization has colored people's views about health, wellness, disease, and treatment across the board, we should not be surprised to learn that it has also affected people's views about disability, the treatment of people with disabilities, and perceptions about appropriate accommodation of disability, or that it has framed students' assessments of their academic institutions' disability policies. Insofar as students have been led to believe that (alleged) learning disabilities like ADHD, mood disorders like depression, and emotional/affective problems like recurrent anxiety can and should be treated with drugs, they may well have trouble feeling sympathy for classmates whose well-being and performance are affected by such things: Why can't these disabled classmates simply seek out the drugs they need to treat (or cure) their disabilities? And correlatively, they may be more hostile to proposed academic accommodations they perceive as providing unneeded special advantages to these classmates. Ubiquitous medicalization may lead students—as it has, to some extent, led us all—to suppose that effective treatment for invisible disabilities is something straightforward and easily obtainable by prescription. And so they may conclude that classmates with disabilities do not really need special treatment from their college.

I have explained how postwar discussions of disability policy gave voice and weight to skeptical doubts about who was "really" disabled and about who was merely lying about their pain or malingering. I have also suggested that current discussions of disability policy in the academy continue to trade on some of the assumptions that underlay those discussions, and that, more specifically, distrust of classmates' claims to have disabilities, and suspicions about the probity of professionals' appraisals, may often engender or abet resentment. I have also suggested that the extensive medicalization of (even minor, trivial, transient, or expectable) discomforts and anomalies may explain why students overestimate the treatability of professed invisible disabilities. Insight and remediation, if they are to be had, may lie in doing more to educate people about the history of disputes about accommodations for disability and in getting them to push back against the totalizing, sometimes infantilizing, and counterproductive framework of medicalization.

CODA

My sincere, although somewhat facile-sounding, suggestion about how to allay students' antagonism toward classmates whom they believe buy dishonest disability certifications to procure unneeded academic advantages is that colleges should stop rewarding this sort of dishonesty. In practice, this means ending reliance on disability certifications or drastically decreasing their use. The difficulties of identifying and removing corrupt medical practitioners are well known. It strikes me as unduly naïve to think that colleges will be able to identify or avoid the bad actors.

I am not here embracing the conservative skepticism of seven decades ago so much as recognizing that it (or something very like it) still influences thoughts and attitudes, and thus seeking to defuse it by avoiding reliance on professionals' assessments of disability. In my teaching, I do not, in fact, rely on disability accommodations but attempt instead to employ a kind of academic universal design. When possible—as it often has been—I have redesigned courses to reduce or eliminate time-sensitive and stressful requirements, and I have offered students a variety of options for meeting the course requirements. I eliminated timed, in-class exams in favor of (different) take-home exams with a potential low-key in-office oral component. That has enabled me to ascertain whether the students had done their own work and whether they actually understood the written answers that they submitted. I have also employed strategies that afforded students some flexibility regarding assignment due dates and enabled me to have varied and robust ways to assess work submitted at different times. The credo "verify, but trust" has informed this attempt at implementing my version of academic universal design.

When an instructor must evaluate students' mastery of more complex technical material in greater detail, the techniques that have worked in my philosophy classes may, of course, not be applicable or appropriate. But the overarching goal should be the same. Insofar as it is possible, instructors should avoid offering options to some students that they do not offer to others: these will be perceived as special advantages and resented.

The larger question of what can be done to defuse student distrust more globally is one I cannot answer. I do not think that anyone really has a compelling answer to offer just now. We are living through an angry and mistrustful time and struggling to stay afloat in treacherous waters. Sadly, many of us do not trust each other to be competent or goodwilled fellow navigators. The misbegotten belief that it must be possible to find a fairly simple way to prevent or defuse dishonesty was one of the principal drivers of conservatives' objections to expanded disability policies many decades ago. Because, in fact, preventing dishonesty or bad faith is not possible, these worries have not been dispelled, nor is it clear how much can actually be done to dislodge them. We cannot prevent academic dishonesty, and colleges would do well to acknowledge that.

But this does not mean that colleges' disability policies must continue to feed mistrust or engage in practices that so many students view as fundamentally unfair. What colleges can do is decrease reliance on procedures, techniques, and certifications that we know have been rife with abundant opportunities for dishonest manipulation. I believe that greater transparency, flexibility, and attempts to implement some form of academic universal design can help dispel some of the resentment and mistrust that currently attach to colleges' disability policies. That said, I have been teaching long enough to have developed a lively awareness of how widespread cunning and lack of character truly are, and a healthy skepticism about just how much success we can hope to achieve here.

Part VII

THE FORGOTTEN

Chapter 15

Overlooking Community Colleges and the Working Class

James F. Keenan, SJ

In any work on university ethics, the unacknowledged elephant in the room is the community college. As we will see, this system is an enormous component of the overall higher educational strategy in the United States. Yet, until very recently, researchers from education, history, and ethics have long ignored these colleges.

This essay will cover six issues. First, we will consider how the community college has been overlooked. This lack of attention is itself the greatest liability for these colleges, whose challenges and related ethical issues have long gone unaddressed. Without appreciating the institutional habit of overlooking the community college, we cannot begin to entertain the considerations at hand.

Second, we need to consider the recruitment rhetoric that persuades us community colleges are a near-perfect solution for the prospective candidate. Seductive and pervasive claims prevent us from seeing what lies beneath them. Only with more in-depth investigation of these matters can we begin to understand how we should study the purposes of community colleges and how effectively these institutions attain their ends.

Third, we turn to some data, the first of which is the crisis of enrollment decline in community colleges. Fourth, we look at the rate of student degree completion, particularly the Catch-22 of community colleges whose student body is literally at work. Fifth, we attend to the other problematic issue of transferring credit to a four-year college.

Finally, we conclude where we started: on the habit of overlooking. Here we consider the contingent faculty, who themselves have long been overlooked.

FAILURE TO RECOGNIZE THE COMMUNITY COLLEGE

The academy's failure to recognize the situation of the community college exacerbates the unacknowledged struggles of these institutions.[1] Research on the community college is difficult to find. My own investigation revealed no work on this topic by any other ethicist, a deficiency that strikes me as deserving considerable reflection about the nature of our own vocation. For if there are evident crises in higher education, they are ethical ones. But ethicists who teach at universities do not study or engage the challenges at their fellow institutions.

In the conclusion of this essay, I reflect on how contingent faculty are integral to the community college. Yet this is clearly the population most ignored at the university. And again, just as researchers and ethicists ignore their sister institutions, the community colleges similarly ignore the situation of their fellow colleagues, the contingent faculty. This double oversight needs to be acknowledged.

Why ignore the community colleges? The answer is revealing: they are not deemed relevant for research. Paul Hutcheson, professor of higher education, discloses that historians have decided community colleges are not schools of higher education and therefore not worthy of study, quoting Laurence Veysey in *The Emergence of the American University* to support this remarkable claim: "On its face, the development of junior and community colleges after World War II might seem to contradict this assertion . . . Yet these institutions are so closely related to the public school system that it may be questioned whether they are part of 'higher education' in more than a nominal sense." Hutcheson concludes that "the community college does not exist in historical terms. It is not real in higher education; in exists only K–12 terms. To a significant degree, historians of higher education have treated the community college in just that way."[2]

Not only have historians decided that colleges are not colleges, they have also described their students as "disadvantaged," a dubious label for the population colleges attract and for whom appropriate curricula or trained faculty are supposedly lacking.[3] In effect and in toto, the academy has dismissed the community college.

THE SELLING OF THE COMMUNITY COLLEGE

Still, the 12 million students at community colleges make up 41% of the general undergraduate student body in the United States.[4]

Is that fact surprising? For the past year I have routinely asked fellow faculty for an educated guess about this percentage. No one has come close. Juxtaposing my informal survey with the fact that we rarely acknowledge the community college, we ought to ask ourselves what do we know about community colleges. Not until scientific inquiry generates data will we begin to cast off long-mistaken presuppositions and finally recognize what is at stake for these institutions and their populations.

Believing the hype about American community colleges tends to dull our research interest in them. The Web roundly touts their financial appeal as a pathway to a four-year university degree. The argument is that higher education is expensive, but if you belong to the working class or to the middle class, or even if you are just fiscally conscious of the expense of higher education, then spending the first two years at a community college before transferring to a four-year university is simply the wisest move one could make. After all, the average annual cost for tuition and fees at a public community college in district versus a public university in state is the difference between $3,660 and $10,230.[5] That's enough to make a community college more attractive, but for those considering the even more expensive private college or university, the differential cost analysis is even more compelling.

This argument appears frequently in any search for "community colleges" along with additional proclamations such as these institutions are much better than they once were: "Community college used to have a reputation of being less academically serious than traditional four-year universities. But a lot has changed in the world of community college. Most importantly, academic standards have risen, as have the qualifications of the teachers. . . . it has never been easier for students to transfer credits between the two."[6]

Such assertions are powerful. High school students wondering whether they should go to a community college or to a four-year university will be overwhelmed with unqualified arguments along the lines of "Don't think twice. Choose community college." When you dig deeper, though, many of the positive claims regarding associate degrees dim or vanish. Sure, the average annual tuition and fees for public community colleges are rightly more affordable. That was the entire reason for establishing them! But the hype masks questions that most are not asking, about the length of time for completion and its costs, and about the percentage who do not attain a degree. Similarly dubious is the presumption of the ease of transferability of courses anywhere. And, finally, no one talks about the inherently unsustainable policies of hiring almost exclusively part-time adjunct faculty.

We will get to those issues shortly, but here I should note that not every review raves about the community college experience. For example, Jeffrey Selingo in the *Washington Post* notes, "Only 17 percent of community-college students end up earning a bachelor's degree within six years of starting school." Clearly, this statistic casts doubt on the purportedly straight shot from a community college to a baccalaureate degree. Still, as an end in itself, sometimes the community college is a good option, especially "for 'middle-skills jobs,' positions that demand more than a high-school diploma but less than a bachelor's degree. There are roughly 30 million of these jobs today."[7]

As Selingo rightly suggests, student successes on one trajectory ought not be confused with student failures on another. If students see a local community college as a route to a better job in their locality, then that community college indeed affords realistic promise. These students will be very different, however, from the 81% of the student population seeking solely to transfer into a four-year institution. Whether courses transfer and whether yet more obstacles loom in receiving institutions are constant concerns for working-class students who enter a community college for an eventual baccalaureate elsewhere.

CRISIS OF ENROLLMENT DECLINE IN THE COMMUNITY COLLEGE

Consider the disturbing opening to the executive summary of the American Association of Community Colleges' 2019 report on college enrollment: "Community college enrollments mostly grew during the first decade of the 21st century, accelerating rapidly at the end of that decade as the Great Recession hit. Since a peak enrollment in 2010, the total community college enrollment has decreased each fall, declining by more than 1 million students nationally (14.4%) between 2010 and 2017"[8] and an additional 3.2% the following year.[9] Notably, full-time student enrollment declined at a faster pace than part-time between 2010 and 2017. The falloff in community colleges within the State University of New York (SUNY), for instance, has been even more precipitous: a 45% decrease from 2010–2019.[10]

Far from validating the recruiting hype, the recent AACC report sounds an alarm, one remarkably few have heard. Searching for comment, I could find only two bloggers writing about the matter. To the extent the report, like the community college itself, is ignored, the 41% of our undergraduate population will not be well served.

RATES OF COMPLETION FOR A STUDENT BODY THAT WORKS (NEARLY) FULL TIME

We need to recognize that the community college serves a very complex student body, and it needs to attend to that complexity, in particular, its labor-intensive population, not unlike the faculty whom we will meet later. Here, before considering the completion rates at community colleges, we would do well to attend to who these students are in the first place.

Literally hardworking people from a wide spectrum of the American working class, approximately 80% of community college students work, 39% full time. Yet only 2% receive any Federal Work-Study aid, compared with 14% of undergraduates at private nonprofit four-year colleges.[11] Even many full-time students work full time. Community college students are twice as likely to work full time as full-time students in public and private nonprofit four-year sectors. Their job and family responsibilities often mean selecting courses when they are actually free to attend a class. Moreover, some need specific foundational courses whose times are a premium.

Economist Charles T. Clotfelter describes the diversity that characterizes the community college and its student body: "Compared to 4-year colleges and universities, community colleges serve a more diverse population" and therefore provide "a wider variety of educational programs."[12] As Selingo did earlier, Clotfelter notes how responsive the community college has been to those growing up in the working class, having "assumed an increasingly important role in this country's postsecondary education since World War II, as American employers have demanded workers with enhanced technical skills." While noting that in recent times, "community colleges have added to this role in technical training a growing emphasis on providing a stepping stone to baccalaureate degrees," he asserts that "community colleges have expanded their mission to include short-term training programs designed to serve the interests of local business, courses to enhance the skills of adults, programs to allow high school dropouts to obtain a high school equivalency degree (a GED), and programs intended for recent high school graduates interested in gaining skills for a job or preparing for further education."

Yet these needs are not being met. Completion rates highlight that problem. As the *Chronicle of Higher Education* notes: "Graduation rates at two-year public colleges are notoriously low, and have long been criticized for inadequately reflecting the value of these colleges to students."[13] According to the National Student Clearinghouse Research Center 2018 Signature Report, "Overall, 15.8 percent of two-year starters had completed a degree at a four-year institution by the end of the study period, with or without first earning a degree at a two-year institution."[14]

This is not simply a recent trend. In 2007, James E. Rosenbaum, a sociologist who often writes about those overlooked in higher education, observed: "Community colleges have shockingly low degree-completion rates. In fact, many students leave with no new qualifications: no degrees and often no credits. For students who get no degree, College provides little or no labor market benefit."[15] He adds: "Although they sometimes post job listings, send out transcripts and offer general career counseling, public two-year colleges do little to connect students with jobs."

Sociologist Sara Goldrick-Rab brings us back to a fundamental question. Why is it that these completion rate issues are not better addressed? "Unfortunately, much of the best evidence on potential reforms is new—and scarce. Many studies purport to identify a set of best practices but are only able to produce suggestive conclusions that cannot tell policymakers how any one practice could create higher rates of student success. A much more rigorous research agenda focused on community college students is needed to inform and evaluate future actions."[16]

For Goldrick-Rab, the lack of research is clearly an overriding concern: "Some students enroll at two-year colleges because they want to, others because they feel they have few other options. That so many fail to make progress, getting stuck often very early in their trajectories, is evidence of both the numerous barriers that these students face and a failure by colleges and states to identify and implement effective reforms. We still know far too little about what works, but what evidence we do have indicates a need for a multifaceted approach that is flexible enough to accommodate the variety of student needs and ambitious enough to create meaningful change."[17] Yet we do not know their needs, nor do we know how they play out at different schools in the different regions around the country.

TRANSFERRING TO FOUR-YEAR COLLEGES

Given the disinterest and lack of research, we ought not be surprised at the considerable lack of information on the community college.

Sociologists David B. Monaghan and Paul Attewell investigate why students who begin at a community college are less likely to earn a bachelor's degree than those who begin at a four-year school. Their findings are remarkable. They conclude that "inferior academic preparation does not seem to be the main culprit: We find few differences between students' academic progress at each type of institution during the first 2 years of college . . ."[18] Challenging the bias about "disadvantaged" students, their study shows that at the end of two years, overall competency for the baccalaureate degree does not differ for students trained at either institution.

What they did find was a substantial, frustrating, and expensive credit loss that considerably alienated the transferring student. Because of the receiving institution's changing policies, some transfer courses are literally discredited before they can be transferred. As a result, these students may fall behind their class cohort and need to redo courses at either their community college or later in their new home institution. In either case, they must scramble to reorganize their course schedules, with added costs both monetary and psychological and with the understanding that they may not graduate in the anticipated time. And some do not graduate at all due to "the widespread loss of credits that occurs after undergraduates transfer from a community college to a 4-year institution; the greater the loss, the lower the chances of completing a BA." Earlier critics blamed the vocational emphasis of community colleges for the disparity in graduation rates; Monaghan and Attewell point instead to the significant impact of credit loss.

At the heart of their findings are these particular ones: "In fact, about 14% of transfer students in this study essentially began anew after transferring: Their new institution accepted fewer than 10% of their community college credits. At the other extreme, only 58% of community college transfers were able to bring over 90% or more of their college credits to the 4-year institution. The remaining 28% of transfers lost between 10% and 89% of their credits." Interestingly, if the student shows the same capacity at the end of two years at either type of school, why then deny the transfer? Moreover, why are some programs so draconian? These questions reflect neither on the sending school nor the transfer student but rather on the receiving school.

Higher education reporter Mikhail Zinshteyn explains well their findings: "Where past research pointed the finger at community colleges' focus on vocational training, Monaghan and Attewell examined how many credits universities accept from students coming from community colleges. The figures are stark: In their national sample of such students, only a little more than half of the receiving institutions accepted all or most of the credits. One in 10 four-year institutions accepted virtually no credits. This credit 'choke point' affects a huge swath of the college-going population because nearly two-thirds of community college students who have passed enough coursework to enter a four-year institution move on to such a school."[19] Zinshteyn concludes, "Fix the transfer bottleneck, and graduation rates for students seeking a bachelor's degree would jump by a quarter, they note."

The Catch-22 of the community college is that historians, educators, and researchers do not consider the schools credible when credibility is precisely what the schools are trying to improve. The Monaghan and Attewell study highlights, however, that older assumptions about the students are not true, nor has the community colleges' accommodation of vocational offerings compromised the integrity of an associate's degree. In other words, the study not only highlights ways of addressing the "choke point" but also the blinding premises that led to the "disinterest" in conducting such studies in the first place. From these researchers, we learn that research can unmask the subjective biases and address the actual, objective challenges.

We need to seriously consider unexamined presuppositions about the inadequacy of the student or the sending institution, recognize these people and schools, and address their challenges; that interplay pays off. According to *U.S. News and World Report*, "Several states—such as Wyoming, Delaware,

California, Washington and Rhode Island—have taken steps to ensure a smoother transfer process between state community colleges and local four-year institutions."[20] Giving community colleges the recognition they deserve will finally help us understand how both the colleges and their students could have a real chance of success.

CONTINGENT FACULTY

As no less than Derek Bok, the former president of Harvard University, has noted, adjunct teachers are as effective at teaching as are tenured faculty.[21] Studies show, in fact, that many adjunct faculty are even more dedicated and successful instructors than tenured faculty, especially at major universities where they are often full time and have greater security, renewable contracts, healthcare benefits and, most importantly, an office. Most community colleges, however, do not provide their adjunct faculty, who are predominantly part time, with any such stability.

Many community colleges fail their predominantly part-time adjunct faculty, who are in turn often unable to serve their students. Running from one school to another, adjunct faculty may maintain contracts at two, three, or even four different local institutions—without healthcare benefits, job security, or an office. Among other reasons, community colleges are affordable because their faculty are often paid piecemeal, one to two courses at a time. It is not that these adjunct faculty do not want to advise their students; they have neither the time, place, support, nor energy to do it.

The Center for Community College Student Engagement at the University of Texas reports that community colleges are hiring more and more part-time contingent faculty: "It is not uncommon for part-time faculty to learn which, if any, classes they are teaching just weeks or days before a semester begins. Their access to orientation, professional development, administrative and technology support, office space, and accommodations for meeting with students typically is limited, unclear, or inconsistent." The report adds: "Moreover, part-time faculty have infrequent opportunities to interact with peers about teaching and learning. Perhaps most concerning, they rarely are included in important campus discussions about the kinds of change needed to improve student learning, academic progress, and college completion."[22]

Inside Higher Ed's Paul Frain captures well how we leave behind both working-class students and adjunct faculty *together*: "More than half the nation's most vulnerable college students are in courses taught by part-time, adjunct faculty members who lack the job security, credentials and experience of full-time professors—as well as the campus support their full-time peers receive." He adds, "Part-time faculty teach more than half (53 percent) of students at two-year institutions. Students who need the most help and are the least likely to succeed in college in particular lack access to full-time professors. That's because fully three-quarters of faculty members who teach remedial courses are employed part time."[23]

The present trajectories of the community college highlight some of the challenges for the well-motivated working-class student. When faculty are unavailable, students must learn how to proceed on their own. During their two years, as they are working, they need to determine which courses they can take and which ones they need. They do not have advisors who can warn them about some receiving institutions as opposed to others, nor those who can explain why one course might be more appropriate than another for a major. The skeletal staff for advising and the demoralized state of the faculty should make us marvel at the resiliency and the fortitude of the student who does succeed.

CONCLUSION

As Ryan Craig writes at *Forbes*: "But no matter how much policy makers laud community colleges, the fact remains that these institutions are only fulfilling a fraction of their enormous potential. Completion and transfer rates remain abysmal, almost without exception."[24] The newly emerging recognition and its attendant research show us, however, that completion rates can be improved and transfer issues can be resolved. But there must be recognition in the first place, even after a long period of historians, researchers and other educators acquitting themselves of their responsibilities to respond to these clearly civic and academic institutional challenges.

Think of it, before you read this essay, did you know that although 41% of the undergraduate population are at community colleges, these institutions are experiencing an enormous, historic decline in enrollment? Did you know too that the greatest challenge for transfer students is not their own preparation but a choke point placed by receiving institutions?

What is also astonishing is that in all probability, you the reader are an educator. We are not talking about problems at hospitals, car manufacturing plants, or at the stock exchange. We are talking about teaching institutions that we apparently know so little about. That we faculty know so little about the academy is extraordinary. Ours is the field that teaches others to write, investigate, and learn. We contend that the unexamined life is not worth living, yet we fail to examine our own institutions. In fact, as we have seen, some eschew their own responsibilities to examine community colleges because these schools are not, in their estimation, worthy.

This essay argues that overlooking the community college has hurt those institutions. In fact, the community college, its predominantly working-class students, and its contingent faculty are in this situation largely because of decisions made by faculty and administrators at *other* more stable, privileged universities.

We could argue that the convenience of overlooking serves the rest of higher education well. But that expediency too is also overlooked. Rather than investigate that question, we need to insist that the academy attend first to its community colleges. This is the key ethical issue. We are just beginning to research the challenges of our sister institutions and, as this essay highlights, the study of university ethics is really at its early stages.[25]

Chapter 16

The Cruelty of the Adjunct System

Alexandra Bradner

Tenured professors are permanent employees of their institutions. They enjoy a unique level of job security for a number of reasons that are often hard for laypeople to understand. To solve emergent problems and innovate, our society must nurture and protect a community of people with deep, hard-won knowledge of their very particular subject areas on the chance that a few might produce something curative, transformative, or new. Knowledge can take a long time to emerge, and it can have fits and starts. You might miss it if you fire someone with advanced expertise just because their early ideas have not panned out. Knowledge is also socially produced. We have the best chance of generating it when we can assemble communities of experts who can support and talk to one another for extended periods of time.

Non-tenure-track (NTT) professors are generally people who have earned doctorates, like their tenure-track colleagues, but who are not allowed to apply for tenure. The working conditions of some NTT faculty are similar to the working conditions of most working people: as long as they do a good job, they won't be fired unless their employer is forced to cut staff. But most NTT faculty do not have automatically renewable contracts. To ride the waves of shifting enrollments and tenure-track faculty leaves, colleges and universities have moved to a system—the adjunct system—in which NTT faculty are hired temporarily (i.e., "contingently") at comparably minimal wages by the single semester or academic year. These itinerant teachers move from institution to institution, patching together different low-paid teaching gigs until they are earning a living wage.

I have worked within this system for fourteen years at a wide range of institutions up and down the academic food chain: elite research universities, flagship state research universities, top fifty liberal arts colleges, regional comprehensives, religious institutions, and two-year colleges. Conditions for adjuncts vary among institutions according to the resources available and the prevailing ideas on campus about the value of education. At wealthier, higher-ranked schools, adjuncts are typically treated equitably as valued members of the faculty. At under-resourced, lower-ranked schools, adjuncts are typically underpaid and marginalized. My intention in this essay is to draw attention to the many sources of wrongness in the adjunct system without blaming, offending, or minimizing the supportive individuals who have made my career possible. Adjuncts rely for their livelihoods upon the goodwill of department chairs and their tireless efforts to push past existing institutional constraints. The system is unjust and cruel. But reflective individuals working within it give everyone hope for a better day.

The National Center for Education Statistics (NCES) Integrated Postsecondary Education Data System estimates that part-time, non-tenure-track (NTT) faculty in 2011 represented more than 51.2% of the instructional faculty among nonprofit institutions, while full-time NTT faculty constituted 19.1%. Tenured and tenure-track faculty, on the other hand, composed only 29.9% of the faculty, down from approximately 78.3% in 1969.[1] More recently, the NCES reports that in 2018–2019, 45.1% of faculty at institutions with a tenure system had tenure, down from 56.2% in 1993–1994. These percentages were even lower at four-year doctoral institutions (which fell from 47.6% to 37.6%) and at two-year colleges (which fell from 47.9% to 28.8%).[2] More than half of the faculty teaching right now are temps.

Data on the NTT faculty population is difficult to gather because institutions are reluctant to report unflattering numbers; the NTT faculty population is transient; and the working conditions of such positions vary widely. But additional data is available from the Coalition on the Academic Workforce (CAW, 2012), the House Committee on Education and the Workforce (2014), TIAA-CREF (2015, 2021), the New Faculty Majority (http://www.newfacultymajority.info/), and the Delphi Project on the Changing Faculty and Student Success (https://pullias.usc.edu/delphi/, 2012, 2014, et al.), which has published a number of valuable reports and assessment tools for institutions hoping to improve the climate for NTT faculty, such as Adrianna Kezar et al.'s 2004 "The Imperative for Change."

INJUSTICE AND DECEIT

The unsatisfactory working conditions of nonunionized NTT professors have been widely reported for more than a decade:

- Short-term (one-year or one-semester) contracts that are renewed unpredictably, if at all.

- Low wages, ranging from $1,800 per course part-time and $24K full-time at public institutions to $7,500 per course part-time and $60K full-time at private institutions, regardless of length of service. The 2010 per-course median was $2,700.[3]
- No health insurance for part-time positions.
- No retirement account contributions.
- Last-minute hiring and firing without due process as enrollments shift.
- No limits on hours worked for those who must cobble together a living wage by teaching at several different institutions.
- Heavy course loads of up to six courses per semester to get to that living wage.
- Expectations to work for free before and after one's contract: designing syllabi, writing recommendation letters, grading incompletes, etc.
- No private offices (necessary, among other reasons, to prevent FERPA violations).
- No faculty development or travel funding.
- No take-home tech and no reimbursement for the personal computers, glasses, or internet services that one needs for work.
- No staff support for nonteaching professional activities.
- No scheduling preferences or parking privileges for those who have to travel between campuses in the middle of the day.
- And no meaningful representation in university governance.

Like other short-term positions in the gig economy, where workers are paid by the task, laboring in the "gig academy" is precarious. People can quickly adjust to unpredictable changes in the weather. But changes every five months in one's salary, housing, and medical access are harder to absorb. Moreover, realities specific to adjunct teaching make the gig academy an especially difficult corner of the gig economy. Adjunct professors have specialized areas of expertise. The threshold of entry for these positions is high. You spend five to ten years in training to land a job that lasts only five to ten months. And you cannot work just anywhere. Like the army, you must move to wherever there is an opening, which might mean across the country, away from your support systems, to where your partner cannot find work, and so forth.

Despite these overwhelming challenges, NTT faculty dutifully fulfill their stated job requirements. The members of this contingent army show up, deliver their lectures, and grade their papers. Many adjuncts feel lucky to be working at a job in which their body doesn't hurt at the end of the day. They are worldly and educated enough to be aware of their relative privilege. However, there is little feeling that they are part of something larger than themselves, constitutive members of an intellectual community working toward the shared goal of human progress through education. They are bean-counting—calculating the few hours for which they are paid; working up to, and not beyond, that limit; and detaching emotionally from a job that treats them so inequitably. Scholars of student learning in higher ed from the research-based Delphi Project have found that the overreliance on adjuncts has at least eight negative effects on student learning, effects that stem largely from reduced contact time and lack of energy for high-impact teaching practices.[4]

This is not the student-professor relationship that colleges are selling. According to the slick brochures sent to high school seniors and their families, students are educated in small classes by professors who are passionate about their work and singularly devoted to their students' intellectual growth. That message resonates because it feeds into a deep-seated dream on the part of caregivers who want their kids to be excited by school—to be self-driven. Families send their children off to college hoping they will discover a subject interesting enough to sustain them emotionally and financially in perpetuity. And we all know what it takes to light that kind of fire: a happy, well-supported teacher who has the time to attend to the needs of individual students. When institutions staff their courses with NTT faculty, it is a bait-and-switch.

Thus, the adjunct system is morally problematic because it is unjust. The treatment of NTT faculty is unfair in both John Rawls' and Robert Nozick's senses: colleges are paying people with the same credentials drastically different wages for the same work, and colleges are not paying individuals what they deserve.[5] But the system is also morally problematic because it draws institutions into a lie. Families do not pay $20–40K a year to have their kids take classes from a rotating series of newly minted PhDs on five-month gigs whose attention is consumed by their low salary and job insecurity. The alighting of a student's passion, the discovery of a student's vocation, the opening of a student's world, passed down with care from mentor to student, is not a transaction.

NEGATIVE CONSEQUENCES

The move to adjunct labor has set into motion a number of broader, longer-term harms as well. These include the homogenization of the academy, as only well-heeled professors have enough support to last more than a few years as adjuncts and only people without physical challenges can move easily between campuses; the emergence of proprietary teaching materials that disappear with their independent contractors; sourness and pessimism in the ranks, as tenure-track and NTT faculty have been duped into believing that they have conflicting interests; the institutional burden of processing an endless stream of new hires and fires; the growing risk of legal exposure as NTT faculty organize and chairs hire without national searches; an instructional gap that tracks the wealth gap between rich and poor institutions; and the erosion of tenure and ensuing narrowing of the innovator pipeline. Beyond innovation, the erosion of tenure is tied to the erosion of critical reflection. Universities are uniquely valuable to their societies because, unlike other institutions, universities can improve in response to criticism. Tenured professors can raise unpopular but helpful objections without fear of reprisal.

Administrators and state legislators with misaligned, anti-intellectual, mission-hostile priorities are working to minimize and devalue the reflective and stabilizing role of the university in our society. No longer the incubator of open innovation through the nurturing of a community of experts protected from poverty and backlash, no longer a preserver of knowledge through the effort to sustain departments during periods of threat, the university is becoming a mere peddler of transferable skills, a credentialing entity in the service of outside employers. Colleges should exist not to produce winning athletic teams; sustain multilayered administrative bureaucracies; deliver fine food, fancy gyms, and luxury housing; or even find jobs for students. They exist to educate a populace, secure the peace of our republic, seed innovation, and model virtue.

Administrators respond that quality instruction and low-enrolled linguistics/philosophy/French/physics/etc. courses simply cost too much. But this is just silly. Institutions establish priorities to determine where they want to spend their money. Creative solutions abound.[6] You cannot promote yourself as an educational institution and then outsource your *instructional* needs. Perhaps it's reasonable for a serious restaurant to outsource its laundry, but to outsource its menu, food prep, and service? A dedicated faculty is the heart of the institution—the talent. If there were any single cost item into which university administrations should pour resources, a top spending priority, it would be instruction. The professors are the front line, the hour-to-hour face of the institution, the soul of the physical plant.

Thus, the adjunct system is morally problematic because it generates negative long-term consequences for our society. It is shortsighted, ill-conceived, and unsustainable. But there are even deeper, more human concerns. The second half of this essay offers an argument that administrators, legislators, tenure-track faculty, students, and families do not hear, because they are not listening: relying upon adjunct labor is wrong, because it is cruel. The system capitalizes upon the desperation of a vulnerable population, profits from that population's labor, and then willfully turns its back on the needs and suffering produced by the conditions of the population's employment. The adjunct system not only uses people, it uses people up.

MAKING THE CRUELTY VISIBLE

Working as an adjunct professor comes with many of the challenges experienced by people living in poverty. To start, adjunct professors don't just teach six courses a semester to earn their $32K, they usually have a side hustle: driving for a rideshare company, reselling clothes, painting houses, . . . even plumbing. We complain to our institutions when our students try to take a full load of courses alongside a demanding job, but many of our professors are attempting a similar feat. A second job in your back pocket is important. If your teaching contract is not renewed, your annual income can fluctuate from year to year by more than $50k. How can a single parent live or plan with swings like that? Or is being healthy, wealthy, and childless an academic job requirement?

Well-paid professionals outsource their domestic responsibilities so they can use their nonworking hours either to get more work done or to relax and return to work fully restored. NTT faculty, in contrast, return home from work only to do more work: cleaning, cooking, shopping, lawn care, childcare—all of which take disproportionately more time when there is no car, dishwasher, washing machine, or nanny.

Summers are particularly precarious. Unlike tenure-track faculty, whose nine months of pay are divided over twelve months, most NTT faculty do not receive paychecks in June through August. Full-time adjuncts on one-year contracts lose their health insurance over the summer, which adds an expensive COBRA fee to the monthly bills. Of course, part-time adjuncts rarely have institutional health insurance in the first place. The choices reported in the news between one's medication and preventative care, on the one hand, and one's rent, on the other, are familiar to these professionals. Wants are off the table, as adjuncts are always picking and choosing from a long menu of needs, scrambling to do without something vital: dental care, gas money, functional glasses.

NTT faculty move frequently to chase job openings, but few schools offer moving allowances to adjuncts. If you move sixty boxes of books and an apartment full of furniture once a year for four years, that's minimally $12K on your credit cards. You cannot do your job without a computer and internet service, which adds $2K to the bill. Then, without available credit, even if you have a faculty development account, you cannot purchase conference registrations, flights, or books without a cash advance from your institution, which is embarrassing to request, if the option is even available at all.

Young adjunct professors and professors with access to familial wealth can absorb these costs for three to four years. But the financial issues become more serious eight to ten years in as one's debt and exhaustion builds. A single unexpected expense, like a major car repair or health scare, can have ripple effects that end up destroying an NTT professor's career and bankrupting their family. If an adjunct happens to make it through to retirement, they often retire without any 401K savings, for most institutions will only begin retirement account contributions after a worker has served for a year in a position. Conveniently, for the institutions, adjunct contracts are rarely longer than one year.

If the financial barriers sound exhausting, there are physical tolls as well. It is physically demanding to be "on" lecturing at the front of a classroom for 18 hours each week. There are no TAs to do the grading. There is no break in the day (add meetings, 12 to 15 office hours per week, and an explosion of student email to those six three-hour courses), and there are no future escapes to dream about: no monthly dinners out at a restaurant, no annual coastal vacations, and no semester-long sabbaticals to conduct research or design a new course. All of your research, grading, course prep, and service work have to happen late at night, because there is no time during the day for anything but that 6–6 load.

The actual instructional work adjuncts perform is harder due to the low levels at which they routinely teach. Introductory students have more needs than majors. NTT faculty in the humanities, for example, are often charged with the task each semester of teaching eighty intro students how to write. That is simply more taxing than teaching sixteen upper-level majors and eight graduate students something in your scholarly field while advising three to four doctoral students, the typical instructional load for a faculty member on the tenure-track at a research university.

Unlike most tenure-track faculty, who slow down post-tenure to explore a hobby unrelated to their work, adjuncts must perform in perpetuity at the very highest level so their contracts will be renewed. Every position requires new syllabi. Very little can be reused from year to year. There can be no parental complaints, no failed teaching experiments, and no devastating student course evaluations. To enhance your value, you take on extra unpaid and underappreciated departmental, institutional, and professional service, which further constrain your schedule. That service, which should feel like a meaningful contribution to the field, ends up feeling like a waste when it remains invisible and undervalued in fields that promote scholarly publication above all.

NTT faculty are *always* on the job market. Throughout the year, they apply to academia-adjacent positions in high schools, nonprofits, publishing companies, educational software services, and college administrations. Every year around February, they neglect their 150 students to apply to academic jobs, re-calling their recommenders, rewriting cover letters, repreparing applications, arranging interviews, and visiting campuses.

The minor annoyances don't help either. With every institutional move, you have to reprogram all your learning management system course shells. You must transition all your email. You have to learn a new system of general education and major/minor requirements. And you must endlessly retake all the time-consuming tutorials required by each institution on sexual harassment; diversity, equity, and inclusion; cybersecurity; and responsible research. When you work at multiple campuses at the same time, you are always leaving books, keys, and files at the wrong school. Publishers, whose software is programmed to assign only one institution to each instructor, mix up your textbook orders. And you have to spend double or triple the time on each campus making small talk with your colleagues and the administrative staff, attending holiday parties, and going out for Friday night drinks when you have very little unscheduled time available for such frivolities. These are all serious concerns. But we might recognize an even deeper order of damage and destruction in the emotional taxation and in the destruction of intellectual community, that is, in the corrosive effect of the adjunct system upon one's relationships with one's tenure-track colleagues.

The low wages and the frequent moves can destroy a family unit. Your children are forced to master a series of new schools, teachers, and math curricula. Teenagers have to leave their friends. Partners must leave their jobs. You never have the clothes, braces, trips, and houses of the Joneses. Worse, as someone who values education, you cannot afford to live in the best public school districts or send your kids to the best independent schools. You are certain that your self-interested career choices are clipping your children's wings. Your own precarity transforms into pressure on them to succeed. You frustrate and alienate your partner. You worry about money all the time. And these anxieties, in turn, affect your health, your job performance, your children, and your most important relationships. Scarcity, as we know, eats away at our cognitive and emotional resources.

Beyond regret, sorrow, anxiety, and fear, NTT faculty live with toxic feelings of failure. Nothing has turned out the way it was supposed to be. None of the brilliant ideas for papers were ever written up. When rare scholarly opportunities come your way, you don't have the time, resources, or knowledge to do your best work. Your students grow up and lap you. There's nothing about your life that your advisor can boast about or that your parents can cheerfully share with their friends. The conference nametag of a middle-aged professor that says "lecturer," "instructor," or "visiting assistant" is embarrassing. No one can see the thirty years of successful teaching and the thousands of students served behind that junior title, which never changes.

There is anger. You are angry at the universe that determined your entire future by the chance number of listings in your field and the chance number of competing candidates who happened to emerge during the two to three years after you completed graduate school. There is anger at your discipline, which values scholarly research over the difficult, socially relevant, and transformative classroom work that you do every day. There is anger at your institution, which hands out teaching awards to tenure-track faculty members for doing with more amenable students only a share of the pedagogical work you do. There is anger at your department for not consulting you on the student and curricular issues you are better placed than they are to assess. Last, there is anger that all this anger interferes with your productivity and, more importantly, with your relationships. And when all this anger begins to feel outsized and aberrant, it morphs into feelings of shame and foolishness.

Then there is the guilt. Every adjunct professor understands, more than most, that landing a teaching job at the college level—any teaching job—is a privilege. One of the benefits of the adjunct life, one of the only benefits, is the expanded capacity for empathy and humility that comes with the territory. Adjuncts live in the mental space between their preoccupation with the injustice of it all and their knowledge that they have no right to complain. During the sharpest moments of self-doubt, when they entertain the possibility that they simply weren't good enough to land a tenure-track job, they feel grateful to work in their chosen field at all, in any capacity and under any conditions.

Feelings of gratitude prepare the way for love, love for the student accomplishments that emerge from struggle, love for your partner's unwavering support of your failed career, love for your graduate mentors' humor and encouragement during the darkest times, love for the camaraderie and commiseration you find among fellow NTT lifers, love for colleagues who send professional opportunities your way, and love for your discipline, which, due to the breadth of your teaching, you know better than most tenure-track faculty members. This last love leads to pride, pride in your ability to teach almost anything and any population well, and pride for the fact that you (kind of) made it—you're a working professor living the life of the mind. Even with the bare bones paycheck, teaching the canonical works of our culture can be an abject thrill.

But mostly, there is overwhelming sadness. NTT faculty do as much as they can for their students within the existing constraints but know that their teaching falls short. More time and attention are needed to get their students where they need to be, to compete with the wealthier kids whose parents hire tutors and test prep companies at the first sight of a B. But there is simply no way to offer developmental assistance to 150 students. It is hard enough to learn their names. So, instead of delivering what these students need (more writing, more close reading, more calculating, more tutoring, more time, more hope, more inspiration . . .), adjuncts are forced, in their daily quest for self-preservation, to look for creative ways to minimize student contact, and this genuinely *haunts* us. Faculty who are given the resources to do their jobs well do not have to carry the emotional burden that follows upon one's daily neglect of the needy.

NTT faculty routinely serve more students and a wider range of students each semester than tenure-track faculty, so adjuncts more frequently absorb the heartbreak when a young person's potential is lost to drugs, alcohol, family dynamics, sexual assault, underpreparation, or financial strain. Tenure-track faculty see only the students who have survived the gauntlet. Roving adjuncts have a front row seat to the structural failings and corruptions of higher ed writ large. A low hum of mourning sets in as they witness the failures of institutions with the potential to rescue underserved students against the successes of institutions designed to catapult privileged students into the stratosphere, just because the former have fewer resources than the latter. Our country showers instructional resources upon students who do not need assistance and withholds resources from students who could most benefit from them.

These are just a few of the thoughts swirling around in the minds of your NTT professors, friends, and colleagues as they process their fragile situations. But the adjunct system does even broader damage. It undermines our intellectual communities, our *collective* minds.

Given the information shared above, how are NTT faculty supposed to feel when they meet a tenure-track colleague at the photocopier, and that colleague, exasperated, rehearses their lengthy to-do list? How should NTT faculty respond when they read about a tenure-track faculty member's research award in a department newsletter or come across a faculty reading group sitting around, leisurely discussing a fashionable new book? How should NTT faculty members react when their department decides to advocate on the part of their (comparatively well-supported) graduate students, instead of their adjuncts, for higher salaries, job market assistance, summer funding, travel stipends, and institutional representation? "What a *monumental* failure of moral imagination" is what the NTT faculty are thinking as they feel themselves becoming more and more emotionally distant from the very people whose power they most need.

True privilege manifests when the work you perform generates some reward. When the work you do never generates any praise, when it never generates any respect, when it never generates any advancement in rank, when it never generates enough money to care for yourself and others, and when it never generates its desired impact, the work takes on an air of futility that is difficult to endure.

IN CONCLUSION

The adjunct system is immoral by any philosophical measure. The system is not equitable—no one would choose the adjunct life from behind a veil of ignorance. Institutions treat adjunct faculty as means rather than ends, so adjunct faculty treat students as means rather than ends. No one is accorded their due dignity. The system will not produce high-quality happiness for our society. NTT faculty have no chance at the good life, without material preconditions and a virtuous community in which to grow. The needs of NTT faculty are not being fulfilled by their more powerful colleagues, who should be attentive and responsive to those needs. And the needs of our most neglected students are not being fulfilled by NTT faculty, who are so mentally, physically, and financially taxed that they can barely care for themselves.

Most uncomfortably, however, the adjunct system is cruel in the useless, unnecessary, and preoccupying disorder it brings to a person's mind, family, and community. If you are an administrator, legislator, tenure-track faculty member, or paying education consumer, and you are not actively fighting against the adjunct labor system in higher ed, you are maintaining it. You are a callous or willfully ignorant person taking part in a harmful deception.

NTT faculty cannot advocate for themselves without threatening their livelihoods. As a vulnerable population without representation, they must have your help. If you are lucky enough to have the security that every human worker needs, please look for ways of extending that security to your needy colleagues. We need longer contracts, representation, benefits, and $8,000 per course. Inaction is threatening the very heart of the academy—its mission-essential and socially vital charge to teach well and to innovate.

Part VIII

ADMINISTRATIVE RESPONSIBILITIES

Chapter 17

Prudent Reserve in Academic Administration

Karen Hanson

Why would a member of a college or university faculty choose to become an academic administrator? Assuming one is drawn to the professoriate by passion for a field of inquiry and a desire to share that field with students, the move to spend a considerable portion of one's work time neither pursuing the issues of one's field nor teaching students to do likewise can seem a bit puzzling. Leave aside the avaricious motives that might be attributed to a newly appointed administrator by some uncharitable academic friends, or former friends, and colleagues. A more honorable motive, and one that typically does in fact move faculty to join administration, is the hope that one can both steward and shape an institution dedicated to enabling the teaching, research, and service that the professoriate prizes. That hope is not unrealistic. There are indeed things that can be achieved most readily, most effectively, and sometimes only by those who are willing to take on responsibilities at the institutional level. What sorts of things are these, and how are they pursued?

Policies and practices that shape the entire institution, that structure many of its core activities, are usually a product of what's called "shared governance," but specific academic administrators typically have a larger role in initiating, developing, and refining those policies and practices—and, perhaps more crucially, the institution's general overall agenda—than do individual faculty members. This can be understood to be mainly a matter of the scope of influence and authority. Given the prospect of greater impact, seizing the opportunity to forward the best aspirations of the academy at this larger scale seems a worthy endeavor—not just unobjectionable but perhaps even praiseworthy from a moral point of view.

But are there also new moral hazards, given the broader scope of authority and the new ranges of responsibility? More neutrally, are there new intellectual and moral challenges that face the academic administrator, challenges that go beyond those faced by a regular faculty member? And if there are, what is required to address them successfully?

Consider first whether the administrative decision-making process itself is really any different from the one employed by a faculty member in, say, structuring a course syllabus or helping to design a major. Isn't the administrator overseeing curriculum and instruction simply employing, at a higher level, roughly the same processes of evaluation as the faculty member building a course—pursuing, perhaps on a larger scale, roughly the same general goals? Sometimes this does seem to be the case. The same categories of excellence pursued by faculty as they design and revise their courses are pursued by the provost who sets in motion a committee to review and revise the general education requirements. The dean or provost who expels a student for repeated cheating is safeguarding the same values of honesty and academic integrity as the professor who gives the student an F for plagiarizing a paper.

But there may also be other sorts of issues, decisions to be made where the guidelines that typically structure individual teaching and research would seem to need thoughtful supplementation. Consider a problem of university capital planning: Suppose both the chemistry department on a regional campus and the foreign language departments on the main campus of a public university make good cases for rehabilitation of the buildings in which they are housed, citing the deleterious impact of their current facilities on their work and the specific enhancements to teaching and research that could be expected from capital improvements to their spaces. The academic administrator who must prioritize one of these building projects over another—say, the new chemistry building instead of a new home for the foreign language departments— sometimes needs to draw on evaluative considerations quite different from those motivating the immediately conflicting demands for new buildings. There may be political considerations that favor the regional investment—for example, the likelihood of securing support from more members of the legislature, particularly those less interested in, perhaps even hostile to, the main campus. Or the political considerations may be more long-term: the chemistry building project would be a highly visible sign of engagement with communities beyond that in which the flagship is located, which might in turn build outstate goodwill and foster greater support for the university as a whole in the future. Even the planned disciplinary foci of the buildings might make the difference between securing the funding and not getting it, as, at some times and places, key legislators and other funders may more readily accede to the importance of chemistry and fail to see the urgent need for language study.

Is there anything wrong with administrators turning to these sorts of considerations to determine what they will put forward as the institution's capital priorities? In this instance, before the weighing of public relations and political considerations, the prioritization of one building over another looks as if it might as well be subject to a coin flip, as academic needs and values are, by hypothesis, roughly evenly balanced. Given that, the addition of purely political calculations can seem not only excusable but prudent—perhaps even wise. It might be plausibly argued, after all, that attending to the long-term best interests of the university requires this sort of political calculation, as the material basis for the conduct of teaching and research will thereby be most effectively sustained and augmented. The university and the administrator seem above reproach if they engage in such a calculation. The constitutive values of the institution are honored as its vital operations are supported and enhanced.

But would this sort of political calculation still be defensible if the immediate academic needs were not so evenly balanced—if, for example, there were few successful science students at the small regional campus and the language labs and classrooms on the high enrollment flagship campus—a campus still renowned for the breadth and excellence of its language departments—were conspicuously dilapidated, impeding instruction and negatively affecting the recruitment of new faculty? We can imagine a set of administrators reaching a well-grounded conviction that, even in these circumstances, when the academic considerations weigh heavily in favor of the language building, a request for funding for foreign language facilities simply would not succeed this year—not with this particular state legislature. But there is a chance that the new chemistry facility would be supported. With these informed political assessments in mind, the administrators might decide to assert—may we say falsely?—that the chemistry building is the university's highest priority.

Are they stepping over to the wrong side of a moral line as they make this pitch? The administrators may assuage any twinge of moral discomfort by rehearsing silently the terms and circumstances of the legislative request: The university perennially seeks state funding to support its core activities, and what resonates with the legislature varies; legislators' receptivity to the university's request may, in the long run, as political circumstances change, align better with what are truly the institution's greatest needs. Better to get a small slice of the pie right now, rather than none at all—even if the pie is the wrong kind and even if what was really needed was not pie but meat and potatoes. Perhaps those can be prioritized in a future year.

So in saying that the regional chemistry building is the university's highest priority, the administrators feel they are not exactly lying. They are saying out loud, "This is our highest priority," but also sotto voce and really only to themselves, "among the requests we believe we have some chance of your granting." The audible assertion will, though, take a toll on the administrators' relations with the language and literature faculty on the main campus, for that will of course be all they hear. They will find this prioritization not just utterly wrongheaded but also dispiriting. It will seem that the administrators either didn't understand or didn't care about their space and equipment needs, perhaps even that they don't really care very much about languages and literature at all. The despair and estrangement can be profound: as the language faculty talk to their colleagues and ponder the institution's stated priorities, they begin to say among themselves that perhaps the administration simply doesn't value the humanities.

The administrators can't explain their public prioritization by saying to the faculty privately, "We didn't really mean that; our public assertion was shaped by a political judgment." First, there is no such thing as a "private conversation" between the administration and the faculty; and second, even if there were, the language faculty, deeply cognizant of their own needs but less attentive— appropriately less attentive—to the vagaries of legislative dealmaking, are still likely to feel that the argument based on academic needs and values should win, would win, if it were put forward forcefully enough. The administration will be judged to be either unenlightened or cowardly or inept.

An administrator may feel absolutely confident that this is wrong, that it is naïve. The administrator may even be right about that. But shouldn't one worry that an unattractive cynicism may be bolstering that confidence? And shouldn't one worry further that, with every instance of an avowal of priorities compromised by political calculations, the administration's capacity to discern true priorities may be slightly degraded? As administrators deploy, as they in fact privately embrace and foreground new evaluative concerns—for example, the likelihood of securing more rather than less overall construction funding in a given year—are they not actually putting aside some of the academic values that the faculty prize most dearly?[1]

There are innumerable circumstances where administrators may be wary of discussing publicly all the considerations determinative of an institutional position and perhaps even more occasions where they are reluctant to disclose fully their own personal positions on an issue. Some of these difficult situations are perennial and present themselves in many shades of gray. For example, a dean may court a potential donor whose social or political views she finds repellent. She tries to avoid engaging on those topics, even when the prospect makes stray comments she dislikes, and even when silence can seem like agreement or acquiescence. She keeps her own views to herself, and, so long as the prospect isn't publicly associated with politically problematic statements or actions, she continues to cultivate the potential donor for institutional support.

Even here, though, where this administrator may be thought to be exhibiting some form of "prudent reserve,"[2] the restraint involved in maintaining silence still seems slightly corrosive. If a truly offensive remark is made in ordinary conversation in a purely social setting, one would not, should not, refrain from expressing disagreement. If the dean refrains, bites her tongue, because she fears angering or annoying the prospect, she demonstrates a loss of faith in the power of dialogue and the search for mutual understanding that might be understood, at least since Plato, as foundational to the academy. Seeking support for the academy, she is at the same time exhibiting a lack of confidence in its methods and strengths. That is an uncomfortable duality, one that should stir disquiet in the dean's soul. If this concern seems a bit precious, or too focused on the integrity of her character rather than on whether her behavior is flatly wrong or right, it should at least be clear that the dean is beginning to treat this prospect as primarily a means to the end of a donation; and given the generally sociable circumstances—or faux-sociable circumstances?—of prospect cultivation, that is not a particularly attractive mode of human interaction. We do not even have to assume the dean's political views are "better" than the potential donor's; we just have to notice that there is a *deliberate* lack of sincerity that taints the dean's conversation.

There are yet other situations confronting administrators that are highly fraught and so irredeemably complex that an administrator may decide to refrain from articulating a clear position—even if she has one—because she counts on the fullness of time to help settle or at least lower the heat on some contested issue. Consider recent calls for police reform, and consider, in particular, calls from some university communities to eliminate university police forces. A president navigating such a call may know that immediate elimination of the university police force will simply make the university dependent on the surrounding city police. She may believe, let's say with reason, that the culture of the university police department has been carefully and genuinely shaped by an ethos of protection and service that is rather different—let us say more community-friendly—than the police department of the surrounding city. She may fear, however, that simply rebuffing student and faculty demands to eliminate the police will seem insensitive to their justified outrage about nationally prominent cases of serious, deadly police misbehavior. She may also and equally fear that simply acceding to the currently pressing student and faculty demands will provoke outrage in sectors of the public—and perhaps the legislature—that could harm the university financially. She may also sincerely believe that the campus will be less safe without its own police department, and she knows that a campus that is or even seems unsafe will face additional difficulties in student and faculty recruitment. Mulling these thoughts, she may find it attractive to engage with the controversy in a way that in fact postpones a decision, wrapping the issue in many layers of public discussion and "governance" processes, in the hope that some of those expressing the sharpest sentiments will grow tired and distracted—or simply graduate and move on.

Let us leave aside the hard—perhaps unanswerable—question of whether it would be right or wrong in a given case to eliminate the campus police force. Let us notice instead that so many of the considerations upon which this particular president is ruminating are ones that she would be unlikely to want to voice publicly, to own straightforwardly, as pertinent to this decision. Does she want to be, or want the university to be, the face of implied opposition to the city police department? How difficult would it be, on the one hand, to manage predictable public outrage at what will be seen as a politicized elimination of the campus police force, and how difficult, on the other, to manage student and faculty agitation if demands for elimination are flatly rebuffed? For any president immersed in this sort of situation, these questions are pertinent—one might even say it is an obligatory part of the president's university stewardship to consider them—but publicly foregrounding such considerations is likely to make a tense situation worse. Making a decision on the basis of these sorts of considerations can seem unprincipled—as if one is not even looking directly at the crucial issue and trying to determine the morally preferable course of action but is instead looking to the side and over one's shoulder, looking at public relations, for a solution that will play well, for now, with the broadest public, or play well with the public that matters most at this moment.

Again, there may be ways in which one can rationalize this sort of administrative thinking so that, *if* the case is truly and fully described (as this example, a mere sketch, admittedly is not), a decision that is shaped by private rumination about material consequences and public perceptions *is* one that actually satisfies the moral demands of the moment. Still, there is something worrisome, something morally burdensome, about the practice of keeping these largely consequentialist concerns private. Keeping these calculations to oneself or hashing them out with only a small circle of trusted fellow administrators seems at odds with the reverence for free and open inquiry the university consistently avows and claims to honor. A whiff of duplicity arises if all public pronouncements on a contested subject omit considerations that really did influence an administrative decision. The conscientious administrator should at least begin to ponder whether "prudent reserve" here really amounts to dissembling.

These last two examples—courting the obnoxious donor to secure institutional funding and obscuring the processes used to reach institutional conclusions—can seem like pale versions of the "dirty hands" problem.[3] If so, they are very pale, for it is not obvious that the administrator is really, for the sake of a great good, doing something that is clearly and unequivocally morally wrong. She is, though, doing things that may depend for their success on a level of secrecy, insincerity, and social manipulation that is somewhat disconcerting. We might worry about the character of a person who finds it easy to treat people as mere means to an end, even a worthy end, or the character of a person who is determined to distract interested stakeholders earnestly trying to engage directly on a matter of manifest importance.

Of course, the administrator may *not* find these things easy. She may struggle with what she feels called upon to do in order to act in the best interests of the institution. She may well recognize that most of the complex situations she faces are ones where different and often contending values are at stake. That is perhaps no different from the complexity of much of adult life. But her understanding of her role responsibilities—stewardship at the institutional level—may canalize her choices along paths that prioritize the material necessities of institutional survival or, less dramatically perhaps, institutional flourishing, all things considered. Attention to more delicate moral issues may, because of those responsibilities, fall by the wayside.

Again, all complex jobs may require some distasteful compromises, and one should probably not expect a job at this level to offer only easy choices and clear pathways to solutions that completely harmonize all contending considerations. What may be importantly different here, though, is that the academic administrator may too frequently be called upon to sacrifice some of the core values to which her job is ostensibly dedicated. The university avows its allegiance to free and open inquiry, to examining ideas on their merits, unconstrained by political fear or favor. The administrator may in private, or with a small circle, engage in robust inquiry, a thorough examination of available options for some administrative action or policy adoption; but if all the considerations in play really cannot, for good prudential reasons, be brought beyond that inner circle, the administrative decision will not seem, will in fact not really be, a product of open inquiry.

That administrative practice sometimes seems to demand this retreat from openness can be a significant source of tension not only between administrators, on the one hand, and faculty and students, on the other. It can also be a source of disquiet within the soul of the administrator herself.

The foundational ideals of the modern secular university are essentially epistemological. The university is dedicated in both its teaching and its research activities to the search for knowledge; and, in principle, that search involves open processes of inquiry, a commitment to robust and unconstrained interrogation of both received opinion and novel ideas. We know individuals can have other, less high-minded interests propelling their research and teaching. Some professors may want the fame or the patent rights that accompany a scientific breakthrough, the social admiration or disciplinary renown that stems from a successful book. Some students may be focused most intently on the market value of a degree rather than valuing for their own sake the concentrated inquiry and knowledge acquisition the degree is supposed to certify. But whether or not these sorts of personal goals and motivations are thought shallow or base, individuals spurred by them can, in being thus driven, push full-throttle into research and learning. These personal interests or needs are not inherently in conflict with the epistemological presuppositions of the university.

But there is such a conflict—a fundamental contrariety—when an administrator deliberately shields from public examination, discussion, or debate some of the considerations that are in fact shaping her decisions. It may be too harsh to think of this as an outright betrayal of the ideals of the academy, especially if the administrative maneuvering is genuinely meant to be in service to the university. And perhaps the idealized picture of the academy—as committed to open inquiry and democratized debate—is *too* idealized. Universities do have a business side; they do have to manage their finances. They are also social institutions; they affect and are affected by political processes.

The fact is, however, that it is precisely the idealized picture that draws most academics to the academy. They want to study, do research, and teach in an institution that is dedicated to open inquiry. The faculty member who then takes up an administrative role to manage and support the sort of institution where that ideal can flourish, but who finds herself unable to operate with the intellectual frankness and forthrightness that are prized privileges of an academic life, will be in an uncomfortable place. She has gone into this administrative work to preserve the conditions of discourse that support an ideal, but to achieve that goal she may sometimes judge it necessary—sometimes be required—to refrain from full and frank participation in common—democratized—institutional discourse.

We should assume, nevertheless, that people go into university administration with eyes wide open, knowing they will have a responsibility to be mindful of certain matters, including public relations and institutional politics, that did not much concern them in their faculty roles. We may also assume that an academic administrator may find her work fresh, interesting, and satisfying, and she may feel it enhances the development of certain executive virtues, such as self-control. If she is clear-eyed, though, she should notice that this work, dedicated as it may be to sustaining and fostering the conditions in which academic values can flourish, sometimes seems to narrow the options for her to exercise the very freedoms she now protects and that she formerly enjoyed in her professorial role.[4] Her dedication to academic values may be a reason for her to take up an administrative role. It may also, in the end, after a time, be a reason to leave it.

That is not a bad prospect. There is great institutional strength in the common practice of faculty cycling in and out of academic administration. Each new administrator brings experience and perspectives derived from a particular disciplinary and generational position in the academic landscape. Those experiences and perspectives color the lenses through which the administration views academic issues, informing and refreshing the administrative outlook. That is a reason to bring new people in. If it is also the case, however, as argued here, that fulfilling administrative responsibilities not infrequently involves sacrificing the openness and epistemological transparency that should structure all academic inquiry, that is a reason for people to rotate out. An academic shouldn't become too comfortable with these sacrifices. Even if such sacrifices sometimes have to be made in the interest of the institution, we do not want them to be made too lightly. We do not want a lack of candor to become routine. We do not want the university to be led by academic administrators who have ceased to care about openness and unfettered inquiry.

Chapter 18

The Discretion of Academic Administrators

Anita L. Allen

Discretion is one of the core ethical responsibilities of leadership. Professionals of all sorts are required to exercise it—from judges, highway planning officials, and police officers to academic administrators in higher education.[1] Yet many struggle to make sage discretionary choices, decisions well-informed and insulated from undue emotionalism, favoritism, and "the imperfections of human nature."[2]

Often, the stakes are high in discretionary decision-making. A judge may determine important rights with life-or-death consequences. The decision of a highway planner not to place barriers between traffic lanes could cause traffic fatalities, and a police chief who ignores an officer's pattern of misconduct could result in needless civilian deaths. Flawed exercise of discretion in public and private colleges and universities may be less harmful on the whole than these examples illustrate, but academic officials also have ethical obligations to act with wisdom and integrity so not to jeopardize justice in the tug of war between "prioritisation of efficiency, accountability and compliance" and "the human elements."[3]

While fear of the abuse of power or arbitrary and capricious decision-making has encouraged specific, detailed, and inflexible rules in public administration, the exercise of discretion often remains unavoidable for a number of reasons. First, no system of rules, however tightly and precisely drawn, can render leadership purely mechanical or ministerial—the need for choice and judgment remains. Second, given the limitations of human policy making, exceptions consistent with institutional mission and values need to be made on a discretionary basis to achieve important goals. Third, good governance often includes a combination of specific rules and general standards that expressly provide discretionary powers for designated leaders such as, in higher education, trustees, presidents, provosts, deans, and department chairs.

Like some judges, some academic administrators may be philosophically inclined to see themselves—or present themselves to others—as rigidly bound by rules and policies. But it is a myth or at best a Platonic "golden lie" of leadership that academic administrators are mostly ministerial agents. Applicable rules and policies presumed to require simple application and "tie one's hands" may in fact be ambiguous or unclear, calling for professional judgment. A policy whose tone is strict may still confer the power to grant exceptions or waivers and modify or scrap old rules. Moreover, occasions for novel decisions can arise in higher education that are not be governed by established rules or norms at all.

Although a source of pride and power in office, possessing the freedom to decide, with its attendant ethical responsibilities, can also be a source of discomfort and stress. This is especially true among leaders who understand—or misunderstand—their roles as restricted by rules or politics that shade exercises of discretion as inherently transgressive, even if the consequences are empathetic, moral, and just. While appropriately constrained by the politics and other realities of an organization, strong leaders still have the gumption when needed to do what is right rather than what is expected.

A central question informs the following analysis of a series of hypothetical illustrations about ethical discretion: what is the type and scope of discretion called for in the situation and what characterizes its ethical challenges and pitfalls? I seek to identify and illuminate typical and recurrent concerns that academic administrators face today, violations of professional ethics that may not entail formal negative sanctions such as written reprimand, censure, termination, or legal action. Although discretion both as a virtue[4] (requiring discernment and selective secrecy) and as final, interpretative, or wide authority[5] (requiring judicious deployment of power) are relevant to higher education, I focus on the latter, "the power to choose between two or more courses of action, each of which is thought of as permissible."[6] As a touch-point for ethics relevant to higher education, I assume commonly held values and clusters of ethical concern referenced in ethical principles promulgated by a professional organization of academic administrators.[7]

DISCRETION AT ITS BEST

Wise and ethical exercise of discretion cannot be reduced to a simple formula. Yet academic administrators faced with a discretionary decision can take specific steps to help stay on track ethically. The first is to consider whether duly enacted institutional rules, standards, or policies bear on the decision at hand. These outrank the personal moral authority of a president or provost. Although colleges and universities may not be democracies, "autocratic" does not describe a virtue of good leadership in higher education. Thus, as a threshold ethical matter, in the interests of accuracy and transparency, administrators should always seek to uphold rules appropriately established by their institutions. Consistent with this ethical requirement, administrators should do their best to change ineffective rules and access appropriate channels for challenging guidelines and practices that do not align well with institutional mission and values or that violate ethical values.

Identifying which standards apply is not a solitary activity but a collaborative one that may require research. Often peers or subordinates with responsibilities related to a given decision have superior knowledge of and access to relevant policies and rules. If the issue at hand relates to personnel benefits, for example, confidentially consulting someone in human resources may be useful. Administrative leaders prioritize the search for relevant rules, standards, and policies because these reflect institutional mission and values they are ethically bound to uphold.

Once identified, relevant rules and polices must be skillfully analyzed and judiciously interpreted by the administrator. Their implications for an issue at hand may be clear cut. For example, a rule of maximum reimbursement of $2,000 for foreign travel is an unambiguous rule.

Yet allowing an exceptional reimbursement of $3,000 might be warranted if the purpose were to receive the Nobel Prize or to serve as a translator for the college president on a business trip to China. A policy to hire "highly qualified instructors," for instance, is vague. Where ambiguity or vagueness complicate decision-making pursuant to a guideline, an administrator will need to consider its intentions, goals, and purposes. At a school whose strategic plan calls for increasing the percentage of its PhD-holding faculty, a talented job applicant with a master's degree could be judged not "highly qualified" per the standard.

Before a final decision is made, an administrator should consider whether general features of fairly applied rules, standards, and policies are present. Two general features strengthen the ethical case for their application by administrators: notice of the rule by official publication, along with general enforcement and compliance. Enforcing a rule that is obscure or rarely applied can be exceedingly unjust. Also unjust is not enforcing a rule that has always been applied to others who were similarly situated. Not following established precedent damages reasonable expectations and exposes the administrator to charges of being capricious and unfair.

THE TICKING CLOCK

Fairness and equity, important ethical values in higher education administration, become particularly significant in the appointment, promotion, and tenure decisions for faculty, processes that require the utmost of discretion. Academic positions, a scarce resource and highly attractive form of employment, are often subject to stiff competition. Getting promoted in research universities may require one to "publish or perish." Perceived quality and volume of teaching, service, and scholarship are paramount. The harshness of "up-or-out" rules, however, is tempered by other rules that extend the tenure clock.

> Illustration 1: The Vice Provost for Faculty (who reports to the Provost) is responsible for reviewing requests for extending faculty members' default six-year tenure clocks. The faculty handbook states clearly and unambiguously that a faculty member "shall be reviewed for tenure in their sixth year of employment, unless they have applied for up to four one-year extensions based on illness, caregiving, childbirth or military service within one year of each such an occurrence." The policy adds that "faculty may appeal to the Vice Provost to grant exceptions in extraordinary circumstances," and that "the decision of the Vice Provost is final." An assistant professor who had a child but failed to apply for an extension within one year requests an exception as she nears the start of her sixth and default tenure-review year. She missed the deadline, she states, because she "lost track of time."

As illustrated, higher education officials must sometimes render a decision under a clear and unambiguous rule that explicitly allows for exceptions. A variant of this situation is officials, by custom and practice, granting exceptions to a clear and unambiguous rule.

In the instance of Illustration 1, granting an exception to a well-known, clear, and unambiguous rule could seriously violate fairness and equity. Still, unless it is known that others who missed the deadline went without extensions, granting the exception to a faculty member otherwise entitled to an extension who missed an administrative deadline might not greatly compromise fairness, depending upon the circumstances. Missing the deadline due to a hospitalization for a debilitating illness, for example, rather than absentmindedness would make the decision easier. This exception could be granted as an extraordinary instance, with less offense to the ideal of fairness.

Suppose, for example, a faculty member requests an extension after losing research materials in a hurricane, a catastrophic circumstance that would seem to warrant consideration although it's not explicitly identified in the rules. By contrast, a junior faculty member requesting an extension to finish writing a book, for instance, is not exceptional. In the interest of fairness, the Vice Provost should reject an appeal to do what is routinely expected to qualify for tenure within six years. Deans or department chairs might throw their weight behind such requests out of special regard for that faculty member. But as leaders, provosts have an ethical responsibility to rebuff the political pressure of favoritism that threatens the integrity and fairness of the promotion and tenure process, and all institutional processes for that matter.

An extension granted solely to complete research would violate the rule more significantly than that provided due to a missed deadline for an expressly justified extension as in the given scenario. Avoiding special favors or waivers is especially important when faculty members are competing for tenure. While additional time to complete the necessary scholarship may be exactly what a particular individual in an up-or-out regime needs to succeed, this would constitute a seriously undue advantage. Yet empathy—the human element—may tempt a leader with discretionary power to act against institutional long-term interest as well as fairness.

SUDDEN DEATH

Higher education officials must sometimes render a decision under a clear and unambiguous rule that does not allow for exceptions either expressly or in institutional practice.

> Illustration 2: Under a university policy aimed at incentivizing voluntary retirement, faculty members between 62 and 68 years of age with 20 years of service are eligible to a receive a lump sum cash payment of $200,000 upon retirement or other termination of employment. At age 67 with 25 years of service, a professor dies unexpectedly in a car crash just a few days before having planned to submit a formal letter of resignation for retirement but after having already discussed retirement with the department chair. Believing the university should "do the right thing," the decedent's spouse informs the dean of the family's expectation that the university honor 25 years of service and award the decedent's estate the $200,000 paid to voluntarily retiring faculty.

Again, in this example, we have a clear, unambiguous, published, and, I will stipulate, generally complied-with rule. It does not authorize exceptions for either almost retired faculty or deceased senior faculty. Hopefully, the dean's office would recognize that what the surviving spouse wants is out of line with university practice and possibly unlawful under the Employee Retirement Income Security Act of 1974 (ERISA). Institutional retirement policies are complex, and the surviving spouse may mistakenly believe the incentive plan works like an additional life insurance plan, providing income for the families of faculty members as a key goal. This is a delicate and consequential situation in which the exercise of discretion should aim to place the interpretative authority and the ultimate decision in the most expert and authoritative hands, likely by kicking the matter upstairs to a human resources vice president, general counsel, and/or the provost's office.

No senior administrator should readily grant the spouse's request, since exceptions are without precedent and neither explicitly nor implicitly authorized. Legal compliance is an important prima facie ethical obligation of administrators. It may be unlawful to bend the rules of a retirement plan for the benefit of a single employee. Furthermore, paying the benefit to one family but not to others who could have but did not make a similar request would be arbitrary and unfair. But the strongest reason for not granting an exception in such a case is frustration of purpose. Supporting the reasonable interests and mission of their institutions is an ethical responsibility of administrators. The purpose of retirement incentive programs is to help colleges and universities revitalize their faculties and provide an attractive retirement path for faculty whose best years as teachers and scholars may be behind them. An unexpected death such as this, while tragic, obviates the need to incentivize retirement, a financial windfall for the university.

HUSHING UP

In some instances, an administrator faces a choice that lacks the clear guidance of a university rule or policy. These are occasions for exercising wide discretion.

> Illustration 3: A former assistant professor in a senior faculty member's department left the college before his tenure decision. He is now being excitedly recruited to return as a full professor with tenure. Ten years ago, when the senior faculty member was chair, the recruitment target egregiously violated college policies by having a sexual affair with an undergraduate in one of his classes, who later alleged sexual harassment. The policies violated state that: "Any sexual relations or dating relationships between a faculty member and an undergraduate student are prohibited." Before the matter could be addressed, not wanting to face publicity and discipline, the faculty member resigned and found a position elsewhere. The current dean, department chair, and most faculty members are unaware of these undocumented allegations from a decade ago.

Should the senior faculty member tell the current chair or dean about this past misconduct or keep quiet and let sleeping dogs lie? The college's rules prohibit disclosing employment records but not "disclosures of information that are made on the basis of personal knowledge or recollection." As no institutional rule directly governs the choice to disclose, confidential consultation with a superior or peer stakeholder might be ethically prudent here.

An ethical obligation to say nothing may apply precisely because the former chair is no longer an administrator and acquired the relevant knowledge while in a customarily confidential role. This senior faculty member may also believe silence appropriately protects the recruitment target from embarrassment and loss of an opportunity while protecting the former student who alleged harassment from revictimization. Weighing in favor of disclosure is the potentially great harm of prioritizing confidentiality and privacy over a great number of other ethical considerations.

Sometimes the exercise of discretion and its attendant ethical responsibilities fall on faculty members who no longer hold administrative positions and may lack final, interpretative, and wide authority. In this case, the former administrator might need to convey important information to their current chair or dean. A conversation with a campus Ombud might be a way to talk through the matter in confidence and devise a plan for appropriate disclosure or continued secrecy. My assessment is that the college's interest in creating a safe space for students by hiring faculty of high moral and ethical character outweighs the two individuals' privacy and confidentiality interests. The fact that the alleged rulebreaker left before an adjudication and disposition of the matter might give pause, but strategies of avoidance whereby serial offenders escape discipline and consequences by moving to another school only damage the culture of higher education.

ACHIEVING REAL DIVERSITY

How should diversity funds be dispersed? Fairness and equity, process goals in higher education, are also the basis of substantive policies aimed at addressing historic racism and discrimination in majority White colleges and universities. But is racial and ethnic diversity more important than other forms of faculty diversity?

> Illustration 4: Building a diverse and inclusive faculty is a mission of a university where a Deputy Provost controls allocation of a $4 million fund to the schools for the purpose of recruiting and retaining faculty. The funds were made available pursuant to the university's "Initiative on Faculty Diversity and Inclusion" for "recruiting, retaining, and mentoring a distinguished faculty embracing all races, cultures, genders, ethnicities, sexual orientations, historical traditions, ages, religions, disabilities, veteran statuses, interests, perspectives and socioeconomic backgrounds." The Initiative was adopted at a time when the faculty was 90% White, 5% Asian, and 80% male. Currently, the percentage of faculty who are Black/African American, Hispanic, or Native American at the university totals about 8%. Asian faculty constitute 12%. The percentage who are women is 33%. Thus far 100% of the grants awarded by the Deputy Provost have gone to recruit Black, Native American, Asian, and Hispanic faculty members. The Dean of the School of Art and Architecture requests a $120,000 grant from the Deputy Provost's fund to help retain a White faculty member entertaining an outside offer. A first generation college graduate in his family and a combat veteran who served in Iraq, the retention target is a third-generation Italian American whose father was a carpenter and whose mother was a seamstress.

The Initiative lacks specific guidelines for awarding diversity and inclusion grants. Yet the Deputy Provost, who has final and wide authority, might well assume that everyone knows these funds are intended for recruiting and retaining minority group members and women, especially underrepresented minorities, not White men. The Initiative's inclusive language would appear to allow a grant to retain a White male colleague who is a veteran and whose parents did not attend college. To promote the university's policies of diversity and inclusion on behalf of the most excluded racial and ethnic groups, the Deputy Provost could reasonably deny the request. But the written diversity and inclusion policies also provide grounds for awarding a grant.

The Deputy Provost might want to consider the reasons behind the request. Suppose a dean, in an effort to game the system by accumulating any and all resources for their school, decided to request diversity funding only after someone pointed out in passing that the faculty member was a veteran and a first-generation college student. In this instance, denying a request that does not genuinely aspire to greater faculty diversity and inclusivity would be justified. By contrast, suppose the Deputy Provost is informed that the faculty member is an expert in urban planning, strongly identifies as both a first-generation college graduate and a veteran, and has created an academic mentorship program for first-generation students. Under the broad language of the policy, the Deputy Provost could grant this strong case for a diversity and inclusion grant without straining the purpose of the fund or encouraging a flood of applications from cash-strapped schools.

UNCIVIL DIGITAL CULTURE

In the digital age, faculty communicate to and about colleagues and students by campus email. Increasingly, faculty convey their ideas, opinions, and news through social media such as Twitter, Facebook, and Instagram. When faculty are uncivil or offensive, campus administrators may be asked to take action.

> Illustration 5: A tenured faculty member in the small political science department of a college repeatedly sends sharp, nasty, angry and critical emails to colleagues, incivility that is putting everyone on edge. The college has an open expression policy responsive to the digital age. It states that: "The rights to freedom of thought, inquiry, and expression are paramount values of this community. The commitment to open expression extends to and includes the electronic information environment, and interference in the exercise of those rights is a violation of this policy." The chair of the department requests guidance and appropriate action from the dean of the college.

In such a situation, the dean has wide discretion but few practical options. The dean can offer or not offer advice. Declining may be impolitic and an abrogation of responsibility as the chair's supervisor. It's an internal departmental matter, to be sure, but one that implicates college-wide policies. A wise first step could be conversation initiated by the dean with the faculty member to ascertain general personality and character in addition to specific issues in the individual's personal or professional life that could account for their behavior in the electronic workspace. Hearing directly from the faculty member is important because they could be responding to real or perceived exclusion, racial or ethnic bias, or bullying. Moreover, sometimes uncivil communicative behavior is tied to addressable unacknowledged mental health problems revealed only through sensitive, objective listening.

Should it turn out that the chair is dealing with an inexcusably troublesome individual, then, on that basis, the question of whether the email conduct must be tolerated can be addressed. In public institutions where college officials are state actors and constitutional rights of free speech pertain, special care should be taken not to punish mere incivility. Private institutions have greater latitude, even those that voluntarily embrace tolerant First Amendment values. Curtailing access to email or criticizing speech could attract unwanted publicity and spark protests. Yet doing nothing seems wrong. Good people skills and wise judgment, as well as ethical exercises of discretion, are called for to confront incivility. The dean may need to focus on improving the chair's leadership skills as well as the faculty member's communication skills. Counseling, coaching, and moral suasion are possible approaches in this situation.

STAYING ON TRACK

I end with an illustration involving the preservation of distinct faculty tracks. Rules and policies defining the privileges and responsibilities of faculty members by track are commonplace at large research universities. Designated tenure, research, clinical, practice, and so on, these tracks serve a variety of institutional needs.

> Illustration 6: An institution hires faculty in several tracks. They include a tenure-eligible teaching track and a non-tenure eligible research track. The school's faculty handbook states "the purpose of research faculty appointments is to increase the quality and appointment of non-tenured scholars to the faculty in order to collaborate with the research efforts of other faculty or carry out independent research." Members of the research faculty may not take responsibility for courses or seminars in the university, nor may they supervise doctoral dissertations, unless prior approval of the provost is obtained for each such activity. The provost may approve or deny any request.

In Illustration 6, under a published rule, research faculty may not engage in certain activities unless the provost exercises discretionary power of approval. The benign rule appears to grant the provost wide and final authority to decide whether a research faculty member may perform tasks other than research. Two ethical guidelines seem most clearly implicated here: upholding fairness and equity, and maintaining the mission and reasonable interests of one's institution. To respect fairness and equity, the provost could not approve one self-selected research-track faculty member's request to teach unless the provost were prepared to approve all similar requests. And one approval might open the floodgates to similar requests whose approval would be inconsistent with the institution's mission of developing and sustaining excellence in both research and teaching through dual faculties.

By contrast to the fact pattern in Illustration 6, suppose a teaching faculty member is suddenly unable to teach a core course needed by a school due to a sudden serious illness and the dean requests that the provost allow an able research-track faculty member to step in and teach the course on a one-time basis. Here the provost sets a precedent for granting exceptions but without raising serious concerns about fairness and equity and without compromising the goal of excellence in teaching and research. The precedent set is that in an emergency, a research-track faculty member may be permitted to teach on a one-time basis.

Similarly, consider a research faculty member who requests permission to teach three weeks of a fourteen-week course in their area of expertise. The provost, using interpretative discretion, might conclude that teaching a small portion of a course is not "taking responsibility for a course" as contemplated by the prohibitive rule. This interpretation does little harm to the goal of research excellence in the short run; but even so, it might raise fairness and equity concerns if the provost is prepared to permit other research faculty to teach a portion of courses for which teaching-track faculty are responsible. Note that there may be a nonethical administrative burden ("paperwork") with accounting for course sharing by research-track faculty.

Suppose, however, that the policy stated in Illustration 6 did not include a provision for exceptions made by the provost, but by custom and practice, faculty chairs and deans can appeal to the provost. I would argue that the same ethical considerations would bear on the decision. No exceptions should be granted that introduce inequity and unfairness among similarly situated faculty or frustrate the school's interest in research and teaching excellence.

CONCLUSION

The discretion that is an inevitable aspect of academic leadership is risky but salutary in the long run, especially where due attention is paid to ethical values identified here. Drawn from the contemporary landscape of higher education marked by debates over various issues such as tenure, benefits, diversity, and digital incivility, my illustrations explore some of the many ways in which challenges for leaders with a range of discretionary powers arise. Ethical discretion remains a core responsibility of higher education administrators, who best reject any pretense that their opportunities to exercise this power are either rare or avoidable.

Part IX

TECHNOLOGY

Chapter 19

Ethical Online University Instruction

Shelley Wilcox

INTRODUCTION

In 2020, many colleges and universities abruptly canceled face-to-face classes, including labs and other learning experiences, and moved their courses online in response to the COVID-19 pandemic. Although expected to be temporary, this period of emergency remote teaching has prompted many institutions to consider permanently expanding their online course offerings. This paper explores the ethics of online university instruction. I argue that if online programs are to be ethical, they must reflect three core normative values: equity, academic excellence, and distributive justice. To make my case, I draw upon two recent experiments in remote learning: massive open online courses (MOOCs) and emergency remote teaching. I argue that although these modes of instruction differ from regular online university courses in salient respects, their shortcomings provide important lessons for the design and implementation of ethically responsible online instruction.

MOOCs AND THEIR CRITICS

Educators and administrators have long looked to technology to address issues of scale and affordability in higher education, with online learning playing an increasingly central role. Yet massive open online courses captured the imagination of administrators, policymakers, the media, and investors like no instructional technology had ever done before. MOOCs are massive, free online courses, open to anyone with internet access. A typical MOOC provides self-paced, on-demand instruction through short lecture videos and automatically graded exercises. Some MOOCs supplement this instruction with reading assignments and discussion forums. Students typically do not interact directly with a professor in these courses, however, and few assign written work.

MOOCs gained national prominence in 2011 when Stanford offered three free online courses that quickly attracted hundreds of thousands of students from around the world. A number of elite universities, including Harvard, Princeton, and MIT, soon joined in, creating their own MOOCs and partnering with providers, such as Coursera, Udacity and edX, to develop additional courses. By August 2012, nearly two million people had registered for MOOCs through these three companies. Although early MOOCs did not carry university credit, supporters predicted that these classes would revolutionize higher education by increasing global access to university courses, improving the quality of instruction, and lowering costs. Despite this widespread enthusiasm, however, critics voiced three powerful concerns about MOOCs.

Poor Student Success Rates

The first is that MOOCs have poor student success rates. Proponents claimed that MOOCs would democratize education by enabling anyone, regardless of their academic preparedness, socioeconomic status, or geographical location, to access a free, flexible, and high-quality university education. Implicit in this claim is the assumption that educational access should be measured in terms of the opportunity to enroll in a course. However, MOOC critics insisted that meaningful educational access means more than mere enrollment.[1] For access to be meaningful, "students must have a real chance, if they work hard, to succeed in getting a quality education."[2] Yet MOOCs have extremely high attrition rates. Data suggests that although hundreds of thousands of students had signed up for MOOCs by 2013, fewer than 10% of these participants completed them successfully.[3]

Critics also raised concerns about the demographics of the students who did succeed in MOOCs: the overwhelming majority were older, affluent, and academically well-prepared.[4] Some skeptics attributed this disparity to the so-called digital divide. To successfully complete a MOOC, participants need access to a computer and a reliable internet connection. Yet technology is not equally distributed, globally or within the United States; low-income or marginalized communities typically have less access to technology than more affluent communities. Other critics linked these skewed success rates to the preexisting learning skills needed to succeed in a MOOC.[5] Because these courses are self-paced and involve little or no interaction with professors, their successful completion requires that students already be adept in self-regulated learning strategies, such as goal setting, time management, and help seeking. This tends to favor experienced students because these skills are usually learned over time in traditional university contexts.

Given this data, critics concluded that MOOCs could not dramatically expand meaningful access to higher education. At best, these courses serve a fairly limited audience—namely, relatively privileged, already-educated adults interested in advancing their learning or gaining professional credentials.

Faulty Pedagogies

The second main criticism of MOOCs is related. It maintains that MOOCs fail to provide the same quality of education as traditional university courses. This concern gained currency in 2013 when policymakers in California and Florida introduced bills that would allow students at public colleges and universities to take MOOCs for credit. These proposals triggered a national debate over whether MOOCs produced in partnership with elite universities are academically equivalent to the traditional in-person and online programs offered by less prestigious institutions.

MOOC skeptics in this debate raised two specific charges. The first is that MOOCs are suitable for only a narrow range of academic disciplines. Early MOOCs focused on topics in quantitative and computational fields. Some policymakers and college administrators, however, envisioned a future in which MOOCs replaced courses in most, if not all, disciplines. In response to these proposals, critics insisted that inherent features of MOOCs are inappropriate for teaching in many university disciplines, including those in the humanities.[6] Most obviously, because MOOCs are wholly virtual, they cannot offer students the same hands-on experience as traditional in-person labs and other experiential learning modalities. Furthermore, they argued, because MOOCs favor huge enrollments, their assignments must be graded automatically. Yet although automated graders can score some types of exercises, such as problem sets and multiple choice exams, they cannot provide meaningful feedback on student essays, an essential core assignment in many humanities courses.

The second charge is broader and more philosophical. It claims that MOOCs are unable to provide a high-quality, general university education. According to this critique, universities should strive to achieve a twofold goal: (a) to enable students to gain broad knowledge in a variety of academic disciplines, along with in-depth knowledge in at least one subject; and (b) to equip students with the skills they need to become good learners and active participants in all aspects of society. The San José State University Philosophy Department offers a prominent version of this critique. In their view, good university education must enable students to attain both literacy in a range of academic disciplines and general intellectual skill and virtue. To achieve literacy, students must gain an understanding of the academic subject at hand. Developing intellectual skill and virtue, in contrast, involves "learning how to think, learning how to analyze and interpret, learning how to learn, developing epistemic virtues such as open mindedness and attention to evidence, and acquiring tools to continue learning."[7] Notably, they insist that intellectual skill and virtue "is more important than, and a necessary condition for, literacy."[8] In fact, it is precisely these intellectual capacities that enable experienced learners to succeed in MOOCs.

The SJSU Philosophy Department identifies three useful pedagogical methods for teaching students to become more skillful and virtuous learners: dialogue, active engagement, and evoking affect. Although specific teaching strategies will vary across disciplines, substantive feedback is essential to all three methods. Students learn to ask good questions, listen carefully to the views of others, challenge and defend their own thinking, and develop their own positions by receiving substantive, dialogic feedback from their professor and fellow classmates. Students are encouraged to engage actively in their own learning and to care deeply about a subject when professors display these commitments, offer inspiration and guidance, and provide positive feedback and reinforcement. Because MOOCs omit substantive feedback, the SJSU Philosophy Department concludes, they are inherently pedagogically inferior to traditional university courses. MOOCs can at best help experienced students gain some degree of literacy in a particular subject; they cannot foster intellectual skill and virtue.

Churchill makes a similar point with respect to liberal arts education.[9] In his view, a good liberal arts education enables students to attain various general goods, which he calls external goods, including persuasive communication, strong critical thinking skills, intellectual curiosity, self-esteem, and other abilities that individuals need to engage productively in society. Students can attain these goods by striving for excellence in a particular academic discipline. For instance, philosophy majors can become effective communicators by struggling to interpret difficult philosophical texts and engaging in constructive philosophical discourse. Here again, active engagement and substantive feedback play a critical role in the learning process. To teach students how to excel in their field, professors must model the skills and virtues required for proficiency and provide students with substantive feedback as they attempt to develop these capacities. Moreover, because academic fields are cooperative practices, instructors must engage actively in the relevant disciplinary practice along with their students, exploring challenging ideas together, working out difficult problems, sharing exciting discoveries, and so on. Enabling students to achieve disciplinary excellence also requires professors to be good mentors, and this too requires working closely with students. Instructors must get to know their students and appreciate their lived experiences, needs, expectations, and perspectives. Because MOOCs are inherently incompatible with these relational pedagogical methods, Churchill concludes, they are also incompatible with the ethics of teaching.

Injustice

The third objection to MOOCs builds on the student success and pedagogy critiques. It claims that a policy of offering MOOCs for credit at public colleges and universities is unjust in three respects. First, it would deepen existing educational inequalities. If MOOCs are pedagogically inferior to traditional college courses, as Churchill and others argue, then integrating for-credit MOOCs into local and regional college curricula would reproduce and intensify broader structural injustices. Rather than democratizing higher education, as MOOC supporters claim, for-credit MOOCs would deepen the divide between well-resourced elite private and flagship public institutions, on the one hand, and resource-starved local and regional public institutions, on the other. As the SJSU Philosophy Department puts the point, for-credit MOOCs would essentially create two classes of universities: "one, well-funded colleges and universities in which privileged students get their own real professor; the other, financially stressed private and public universities in which students watch a bunch of videotaped lectures."[10]

Second, some critics contend that for-credit MOOCs are aligned with a neoliberal political agenda that is hostile to public education.[11] Neoliberalism is a political ideology that promotes free market policies, reduction in government spending, deregulation, lower tax rates for businesses, and greater participation of private entities in public services, including higher education. Critics are particularly concerned that offering MOOCs for university credit would enable further privatization of higher education. Specifically, it would transfer core university functions—control of the curriculum and pedagogy—from faculty to outside vendors. For-credit MOOCs would also accelerate the trend of shifting responsibility for the financial cost of higher education from state governments to individual students. As part of their tuition at traditional institutions, students receive access to libraries, study spaces, specialized learning facilities, and classrooms, all equipped with furniture, instructional technology, equipment, heat and cooling systems, and high-speed internet access. In for-credit MOOCs, however, students would be expected to supply their own internet access, materials, computer, and study space in addition to regular tuition.

The final justice-based concern warns that treating for-credit MOOCs as an easy solution to the problems facing higher education deflects our attention from the root causes of these problems. For-credit MOOCs are marketed as an answer to cost-efficiency problems, but this conceals the fact that rising tuition results largely from political decisions to defund public education rather than increases in instruction-related operating expenses.

IMPLICATIONS FOR ETHICAL ONLINE UNIVERSITY INSTRUCTION

These critiques, together with the well-publicized failure of a number of for-credit MOOC experiments, quickly diminished enthusiasm for MOOCs. The trend toward online instruction continued, however, as colleges and universities stepped up development of their own online courses and programs. This process accelerated dramatically in 2020 when many institutions responded to the COVID-19 pandemic by abruptly canceling face-to-face classes and moving their courses online. Advocates of online education are careful to distinguish this period of emergency remote teaching from regular online university instruction. The former, they argue, was meant to be a temporary stopgap measure to maintain instructional continuity and prevent universities from shutting down completely. Online instruction, by contrast, is a regular part of the university curriculum. Whereas faculty were given little time to move their existing classes online during the emergency remote period, online instruction can be intentionally planned and designed. This gives faculty, instructional designers, and administrators an opportunity to ensure that their online courses and programs are ethically responsible. But what values ought to guide the design and implementation of online university instruction? In this section, I will draw upon the various shortcomings of MOOCs, together with the emerging literature on emergency remote teaching, to argue that ethical online instruction must reflect three core normative values: equity, academic excellence, and distributive justice.

Equity

The first value is equity. Ethical online instruction must be equitable, interpreted broadly to include equity in access, treatment, and outcomes. Although nearly a decade has passed since critics linked MOOCs' dismal student success rates to the digital divide, unequal access to technology continues to pose an obstacle to achieving equity in online instruction. As we have seen, students have long needed a computer and a reliable internet connection to succeed in asynchronous online courses. However, many courses are now taught synchronously through Zoom, and these courses require additional technology. To succeed in synchronous online courses, students need a computer or device with a working microphone and camera (I will return to the issue of camera use below) and a high bandwidth internet connection. Yet students in low-income, rural, and Black and Latinx communities are less likely to have consistent access to high-speed internet than students in affluent, non-rural, and White or Asian communities.[12] Even households with a fast internet connection may experience connectivity problems when multiple members are online simultaneously.

Many colleges and universities have attempted to bridge this divide by providing tablets or laptops, internet hotspots, and technical support to students who need them. But promoting meaningful equity in online instruction requires more than simply ensuring that every student has the technology required to access their courses. Many students struggle to find a quiet, private location to participate in their online courses.[13] Lack of an adequate study space can negatively impact students' performance in their online courses in numerous ways. Students who are frequently interrupted during class may find it difficult to concentrate on the course material. Students who lack a private study space also may not feel comfortable turning on their cameras on during synchronous class meetings. This concern has led many instructors to adopt a camera-optional practice for teaching through Zoom. Low camera use, however, may diminish the educational experience.[14] Professors rely on nonverbal cues from students to inform their teaching in real time. Students, too, report that seeing each other onscreen helps to build the trust and rapport essential to their learning. In short, classes with low camera use lack the social context of living classrooms—the essential human connection—that reinforces teaching and learning.

Many students also struggle to find the time needed to succeed in their online courses. Although remote learning provides welcome flexibility, working from home introduces new challenges. Carving out uninterrupted time to study is particularly difficult for caregivers with young children or other family members who need close supervision or care. Single parents and women, who are still expected to do the majority of childcare and housework in heterosexual relationships, have a particularly difficult time juggling family responsibilities and coursework. Students of color are also more likely to experience this challenge than white students.[15]

Unequal access to technology also affects institutions. Nearly all colleges and universities provide some technical support to students, faculty, and staff, but affluent schools can devote more resources to maintaining and supporting instructional technology. Well-resourced institutions are also able to offer more funding to faculty and instructional designers experimenting with new technologies. Instructors who are well supported have more planning time and professional development opportunities, which enable them to explore new approaches and take the pedagogical risks that are essential to innovative, high-quality online teaching.

This brief discussion suggests that colleges and universities seeking to expand their online programs need better strategies for promoting equity in online instruction. To address the continuing need to eliminate student achievement gaps for low-income students and students of color, institutions must acknowledge the challenges that learning online can pose for these students as well as others. Online courses must be designed in ways that work for students with poor internet connectivity, limited access to technology devices, family and job responsibilities, and no designated place at home for doing coursework while also maintaining high academic standards.

Academic Excellence

The second value is academic excellence. Ethical online instruction must provide a high-quality university education to all enrolled students. As we have seen, detractors insist that MOOCs are inherently academically inferior to traditional face-to-face university courses. Yet even the most outspoken MOOC critics believe that pedagogically sound online courses are possible, provided they are carefully designed to meet the needs, satisfy the interests, and reflect the experiences of the particular students they serve. The emerging literature on emergency remote teaching, however, suggests that developing such courses using existing instructional technologies can be challenging.

Course management systems, together with videoconferencing platforms such as Zoom, made emergency remote teaching possible. But these technologies cannot replicate some of the most valuable aspects of in-person teaching, particularly in large classes. There is broad consensus that class discussions in large synchronous courses are considerably less effective than those in traditional in-person courses. During the emergency remote period, some of this disparity could be attributed to the fact classes were moved online so quickly, before faculty could be trained in the appropriate teaching methods. However, the technology itself also plays an important role. For example, in large Zoom classes, faculty without teaching assistants must attempt to facilitate class discussions about even the most complex and controversial issues via built-in Zoom features, such as polls, unmoderated breakout rooms, chats, and reaction emojis. These features are surely useful in some contexts, but they also tend to flatten class discussions and homogenize teaching when used regularly.

It can also be challenging to build a sense of community in classes where participants lack face-to-face contact, even when students choose to use their cameras. Instructors often find it difficult to build meaningful relationships with online students in the same manner as with in-person students, and without this critical component in place, online students may experience diminished interest in the course and less overall satisfaction with their learning experience.[16] Students who lack an emotional connection to a course also tend to produce a lower quality of work. These effects are compounded if social distance impedes the instructor's ability to provide students with adequate support. This is especially important for low-income students and students of color, who may be disproportionately impacted by the social distance, lack of support, and lack of structure common in online environments.[17]

These findings suggest that institutions seeking to expand their online programs need effective techniques for developing rigorous, pedagogically sound online courses within the constraints of existing instructional technologies. Instructional designers have recommended several best practices for high-impact online teaching, including enhancing faculty presence in courses, providing personalized feedback and assessment, cultivating meaningful peer and instructor-student relationships, and assigning frequent, low-stakes assignments that give students a chance to reflect on what they have learned. Some MOOC critics, such as Churchill, insist that high-quality online humanities courses must engage students in cooperative textual practices and provide extensive, substantive feedback on their written work.[18] Different specific teaching methods will be appropriate for different academic disciplines, of course, but a common thread runs through all of these various recommendations: high-quality online courses should be relatively small, and purposeful academic and social support must be readily available to students through multiple means.

Distributive Justice

The final value is distributive justice. Ethical online instruction must align with distributive justice, broadly understood as the fair distribution of socioeconomic benefits and burdens among members of a society. As we have seen, critics contend that for-credit MOOCs are unjust because they would deepen existing educational inequalities, privatize core university functions, and deflect attention from the root causes of the problems facing higher education. Similar concerns could be raised about emergency remote teaching. Although faculty, staff, and administrators worked diligently to ensure that courses were transferred online as equitably and efficiently as possible, a disproportionate number of low-income and minoritized students reported having problems, and often major problems, learning in online courses.[19] Overall college enrollment also fell precipitously during the pandemic, with community colleges suffering the steepest decline.[20] Emergency remote instruction also furthered the privatization of public higher education by shifting additional instructional and operational costs onto students. When physical campuses closed and staff were laid off, students lost access to valuable campus services, including libraries, labs, study spaces, dining halls, and recreation centers, without receiving a corresponding decrease in tuition. Many students also incurred additional expenses by learning from home, such as internet upgrades, new computers or tablets, office furniture, and utilities. Some commentators attribute these outcomes to disaster capitalism, defined as the opportunistic propensity of governments and/or corporations to exploit crises to impose neoliberal reforms.[21] According to this critique, universities have used genuine pandemic-related economic difficulties to justify further restructuring and privatization of higher education.

Does regular online university instruction fare better with respect to distributive justice? Provided that online programs are equitable and pedagogically sound in the ways I have outlined, expanding these programs would increase educational access for working students, rural communities, and other marginalized groups, thereby promoting equal opportunity and helping to mitigate socioeconomic inequalities. There is a caveat, however. Designing and teaching equitable, pedagogically sound online courses is both time-consuming and expensive. To prevent these costs from unfairly falling upon students, faculty, and instructional staff, universities must provide robust institutional support for their learning, teaching, and professional development. As we have seen, this must include material support for students who have difficulty accessing needed technology. But achieving justice in online instruction also requires universities to provide faculty with the institutional resources, including release time, they need to develop and teach innovative online courses. Institutions must also ensure that students are adequately supported in the social elements of learning by providing effective virtual advising, mentoring, and peer support. Because ethical online courses are likely to be more, rather than less, expensive than traditional face-to-face courses, increased public funding will likely be necessary. Attention also should be paid to the effects that a shift toward expanded online instruction would have on local communities, whose livelihoods, cultural opportunities, and even identities may be tied to the flourishing of brick-and-mortar campuses.

CONCLUSION

This paper has explored the ethics of online university instruction in the context of two recent experiments in remote learning: massive open online courses and emergency remote teaching during the COVID-19 pandemic. I have argued that the shortcomings of these modes of instruction suggest that ethically responsible online instruction must reflect the core normative values of equity, academic excellence, and justice. Although various factors complicate the design and implementation of ethical online programs, my analysis suggests that such programs are possible, provided they are adequately resourced and intentionally designed to meet the needs of the students and broader communities they serve. In this way, ethical online university instruction can be one part of the solution to the complex problems facing higher education.

Chapter 20

Improving Fully Online Instruction

Laura M. Howard

Fully online instruction (FOI) in higher education is now commonplace. More than 500 colleges and universities offer a total of more than 8,800 fully online bachelor's degree programs and 25,000 fully online graduate degrees and certificates.[1] In fall 2019, some 36% (6 million) of all undergraduate students enrolled in at least one distance education course, and 15% (2.4 million) took exclusively distance-education courses.[2] Online instruction proliferated following the economic crash of 2008, a profit center for many academic departments that saved them from extinction. Evolving online instruction has provided a path to education previously inaccessible to many people. And FOI saved the academic year during the COVID-19 pandemic.

But for all its advantages, benefits enjoyed by students, faculty, colleges, and universities, fully online instruction also has significant disadvantages that require further examination. A profound pedagogical shift has accompanied the physical move from the classroom to the internet. What has been lost in this transition? This essay explores the ethical question of whether educators can fulfill their duty to deliver a maximally effective and enriching learning experience in a largely or fully online program. The first three sections address the harmful consequences of FOI in higher education for students, the fourth discusses its negative effects on instructors, and the fifth concludes with some recommendations for improving fully online instruction.

ACHIEVING LEARNING OUTCOMES IN FOI

The seven regional accrediting commissions for institutions of higher learning in the United States now expect colleges and universities to expressly articulate the purposes, content, and intended learning outcomes of their undergraduate general education requirements. Every syllabus should include measurable learning outcomes that state specifically what students should be able to do after completing a course. Outcomes are content specific to each course subject, but many of the actionable skills are the same across the curriculum: Students should be able to apply (theories, methods, strategies, algorithms, etc.), to analyze (narratives, arguments, study results, etc.), to construct (experiments, historical timelines, reports, etc.). In my discipline, moral philosophy, the ability to analyze and construct arguments and counterarguments is a key skill to cultivate in students.

Long before the advent of online instruction and the ubiquitous presence of laptops in the classroom, I enjoyed introducing students to morally charged thought experiments that surprised and engaged them, requiring creative thought to come up with unique responses to the ethical problem. In today's classroom, let alone in online courses, the element of surprise is gone, and the slower, contemplative process that yields deeper thought has all but vanished as well. With a few keystrokes, students can generate millions of Google hits that provide one-sentence explanations of a thought experiment along with the most popular scholarly arguments about it. In the digital environment, students are conditioned to look up the answer rather than think through the problem on their own. I call it the thought-replaced-by-search-engine problem. In the classroom, disallowing laptops and phones during discussion periods can somewhat control this disappointing phenomenon. But with FOI, this kind of benevolent paternalism is impossible. I claim that the exercise of original thinking is crucial for learning, and fully online instruction can have a crippling effect on developing this capacity into a competency applied to problem-solving.

Another problem that diminishes success in achieving learning outcomes involves the well-known distraction factor. A quick internet search of "online video lectures distractions" (yes, I used Google and read only the first sentence of each result) yielded over six million hits. There, in the digital world, students can find an abundance of advice for how to avoid being distracted by the digital world. Social media, video sharing platforms, texting, and gaming are powerful competitors to an academic lecture. Software programs aplenty track "student engagement," time spent watching prerecorded lecture videos, for example. But does this data provide evidence that students are actually watching the video lectures? A digital footprint tracks connection but not attention. Students have admitted to me that in courses where they earn points for watching a lecture, they often minimize the screen, turn off the volume, and play video games instead. Of course, the classroom does not guarantee that students are paying attention either. Undergraduates can be very creative at undertaking all manner of extracurricular activities during class lectures. But in the classroom, the instructor at least has a shot at identifying students who need help to reengage, and this can be accomplished in several ways.

In the faceless online environment, however, this is either unfeasible or impossible. Might a webcam requirement help? Educators, psychologists, and others continue to debate whether requiring students to turn on their webcams during synchronous online courses is ethical, and some institutions prohibit such a controversial mandate. Among the reasons for not requiring students to use webcams are the following: an attitude of compassion and adaptability calls for teaching choices that acknowledge students who suffer from trauma, depression, or other mental health challenges; principles of diversity, equity, and inclusion support flexible approaches and multiple means of engagement; cameras are not the only option for engagement; many students may not feel comfortable or safe appearing on camera and revealing their home environment.[3] These are concerns worthy of our careful consideration. In some cases, it is best to relieve certain students from attendance requirements—either in the classroom or online. Instructional design that includes more and varied modalities for engagement and learning is always preferred. But in the online environment, this does not occur without considerable labor.

To reach the distracted student, engage the isolated student, and respect the needs of a diverse student population, online instructors can consider this short to-do list of teaching aids to help ensure attendance and participation: a note-taking template to help students focus; small breakout rooms within the course management system and rotation of student group assignments to those rooms; lectures in smaller chunks and embedded automated quizzes within the lectures; a collaborative real-time document for students to share; screencast software with presentation slides that link to the relevant lecture sections; a multimedia slideshow that allows students to leave comments. Notice at least three things. First, this is the short list. The range and scope of online instructional tips and tricks are mind-boggling. Second, the many hours required to produce such a substantial number of digital aids reduce the time left to research and curate actual course content. Few institutions currently have the IT resources to help all faculty produce their teaching tools. And even where they do, the burden is still upon the instructor to devote time to learning how to use the software.

Third, and most important, students can also find technology daunting. It's a misconception to think that every young college student is totally tech-savvy. Like many instructors, they also struggle with technology overload, as illustrated by these comments from remote learners during the pandemic:[4] "I can often feel overwhelmed with having to learn new technology every semester." "It [a screencast software program] was very complicated to use. I struggled a lot to find the videos I needed for the lecture and I have heard it is super complicated to upload videos. Once I figured out how to use it, it was helpful. But at the start, since I was confused on how to use it, I got behind on my class and had to rush through the lectures later on." "Some of the tools can be intimidating to use at first, making them difficult to enjoy. For me this was . . . a software used to create digital 3D Models. The unfamiliarity of this particular tool and the expectancy to adapt to it quickly made operating it even more difficult." If these are the feelings and impressions of a large number of online students, we should not be surprised to experience diminished success at achieving our learning outcomes—unless the learning outcome is to master technology. In some disciplines, learning to use sophisticated tools of technology is central to the field of study. But in many, if not most majors, asking students to spend so much of their time learning technology simply to learn what they signed up for may undermine our objectives.

I will close this section with what some may see as an appeal to emotion. But it's an argument worth considering if we start with the premise that learning ought to be fun and engaging while stimulating the desire to learn more. Really exciting lecturers are out there, although they may be few. But for the lucky student who ends up achieving an educational and career dream because of that one professor who delivered an unforgettable, stirring lecture, the opportunity to have sat in that seat, in that moment, was life changing. These kinds of moments are much less likely to occur in the online environment. It's not that a lecturer can't give a rousing prerecorded speech in front of a camera; some excel at it. But something about a live presentation with a live audience fuels both the presenter and the listeners, generating a collective excitement and passion for the given subject that is hard to replicate elsewhere. Many instructors report that lecturing online, whether in a synchronous or prerecorded platform, is uninspiring and much less satisfying than in the classroom. Without the student feedback and the shared energy of being together in one room, the computer screen often greatly lessens the impact of an otherwise outstanding lecturer. So, if "after completing the course, students should yearn for more" is one of our learning outcomes, then we should question whether FOI can deliver on that promise.

DEVELOPING ACADEMIC AND INTERPERSONAL COMMUNICATION SKILLS

The higher education experience has always been about more than just applying, analyzing, and constructing academic ideas and concepts. Competence in interpersonal communication helps students use what they have learned and apply it outside the walls of academia. An enormous volume of work from psychologists suggests that immersion in the digital world is diminishing the ability of children and adolescents to interpret nonverbal cues such as facial expressions that convey emotions. An unfortunate, if unsurprising, occurrence, but what does it have to do with delivering a maximally effective learning experience in higher education? I've observed that much student learning occurs in classroom discussion, perhaps more so than in face-to-face, synchronous webinar environments such as Zoom. Classroom students modulate in real time, individually and as a group, to one another. They read each other's body language. They look to other faces for subtle cues that confirm everybody else is confused too. It's an important moment when everyone in the front of the class turns around to see the student seated in the back who said that interesting thing. This interaction may make some uncomfortable, but it's also part of the collaborative learning experience. Students jumping in together to emphasize a point punctuates the importance of a topic. Even those too shy to speak learn from observing how expressive peers react to one another.

In a classroom, it's also possible to hear and understand two people speaking simultaneously. In a webinar, if more than one person speaks, no one hears anything. And when the transmission breaks up, a lot gets lost. Discussions are often stilted and irritatingly time-delayed; interruptions of even a fraction of a second have a chilling effect on conversational momentum. Of course, this also means that synchronous online discussions rarely get heated, a contrast to asynchronous online discussions, where a faceless environment can embolden students who would be unlikely to demonstrate aggression in the classroom. Here again, though, a learning opportunity may be lost. When a classroom discussion degenerates to ad hominem attacks, a good instructor can respond immediately to defuse a tense situation and stress communication that respects others and focuses on the topic.

Communicating respectfully, adjusting one's thinking in real time as others present their views or share information, and assessing states of mind are cognitive skills that complement the other practical skills we hope the experience of higher education provides students. A serious examination of how effectively online instruction promotes these skills that propel success in nearly every career can help clarify our goals and strengthen our educational mission.

FOSTERING ACADEMIC AND PERSONAL INTEGRITY

Everyone knows that cheating is a big problem in the online learning environment. In addition to plagiarism, various violations of academic integrity plague test taking. These include unauthorized collaborating or even substituting a ringer and relying on books, notes, or the internet. But fostering integrity in our students should be about much more than preventing cheating. Integrity is an all-encompassing moral virtue that exemplifies one's wholeness as a flourishing human. Higher education should foster integrity by giving students opportunities to develop maturity, independence, and a sense of honor for having accomplished something important. To that end, requiring attendance and submission of assignments by deadline is one way to promote necessary self-discipline.

During my time as a director of undergraduate studies, I met with countless students who were failing because they had mismanaged their online courses. Many lamented having fallen victim to fatal procrastination because they didn't have to physically appear in the classroom. The appeal of skipping a class that convenes once at a specific time is not as great as the temptation of putting off a prerecorded lecture in an asynchronous online course. Unlike online students, who often have flexible deadlines, classroom students can't simply "do it later."

Online students don't intend to fall behind, of course, and they feel bad when they do. Is some of this our fault as educators, though? In our zeal to ramp up asynchronous online offerings, are we enabling their failure? Surely the problem of cheating on tests and other assessments is at least partially a function of scrambling to catch up after lengthy procrastination. Add to that the distrust students feel while an unknown proctor watches them through their webcam during a test, and it should be no surprise that academic achievements do not inspire a sense of honor for many online students. I'm not suggesting that the traditional classroom is beyond reproach; procrastination and cheating have always been prevalent in higher education and elsewhere—long before the move to online instruction. FOI exacerbates these problems, however, and as this practice evolves, our obligation to create an environment that encourages rather than discourages integrity should remain a priority.

CONSIDERING THE INSTRUCTOR'S BURDEN

FOI is no paradise for instructors either. Those new to online instruction may expect a wonderful break from the task of preparing and delivering lectures in the classroom. But they soon learn that the upfront workload for creating a fully online course is enormous. Lectures must be segmented, condensed, recorded, produced, and uploaded with multiple device compatibility. The first section of this essay outlines many pedagogical tools instructors are expected to employ to promote engagement. Creating and making them functional takes hours upon hours. Instructors who teach the same online course again should expect to write new versions of assignments and exams, since those will be copied and distributed worldwide before the first class is even over.

I'm not claiming that classroom exams and assignments don't need to be freshened regularly, they do. But the extra work involved in testing for comprehension when the test answers are a click away is not insignificant. Add to all this the fact that the visual optics, navigation, and design of digital instruction are changing at a pace that challenges even IT experts, and it is not hard to see why instructors are frustrated. Many seasoned professors who shine in the classroom have elected to call it quits rather than take on the task of mastering so much technology. Others simply ignore the expectations and launch a "self-paced" course that is really more of a "teach-yourself" class. I have reviewed many online courses composed of nothing but a list of reading assignments, where the instructor is effectively absent. Inconsistent quality of instruction has long been an issue for education at every level, but variability in the effectiveness of online teaching can be particularly pronounced. To combat this, many institutions expect faculty to satisfy standardized teaching rubrics. And online instructors are subject to greater pedagogical oversight than their classroom colleagues, a disparity that may widen the chasm between research faculty and teaching faculty and potentially cause ill feelings among instructors teaching the same subjects but in different modalities.

In brief, the surge in online courses, usually at the behest of administration, has caused considerable discontent, dissatisfaction, and disinterest among faculty. As these reactions can negatively affect the student experience, we should be asking if the shift away from the classroom comes at too high a cost for many educators and those they hope to educate.

MITIGATING THE NEGATIVE EFFECTS OF FOI

This essay has focused on the potentially negative consequences of FOI, outlining numerous ways in which the higher education experience that lacks face-to-face interaction may be less effective and enriching for both instructors and students. But online instruction also offers many advantages, especially for students and faculty who delight in new technology and flourish in the digital environment. Admittedly, some things that can be done in the digital space cannot be accomplished as effectively in the classroom. Online instruction also makes a college education and credentials available to those unable to physically attend classes on campus. And for students who can no longer be on campus but are close to graduating, online offerings can save their degree program. Clearly, the merits of FOI must be assessed on a case-by-case basis. Many of the thousands of students I've taught in fully online asynchronous courses have told me how much they learned and enjoyed the class. Still, I remain skeptical that *fully* online instruction is best for some people or even most people, especially first-year students straight out of high school and living on campus.

That said, many negative consequences of FOI can be mitigated. To start with, the internet itself needs upgrades for greater access in rural areas, affordable access for everyone, and better access that is faster and glitch-free. Colleges and universities should invest in tech support, instructional designers who don't merely assist in course creation but make other substantive contributions to help make instruction less labor-intensive for FOI instructors. Stipends should compensate faculty for the time they invest in relearning how to teach effectively in the digital space and avoid potential FOI pitfalls, only some of which I've outlined here. And pedagogical oversight should be fairly instituted for all teaching faculty. Academic advisors should be trained to counsel students one-on-one about their potential for success in a fully online program. Creating an exciting and enriching online experience that differs from the traditional classroom is possible, but whether it will be better remains a question. As we design bigger, fancier, splashier online programs, our guiding ethic should be our duty to deliver a *maximally* effective and enriching learning experience, and we must continue to ask if our online programs hit the mark.

Part X

ADMISSIONS

Chapter 21

Merit, Wealth, and the Ethics of College Admissions

Meira Levinson

In 2019 news broke that dozens of wealthy parents had secured admission for their children at prestigious universities by paying off private college admissions coaches to falsify their students' standardized test scores and resumes, and bribing university coaches to recruit their children for spots on teams that they would never fill—often because they had little or no experience with the sport.[1] These cases, code-named "Varsity Blues" by the FBI investigators, plainly represented instances of morally impermissible bribery, and condemnations of the parents predictably followed. News media were especially taken by the images of actress Felicity Huffman being hauled off to jail for paying a bogus $15,000 "charitable contribution" that was supposedly given to "provide educational and self-enrichment programs to disadvantaged youth" but was instead used to pay a corrupt SAT proctor to raise her older daughter's score by 400 points.[2] There was similar breathless coverage of other celebrity takedowns and self-pitying white-shoe lawyers explaining that they shouldn't be condemned simply for trying to ensure the best for their children.

At the same time, many people raised questions about how materially different these parents' efforts were from the perfectly legal—and socially permissible—expenditures made by other ultra-wealthy families to get their children into college. What distinguishes the $6.5 million paid by one couple to get their daughter into Stanford by bribing the sailing coach and falsifying her credentials,[3] for instance, from the $2.5 million promised to Harvard by Jared Kushner's father mere months before the younger Kushner was improbably admitted to Harvard despite his poor test scores and grades?[4] Maybe the right conclusion is simply that Harvard admission could apparently be purchased on the cheap back in 1998, and one hopes they've raised their rates for building and scholarship "donations" since then.

In fact, the challenge of distinguishing bribery and fraud from "donations" and "special treatment" is at the heart of some of the defendants' arguments for why they should be deemed not guilty in the Varsity Blues racket. One defendant's lawyer cited email exchanges among University of Southern California (USC) officials discussing a walk-on water polo player's family as "a high-level prospect with 1–5M potential" and another hyper-wealthy applicant as "good enough to shag balls for the tennis team" despite his poor academic qualifications.[5] These were evidence, the lawyer argued, that university officials themselves were complicit in admitting students on grounds that they themselves knew were sketchy in exchange for high-level donations. Another defendant's lawyer argued, "Giving money to a school to help with the hope that helps your child get in is not a crime," and that giving it to a middleman was no worse than paying it directly to the school.[6]

Furthermore, the defense might have pointed out that middlemen have long profited perfectly legally off parents' college application anxieties. Whole industries in the United States are based on parents' spending four-, five-, and even six-figure sums specifically to boost children's college admission prospects. Wealthy parents may pay $6,000–$8,000 to purchase a neuropsychology assessment to get their child extra time on the SAT, thousands more for private SAT tutoring, and $10,000 or more on bespoke college counseling services that promise to increase elite college admission chances by up to 500%.[7] William Singer, the corrupt college admissions advisor whose cooperation with the FBI was essential for blowing open the Varsity Blues case, was only one of hundreds if not thousands of high-end admissions coaches—most of whom presumably are not corrupt but who are nonetheless earning a very comfortable living helping wealthy children get into highly selective colleges and universities.

It may even be a mistake to focus on these "end of [high school] life" expenditures in trying to understand the impact that family income has on elite college admissions. As the economist Raj Chetty and others have brought to light, most elite and highly selective colleges serve a stunningly disproportionately high-income student body. As of 2017, thirty-eight colleges and universities enrolled more undergraduates who came from the top 1% of the income scale than came from the bottom 60%.[8] Barely 10% of students from the bottom income quintile (lowest 20%) attended even a selective college (meaning one that received more applications than it had spots and hence rejected at least some applicants who met the minimum benchmark). By contrast, over 80% of students from the top 1% attended selective colleges or universities; in fact, over 50% of those students attended a highly selective college and a full *third* of students from the top 1% attended an "elite" college such as an Ivy league school or other highly prestigious liberal arts college ("elite" refers to the top 100 or so colleges in the nation, such as MIT, Wellesley, or UCLA). This is not to suggest that one needs to be in the top 1% to gain disproportionate access to elite and highly selective schools. Children from families whose income puts them in the top 20% attended highly selective schools at rates 8–10 times higher than children from low-income (bottom quintile) families; their likelihood of attending elite and Ivy-plus schools is not even comparable, because too few low-income students do so for it to register on a graph.

Why is this? It's not because of fraud; very few of the families in the top 20% (or 1%) are attempting to bribe or falsify their child's way into college admission. Nor is it because of collegiate strong-arming for donations (let alone whole buildings). Admittedly, Harvard does maintain a "Z list" of high-net-worth but underachieving applicants who are awarded a spot in the freshman class on the condition that they first take a "gap year" to mature (and presumably consider making a significant donation in the process). Other universities apply similar affirmative action policies to super high-net-worth applicants. But these amount to only a few dozen spots per year at most schools; the rest of the seats are awarded through standard admissions procedures.

No, corruption isn't what is making the student body at highly selective colleges disproportionately wealthy. Rather, the problem in a hyper-unequal society is money itself: or rather, money's capacity to buy merit. Money sloshes around wealthy families before children are born.[9] It buys mothers high-quality prenatal care and partial protection from the traumas of poverty that can lead to lower birth weight or emotional dysregulation. Money shields children from the toxic stress that accompanies such adverse events as becoming homeless, seeing a parent be fired from a job, or going into foster care. Money pays for high-quality childcare, for houses priced at a premium because they are in neighborhoods with highly ranked public schools, for music lessons, travel, summer camps, and academic tutors. Money enables affluent families to spend over six times what poor families spend annually on children's "enrichment" activities; these expenditures match or even exceed schools' annual per-pupil spending, meaning that high-income families in essence double educational expenditures on their own children as compared to low-income children.[10] Money buys access to therapists, medication to treat anxiety and depression, healthy breakfasts before a child is dropped off at school, a quiet place to work at home, reliable internet, one-to-one technology for each member of the family, participation in club and travel sports teams, and attendance at private schools that can cost as much as $55,000 per year from age three through high school. Money buys books, special education diagnoses and advocates to ensure that children's Individualized Education Plans (IEPs) are being followed, houses in neighborhoods where it is safe to play outside, and professional degrees that prepare one to help one's children with homework and to be treated with respect by teachers, administrators, and district officials when one shows up to make a request or register a complaint.

A predictable result of these disproportionate expenditures on children's learning and well-being is that children from high-income families typically acquire and can demonstrate more of the knowledge, skills, and achievements that highly selective colleges look for than children from low-income families. On average, high-income children read better than low-income children. They pass calculus at higher rates. They complete more AP courses and earn more passing grades on exams. Wealthy children participate in more extracurricular activities than low-income children; they have higher grade point averages and test scores, and they are more likely to master an orchestral instrument and to be included in a gifted-and-talented program. In sum, children from high-income families are more likely to meet the admissions criteria set by highly selective and elite schools than are children from low-income families. Not just a little more likely. A lot more likely.

As a result, even elite colleges that do need-blind admissions, guarantee full need-based financial aid, and offer grants rather than loans so students avoid crushing debt end up with a student body strongly skewed toward the wealthy. The numbers are even worse for the many highly selective institutions that cannot afford to be indifferent to students' capacities to pay full tuition and that cannot guarantee students financial aid adequate to meet their needs. It is true that part of the problem is a skew in who applies. Many high-achieving students from low-income households assume they could not afford to attend highly selective and elite colleges or would not succeed there even if it were affordable; many choose to attend a lower-ranked college closer to home to meet family obligations or maintain family ties; some have never heard of highly selective colleges given the paucity of college guidance counselors in schools serving low-income students and the lack of personalized outreach by colleges to exurban and rural students.

But even if this "undermatching" problem were solved tomorrow, a serious income gap would remain. For instance, Chetty and his colleagues found that under the most optimistic scenario for elite college applications and admissions, where qualified low-income students applied and were admitted at exactly the same rates as their equivalently qualified higher-income peers, the percentage of the student body that came from the bottom income quintile would barely budge, rising perhaps from 3.8 to 4.2%.[11] Working-class and middle-class students would increase their representation significantly more, but students from the bottom 60% of the income distribution would still make up only 29 to 35% of the total student body in highly selective and elite colleges.[12] This is barely half the representation they should have in such schools if income did not predict college matriculation outcomes.

So, this is the ethical question at the heart of selective college admissions in an era of hyper-inequality: namely, what should colleges do about the fact that money buys "merit," whether measured by GPA, test scores, achievement in sports and in the arts, writing skills, scientific knowledge, or whatever combination of features a college chooses to elevate in their admissions process?

One option is that they should do nothing. Highly selective and elite colleges may reasonably argue that the fact that students from higher-income families are able to acquire more of the knowledge, skills, and dispositions that they (the colleges) value is unfortunate and should be changed, but the colleges aren't the institutions that need to do the changing. Rather, we need broader structural and social reforms to avoid inscribing into eighteen-year-old college applicants the inequities of the environmental and economic conditions in which they are raised, the relative qualities of the elementary and secondary schools they attend, and so forth. Colleges might even advocate for some of those changes, as long as their advocacy doesn't jeopardize their nonprofit status. They might host a conference series, for example, about improving urban and rural schools or host legislators to learn about strategies for lowering the Gini index (an internationally comparable measure of economic inequality inside countries; the United States is comparatively high and hence unequal). But what wouldn't make sense, according to this argument, is for highly selective colleges to change their admissions criteria simply to accept more low-income students. Rather, elite colleges should keep the stringent admissions criteria that allow them to continue to teach intellectually rigorous courses that set the standards for academic excellence, push the frontiers of knowledge, train the next generation of leaders, and accomplish all the other high-minded aims that universities may claim as research and teaching institutions.

This argument is potentially compelling in the abstract, on the assumption that universities are solely interested in bringing together academically outstanding students to engage in highly demanding, rigorous classroom learning. Universities in the United Kingdom often make these arguments, for instance, on the grounds that they admit students solely on the basis of academic merit as measured by A-level scores (and interviews in the case of Oxford and Cambridge). Highly selective universities in the United Kingdom do have robust sports teams, dramatic societies, orchestras, debate clubs, and other exemplars of extracurricular undergraduate life. Insofar as they select students solely for their demonstrated academic prowess in a specific discipline, however, these universities can plausibly argue that not only do they bear no responsibility for redressing economic inequities among applicants at the point of admission, but doing so would actually undermine their mission. Such an argument wouldn't be dispositive—in fact, I believe that there remain very strong civic, economic, and even intellectual reasons that U.K. universities should admit a more economically diverse student body, which I won't take the time to review here—but the argument is at least valid, if not sound.

The story is different in the United States, however, given the admissions criteria currently in use at highly selective and elite colleges. As we have seen, it is *already* the case that some students are admitted because their families are outstandingly wealthy and have donated or are expected to donate significant sums to the university. Other students are *already* admitted because they are outstanding tennis players, knockout trombonists, or professional actors, sometimes regardless of their academic achievements. After all, this is exactly how William Singer was able to guarantee some students admission to schools like Yale, USC, or Georgetown, by bribing coaches to send their names to the admissions directors for automatic approval. Furthermore, highly selective colleges across the country also give a boost to thousands of applicants each year because their parents or grandparents attended the college (i.e., affirmative action for legacies) or because, say, they add geographic diversity (e.g., affirmative action for North Dakotans).

Consider the Stanford undergraduate class of 2023, for instance, which matriculated in 2019. We don't know exactly how many or what percentage of students were athletic recruits, although we do know that as of Spring 2021, 520 "scholar-athletes," or about 130 students per class across the four years, are currently receiving "some amount of athletic aid."[13] More informatively, the Stanford athletics department recently announced that it will be piloting a program to enroll up to fifteen athletic recruits (mostly football players) a semester early to compete with other powerhouses such as USC and Notre Dame.[14] They must "be academically qualified for Stanford and have graduated from high school," but they are not admitted as part of the normal admissions pool. We also know that there are thirty-six varsity sports at Stanford, and the Varsity Blues debacle revealed that even sailors at Stanford—not a highly visible or high-status sport—get a special admission pathway. So, if football gets fifteen early-admit recruits, some of the other high-status sports like basketball or swimming get even just five special admissions recruits each, and the lower-status sports get one each, a bare minimum of 70–100 students per year—or about 4 to 6% of the entering class—enter through the "back door" of athletics.

Thanks to a state law passed in the wake of the Varsity Blues scandal requiring California colleges to report their undergraduate admissions preferences for legacies and potential donors, we have many more specifics about both legacy and philanthropic admits at Stanford.[15] As the Stanford provost was forced to report:

> In the undergraduate Class of 2023, which was admitted for Fall 2019 entrance, 16.2% of the enrolling class (302 admitted students and 276 matriculating students) were the children of Stanford graduates. For some of these students, their admission files also noted a history of philanthropy. An additional 1.5% of the enrolling class (34 admitted students and 26 matriculating students) had no legacy affiliation with Stanford, but their admission files noted a history of philanthropy. Together, those with either of these two characteristics totaled 302 students in the enrolling class, representing 17.8% of our 1,701 entering students.[16]

Of course, many of these students might have been admitted entirely on their merits independent of their legacy or potential donor status. It would be wrong to conclude that 18% of the student body had secured admission simply because of their parents' net worth or alma mater. But it is also clear that these characteristics are not merely incidental at the time of admissions. As the provost went to pains to explain in the same report, "Philanthropy plays a significant role in supporting the opportunities available to all students at Stanford, including the ability to attend the university through our program of need-based financial aid."[17] Evidence from Harvard, University of Chicago, and elsewhere suggest that Ivy League and similar colleges may offer seats to between twenty and fifty applicants each year, or about 1.5 to 4% of the entering class, on grounds driven more by development needs and legacy considerations than by applicants' quality.[18]

Taken together, even by the most conservative estimates, at least 120 students, comprising 6 to 8% of each entering class, are apparently admitted to Stanford on grounds other than applicants' academic qualifications if they surpass a minimum threshold. Not all highly selective and elite colleges are as significant academic or athletic powerhouses as Stanford, and similarly, not all have the same draw to ultra-high-net-worth families as do places like Stanford and Harvard. Let's be even more conservative, then, and cut this percentage by two-thirds for the average highly selective college. This would lead us to conclude that at a minimum, highly selective colleges and universities in the United States admit 2 to 3% of their student body each year solely on the basis of their athletic achievement or high net worth, once these applicants have passed the basic academic bar for admission.

In light of this data, there just isn't a case to be made that the highly selective or elite U.S. university experience, universities' standards, or their aims are violated by admissions practices that discount or even ignore academic achievement for a substantial number of students. Clearly, universities think that they can achieve their aims even while (perhaps *especially* while) admitting dozens and even hundreds of students through the back door of athletic admissions or their families' "history of philanthropy." In fact, University of Southern California (USC) administrators have gone so far as to claim that donor-sensitive admissions are essential to achieving its greatness as a university: "Without philanthropy, USC would not be able to award over $640 million each year in student aid, conduct cutting-edge research, and hire and retain exceptional faculty and employees."[19] From this perspective, there is a direct and positive relationship between admitting wealthy children and promoting the university's mission as a teaching and learning institution.

So, this brings us back to the core question: In an era of heightened attention to systemic inequity and injustice, how, if at all, should highly selective and elite colleges change their admissions policies to address the outsize impact of money on students' desirability? I recommend that they take two specific and related actions. First, directly auction off a limited number of admissions slots every year to the highest bidders, or invite wealthy families to buy admissions lottery tickets at a fixed price and then run the lottery for the same number of places as one would have auctioned off. (As I am not an economist, I don't know which approach is more likely to generate revenue.) Keep the number of seats allocated this way small enough to maintain the tenor of the college: say, 2% of the available slots or fifty seats, whichever is smaller. Second, allocate at least 75% of the money earned from the auction or lottery to increase outreach, recruitment, need-based financial aid, and on-campus academic, social, and related supports for low- and middle-income students. (I recommend 75% rather than 100% because as USC's and Stanford's statements make clear, the universities are already dependent on these admission-related donations to pay for other financial commitments such as research labs, libraries, and ice cream sundae bars in the cafeteria.)

Although my suggestion that seats be sold to the highest bidder (or won by the luckiest lottery-ticket holders) may seem shocking, remember that these seats are *already* in effect being sold, just in secret, and often only in anticipation of a donation rather than a guaranteed gift. By openly selling the seats instead, an elite university like Harvard can better live up to its guiding ideal of *Veritas*, or Truth. It can be transparent and above board about its interest in admitting high-net-worth applicants for the sake of revenue generation rather than squirming in the witness box.[20] Furthermore, by directly selling a small number of seats, highly selective universities can reduce the excess rents paid by wealthy parents to middlemen like ultra-exclusive college admissions coaches and redirect the money toward the university.[21]

It is equally important, however, that universities use a significant portion of these revenues to increase access and attainment for applicants from the bottom 60% of the income distribution. I mentioned earlier that students from lower-income families tend to "undermatch" with highly selective colleges and universities; in other words, they apply to less selective or often only to nonselective institutions even as higher-income peers with identical (or worse) academic records apply to and matriculate at more prestigious colleges.[22] Expanding carefully designed outreach and recruitment efforts by highly selective colleges could reduce this disparity.[23]

An even more powerful intervention is to lower real tuition prices from the stratosphere and make them visibly affordable to middle-class, working-class, and low-income families.[24] There is good evidence that if low- and middle-income students can see from the start that attending a selective college is affordable, rather than being shocked by the sticker price and receiving aid only if and after they gird themselves to apply anyway, then they are much more likely to apply and matriculate. To make themselves visibly affordable, however, colleges and universities need to engage in personalized outreach to students and their families. Generic brochures or websites that claim financial aid is available to those in need are not enough; rather, students and families need to receive specific information from each highly selective college showing what their actual cost will be to attend.

And then, of course, colleges need to make themselves actually affordable, which means increasing need-based financial aid to admit more middle- and low-income students. Barely 100 American colleges and universities currently engage in need-blind admissions; the vast majority of higher education institutions turn down high-achieving low- and middle-income students whom they would like to admit because they can't afford to take them. Furthermore, only about 50% of colleges that are need-blind during the admissions process also guarantee aid that meets admitted students' full financial needs. So, even if, thanks to need-blind admissions, a high-achieving working-class student is admitted to Boston University, for instance, she may be unable to attend unless she takes out terrifyingly large loans since BU does not guarantee aid to meet her full demonstrated financial need across all four years. Significantly increasing need-based financial aid thanks to an annual admissions auction or lottery could enable highly selective colleges like BU to admit an equally meritorious but less disproportionately high-income class of students.

Admittedly, colleges and universities cannot redress the ethical complexities of admissions in an era of hyper-inequality solely by recruiting and admitting low- and middle-income students who are already as high achieving as their high-income (particularly their ultra-high-income) peers. As I pointed out earlier, money really does buy merit, if we take "merit" to mean all the various forms of achievement and accolades that highly selective colleges value in admissions. Students from families with very high levels of income will thus continue disproportionately to merit admission to highly selective and elite institutions. To address this problem, colleges committed to combatting systemic inequities and injustices prevalent in an era of hyper-inequality will need to admit able but less well-prepared middle- and low-income students and then provide additional assistance to ensure success once they've matriculated. By systematically offering academic, social-emotional, vocational, and other supports, highly selective colleges can admit clearly great people and hard workers who could succeed with help but who haven't necessarily attained all the markers of success acquired by some of the upper-income applicants they might otherwise have accepted.

Defenders of a particular ideal of highly selective and elite universities as bastions of intellectual achievement, rigor, and "the best of the best" may balk at this suggestion that admissions standards be "lowered" to admit more low- and middle-income students. But again, remember that virtually all these institutions have already committed to filling at least 6 to 8% of their seats with applicants selected primarily on the basis of their athletic or philanthropic promise rather than their academic prowess or even overall merit. (It is also worth remembering this doesn't even account for seats awarded via affirmative action for legacies.) These institutions have also figured out how to support these students whom they deem deserving of admission despite lower-than-average achievement. Athletes, for example, benefit from an enormous range of wraparound supports.

These include special study hall and tutoring sessions, academic counselors who help them choose their courses and check in regularly with professors to monitor their progress, special meal provision when practice goes late or they must stay during breaks to train, and access to on-demand mental health services in addition to top-notch physical medical care. There is no reason that highly selective and elite colleges would be unable to provide similar assistance to low- and middle-income students who need the extra support, if these institutions so chose.

Furthermore, there is good reason to think that such a policy would significantly benefit not only these students and their colleges and universities but also society as a whole.[25] As individuals, lower-income students are likely to have better jobs and higher lifelong earnings if they attend a highly selective or elite college—a benefit notably lacking for the high-income students who currently gobble up these seats, as they seem to do equally well in the labor market on average no matter what college they attend.[26] Both lower-income students and their higher-income peers are likely to experience real educational benefits from being in socioeconomically diverse cohorts in classes, dorms, and extracurricular activities. And insofar as these colleges and universities prepare a high proportion of those with elite political, cultural, economic, and professional status in the United States, preparing a more economically and experientially diverse leadership class has real civic benefits.

Admittedly, even the most cutthroat auction for seats will not yield enough additional funds to support fully the initiatives I have outlined. Boston University awards almost $330 million in undergraduate financial aid each year; it spends millions of dollars more on student support services such as writing centers, librarians, mental health counselors, and affinity spaces. No auction or lottery will raise amounts sufficient to transform these budgets. Still, it would behoove highly selective colleges and universities to be more honest with prospective students and parents, the public, and themselves about what they do consider their ethical obligations as admissions gatekeepers and assessors of merit in an era of hyper-inequality. If bribery is clearly unethical, but raising money even through the admissions process is nonetheless deemed essential, then the only ethical response seems to be openly and transparently selling seats. If colleges maintain their elite status by restricting access to those deemed to demonstrate extraordinary merit, but children of families with extraordinary income are orders of magnitude more likely to "merit" entry to elite colleges than are low-income children, *and* these colleges also consistently waive merit requirements for other disproportionately wealthy students such as donors and lacrosse players, then the only ethical response seems to be to change admissions standards and on-campus services to support low- and middle-income students. Such initiatives won't eliminate structural inequity or even ensure fair equality of opportunity. But they would be a good start.

Chapter 22

The Ethics of Doctoral Admissions

Bryan Warnick

The supply of PhD students is far outstripping demand for jobs in the professoriate, yet their number seems to be increasing. According to the *Economist*, "America produced more than 100,000 doctoral degrees between 2005 and 2009. In the same period there were just 16,000 new professorships."[1] A more recent estimate puts the U.S. rate of PhDs absorbed into faculty ranks at only 10 to 16%.[2] Not only are American universities pumping out PhDs, universities across the world are manufacturing these graduates at an apparently alarming rate, most of whom face a dismal employment market.[3] The job outlook is particularly grim in the humanities but also surprisingly bleak in science and engineering programs.

THE ETHICAL ISSUES

Why might it be an ethical problem for programs to continue to admit PhD students in large numbers when so few jobs are available? There are two issues. The first is the possible harm to PhD students themselves. By offering and promoting PhD programs structured largely to prepare future faculty members, universities are perpetuating a type of deceit, luring students onto a career path where up to 80% of the graduates hit a dead end. At the same time, universities often use these graduate students as a source for low-cost undergraduate teaching and for other forms of unglamorous academic labor. As Thomas H. Benton points out, this could all be seen as exploitation: "For universities, the impact of graduate programs on the lives of those students is an acceptable externality, like dumping toxins into a river."[4]

Beyond the harm to PhD students, the second issue concerns the economics of higher education, how universities allocate resources. A PhD program is expensive, requiring intensive faculty time and attention. The faculty currently teaching small doctoral seminars could be reassigned to teach undergraduates. Fewer adjuncts and funded graduate student positions would then be necessary, savings that could make undergraduate education more affordable and increase access for all students. Consequent gains in institutional efficiencies could be substantial.[5]

Both these problems pit the perceived interests of faculty members against the perceived well-being of graduate students, institutional efficiencies, and even the greater social good. Faculty members are often quite invested in their graduate programs that provide influence and status. Supervising graduate students is intellectually enriching work that can advance the vitality of a field by, for example, increasing classroom enrollments in highly specialized courses or by growing professional organizations, conferences, and other activity in a cherished discipline. Graduate faculty often care deeply about such things.

A number of solutions have been proposed for these ethical problems. The first solution involves "academic birth control," cutting back on the number of degree-granting programs. In many disciplines, "right sizing" would lead to a fairly drastic reduction in programs—at least eliminating the doctoral programs at regional universities and smaller institutions, and perhaps at some major research universities. After all, just a handful of PhD programs would be necessary to prepare research specialists in fields like history and philosophy. The potential savings to universities could be substantial. Another related option would be to significantly limit admissions into existing programs rather than reducing the number of programs.

A second proposed solution involves reenvisioning the PhD degree itself. Often this entails cutting back on the time and cost of graduate school, making it more flexible, less risky, and less focused on preparing students for the professoriate alone. A report by the Modern Language Association (2014) recommends a structure that allows students to realistically complete a PhD in five years with full funding for the duration of the program. It argues that dissertation projects should be rethought to connect with a wider range of intellectual interests and professional trajectories, with more training in teaching, pedagogy, and technology. PhD programs should help build student networks inside and outside academia. Together these reforms are intended to (1) expand the purpose of the PhD beyond simply preparing professional researchers and academics, (2) improve the quality of life for PhD students, and (3) limit the investment of time to complete the PhD. More efficient for the institution, these reforms also make the PhD degree less risky, more flexible, and more marketable outside of academia for students.

PROBLEMS WITH ACADEMIC BIRTH CONTROL

Of these two solutions, we should reject the option that involves academic birth control: eliminating departments or decreasing admissions. These options can be paternalistic. Paternalism, taking choices away from others because we believe it is in their best interest, connects more to the first ethical problem, that over-admitting is unfair to the students themselves. Some people see their personal flourishing as involving, in part, advanced study in and continued, even lifelong, engagement with an academic subject. Liberal societies allow people to make risky decisions (even bad economic ones) because this freedom respects the human ability to make choices, to think independently, and to follow different pathways through life. Consider whether we should limit the number who study art, music, or dance in high school or as university undergraduates. Although these pursuits rarely lead directly to a job in the field, they enrich areas of human life that should be open to personal exploration.

The academic birth control position overemphasizes the economic side of doctoral study and assumes the only purpose of a PhD is obtaining an academic job. Someone might legitimately pursue a PhD for many other reasons, however. Some might find advanced study useful in an already established career. Some might be seeking resources to help solve a particular social problem. Some might think that advanced study is intrinsically valuable and view a PhD as a project of self-development. Indeed, a PhD program might be an enriching chapter of one's life, valuable in itself and not for what comes after. It should be up to the individual to decide whether the costs and benefits—and risks—are worthwhile.

The objection to the self-enrichment argument is that, while people have the right to make bad choices or pursue self-development, the larger society is under no obligation to subsidize those choices, particularly given competing priorities such as university access and affordability. We would need to explain, then, why institutions of higher education should be the vehicles for these options rather than other options for self-enrichment available through the market. People may be passionate about, say, mastering barbecue, but helping them develop this talent is not a social obligation.

Four points challenge the objection to university support for projects of self-development. First, PhD programs feature technical expertise difficult to master through amateur study. Think of the differences between the study of physics and barbecue. While both subjects inspire passion as vehicles of growth and individual enrichment, one can learn plenty about barbecue from books, the internet, television shows, and so forth. Much can be learned about physics from public sources, too, but specialized training in that area requires intense study guided by experts and institutions dedicated to its mastery.

Second, advanced academic study introduces important public goods in several ways. The existence of graduate programs improves the quality of university departments. Engaging with PhD students, who are often more likely to question the status quo and more receptive to new ways of thinking, helps keep faculty honest and up to date. Moreover, faculty members across departments often work together with PhD students. Dissertation committees, for example, reveal interdisciplinary connections and common ground. PhD students, therefore, benefit university life, but realizing these benefits requires a critical mass of graduate students.

Another advantage for institutions is PhD student teaching. Although shifting from more knowledgeable tenured faculty to graduate students is in some ways a regrettable trend, here is a little secret rarely discussed in the debate about college teaching: PhD students are often exceptional teachers–with more energy, ideas, and ways of connecting with undergraduates, who are often closer to them in age. Indeed, one study suggests that undergraduate students are more likely to choose a major in an area where their first instructor was a graduate student.[6] PhD students, in short, bring real value to universities and are not simply draining resources.

Third, the practice of academic birth control will almost surely make graduate programs and the professoriate less diverse. Restricting the PhD to only certain elite programs and restricting admissions in those programs to only the very best will shrink their diversity. The few remaining slots would become highly competitive, and faculty would need to become highly selective. Fierce competition could promote hyper-attention to disciplinary norms and magnify certain problematic selection criteria. In such conditions, research suggests that faculty look for students most like themselves as the ultimate standard for admission and rely more heavily on dubious weeding-out mechanisms such as the GRE.[7]

The fourth reason to resist such restrictions involves larger societal health, namely, creating what we could call a knowledgeable and critical "culture of substance." I admittedly do not know how to bring any evidence to bear on this speculative argument, but its central idea is this: our cultural life improves when we have individuals who have undertaken advanced study in important topics. People with deep knowledge of the arts, humanities, and sciences enrich our cultural conversation, whether those people are academics or whether they are citizens, parents, business executives, or community leaders. To claim that PhD programs help build such a culture is perhaps more an expression of faith in education than an argument. If we lack this faith, however, then our issue may be with the mission of universities more broadly than with PhD programs specifically.

In addition to establishing a larger social justification for nonvocational PhD programs, these arguments suggest, in response to the second ethical problem, that universities should be wary in cutting PhD admission for the purpose of resource redistribution. They also suggest that the dilemma of graduate admissions is not simply a conflict between self-promoting faculty, obsessed with status and legacy, and the well-being of students. Although faculty self-centeredness does exist, a critical mass of students engaging in doctoral study produce legitimate individual and social goods. The tension, then, is between two opposing moral goods rather than merely between faculty self-interest and morality. Eliminating the conflict between these different moral goods becomes the task. That is, we should proceed with doctoral admissions but in an ethically transformed way.

TRANSFORMING PhD ADMISSIONS: INFORMED CONSENT

I have argued that limiting graduate study to smaller numbers of students is problematic. Many current practices, however, also prevent students from making good decisions about graduate school. Rather than limiting PhD admissions, then, we should instead try to develop an ethics of admission. Under what circumstances is it justifiable to admit students into PhD programs with risky future employment prospects? Of relevance here is the notion of informed consent: individuals must agree to interventions administered by professionals that affect their lives. Valued for several reasons, informed consent is important to protect the welfare of individuals, who are themselves the best judges of what constitutes and promotes their welfare. Informed consent also helps establish or restore trust in social institutions.[8] When a social institution tramples the preferences of individuals under their care, trust is broken, making the organization less able to fulfill its role. Finally, informed consent is important to preserve autonomy, the right of individuals to make their own decisions about how to live.

What does it mean to be informed? Developed after World War II, the Nuremburg Code states that an individual should "have sufficient knowledge and comprehension of the elements of the subject matter involved, as to enable him to make an understanding and enlightened decision."[9] Note here the emphasis on knowledge and comprehension and not simply on disclosure of risks. Fuller and more robust understanding is needed before consent can be considered valid. Surely, lying about pertinent facts involved with a risky decision constitutes a violation of informed consent, but so too does non-lying deceit that intentionally or unintentionally gives a false impression. Emotional manipulation, such as putting positive news before negative news, or emphasizing positive news over negative realities in other subtle ways, may also violate informed consent.

The authors of *A History and Theory of Informed Consent* develop a conception of "substantial understanding" as the professional gold standard.[10] Full understanding of a medical procedure, for example, is generally not needed and may even impede understanding through information overload. A patient need not know the name of a particular instrument required to make a certain incision, for instance. Information "material to the person's decision" to authorize a procedure is necessary, however.[11] The role that subjectivity plays here is notable: what professionals are required to disclose depends on the values, needs, and interests of the subject. This extends beyond that which would directly impact a decision, the causal efficacy of the information, to what people would like to know. Although patients may not base a decision about surgery on the degree of expected scarring, many would still like to know this information.

Obtaining informed consent first involves a "core disclosure." Core disclosure includes (a) what individuals usually consider material in making decisions, (b) what the professional believes is material, and (c) what needs to be said to establish the conditions for consent. Beyond that, though, the core disclosure is given only to "initiate the communication process necessary for substantial understanding."[12] The professional's focus is not simply to provide facts but also to find out what questions are important to the patient and to establish a sense of trust and openness: "Professionals would do well to end their traditional preoccupation with disclosure and instead ask questions, elicit concerns and interests of the patient or subject, and establish a climate that encourages the patient or subject to ask questions."[13] Answering these individualized questions constitutes the second disclosure, the "subjective disclosure."

What might graduate programs include in their core disclosure to prospective students? Given the harsh realities of the academic job market, employment constitutes a major risk. Of course, many students rightly ask about the ability of this or that program to place graduates in academic jobs. But answering these questions may not give students the necessary information concerning larger trends in a given field. Students should be informed not only of past successes but also of current trends. Graduate programs avoid full disclosure of employment realities in many ways: They may brag about successes while deemphasizing or hiding the cases where students did not get faculty jobs. Or, alternatively, unemployed students may be blamed for not working hard enough. Core disclosure should eschew evasions or distortions.

Other items of information should also be part of the core disclosure. Applicants should, for example, understand if job prospects differ by specialization within a program. If graduates only get jobs after spending years in adjunct positions, this should be explained. If only students with a long list of publications in prestigious journals find jobs, they should be informed of this and know that extraordinary sacrifices (and some luck) might be required to succeed on the job market. Applicants should know about any characteristics important on the job market—particularly if the program itself does not develop or provide these characteristics. Consider, for example, the field of education, where job seekers often need K–12 teaching credentials and school experience to succeed in the job market in higher education. This is not something that PhD programs provide.

What else should be part of the core disclosure? The job market is not the only thing that students should know about. Students need to understand what to expect of the experience itself. Suppose we grant the idea that pursuing a PhD will not always lead to an academic career but might still be worthwhile as a project of individual or professional growth. If we grant this (as we should), then the lived experience of the PhD program should be disclosed and clearly understood by the applicant. Applicants should also know how much funding they should expect, for how long, and what they must do to maintain their funded positions. They should understand the cost of living in the prospective location and the realistic timeline to graduation.

Applicants should also have some idea about the quality of their lives: Will they have a robust student community, or will they be toiling away in relative solitude? What is involved, exactly, with their teaching or research assignments? How many hours will be expected of them? How much interaction with their faculty advisors can they realistically expect? What sort of advising relationship can the potential advisee expect (close and friendly, distant and professional, etc.)? All of this should be offered to the students up front as part of making an informed decision. Meetings with current program students are often helpful in helping applicants grasp the nature of the experience they are to expect.

In addition to the core disclosure, subjective disclosure should address the specific needs and questions of individual applicants. The core disclosure should provide opportunities to discuss topics in more detail or introduce new topics. Formal interviews are important, but subjective disclosure depends on moments of genuine communication in a context of trust and comfort difficult to achieve. Applicants trying to impress program faculty may not be willing to open up with personal questions that might betray a potential weakness—a challenging family situation, perhaps. Such questions will not always come up in one-off interviews, particularly over the phone or by web-conferencing. While still not ideal, campus visits can play an essential role in building a minimal relationship that allows for personal questions to be raised.

Informed consent should be an ongoing feature of the graduate school experience. As high as 50%, much of the attrition in U.S. doctoral programs occurs after years spent in the program when the opportunity costs of dropping out have increased. There should be various decision and exit points, particularly early in a student's program. Perhaps mid-program certificates can be created to document certain competencies, so that student time has not been completely lost from an economic perspective. Rather than stigmatized or ridiculed, earlier exits should be honored and respected.

PhDs WITH A FLEXIBLE FUTURE

It may be tempting to think that the responsibility of PhD programs to their students ends with the notion of informed consent: if students know exactly what they are getting into, then they alone are responsible for what happens. This is a mistake—student preferences change, and graduate programs should account for that fact. Sometimes self-knowledge changes. Some students will grow to want academic jobs even though that was not their intended path in the beginning; others who thought they wanted to be tenured professors will decide to leave academia. PhD programs have a responsibility to respond to these natural and unavoidable shifts. Moreover, information provided to students about the labor market or the graduate program itself may be incomplete or outdated by the time students graduate. Since both student and context will change, graduate faculty cannot place all the ethical weight on students' initial choice to matriculate, however informed that decision.

An ethical graduate program will create alternate pathways that allow for a flexible future by providing a host of useful soft skills, such as writing, speaking, overall communication, teamwork, teaching, and conceptual and empirical analysis. While a doctoral program may not lead directly to a marketable credential, it may still impart proficiencies valuable across a range of occupations, so time spent in a PhD program is not simply time lost, economically speaking. Graduates should be encouraged to think about what they do in relationship to other economic sectors such as the business and nonprofit worlds.

> PhDs typically have an exceptional ability to organize information. They understand the need to read and learn widely and deeply in order to understand something (including looking behind the immediate subject area), and they can carry out that task with minimal supervision. They can manage long projects and work on their own—and of course their dissertations demonstrate their ability to finish these projects.[14]

A graduate program should teach students how to describe these skills on a general résumé. To that end, as mentioned earlier, such skills could be codified with official certificate programs in, for example, "data analysis" or "institutional research." Programs can offer additional opportunities to develop marketable skills beyond what students acquire through their normal studies. For example, students can play leadership roles on teams or supervise staff or other students. These soft skills may not be enough for gainful employment, but they will be a solid asset when paired with other types of training programs such as entrepreneurship or web design.

The culture of unrelenting professional socialization that too often exists in academia should be challenged. By this, I mean the different ways that professors send the message that students should be aiming for tier-one academic jobs and that anything less constitutes a professional failure. The application process itself encourages students to present themselves as potentially successful researchers and scholars, not teachers or public intellectuals. Professors reinforce this old-fashioned training in different ways, promoting a focus on what is of value in a narrow specialty but not in the larger world. Faculty urge, for example, exhaustive dissertations devoted to highly focused and esoteric topics. Professors carefully track and hold up as exemplars students who attain prominent university positions, and not so much those who have gone on to do other important things, perhaps outside academia altogether. Fighting these aspects of narrow socialization is necessary to make the PhD more relatable to and more valuable in the outside world.

INCREASING THE SOCIAL AND INSTITUTIONAL VALUE OF PhD PROGRAMS

Another reason for PhD reform harkens back to my earlier arguments for the social value of doctoral work. Beyond preparing future faculty, PhD programs have the potential to enrich university and cultural life and are not simply expensive playgrounds for self-development. Graduate faculty have an obligation to actualize the social and institutional values that arguably justify the existence of these programs. If they do not live up to these responsibilities, then their resources should indeed be removed and redistributed across the university to improve access and affordability.

How well PhD graduates enrich social life and further a culture of substance is a measure of their program's worth. Students should therefore be given opportunities to see how their academic work connects to the ongoing social drama around them. They should be taught to write for public audiences and not just for academic committees, and they should be able to communicate in whatever media is relevant to their training—film, the internet, graphic novels, and so on. Students should be encouraged to focus on less specialized and less technical research projects. Research topics should be evaluated not only for their scholarly contribution but also for their ability to capture the attention and imagination of audiences outside of their narrow specialty.

Other opportunities to engage with the larger social world should be an important part of PhD reform. When we think of service learning, we often think of the undergraduate experience. Yet engaging actively in community life, connecting with problems of concern to the larger community, will also augment the social value of doctoral programs as it increases their economic value and yields more applied research and scholarship.

CONCLUSION

This essay argues that academic birth control is an inadequate response to the overproduction of PhDs. Limiting the number of programs and admissions can be paternalistic and often wrongly assumes that achieving an academic research position is the only purpose of PhD programs. An important part of the flourishing life for some individuals, doctoral programs can enrich already existing careers. Limiting production will necessarily make the PhD corps less diverse, decrease the quality of university departments, and emaciate cultural life. Still, changes are necessary. Graduate faculty have the responsibility to maintain continuous informed consent, involving core disclosure and subjective dialogue that help ensure student understanding of the job market along with the realities of life as a graduate student. In addition, because both the students and the economic landscape change over time, graduate faculty should make the PhD more marketable, helping students develop skills and credentials useful to life outside of academe. Finally, faculty have the responsibility to create and maintain PhD programs that realize their potential for enriching social life. All these factors are necessary in a complete consideration of an ethics of admission.

Part XI

STUDENTS

Chapter 23

The Goals of Campus Discipline
David A. Hoekema

Considering the system of student discipline in its broadest application, ranging from physical or sexual assault to stolen textbooks and offensive graffiti, it is helpful to identify three distinct goals that a system of campus discipline seeks to achieve. In both practice and theory they are separable yet closely related. Measures that advance one of the three are likely to contribute to the others as well.

TO PREVENT EXPLOITATION AND HARM

The first goal of a system of student discipline is to prevent exploitation and harm to students. Policies and procedures related to student conduct should protect students so far as is reasonably possible from others who would prey on their vulnerability if given the opportunity. This is the foundation for rules prohibiting many kinds of serious misconduct such as theft, physical violence, sexual assault, verbal harassment and denigration, and sale of mind-altering drugs. Academic dishonesty is also a form of exploitation. A student who copies another's work not only deprives the source of proper credit for her work but also undermines the essential but fragile system of academic evaluation in the institution. By enacting and enforcing policies against exploitation and harm, the university seeks to protect students against others' malevolence.

What is the moral ground for a university's concern with preventing harm? No more and no less than our fundamental obligation to protect others from injury, especially in circumstances in which another is vulnerable to harm that could be averted by one's words and actions. Every ethical system recognizes this basic duty to prevent harm, whether it then traces the ultimate ground of this obligation to a Kantian conception of autonomy and universalizability, an Aristotelian concept of virtuous habits forming a virtuous character, a theological concept of the respect due to all created persons, or a morality based on the weighing of good and bad consequences.

Those who govern an institution such as a university have the same duty to protect others that applies to them as individuals. But their official capacity to set policies and direct practices on campus greatly enlarges the consequences of their actions and therefore their responsibility to act. Of course, it is impossible to prevent all harmful and hurtful acts committed by members of an academic community or of any other community. But a carefully framed and rigorously enforced policy regarding physical assault, for example, may deter many attacks that would have occurred under circumstances of institutional laxness and inattention.

The primary goal of campus rules of conduct is to prevent students from harming fellow students. The reason is not that students are more prone to misconduct than outsiders. Indeed, they are surely less likely to injure each other intentionally than are a random collection of individuals, since their shared status as students contributes to a sense of common purpose and their shared participation in campus life makes them something more than strangers to each other. Only students, however, are directly answerable to the institutional code of conduct. Campus disciplinary officers can impose potent disincentives to deter students from harming others and a range of sanctions if they do. Their authority over outsiders is far more limited.

Note the overlap, but also a great deal of difference, between what is legitimately prohibited in a campus environment and what is prohibited by law. Actions liable to criminal prosecution—rape, assault, theft, embezzlement—are not the primary focus of a university disciplinary code. When these crimes occur on campus, administrators must cooperate with local authorities in conducting an appropriate investigation. Universities should remind students that living on campus is not living outside the law. Students gain no immunity from criminal law and surrender none of the protections of those charged with breaking the law.

Prevention of crime should be a priority, all the same, in other aspects of the life of a university. Building design, campus lighting and landscaping, student transportation options, and the work of campus safety officers can greatly enhance the safety of students and reduce the incidence of violent crime. This is not the domain of disciplinary codes but an important contribution to their effectiveness.

Students are especially vulnerable to some sorts of harm that fall outside—or just at the borders of—the criminal code. The possibility that one's work will be stolen and used dishonestly, for example, is an inherent risk in any academic enterprise. Undergraduates, graduate students, and established researchers sometimes succumb to this temptation. Some institutions, including many elite undergraduate colleges and the nation's military academies, seek to combat plagiarism through promulgation of an honor code to which all students must subscribe. Others disseminate detailed guidelines that distinguish legitimate from illegitimate borrowing in academic research and writing. Studies that I reviewed in writing my book on student conduct indicated that neither system was, in general, more effective than the other. A newly drafted honor code, however, seems to be less effective than one that has long been part of campus culture.

Consider too the issue of acquaintance rape. It is by no means unique to university communities, but the close personal relationships and powerful peer pressures that obtain in college, together with ready availability of alcohol, heighten the danger of such assault. Whenever one person is induced to engage in sexual activity through coercion or threats, a sexual assault has occurred. But campus cultures too often discount the testimony of victims and give too much credence to an assailant's assertion that the act was entirely consensual.

The rules for responding to allegations of sexual harassment in educational settings have become a contentious issue as three U.S. administrations sought to interpret the requirements of Title IX of the Higher Education Act, which guarantees equal treatment and protection against harassment. In brief, the Department of Education under President Obama issued guidelines for investigating and adjudicating allegations of abuse that were intended to uphold victims' rights and remove impractical evidence requirements, but under President Trump new guidelines were issued that set a higher standard for evidence of wrongdoing and allowed alleged perpetrators to question anyone testifying against them. Under President Biden, as a major policy review moves forward, the last requirement was revoked in August 2021. Universities will no longer be required to allow the accused to cross-examine the complainant, and more extensive revisions are expected soon.[1]

In many cases of plagiarism and acquaintance rape, no laws have been broken, so victims cannot call on the police or the courts to come to their assistance. Copyright laws are not intended to apply to unpublished work by students. Criminal penalties for rape are severe, but the circumstances of acquaintance rape make it difficult for the victim to prove that an assault has occurred and easy for the guilty to escape punishment. Institutions have a special obligation to address the issues of cheating and sexual assault because there is little likelihood of legal redress for these harms imposed by some students on other students.

The same is true of the prevention of alcohol abuse and illegal drug use. No academic community can hope to be entirely free from such practices, which are widespread on campus and off. But the intense social pressures that bear on students in a campus setting need to be balanced by clear and firm campus rules, backed by effective measures of enforcement and consistent penalties when violated.

The aim of averting harm is inevitably to a certain extent paternalistic. The university no longer claims to be a moral arbiter standing in loco parentis, an institutional chaperone guiding young men and women on the path of virtue. With rare exceptions, no institution today wants to reclaim this role, and in any case, students would not tolerate it. The college's concern, however, is not limited to protecting students against harm done to them by others. It extends also to protection of students against themselves, antiquated and condescending as that phrase may sound today.

The harm of drug and alcohol abuse is suffered primarily by the individual who engages in such behaviors, not inflicted on others. All the same, it is a serious form of harm and a legitimate concern of a university, not merely because it is likely to be a contributing factor in other graver harms, such as physical injury and, especially in the case of alcohol, sexual assault. Diminished capacity for academic work and for responsible behavior due to such substance abuse is itself a harm to the individual and to others that the institution should seek to prevent.

An institution places itself in a position very similar to that of a parent in saying to students: We seek to protect you from grave harm, even when you bring it upon yourself and would suffer it willingly. The goal of disciplinary rules in this instance is to deter students from acting in a way that amounts to an assault against themselves and a diminishment of their future prospects. In my study of student discipline I suggested, with tongue in cheek, that institutions that want to disavow their role in loco parentis as a vestige of the distant past might adopt a change to the metaphor. Consider the difference between advice given by a parent and that offered by a grandparent, for example, which is likely to be less directive and more empathetic. Or think about how one might intervene to dissuade a niece or nephew from making foolish choices, knowing that one cannot directly tell them how to behave but can expect them to consider one's counsel seriously. Perhaps today the university should stand *in loco avi* (in place of a grandfather), then, or *in loco avunculi* (in place of an uncle). Although not as familiar as the parental variant, these Latin phrases may be more appropriate.

So much for prevention of harm. To acknowledge this first goal and no others, however, would be to confuse the function of the entire system of student discipline with that of a campus security department. Colleges and universities also pursue two additional goals no less important to the life of the institution.

TO PROMOTE AN ATMOSPHERE OF DIALOGUE AND DEBATE

A second essential goal of student conduct rules is to sustain an environment conducive to free discussion and mutual learning. The campus is not merely a place where students can go about their lives and studies relatively free from fear of assault and exploitation. It is also characterized by free and open exchange of ideas, arguments, and ideologies. A university is a place for vigorous debate of issues important to students and their communities, where ruling orthodoxies confront new evidence and new interpretations. Even one's most cherished beliefs and ideals are open to challenge and possible revision in a healthy academic environment.

The moral ground of this second purpose is different from that underlying the first, but it too is a principle widely embraced: A healthy community grants its members as broad a range of personal and political freedom as is consistent with respect for the rights and the liberties of others. Although similar ideals of religious and intellectual freedom motivated the founding of the United States, they have frequently been compromised because of the pressures of social conformity. From their inception, universities have held themselves up as beacons for a broader vision of freedom. Yet there is a continual struggle on many campuses between the ideal of free and open discourse and the tendency of institutions to adopt and enforce an official ideological vision.

Cultural critics on the political right make this point frequently and stridently. They allege that universities pay only lip service to academic freedom and open dialogue while imposing a stultifying intellectual orthodoxy. Instructors who venerate Marx and Foucault and scorn Friedman and Hayek, they claim, force-feed students a diet of socialism, secularism, and radical feminism. Conservative voices are silenced or scorned.

Are these allegations accurate? Surveys of the political leanings of college and university faculty do indeed show a tilt to the left but not an absence of voices on the right. In a 2006 survey, 44% of faculty respondents identified as liberal, 46% as moderate, and 9% as conservative.[2] Periodic surveys of undergraduate faculty conducted by the Higher Education Research Institute at UCLA show, over recent decades, greater numbers calling themselves "liberal" and "far left" than "conservative" and "far right." In the 1990s, the largest number selected "moderate/middle of the road," followed by a shift to the left and then, in the most recent surveys, a shift back to the center. One notable finding in 2016–2017 was a substantial increase in those choosing "encouraging students to think and act critically" as an important priority.[3]

Allegations of liberal bias also highlight campus agitation against controversial speakers. In 2016 conservative watchdog groups counted forty-three incidents in which students and faculty demanded "disinvitation" of speakers, most of them identified with the political right. But only half these efforts succeeded. Moreover, according to a nonpolitical organization, by 2018 the number of such incidents had dropped to just nine, five of them successful. The organization also noted that, where twenty-eight faculty members had been dismissed or demoted in 2017 for inappropriate political speech, that number dropped to just eight in 2018, four of them targeted by conservatives and three by liberals.[4]

Conservative perceptions of a liberal stranglehold on campus are unfounded. And yet the right's critique of campus culture serves as an important reminder that free and open discourse requires active monitoring and vigilant defense. On every campus, some factions seek from time to time to silence others, and the danger that a ruling orthodoxy will stifle dissent is never wholly absent. Claims that a particular party line has gained the ascendency on the nation's campuses, whether that be an ideology of the left or the right, Marxism or libertarianism, should provoke our skepticism. All the same, the atmosphere of openness and readiness to listen to others who hold sharply different views is a rare and fragile thing, not just on campus but in other communities as well. It needs to be nurtured and defended against social and political pressures that threaten it.

The goal of upholding freedom of thought and expression mandates broad discretion for students—and faculty members—in planning debates, inviting speakers, publishing opinions in campus newspapers, and the like. Some student codes of conduct underscore the importance of these provisions by including a formal "bill of student rights" in their discipline code, setting out the extent of students' freedom to speak and act.

The goal of facilitating open discourse entails another objective with which it might appear initially to be in conflict: minimizing the incidence of abusive and degrading speech and writing. Conflict does occur between these two objectives, but it need not. If carelessly and vaguely written, a speech code intended to prohibit racial and gender abuse can cast a pall over discussion of controversial issues and deter open expression of unpopular ideas. Disciplinary rules need to target precisely those rare sorts of abusive speech that cast some out of the community of discourse and treat them as less than human. If narrowly worded and carefully framed, hate speech policies contribute to an environment conducive to learning and constructive discourse, barring the door only to those who by their very choice of words would exclude others on the basis of race, gender identity, or sexual orientation.

Upholding an atmosphere conducive to free and honest discourse has implications in what might appear to be an unrelated realm, that of on-campus housing. Clear rules, consistently applied, concerning alcohol use and overnight guests in residence halls contribute to an ethos in which students' social and academic lives are closely integrated, each supporting and advancing the other. Absence of such rules, on the other hand, or their effective absence owing to lax or inconsistent enforcement, makes residence halls essentially useless for purposes of study, especially in evening hours. On far more campuses than the admissions brochures and student life administrators acknowledge, drinking and partying and hooking up in dorm rooms effectively opens a wide gulf between the academic enterprise and the social community in which students live. Not only does it impede academic study, it also inhibits thoughtful political and intellectual discourse.

What sorts of regulations are appropriate in student housing? The traditions and the character of a particular institution make it difficult to generalize, as does the architecture of student housing. A building with a separate wing for study, well away from social gathering spaces, poses fewer challenges than a complex of small rooms. The parietal rules of earlier generations rested on moral dogmas that students might have rejected if asked. But we need not invoke an outmoded moralism to justify promoting a healthy environment for learning.

In effect, student life staff today are invoking old means to new ends. No campus administrators claim the prerogative of acting in loco parentis to prohibit drinking and cohabitation today. But if they do not set some rules for student life—acting *in loco avunculi,* like a concerned but not controlling uncle—then students must live in what are merely and literally "dormitories," places for sleeping and partying but not for studying or serious conversation. To leave students to behave as they will without restriction in on-campus housing is not merely to set aside the moralistic ambitions of an earlier era but to compromise the obligation of the university to maintain an atmosphere for students in which study and learning can flourish.

An interesting trend has emerged recently in campus housing: more and more campuses offer options for "substance-free housing," residence halls whose residents promise not to use tobacco, alcohol, or recreational drugs. One source lists forty institutions offering this option, implicitly acknowledging that discipline codes alone do not guarantee an environment conducive to study, and no doubt there are many more. I have not found any studies assessing the effectiveness of offering such options—how many students choose them and how well they comply with the rules. On online forums, some students say they are glad to be in environments free from wild parties, but others say the wildest parties on their campuses tend to happen in the supposedly substance-free halls. Clearly much depends both on student compliance and on institutional oversight.

TO NURTURE A SENSE OF COMMUNITY

A third essential goal of student conduct regulation is to instill a sense of mutual responsibility and moral community in students. This third aim is both more comprehensive and more controversial than the first two. Some would reject it as extending beyond the proper function of a modern university, which should stick to academics and not meddle in the private affairs and personal relationships of its students. But to neglect this third purpose would be an abdication a critical responsibility of the college and university.

Formation of character was once upheld as a central, if not the primary, purpose of higher education. This tradition is honored rhetorically in the preamble to many a college catalog, where the language of character, citizenship, and moral community is laid on with a trowel. Yet today few colleges, and even fewer universities, take their own lofty rhetoric seriously in planning their programs, hiring new faculty, or shaping general education requirements.

A typical college of the eighteenth or nineteenth century made the behavior of students its business and sought to inculcate moral virtue, which a majority of institutions grounded in religious orthodoxy of one sort or another. In the 1860s, to cite one example, the student conduct code at Harvard was forty pages long. Many college presidents of that era taught a required course in ethics for graduating seniors.

A typical college or university of the twenty-first century proclaims its lofty goals of training responsible and engaged citizens and promoting a sense of moral and social accountability only in the first few pages of the catalog and in fundraising appeals to alumni, while its actions carry another message entirely. I do not intend to suggest that moral growth does not occur in universities, of course. Every issue of every alumni magazine highlights glowing testimonials to the inspiring example of instructors who opened students' eyes to the pressing problems of the nation and the world, leading them into careers in public health or community development. Faculty and their employers can take pride in such stories.

But these stories may not reflect the operating principles of the institution. Indeed, they may result from the readiness of some faculty and administrators to defy an institutional culture of individualism and careerism. At many institutions the core message that can be discerned, in faint letters behind the inflated rhetoric of marketing brochures, might be summarized thus: "We hire excellent scholars for the faculty, we maintain a fine library and provide access to a world of online resources, we cherish our sports teams' trophies, we fill the flower beds each year for parents' weekend, and we sincerely hope that our students will turn out all right."

Whether graduating seniors are paragons of virtue or cynical opportunists is a matter largely beyond the control of the institution and its faculty. Moral character has been largely shaped before students begin university studies, after all. Even in college, other factors—family, peer judgment, mass media, and personal reflection—are likely to exercise a more profound influence on students' ethical commitments and sensibilities than will any acts or policies of the institution. For most students, a few faculty members will stand out, even a decade after graduation, as models of both intellectual and ethical integrity, and I do not mean to understate the effectiveness of faculty-student interaction both in and out of the classroom. But matters such as these cannot be effectively mandated by institutional rules or policies. The goal of producing ethical and engaged citizens is simply not realistically attainable by any institution, whatever the preamble to the college catalog may boast.

All the same, the university can and should seek to create a campus atmosphere of respect, openness, critical discourse, and mutual recognition of both rights and responsibilities. Students learn quickly, as much from unspoken signals as from handbooks and speeches, the limits of acceptable behavior. An instructor who overlooks rampant cheating on the first test of the semester cannot expect better behavior on the next one. An institution that takes no effective steps to prevent and punish alcohol abuse tells its students by its inaction that, notwithstanding the lofty ideals in the catalog, they are students at a party school. Conversely, if cribbing and excessive drinking meet firm and consistent discipline, students learn that they will be held responsible for their academic work and for their actions. And the behavior of administrators and faculty members speaks louder than the conduct code.

When students regularly observe their instructors engaging in spirited and open-minded debates with each other and with students over important moral and social issues of the day, they learn that the institution expects more than transmission and acquisition of knowledge. When a controversy over campus policies or governance is resolved through consultation and cooperation among students, staff, and faculty, students' moral education is advanced, not by a required senior class, or a student handbook, or a presidential dictum ending the debate, but by seeing how the campus community functions. Even in cases where resolution is not reached and controversy continues, the character of a diverse campus community is evident in its modes of discourse.

Modern societies regard moral choices as fundamentally individual decisions. While this ideology has made indispensable contributions to the establishment and protection of a broad range of personal and political liberties, it is grossly inadequate as a description of our moral life and action. We make our choices in social and cultural contexts. Morality is both learned and exercised, above all, in relation to others. This is why a collaborative response to the challenges that confront a campus community is so vitally important: the community itself is the context in which morality arises, is articulated, and is put into practice.

Consider a hypothetical example. Suppose a crisis erupts when members of a fraternity taunt and harass transgender students. Their behavior elicits protests by student groups that serve as advocates for LGBTQ+ students, and then those protests provoke counterprotests from other fraternities. What should be done? Should the students responsible for the initial incidents of harassment be punished? Or should students work out their differences without interference from student life staff?

To allow such behavior to pass without comment suggests that the university either approves or tolerates behavior that falls far below a minimum standard of mutual respect. To do and say nothing is in effect to accept the fraternity members' judgment that trans students are not deserving members of the student body. But disciplinary action alone, punishing the individuals involved without addressing what lies behind offensive behaviors, is also inadequate.

In a campus community that promotes mutual respect and open dialogue, such an incident might yield a process of deliberation and consultation leading to action more wide-ranging and more lasting than sanctions for a few individuals. In discussions that bring diverse viewpoints into conversation with each other, transgender students and their allies would gain a wider audience for their concerns, not just about isolated incidents of harassment but also about difficulties they face in classrooms, residence halls, and locker rooms. Leaders and members of fraternities would be challenged to identify aspects of their past behavior and rhetoric that made misbehavior more likely and to undertake changes in the future. Everyone who attends to this discussion on campus would learn more about the experience of those who face abuse because of others' insecurities and fears.

A process in which all voices are heard, and then paths for future cooperation are mapped out, serves as a concrete demonstration that the campus community can face and resolve its problems. The goals of freedom of expression, freedom of association, and regard for the vulnerable may come into conflict. Balancing them requires patience and wisdom. When students participate in or observe a process that airs differences and finds common ground, they do not simply learn to respect differences and stop shouting insults. They learn what it means to be a member of a moral community.

I do not mean to suggest that every incident of petty harassment warrants such a full-court response. Context is crucial. An isolated incident on a campus where LGBTQ+ students feel fully a part of the community may offer no reason for alarm or for a public response. At the other extreme, if a pattern of repeated and damaging attacks on a campus minority becomes evident on campus, what is needed is a prompt and firm disciplinary response, prompting measures such as suspension and restitution, not an extended dialogue between offenders and victims. In incidents that fall between these extremes, however, what is initially no more than an unpleasant incident can be the catalyst for a vivid demonstration of how a healthy moral community on campus resolves problems.

Unique in American society, the community of learning that exists on campus—both intellectual and moral—is threatened from within and without. The suspicions of legislatures and anxious parents, the economic and political agendas of private and public donors, and the social-media carping of uninformed critics all seek to limit campus freedoms. No less grave a threat to the health of the campus community are the temptations that draw faculty and students themselves into a narrow vision of higher education, lapsing into individualism, careerism, and social and political apathy.

Nurturing an effective community conducive to moral growth is a vital third goal of student discipline systems, in addition to the prevention of harm and the facilitation of free and open dialogue. It is a worthwhile exercise on any campus to assess the effectiveness of rules, enforcement provisions, and daily practices in advancing each of these three objectives.

Chapter 24

The Social Costs of a College Education

Anthony Simon Laden

What does a college education cost students? Familiar expenditures include time, effort, tuition, and related debt. In return, students receive an education along with some mix of valuable credentials, meaningful experiences, and increased earning potential. Consider, however, the unanticipated or hidden costs some students encounter:

> For four months I attended lectures on geography and history and politics. I learned about Margaret Thatcher and the Thirty-Eighth Parallel and the Cultural Revolution; I learned about parliamentary politics and electoral systems around the world. I learned about the Jewish diaspora and the strange history of *The Protocols of the Elders of Zion*. By the end of the semester, the world felt big, and it was hard to imagine returning to the mountain, to a kitchen, or even to a piano in the room next to the kitchen.[1]
>
> The biggest challenge [of being at Renowned] is the pressure to become one of them. When you come here, you become one of the elite. . . . People forget where they come from. They live here for four months and they're not living at home and they forget what it means. Then, after four years, they don't go back home. They go to New York. They're just consumed! Forty percent of people go into consulting after graduation. Forty percent of people don't come into Renowned thinking of consulting. People are transformed.[2]
>
> It was almost like I was given the choice . . . to sacrifice relationships for being able to survive college.[3]

College transformed each of these students, making it hard for them to go back home. Being unable to return or return in the same way to even a difficult home is a genuine cost, one paid both by the students themselves and the families and communities they left. Unlike the price of tuition, these costs are rarely announced up front and cannot be paid by others or waived by the college that may ultimately prepare students for a life that takes them far from home.

This essay explores these social costs, how a college education imposes them, and how colleges can help students bear them. It does so by examining an education's effect on trust. Shaping both our knowledge and our social ties, trust helps explain why certain forms of education impose these social costs. A college education aims to enhance a student's capacities as a knower, what might be called epistemic standing. Colleges do this not merely by expanding a student's storehouse of knowledge or teaching a set of specialized intellectual skills. Colleges also reshape student "trust networks" as epistemic bases for genuine knowledge. But sometimes this reshaping affects social networks as well in ways that incur social costs.

Very different groups of students face these costs, including those whose experiences have been the touchstone of varied criticisms of college. Some religious, conservative, and rural families worry that colleges indoctrinate students into a foreign, left-wing ideology. Working-class, poor, first-generation, and traditionally underrepresented students argue that colleges are often unaccommodating or downright hostile environments for them. Despite the diversity of these groups, they share a concern that these institutions may change whom and what they trust. Identifying this common ground does not deny significant differences among these communities but rather helps us think differently about how to move forward. What follows is a description of the obstacles in question and recommendations for confronting them.

CHAINS AND NETWORKS OF TRUST

I normally trust my senses to provide information about the physical world. I don't try to verify what they tell me or if they are functioning properly. Similarly, I trust the information I get from various instruments, devices, and people. As I go about my day, I believe what my watch says about the time and what my search engine says about where to find things on the internet. I typically follow the directions of a stranger in an unfamiliar city without hesitation or consulting my map. Trusting these sources of information involves adopting what philosopher C. Thi Nguyen calls "an unquestioning attitude."[4]

Trust of this form plays an outsized role in the kinds of knowledge that is the bread and butter of college coursework. My knowledge of U.S. history or theoretical physics comes from reading books and attending lectures. Most of what is in those books and lectures relies on other, perhaps more specialized, sources that also rely on additional sources. Further knowledge mediates even conclusions drawn from basic archival and experimental evidence. Experiments often rely on machinery whose workings the scientist may not understand or question, or on other experimental work that regards this as evidence for that. Treating an archival document as evidence involves processes of authentication and continuity of storage. Trust linking these chains of support makes information at their ends usable. Because I trust my sources of knowledge who trust their sources of knowledge and so on, their information directly informs my further thinking.

Chains of trust then intersect and work together to form broad trust networks that shape what we know and how we add to this knowledge. If I believe a newspaper report about the rate of economic growth in the United States in the last quarter, it is not because I personally know and trust the reporter or that I have independent grounds for believing the figure. I accept what is reported because I trust in a complex background network of institutions and practices: those that hire, educate, and credential reporters, fact checkers, and editors, as well as those that collect data and develop theories for interpreting it. In all these cases, watchdog agencies that call attention to mistakes along the chain of transmission and determination bolster my trust. I believe that there are no such mistakes because I have not been alerted to any. If my trust in any of these institutions or individuals wavers, this erodes my confidence in the reported figure, which I might question more closely or stop believing altogether.

Trusting is an unavoidable feature of human life. We all inhabit some set or other of trust networks. The difference between a college graduate trained in critical thinking who relies on government agencies, scientific bodies, and university expertise and a person without such training who relies on social media, neighbors, family members, and religious authorities is not that one forms beliefs on the basis of trust while the other does not. The difference lies in what and whom each trusts.

Trusting offers others direct and unmediated access to our thinking process, thoughts, and psyche. Like other forms of intimacy, trusting leaves us vulnerable to mistakes, bad judgments, and manipulation, among other things. Like other networks of intimacy, our trust networks also situate us socially. This connection between trust and intimacy goes both ways. We trust those in our social networks and by extension what and whom they trust, giving these people an outsized influence on the shape of our trust networks. Also, and as important, the shape of our trust networks determines who can be in our social networks. Two people with vastly divergent trust networks will have difficulty talking to one another or relating in ways that foster and sustain community. They won't just disagree; we can form close social ties to those with whom we disagree. Rather, they will find each other inscrutable because each works from a different set of accepted facts.

GOALS OF A COLLEGE EDUCATION

Trusted sources of information appear and disappear through all sorts of processes, some reflective and critical, some not. Because network sources and configurations are not all equally trustworthy, we improve our capacity as knowers by improving our ability to discern trustworthiness. A college education works by reshaping and restructuring student trust networks to improve them epistemically. Consider, for instance, three widely touted aims of a college education.

Disciplinary Fluency

Training involves not merely amassing a body of facts but also becoming familiar with the methods and standard sources of a particular discipline. College students learn to read its academic journals, absorb the material it takes as evidence, and work with its distinctive tools. Using these methods and sources fluently involves taking an unquestioning attitude to them, or at least to the background network that brings them to light. Insofar as the discipline has developed credible networks, fluency adds nodes to a student's trust network, expanding it in trustworthy directions.

Critical Thinking

While fluency grows one's trust network, critical thinking prunes it. The habits and skills of critical thinking encourage students to question previously unquestioned sources, which alters their trust networks in one of two ways: they may no longer believe a given source of information, or they may continue to believe it but in a distanced and more suspicious fashion. In the second case, students change their trust network without changing their beliefs, only their relation to them.

New Social Ties

As they make new friends and acquaintances, college students have less time and opportunity to spend with old ones. Colleges make a concerted effort to achieve this natural effect of any change in a social environment for their students. While this phenomenon is most in evidence at residential colleges where students may interact all day with people from unfamiliar backgrounds, it also happens at commuter schools. Commuting students spend time on campus that they might otherwise spend in their neighborhoods and enmeshed in previous social spaces. Both residential and commuter schools foster student involvement with their campus as a student success strategy, consciously and intentionally changing the social spaces their students occupy. Since social ties and trust networks shape one another, by changing where and with whom students spend time, colleges further change whom and what these students trust. And as this third pathway makes clear, the effect of colleges on the trust networks of their students is not merely a result of what happens in classrooms.

These three goals clearly shape the trust networks college students end up inhabiting. A college education thus involves a rather intimate transformation. What justifies such a transformation, if anything does, is that it improves the epistemic standing of the student who undergoes it. A college education promises to make students better at knowing, and that means improving the trust networks they rely on as knowers. But how can we be sure that the trust network students leave college with (if all goes according to plan) is epistemically better than the one they entered with? This turns out to be a harder question than it first appears.

Distinguishing more- from less-trustworthy sources is not a straightforward matter. There is no path of unmediated access to "the facts" for comparison with what a given source reports. We have to interrogate the source's methods, position, constraints, and so forth to decide whether to trust it. In many cases, even experts won't agree completely about which networks are more trustworthy. This is in part due to the complexity and compartmentalization of much of advanced human knowledge.

DYSFUNCTIONAL TOPOGRAPHIES AND THEIR REPAIR

One method for judging the trustworthiness of a given network is to examine what might be called its topography. Trust networks can take on distinctive shapes that create dysfunctions and pathologies in our ability to know about the world. One way a college education can improve students' epistemic standing is to identify, and then repair or reshape, the dysfunctional topographies of their trust networks. To see how this works, consider four topographic features that can contribute to a network's dysfunction, and the remedies colleges offer to improve them.

Epistemic Valleys

Restricting information to locally available sources, epistemic valleys encourage their occupants to make judgments about the world based not only on limited information (we all do that) but on the basis of limits inherent in their epistemic position. Being illiterate, not understanding probability, only speaking a single language and lacking access to translated material, relying on a single news source, or only ever talking to people in your small town, insular neighborhood, online social network, academic discipline or political party, all of whom also only talk to each other, all create epistemic valleys. Colleges lift students out of such valleys by broadening their horizons: exposing them to unfamiliar ideas and cultures, helping them develop new skills and methods of investigation, and teaching them to access new forms of information.

Filter Bubbles

Disguised versions of epistemic valleys, filter bubbles limit access to certain sources of information but hide their filtering. Individual newspapers or news networks can create filter bubbles. The *New York Times*, for example, gives its readers "all the news that's fit to print." Yet the *Times,* by making all sorts of decisions about what is fit, filters and selects the information it prints for readers. Those who get information about the world only from the *Times* are in the equivalent of an epistemic valley, though they may think they are standing on a mountaintop with a broad and wide vista. The algorithms that drive search engines also create filter bubbles. Search results on Google or the contents of Facebook feeds, for instance, are a function of the information they have amassed on users and those who are paying them for access to those users. These results do not provide unfiltered, direct access to what is available on the internet about a given topic. Moreover, Google and Facebook's filters reinforce sources of information we have relied on in the past and thereby further strengthen our bubble. Teaching college students to recognize filters, even when, or especially when, they are not evident, helps them break out of their bubbles. This involves the development of critical thinking skills and may also require learning about the sociology of knowledge or the structure of their media landscape.

Echo Chambers

More sinister than filter bubbles, echo chambers don't block information but encourage their occupants to distrust or reject outside sources. Cults and conspiracy theories create echo chambers, and some scholars argue that conservative media in the United States does as well. People in an echo chamber are primed to distrust or reject new sources of information that might contradict their beliefs. New contrary evidence presented to people in an echo chamber often has the seemingly paradoxical effect of strengthening their original beliefs. Since escaping an echo chamber requires reversing our judgment about the trustworthiness of certain sources, trusting someone outside the echo chamber for other reasons is often required. By fostering close social ties with outsiders, whether they be teachers, staff, or fellow students, colleges can help students combat this problem.

Epistemic Nests

Positive reflections of echo chambers, epistemic nests also shape the attitudes their inhabitants take to sources of knowledge rather than limiting access. Whereas echo chambers work by cultivating distrust of outside sources, nests provide positive social incentives to trust only insiders. (Actual networks often do both in that a shared distrust of outsiders generates a sense of community and vice versa.) Epistemic nests rely on the connection trust networks create between our beliefs and our social ties. The positive social incentives provided by occupying an epistemic nest come via the value of belonging to its community. Communities can form epistemic nests without engaging in the abusive practices that mark echo chambers or by threatening to expel members who stray from a particular orthodoxy. The process can be more subtle: those who have left the nest no longer share the same assumptions and reference points with those still inside, making interaction and conversation more difficult. All three aims of a college education—greater fluency, enhanced critical thought, new social ties—encourage students to leave their epistemic nests or sometimes just push them out. Insofar as staying in an epistemic nest limits your trust network, leaving it improves your epistemic standing. But abandoning an epistemic nest jeopardizes social ties with those who remain. The price of epistemic improvement and an education is the loss of a certain intimacy with a community of which one was once a part.

The social costs of leaving epistemic nests are not borne by all college students or equally by those who do. The trust networks of some new students are already well-aligned with those college faculty and staff inhabit and champion. They come from families and backgrounds that trust credentialed expertise, the peer-review process, and the unlimited and unerring powers of critical thought and reasoned argument. They come from communities that have not been systematically harmed by major social, political, and economic institutions. These students acquire what a college education has to offer, including its epistemic improvements, without really leaving their nests.

Other students start college with very different trust networks. They grew up trusting religious authorities or the wisdom and accumulated knowledge of their communities. They arrive skeptical of the goodwill or reliability of sources colleges teach them to trust. Some of that mistrust may be well-founded as not all institutions that figure prominently in college-fostered trust networks are blameless or harmless. And even mistrust resulting from misinformation or misunderstanding may connect students to their home communities. A college education that achieves its aims radically transforms these students' trust networks and takes them out of their epistemic nests. These students are the ones who bear the social costs of a college education.

RECOMMENDATIONS FOR CONFRONTING SOCIAL COSTS

What, then, ought college faculty and staff do in the face of these social costs? How can they help their students bear them? I end with five broad recommendations. These are not specific policies or practices but regulative ideals that college policymakers should keep in mind.

First, a college must ensure that it is in fact epistemically improving the trust networks of its students. Are curricula and courses well designed for this task? Do they broaden student horizons, for instance, yet fail to offer help identifying and remedying filter bubbles, echo chambers, and epistemic nests? Are colleges and their courses merely replacing one set of dysfunctional structures with another, even if the latter is more widespread among the college educated? Departments and disciplines can form their own dysfunctional epistemic topographies. Sometimes these structures help generate new knowledge by focusing on narrow problems and solutions within a discipline. But teaching from such a perspective can be epistemically harmful to students. Epistemically beneficial teaching may require abandoning or adjusting a design primarily intended to initiate undergraduates into a discipline.

Second, a college education should not only epistemically improve student trust networks but also equip students to assess trust networks, including those the college is simultaneously promoting. This requires courses designed to accept and reveal complexity and uncertainty rather than form certain beliefs and reach certain conclusions. Not only does this entail teaching openness and nondogmatism, it entails teaching that is open and nondogmatic. From having students read opposing and credible views on a topic to exposing them to unfamiliar epistemic networks and ways of thinking, there are many ways this can be done. Beyond helping students develop mastery of material and methods and an ability to find flaws and criticize, it requires teaching students to engage charitably and responsively with material they disagree with or find unfamiliar, and identifying what is interesting or valuable even in positions and perspectives they might ultimately reject. Faculty can model this by discussing charitable accounts of positions they disagree with or even deem wrong and coaching students on how to be critical of views the faculty member accepts or defends. While many college faculty across disciplines do this kind of work in their classes as a matter of course, many do not.

Third, colleges need to earn the trust of their students and the families and communities who send them to college. These institutions and their employees have a duty of care not to exploit the dependency of those who entrust the development of their trust networks to them. Colleges should take care to neither amplify their students' vulnerability nor shape their trust networks for partisan or sectarian purposes. A college education should have the potential to be transformative without being an exercise in conversion. Setting out to convert students to a particular position, value system, cause, or concern exploits the opportunity student trust provides and thus betrays their trust. This is another area where orientation as a researcher or scholar may need to stand apart from orientation as a teacher. A scholarly career will be filled with the development of compelling arguments for particular conclusions. An undergraduate course shouldn't operate in exactly the same way. In addition to ethical reasons for not betraying student trust, there are pragmatic ones: colleges will have a much harder time effectively educating students who do not trust them.

Being trustworthy also involves not heightening the anxiety that may ensue from trusting. If you trust me to take care of your prized Ming vase, I should not juggle with it, even if I am an expert juggler and my juggling the vase does not risk breaking it. Colleges can reduce the anxiety of students, their families, and home communities through outreach and greater transparency about the distinctive features of a college education as well as its hidden social costs. They can also discourage their faculty and staff from taking a high-handed attitude to the networks of their students. College faculty can be haughtily dismissive of epistemic positions they reject or trust networks different from their own. They can be arrogant about the value of their own networks, seeing them not as networks that rely on trust but solely on unequivocal facts, reasons, arguments, and science. Faculty should recognize that their own trust networks, despite their epistemic value, are not unimpeachable or unquestionable. They should remain open to challenge and criticism from students, and keep in mind the social costs for those who abandon familiar trust networks for new ones, even in the name of epistemic improvement.

Fourth, colleges should provide students and their home communities with resources and tools needed to manage the social costs of their education. This starts by offering students a way of thinking about and understanding what is happening, such as the description of the transformation of trust networks offered here. It might also involve helping them reestablish social ties in peril. Colleges could teach students how to move among epistemic nests (through code-switching or other forms of intellectual flexibility). They could also teach students how to build bridges, turning isolated nests into more complex networks by developing new lines of trust.

Finally, colleges are less likely to overlook the costs they impose and their own epistemic limitations if their faculty, staff, and administrators come from a variety of backgrounds or have demonstrated attention to and familiarity with such backgrounds. Note that the faculty diversity required here is not of viewpoint or identity (which is not to take a stand on whether these forms of diversity also have value). Diversity of background concerns where people are from and the attendant social costs of their own college education. Faculty or staff who grew up in a socially conservative rural community or who are first in their family to go to college are more likely to recognize the social costs of a college education as well as college policies and practices that make those costs harder to bear, even if they no longer share the views of their family and community or look like the students who face similar challenges where they work. Beyond merely diversifying faculty and staff this way, this diversity should be made apparent to students, their families, and others on campus. Unlike diversity of identity or viewpoint, diversity of background can go unnoticed if not welcomed and highlighted. In discussions of curricula, teaching practices, and student life policies, it is important to hear and seriously consider the observations and insights of people from diverse backgrounds.

I have argued that a college education can impose social costs through the same processes that improve the epistemic value of its student trust networks. This discussion suggests a number of significant issues for colleges to consider as they develop curricula, teach classes, create extracurricular programs and spaces, advise students, and hire faculty and staff. Determining what precisely a college should do to help its students bear the hidden social costs of a college education requires sensitivity to local context—the particular students being educated, the connection of the college to the local community and the communities of origin of its students, the composition of its faculty, and the nature of its curriculum. But many other values and costs are also at stake in providing a college education. Determining how these various concerns interact and should be addressed, however, is work I leave to involved readers, trusting that they are up to it.[5]

Part XII

THE CURRICULUM

Chapter 25

Why College?
An Education for Freedom

Dan Edelstein and Debra Satz

The content and purposes of college education have long been the subject of debate and discussion. Today, as students face mounting college debt and insecure job prospects, many wonder why anyone should take time to study Aeschylus or French literature. Why shouldn't college be primarily vocational, with the sole purpose of equipping students for productive jobs? What is the value of a broad liberal arts education?[1]

We don't believe that colleges have done a good enough job of answering these questions, despite the fact that very few American colleges are strictly vocational. Although the most popular major in college, according to the National Center for Education Statistics, is business, other majors such as history, political science, psychology, and the visual arts continue to draw large numbers of undergraduates. Moreover, with few exceptions, colleges have distribution requirements so that even a business major will take courses in fields of study like literature, philosophy, and physics.

Unlike universities in most European and Asian countries, American higher education has always emphasized both breadth of knowledge and depth of specialization. We admit students to college, not to any particular major. A broad liberal education, then, has a distinctively American pedigree; it is the broadest kind of education the modern world has known. But our nation's colleges, we believe, do not adequately explain the rationale for this kind of education to students, parents, or even their own faculty. Seemingly entrenched practices such as these still require justification, however, lest they become what John Stuart Mill referred to as "dead dogma." And it is especially important to be clear about the rationale when, as now, the practice itself is under considerable pressure.

We can learn something about the rationale for the distinct American college path from a moment when this issue rose to the forefront of concern. Here we focus on two key debates that occurred nearly contemporaneously toward the end of the nineteenth century. The first, an argument between W. E. B. Du Bois and Booker T. Washington, concerned the kind of education appropriate for the newly free men of Georgia, following the Civil War and the end of Reconstruction. This debate highlights the importance of liberal education for the most disenfranchised and underserved among us. The second debate was between James McCosh and Charles William Eliot, the presidents of Princeton and Harvard, respectively, over the nature of the best education for American college students. Of course, the students they had in mind were among the most privileged in the country. While these two debates focused on very different segments of society, a number of important threads connected them.

Du Bois offered one of the greatest defenses of American liberal education in his debate with Washington, founder and President of the Tuskegee Institute, devoted to technical and vocational training for Black Americans. Washington's hope was to train the freemen of Georgia for the agricultural and vocational trades where they could find productive employment in the jobs that would actually be available to them in the post–Civil War South. By contrast, Du Bois, arguing against the renunciation of broader educational aspirations for African Americans, favored an education that would prepare them for the democratic citizenship they would still have to fight for.

Du Bois makes two main arguments for liberal education. First, such education is vital to reconstructing the South and performing what he refers to as a delicate "social surgery." How can two groups who have lived together only as masters and slaves find their way to relationships of equality? How might the South become more than "simply an armed camp for intimidating black folk?" According to Du Bois, "Such transformation calls for singular wisdom and patience . . . if this unusual and dangerous development is to progress amidst peace and order, mutual respect and growing intelligence . . . it will demand broad-minded upright men, both white and black . . . For this is certain, no secure civilization can be built in the South with the Negro as an ignorant, turbulent proletariat."[2]

We cannot heal the divisions wrought by an apartheid regime in the South, Du Bois argues, without careful and thoughtful Black leaders who understand the possibilities for human cooperation and a more just political order. And to have such leaders requires college-educated Blacks who can help move their community and society forward. A Black proletariat trained only for jobs will not be able to play that role. If we use the market to fuel the supply and distribution of education, it will undersupply the skills, judgment, and ethos that making a new South requires.

This first argument is fundamentally political. The second argument is connected to the first but deepens it by reaching into the "souls" of individuals. Du Bois recognized that how others see us and what they expect of us fundamentally shape the way we conceive of ourselves. Others who view us as inferior and expect little of us shape our own self-conception. The tools of a broad education—an education that provides access to the full scope of human culture—can give people the resources needed to break free of the conceptions and preconceptions of others. This lays the groundwork for a life of freedom and self-development. A broad education is, for Du Bois, a kind of vaccine against servility.

While made in extreme conditions, Du Bois' arguments still apply to our own circumstances. We too as a society suffer from deep social and political divisions that challenge our ability to live together as social equals. We too need leaders from all segments of the population and educated citizens who can weigh evidence, evaluate arguments, and draw on the reserves of human culture to find better ways for our living together. Additionally, all of us are saddled with social expectations and preconceptions, although these constrain some lives more than others. The burden of lowered expectations still casts its shadow on Black lives. And all of us require access to other preconceptions and expectations, developed over the millennia, to figure out who we are and what we fundamentally care about. Otherwise, we are living someone else's script.

At the time Du Bois was writing, however, his vision of college was under attack. Du Bois himself could have witnessed the dramatic changes that undergraduate education was facing when he attended Harvard from 1888–1890 (he stayed on for a master's and doctorate degrees). Driving these changes was Charles Eliot, who had assumed the presidency in 1869. Eliot sought to transform the New England college into the kind of German research university that he had studied during a two-year stay in Europe. Like Booker T. Washington, Eliot also believed that college should be more practical, although in Harvard's case, this outlook led to a greater focus on the professional schools and advanced degrees.[3]

At the undergraduate level, Eliot's principal innovation was the elective system. Previously, most college students had followed a fixed curriculum, which privileged classical languages and the humanities more broadly. Instead, Eliot wanted students to choose classes that interested them. In his system, virtually no requirements dictated what students could study, not even a major. The entrance exam in ancient Greek was abolished, as was mandatory Latin and Greek for first-years.

This revolutionary approach to undergraduate education divided American educators. One of the fiercest opponents was James McCosh, the president of Princeton. In a famous 1885 debate with Eliot, he challenged the idea that eighteen-year-olds were the best judges of their intellectual needs. Under McCosh, Princeton remained committed to a fixed curriculum, a commitment symbolized by the Collegiate Gothic architecture of the campus, a nod to Oxford and Cambridge as opposed to Berlin.[4]

A theological backdrop to this debate pitted the Unitarian Eliot against the Calvinist McCosh. But ultimately their argument can be reframed in terms of rival definitions of freedom. Eliot advocated for the students' freedom to study whatever they choose. This was the vaunted *Lernfreiheit* of the German research university. It was paired with a corresponding freedom on the part of faculty to teach what they wanted: *Lehrfreiheit*. It is still these freedoms that most students encounter when setting foot on a college campus: they get to choose the classes that interest them from a massive list of courses offered by faculty.

But this is not the idea of freedom embedded in the ideal of liberal education. The vision of liberal education embraced by Du Bois and practiced by McCosh drew on a pedagogical tradition extending back to ancient Greece and Rome. It was "liberal," not because students were free to choose what they wanted to study, and certainly not because it was politically on the left, but because it was an education befitting a free person (*liber homo*). It was the kind of education necessary to participate in a free political community, that is, a community that governed and legislated for itself. A personal objective was also implied in this form of education: free individuals must be able to think for themselves and not be dominated by what others tell them to believe. It was this freedom that Du Bois insisted was imperative for Black Americans to achieve. But it was the same freedom that the Stoics had pursued and was thought to come from a liberal education.

Looking back on this debate today, a first observation is that both McCosh's and Eliot's visions fared poorly. Only a handful of schools still have a fixed curriculum, and almost no school follows Eliot's laissez-faire model. Eliot's successor at Harvard, A. Lawrence Lowell, dropped the elective-only system, insisting that every student choose a concentration or major. Requirements crept back into the undergraduate curriculum in the form of departmental mandates and certain general education demands. Even language requirements (albeit not for Latin and Greek) were reintroduced. With significant variations from one institution to the next, American higher education seems to have settled on a compromise, granting students a high degree of personal initiative (electives, individual choice of major) within a framework of university and departmental requirements.

But when we reflect on the fortunes of the two concepts of freedom championed by Eliot and McCosh, there does appear to be a clear victor. It is difficult to see how a handful of general education requirements, plus the very specific courses required by majors, prepare students for the civic demands of self-governing communities or point students down the path of inner freedom. Are American colleges and universities really producing graduates adequately trained to deal with the complexities and challenges of a participatory democracy? And are the students who choose their courses and study principally for economic returns thinking for themselves, or are they simply conforming to the dictates of their parents, peers, and society?

As anyone who has worked on the issue knows well, reforming general education requirements is an incredibly difficult business. The history of American higher education is littered with short-lived programs and outright failures. There are also a handful of success stories. The core curricula at Columbia and Chicago, for example, have weathered many storms but remain popular among students, faculty, and especially alumni. These programs emerged, in part, as a response to the collapse of the fixed curriculum, so beloved by McCosh.[5] They pioneered what eventually became the "Western Civ" model, which many universities went on to adopt as their general education requirement.[6] Where Columbia and Chicago mainly delivered their requirement in a discussion seminar format, others schools (such as Stanford) relied on a lecture-plus-section structure, which proved less stable.[7] Nationally, this model ultimately came under fire during the culture wars of the 1980s and 1990s and has largely fallen out of fashion. Since then, most attempts at delivering a first-year requirement have tacked closer to Eliot than to McCosh, giving students a number of options to choose from—still a kind of *Lernfreiheit*. But this approach can leave students confused: if a university requirement is so important, why can it be filled in so many different ways? It also fails to provide a "core" common to all students. At the same time, arguments over the canon have not subsided, and designing a core curriculum around a shared set of texts is as challenging now as it was forty years ago.

But there is arguably a deeper and more complex problem facing college reformers today, a problem that goes back to the Eliot/McCosh debate. The two freedoms that Eliot brought to Harvard, *Lernfreiheit* and *Lehrfreiheit*, have completely transformed the relations between students and faculty. Few faculty today are particularly connected to the overall education of undergraduate students. We are professionally driven to focus on (and care about) our disciplines and fields, not the undergraduate curriculum as a whole. Who among the faculty understands the complex systems of educational requirements that populate our colleges and universities?

The problem is that this arrangement suits most of us perfectly well. The German research university rests, fittingly, on a Faustian bargain: we, the faculty, won't tell you, the students, what to study, if you let us teach what we want. It was an ingenious bargain, leading to incredible breakthroughs in research. But like all bargains, it had a price: in this case, the soul of undergraduate education. Restoring the balance between personal choice and liberal education will require changing the mindset of many faculty, as well as students. The former may prove more challenging than the latter.

With respect to the first challenge, one way forward is to retain some of the pedagogical goals of traditional general education requirements, but without fixating on a particular set of texts. The curricular content and shape of liberal education should not be viewed as fixed; it is alterable. And its continued alteration as times and context change is part of its ideal. For example, many of the objectives laid out by Daniel Bell in his classic 1966 report on the Columbia Core can be achieved with a curriculum that is not dominated by Western texts. These include "overcoming provincialism," "gaining an awareness of history," "showing how ideas relate to social structures," and crucially *"liberating* young people by making them aware of the forces that impel them from within and constrict them from without."[8] Western Civ courses used an almost off-the-shelf set of Great Books to reach these goals, but with some ingenuity and broad faculty consultation, it is possible to create equally coherent but less geographically confined curricula.

At Stanford, we are designing a new first-year requirement that focuses on these objectives (along with others) but draws extensively on different cultural traditions.[9] Students kick off their college experience by exploring the idea of liberal education itself in a series of linked seminars that mostly share the same syllabus. We use this introduction to higher education as an opportunity to stage an "intervention" and lead students to appreciate what it means—and why it's meaningful—to learn for the sake of intellectual curiosity and personal growth. Such an intervention has proven to be both effective and well received, as students find little joy in treating school like one long test whose rewards always lie ahead in some nebulous future. Authors such as Plato and Mary Shelley are great guides on this journey, but so are Rabindranath Tagore and Tsitsi Dangaremba. This required course forces students to ask whether they are choosing their non-required courses freely or are being compelled by others to do so.

In their second quarter, students consider the civic objectives of a liberal education, pondering what it means to be a good citizen of a nation, as well as a company, a religious community, or an academic institution. Why are collective action and self-government so hard, and why is Hobbes' Leviathan solution appealing to so many? What are the emerging threats to democratic communities, and which among the age-old threats are still a risk? As they explore these questions through a wide variety of readings and case studies, students also practice the art of civil disagreement. They realize that differences of opinion are not signs of heresy, but the inevitable stuff of democratic deliberation and a free society. These seminars are thus designed to be both an exploration of civic problems and a practicum of civic life. In this quarter, a syllabus shared across seminars creates a common background for all first-year students.

Finally, in the spring quarter, students take a class that provides them with global perspectives on a contemporary problem (e.g., climate change or immigration), historical phenomenon (e.g., colonialism or revolution), or cultural practice (e.g., cinema or urban design). Unlike the first two quarters, these courses typically have a lecture component, and take a more disciplinary-based approach and have little overlap with one another. We plan on devising extracurricular programming around global themes to encourage crossover conversations between students.

The coming years will tell whether this attempt to reinvigorate liberal education at Stanford is successful. While current indications suggest that the students find these new courses exhilarating and relevant, we have not forgotten that the faculty are an equally important part of the equation. Thankfully, despite a lasting tradition of *Lehrfreiheit*, faculty interest so far has been terrific, and we are staffing courses with professors from six of Stanford's seven schools. It is gratifying to recognize that many of our colleagues believe in the general mission of the university to provide all students with a robust liberal education. But it is also clear that the incentive structure of the modern research university is stacked in the opposite direction. For administrators hoping to recommit their universities to the ideals of liberal education and civic freedom, finding ways to modify this incentive structure is crucial. Perhaps then we can restore a sense among the faculty as a whole of our shared responsibility—our civic duty as professors—for the undergraduate education of all our students.

Chapter 26

Ethics Requirements in the Liberal Arts Curriculum

Kyla Ebels-Duggan

> What is it to live a good human life? How should you treat other people, other animals, and the natural environment? How should we organize our diverse society politically to secure justice for all? Whom should you trust and what makes for a good reason to believe something? Why make art? Why do anything other than make art?

Reflection on such questions has always been an important aspect—arguably the very core—of a liberal arts education. But a few years ago a proposal that would have deemphasized them, eliminating them from most students' course of study altogether, circulated at the liberal arts college within my university. The proposal would have abolished a longstanding requirement that, in addition to courses in natural science, math, social science, literature, and history, all students take at least two classes to fulfill a requirement then called "ethics and values."

To be fair, the courses that counted toward the requirement at the time were a motley crew. Concentrated in philosophy and religion, they also included classes from literature, anthropology, sociology, psychology, history, and other disciplines. The collection of classes showed no clear unity in subject matter, methods, or aims, so the committee charged with revising the undergraduate curriculum may reasonably have doubted that the ethics and values requirement, as it then existed, served a genuine curricular purpose.

But they also seemed unable to imagine what a genuine, meaningful requirement of this kind might look like or what pedagogical aims it could fulfill. While I don't think that they were alone in this, the ability to articulate and think intelligently about central human questions like *how best to live* and *what we owe to others* is an essential educational goal. Dealing with questions like these is not optional. Everyone has to settle on some answer to them, if not explicitly and reflectively then at least implicitly in practice. You have to decide how to spend your limited time, what goals to prioritize, what to care about, and how to treat those with whom you interact. A meaningful ethics requirement would equip students to think well about the answers to these sorts of questions.

The requirement at my college was threatened because it was failing to meet two important challenges. Carving out a distinctive area of study and pedagogical aim that avoids duplicating other requirements is the first challenge. I will argue that normative questions—questions about values and reasons, about how things ought to be, and what we should do about it—deserve a place in any liberal arts curriculum and that they differ from the descriptive questions addressed by other course areas. But some worry that courses that take up such questions will amount to an objectionable attempt to indoctrinate students. Answering that objection is the second challenge. In what follows, I'll explain how coursework in ethics can help students think well about the answers to normative questions without collapsing into dogmatism.

A problem with the collection of courses that fulfilled the ethics requirement at my college was that many merely talked *about* values. For example, a sociology course examining how different cultural groups approach some value-laden question, say, the organization of families, might have counted toward the requirement. But there was a distinct requirement in social sciences and a course on family structure seemed to fit better in that category. Seeing this pattern repeated over and over, skeptics concluded that ethics was not really its own area of study but rather a topic addressed within other disciplines.

But there is an important difference between descriptive investigations into *what some person or social group thinks* about an ethical matter and the distinctively normative questions with which we began. The former take normative views, or the people who hold these views, as objects of study, adopting an observer's dispassionate standpoint on them to ask about the causes and effects of people valuing what they do. Most social science courses take that approach and actively discourage consideration of whether the views in question are right or wrong, whether they are admirable or contemptable, whether they are ideal or improvable. Those questions are examples of the distinctive subject matter of ethics. Rather than just *describing* what someone thinks about these things, ethics courses ask students to consider what it makes sense to care about, which principles or ideals to live by, whom to admire, and how to approach their relationships with others.

Now, the study of what others think about such matters is worthwhile in its own right, and can be important for thinking about them for one's self. Sometimes we need to know what others value and what they find worth doing to interact with them on better terms. Consider, for example, interpersonal relationships with friends and family. If you care about another person and want your relationship to flourish, you need to work to understand what they care about: what motivates and scares this individual, what this special someone enjoys and loves. And this sort of interpersonal interest in another's views has correlates in larger communities and political units. If we seek to live together in a fair and just society, we need to understand one another's values and priorities. But even if we achieved a full picture of each person's viewpoint, we would still face, and need to settle, further normative questions about how to get along in light of our commonalities and differences.

Understanding what others think can also help you identify and articulate commitments of your own that you might otherwise have taken for granted and possible alternatives. Seeing that others live quite differently from you, or that they value different things, makes it impossible to deny the contingency in how things are done around here. It makes clear that we didn't have to arrange our society and our lives as we have. We don't have to keep doing things the way we have always done them or fulfill all of the expectations others have formed for us. Seeing that your own commitments about what's worth doing and what's worth caring about aren't inevitable raises the possibility of revising or changing these commitments. To see such possibilities is to be able to frame questions about whether some options are better than others. Which social or personal changes would be improvements, which would amount to deterioration, and which are just differences? But noticing that a commitment is contingent isn't the same as thinking that it's bad or unwarranted. That you could revise what you care about does not entail that you should. Clarifying your own values can also help you think better about why you care about what you do, and why it makes sense to do so. It offers the possibility not just of revised commitment but of deeper, more sophisticated, more mature commitment to what you already valued.

So, learning *about* what others value is important and worthwhile, and it bears important relationships to the sorts of questions with which we began. But no description of others' views about how to answer these questions, no matter how accurate or detailed, could substitute for your own attempt to settle them for yourself. It is one thing to learn about a range of possible attitudes toward, for example, work, leisure, and wealth. It is another to ask which of these possibilities, if any, one should endorse. Are the prevailing attitudes in one's own society reasonable or disordered? Should they be upheld and supported or challenged and revised, and what tools could we permissibly use to attempt any such social reform? So, normative questions are distinct. They are *ought* questions rather than *is* questions. They are evaluative or prescriptive rather than descriptive. Students need to be taught to identify and ask such questions, and shown that it is possible to think well about the answers to them.

But focusing on these distinctively normative questions may trigger a new worry about required ethics and values courses. Won't addressing these questions in a classroom setting risk objectionable indoctrination of our students? Behind this worry is a certain presumption about how education proceeds.

On this view, universities are in the business of producing knowledge, and education consists of communicating this knowledge to students. The production and communication of knowledge are, indeed, important functions of universities, and classes in many disciplines rightly instantiate this model. Many courses in the natural and social sciences aim to inform students of authoritative answers to the questions that characterize those areas of study. It's completely appropriate that they do: students of chemistry, for example, need to learn about the chemical composition of various compounds and the behavior of electrons and they are right to expect that their courses will instruct them about these and similar matters.

Classes where professors reported their own ethical conclusions in a way that mirrors scientists explaining the results of scientific research would be dogmatic in an objectionable sense, even if the faculty had come to these conclusions in the most responsible way possible. But a model of expertise drawn from the sciences, and a corresponding picture of education as the communication of expert knowledge, are ill-fitted for areas of normative inquiry.

In fact, worries about indoctrination are almost always overblown. I am often amused by the dramatic powers such concerns ascribe to professors and find it hard to imagine what the worriers think that I will do to my students to bring about the indoctrination that they fear. Do they suppose students will be so impressed by my apparent brilliance that they will simply take my word for it when I tell them what is valuable and how they ought to live? Or do they think, in the space of a ten-week quarter, I can use the power of grading incentives to make them recite my ethical creed until they come to believe it? A course in which the professor reports her ethical conclusions, would be dogmatic, yes, but also boring or perhaps amusing in a farcical way. The influences shaping the moral outlooks of college students are varied and complex. Some are benign and others nefarious. A few are quite powerful. The influence of a single professor teaching a single course will almost always be negligible, and a professor who hoped to exercise such influence would certainly need tactics superior to the mere assertion of ethical views.

More reasonable worries about indoctrination likely involve faculty who fail to make their normative presuppositions transparent or who deny or are unaware that they are making any such assumptions. Most any class will take some normative positions for granted. We do this when we decide what questions to investigate, how to frame these questions, what texts to read, and what standards of evaluation to impose. The formulation of learning objectives, beloved by many administrators, is a paradigmatic exercise of normative thought, one of identifying the goals we will treat as worth pursuing.

Moreover, many areas of study presuppose substantive and controversial normative positions as part of their methodology. Economics courses routinely take for granted an entire theory of practical reasoning, without so much as noting that they have a position. They treat the satisfaction of a preference as a reason—indeed the only possible reason—to do something and the maximization of preference satisfaction as the goal of rational action. This view is often called *rational choice theory,* but which choices are rational and what makes them so are difficult normative issues that philosophers engage with and disagree about in sophisticated ways. In a similar vein, wildly popular classes on the psychology of happiness take for granted that happiness is both the thing worth striving for and a matter of pleasant subjective states.[1] But this shallow view of the good life is far from inevitable, and both historical and contemporary philosophical discussions present more nuanced and attractive alternatives.

That value commitments infuse the curriculum is unavoidable. No education is, or could be, ethically neutral. But where normative positions go unacknowledged, they can go unnoticed, sometimes even by the faculty who advocate for them. By contrast, good courses in ethics and values make these positions, and the questions they answer, explicit. Students need courses in which they read and reflect on literature selected by thoughtful faculty members, but they also need courses in which they can themselves engage with questions about what sorts of texts are worth reading and why. It is worthwhile to study economics and psychology, but also worthwhile to step back from these disciplines to identify their presuppositions about rationality and ask whether those claims are true. Those who worry that students will somehow be indoctrinated into the ethical commitments of their professors direct their concern to the wrong target when they worry about the sorts of classes that should fulfill requirements in ethics, values, or moral thought. Prompting reflective thought about the answers to normative questions is not dogmatism but rather its antidote.

We have seen that courses fulfilling ethics requirements must address a distinctive subject matter rather than duplicating the aims of other areas of study. I have argued that the subject matter in question is distinctively normative, prescriptive, or evaluative. If such a class aimed just to communicate ethical information or report moral conclusions, it might be right to object that it amounted to an attempt at indoctrination—even if, as I have suggested, it would not be likely to succeed. But it would be wrong to think that the communication of information is the only possible, or only legitimate, educational aim. Instead, among the most important tasks that courses in ethics and values can accomplish are teaching students to recognize and express normative questions and giving them resources, both conceptual and substantive, for answering them.

In my experience, most students arrive at the university with both deep moral concerns and passionate ethical commitments. They also arrive with a sorely limited set of concepts for asking their questions and expressing their answers. In the not-so-distant past, they were largely hemmed in by the vocabulary of an unreflective value relativism. Earlier educational experiences taught them that it would be impolite, at best, to assert as true any evaluative, prescriptive, or normative position. As a result they defaulted to the language of opinion or feeling when expressing these sorts of views. They would profess a lack of authority or standing to advocate for any particular answer to a question about values. They would say that it's up to individuals to decide what they think about morally important matters and that no one can tell anyone else what to do or what they should value. They would reject the very idea that we could ask whether some normative position was right or wrong.

But some of these statements can be interpreted as expressing normatively significant positions of their own—and extremely plausible ones at that. Asserting that it's up to each individual to decide what to think about morally important matters might be a way of agreeing with something that I argued for above: each person has to come to some settlement in practice, whether reflectively or not. No one can escape this responsibility for answering a range of normative questions. To say that no one can tell another what to do or value might be to assert limits on what we can permissibly coerce or force from others by way of action. Or it might be to oppose getting in people's faces to condemn their way of doing things. These are all assertions of normative positions that should be taken seriously. But none support the view that there are no truths about value or about what is right and wrong. Instead, they take a position on what some of these truths are.

More recently, in tandem with increased awareness of the seriousness of racial and other sorts of social injustice, students have become more willing to own their normative views. But most, lacking a rich moral and ethical vocabulary, are relegated to using concepts inadequate for the expression of their concerns. My own students, like others elsewhere, increasingly invoke mental health concepts: They object that they will be, or have been, triggered or traumatized by certain views or topics of discussion. They say that certain views harm them or others and frequently claim explicitly that confronting some position has deleterious effects on their mental health.

Mental health and illness, emotional harms, and trauma are all genuine and important phenomena. The development and mainstreaming of the suite of concepts that we need to think and talk about these afflictions has been an important social advance. But these concepts have limits, as any useful concepts must, and should be reserved for the specific medical conditions, symptoms, and reactions they are meant to name. Problems arise when they are pressed into service to express the full range of ethical concerns. On the one hand, these concepts are inadequate for articulating normative questions and the answers to them. On the other, attempting to use them this way threatens to stretch their meanings so thin that it undermines their original use.

Less sympathetic audiences often interpret student claims that a view harms or traumatizes them as an objection to a view that causes personal discomfort. The student's subsequent failure to engage the view promotes criticism for being weak, closed-minded, and demanding to be coddled and shielded from exposure to disagreements. But consider that students who talk this way may be trying to express something more significant than uncomfortable feelings. I think that they are often, instead, trying to reject the view in question in a particularly strenuous way. They are trying to take a moral stand against it, but they lack the language they need to do this well. They talk about harm, trauma, and damage to their mental health where others might describe a view as morally unthinkable,[2] as revealing a corrupt mind,[3] or as beyond the pale. They may be trying to say not merely that they disagree with a view but that they further find it undeserving of serious consideration or engagement. Whether the convictions they would then be trying to express are reasonable ones will depend on the particular view they target. But, in any case, it would be both disrespectful and inaccurate to interpret them as merely whining, or manifesting cowardice, or engaging in self-protection. They are voicing serious moral positions.

Students are not to blame for the inadequacies of their conceptual tools. They have only those concepts that their upbringing, culture, and prior education have afforded them. If they are not able to distinguish carefully among a claim causing them distress, being false, and being so far beyond the pale that it should not be up for consideration at all, this is probably no fault of their own. And, importantly, we owe them the same presumptions of charitable interpretation that we teach them to apply to the texts they read.

But we also owe them more—and we have more to offer them. We can provide a wider, richer range of normative concepts, concepts that will allow them to think, and express, a wider range of thoughts and ask a wider range of questions. They may need concepts of obligation, wide and narrow, or of rights, positive and negative. They may need to understand the difference between demanding resources as a matter of fairness and requesting them as a matter of beneficence, and where each is appropriate. They may need to be able to formulate the distinction between what is worth wanting and what is worth doing, and the distinction between rejecting some normative view themselves and thinking that, further, no person of goodwill could accept it. They may need, more fundamentally, to understand the distinction between the normative and the descriptive, or between describing a normative view and endorsing it. Providing students with indispensable conceptual resources like these should be treated as a central aim of courses in ethics. The importance of having such resources, and the widespread failure of primary and secondary education to supply them, provides the central justification for ethics requirements at the college level.

With better concepts, students can express their existing concerns more clearly. But they can also deepen these concerns, thinking new and better thoughts. They will be better equipped to identify the range of normative assumptions and presumptions that some view, discourse, or discipline takes for granted. They will be able to ask new and better questions of others, and of themselves. They will be able to articulate, and so to consider, a wider variety of ways of addressing these issues and the reasons for holding these various positions. They will be newly able to appreciate the insights of both their own intellectual or cultural traditions and those of others.

All of this will position students to address the sorts of normative questions with which we started. It is essential that we help them do so because such questions are impossible to avoid. Though you might think that ethics and values is a far narrower area of study than, say, the natural or the social sciences, in fact it is of the widest possible interest. Everyone needs to figure out how to act and interact as a citizen, in their jobs, and in their personal relationships. Everyone must determine what to value and by what ideals to live. In a complicated world marked by a host of overlapping challenges, the ability to reflect intelligently on these central human questions is at least as essential to the sort of educated person that we should be sending out into the world as skills like speaking a second language or interpreting statistical data. We cannot educate students in a way that would eliminate the need for reflection on ethics and values. The question is only whether we will equip them to think about these problems well.

Part XIII

THE UNIVERSITY'S MISSION

Chapter 27

Taking Undergraduate Teaching and Learning Seriously

Harry Brighouse

A while ago, at a meeting of the American Philosophical Association, I passed a group of graduate students who were responding enthusiastically as one described a position for which he had just been interviewed. "It's a great job," he told his friends. "There's very little teaching and I'll have plenty of time for my work." I wish someone had reminded him that, in fact, teaching *was* his work.[1]

Steven Cahn could have heard this exchange at a professional meeting in *any* discipline. A professor uttering "my own work" *always* refers to research, not teaching. Insiders understand why. The professional infrastructure that governs the creation, hiring, success, and promotion of professors systematically relegates teaching to a low status. The graduate students in the story were simply conforming to the norms and expectations of the profession they had entered.

I'll argue that the professoring profession, which systematically subordinates teaching, leads to suboptimal undergraduate teaching and learning. Then I'll argue that universities and colleges that contribute to this are thereby committing an institutionalized wrong, a wrong that harms both the public good and many students. The third part of this essay explores what could be done to improve teaching and learning while elevating its status.

THE SUBOPTIMAL QUALITY OF UNDERGRADUATE TEACHING AND LEARNING

Let's call the claim that teaching and learning is worse, perhaps much worse, than it feasibly could be *the suboptimality thesis*. In the absence of rigorous and widely accepted measures of learning and a widely accepted benchmark, it's hard to establish the suboptimality thesis rigorously. But here are some compelling reasons for taking it seriously.

First, the evidence about how much students study and learn in college is not uplifting. The following highlights from the literature review in Bok (2016) are illustrative.[2] One major review of hundreds of studies of student learning concludes that the progress students make in college is nonnegligible but modest.[3] Over a four-year period they improve, on average, .5 of a standard deviation in critical thinking, .77 of a standard deviation in reading and writing, and .77 of a standard deviation in moral reasoning. (A full standard deviation is the gap between somebody performing at the 50th percentile and someone performing at the 84th percentile.) Arum and Roska administered the Collegiate Learning Assessment (CLA) to students in hundreds of four-year colleges first as freshmen and then as seniors, and found gains of less than .5 of a standard deviation on average.[4]

Critics may claim that the tests used to assess learning are flawed. Freshman may take low-stakes tests more seriously than seniors. General assessments may not capture discipline-specific learning well. And one of Arum and Roska's headline findings—that one-third of students did not make any progress at all on the CLA between freshman and senior year—*is* based on flawed statistical reasoning.[5]

Now let's consider evidence about how much students study. In a recent study of how much time students spend studying, Babcock and Marks found that whereas students spent about 40 hours a week studying and attending class in 1961, by 2003 they were studying, on average, only 27 hours a week, and that these reductions in outside-of-class studying accounted for most of this change. In 2004, only 13% of students reported spending 20 or more hours a week studying; one third reported spending less than 5 hours a week.[6] And, as Bok points out, "In America, surveys uniformly show not only that the time college students spend studying has declined, but that it is used less effectively . . . large and growing percentages of undergraduates now 'multitask' while studying by checking for email, using Facebook, texting, and engaging in other forms of social networking."[7]

The most compelling reasons for believing the suboptimality thesis lie in the structure of the academic profession: the training, recruitment, and professional development of instructors in universities and colleges.

Getting students to learn how to do calculus, developing the close-reading and analytical skills taught in some of the humanities, enabling students to succeed in organic chemistry, teaching them to harmonize a melody, inducing them to understand the fundamentals of quantum theory—these are all *difficult* tasks that involve exercising a complex set of skills. The teacher must be able to engage everyone in a room of 15, 25, 80, or 300 students, motivate them to pay attention to the problems at hand and prepare carefully, and know how to use classroom time in a way that optimizes their learning of the pertinent content and skills. Students are often distracted by their own anxieties or thoughts, by the other students in the room, and by their communications devices. Even in selective colleges, a typical classroom contains students whose levels of talent, motivation, and preparation vary considerably.

But instructors—and, in particular, tenure-line faculty—are hired largely out of PhD graduate programs that trained them as researchers, not teachers. Few graduate programs involve significant pedagogical training. A recent study of philosophy found the following:

> With the exception of a handful of programs, (i) the discipline of philosophy requires no, and offers little, teacher training for graduate students; (ii) the training that is offered is delivered by faculty or graduate students with little expertise in teaching and learning; and (iii) the training usually does not go much beyond the introductory level.

And

> A majority of philosophers (i) know little about best practices in teaching and learning, (ii) receive fewer than twenty hours of formal teacher training during graduate school, and (iii) believe they are well prepared for the teaching aspects of the professoriate.[8]

Some of the best-resourced—and hence most attractive to prospective graduate students—graduate schools involve little teaching experience. Harvard University Philosophy Department, for example, fully funds at least five years of doctoral study, requiring only two discussion sections of teaching/semester for only three of those five years.[9] But, according to the department website, of the fifty-nine completed PhDs between 2008 and 2018, thirty-five teach undergraduates in North American universities where the standard teaching load is two or more courses a semester (or equivalent).

Research institutions hire professors entirely, or almost entirely, without regard to their potential quality as instructors, looking only at their accomplishments and/or potential as researchers. At other institutions, teaching potential may play a larger role but, given the lack of training and experience most entry-level candidates have as teachers, judgments are at best educated guesses.

Once hired, professors typically receive little on-the-job training and engage in very limited continuing professional development as instructors. Again, this is starkest in research institutions where senior faculty observations of teaching may play some role in tenure decisions, but where those senior faculty are rarely trained to use suitable observational protocols and tend to have at best haphazard systems for improvement.

If teaching—that is, inducing students to learn at the college level—is difficult, and involves a different, if overlapping, skill set from that which supports high quality research, then, given the neglect of those skills I have surveyed, it would be extremely surprising if teaching in research universities were anything close to as good as it could be. The suboptimality thesis is our best working hypothesis.

WHAT'S WRONG WITH SUBOPTIMAL TEACHING AND LEARNING?

From the point of view of both the student and of the society, deficient teaching is wrong if it results in the legitimate purposes of undergraduate education being less well met than they could feasibly otherwise be met. We can start getting a fix on what the legitimate purposes are by imputing aims to the revenue sources. Undergraduate programs are typically funded by a combination of tuition revenues, government subsidies (directly from state and federal governments, and indirectly via tax credits, deductions, and exemptions), and, in some institutions, endowments (which are enhanced by tax exemptions).

What legitimate interests does the government have with regard to undergraduate education? Any answer is bound to rest on potentially controversial theories of justice and of the good. Here are two defensible purposes. The first relates to the distribution of opportunity. Young people from poor and working-class backgrounds should have meaningful access to an array of educational opportunities for developing human capital. This allows them to compete more effectively for positions to which various kinds of benefits are attached than if they were solely dependent on their families' resources and networks.

The second purpose is contributing to the public good, in substantial part by enhancing the knowledge, skills, attitudes, and dispositions of students so that they can, and are oriented to, making such contributions through participation in the economy, political structures, and civic society. Exactly how best to interpret the idea of the "public good" is contested. My preference is to reference the disadvantaged members of society. Roughly speaking, when someone's economic, political, and civic activity, in harness with the activities of others, benefits disadvantaged members of society, it is for the public good; when it harms them, it is not. But you can understand the public good in a number of other plausible ways. Good education, whoever receives it, enhances the pools of social and human capital potentially available for the benefit of all.[10]

What legitimate interests do students *themselves* have in undergraduate education? Students benefit from a college education in several ways. A degree is a prerequisite for entry into a substantial number of well-paid and interesting professions. Graduates have better health (including mental health), lower stress, longer marriages, live in safer neighborhoods, have more control over their daily lives, and live longer. They also gain the *learning:* students can acquire knowledge and become more skilled in ways that may help them better carry out the responsibilities of whatever positions they occupy and that may be valuable in many other ways. And many students enjoy the social side of being in college, being surrounded by other mostly young, often somewhat interesting, people with whom they can enjoy their leisure time.

How should a full assessment of the costs of suboptimal performance balance the interests of students with those of the government acting on behalf of the public good? For the current purposes, a fine-grained theory of weighting is not needed, because the remediable structural features that give rise to the suboptimality of the undergraduate mission negatively affect the interests of *both* students *and* society: their interests are sufficiently congruent to obviate the need for a theoretical weighting.

We're now in a better position to assess what is wrong with suboptimal teaching and learning.

First, and most obvious, is the cost to the social and human capital of the students. If they learn less, they are less well-equipped to do whatever it is they plan to do in the future. A literature class that awards good grades without having read the novels being discussed, and that does not introduce other classroom or extra-classroom elements to induce students to read the novels, leaves those students less capable than if they had read the novels. A professor of organic chemistry who grades the course on a curve and lacks the skill to explain the material well, or who fails to provide instructional support and materials for novice TAs, leaves the students less knowledgeable and skilled than they could have been.

This cost to the students exacts a further toll: the cost to the pool of social and human capital available for the public good. Universities and colleges educate future nurses, physicians, K–12 teachers, social workers, early childhood workers, counseling psychologists, military recruits, psychiatrists, correctional officers, police officers, public defenders, public prosecutors, human resources managers, to name a few. How humane they are, how competent they are, and how they balance, and how successfully they can reconcile, their own private interests with public service all affect how well the public is served. An undergraduate who has benefited from considerable private and public investment in social and human capital may have the choice whether to pursue a career as a nurse in an urban primary care facility or as a philosophy professor at a research university. Another may have a choice whether to become an elementary teacher and (though this student does not yet know this, teachers can discern it) eventually a superintendent in a high-poverty school district or a corporate lawyer. Good—that is, *highly skilled and well-motivated*—teachers and school district leaders, county social work department leaders, hospital administrators and nurses, human resources managers, urban planners, city managers, and so forth, benefit the public by doing their jobs better, more imaginatively, and with greater commitment.

Even if instruction were optimal in the sense that it enhanced the social and human capital of students as much as is feasible, the public would still bear a cost as long as students are not optimally oriented to public service. Educating students well—intensively building their social and human capital—does not benefit the public much if students deploy that additional human capital entirely for their own private interests. In 2014, in line with the years since the start of the Great Recession (but down from before 2008), 31% of Harvard's graduates pursuing jobs took them in the finance and consulting industries.[11] Capitalism certainly requires hard working and highly capable minds to keep capital and financial markets efficient. But it seems likely that *some* of the phenomenal social investment that has gone into developing the human capital of Harvard graduates could be put to better use than on Wall Street. Maybe *some* of that human capital (as well as some of the human capital going to law school and graduate school) should enter the kinds of occupation that lead to management and leadership of inner-city or rural social work departments, mental health programs, school districts, and housing departments.

Students do not bear the costs of suboptimal instruction equally, as my examples have already indicated. The particular way in which the costs are distributed may have direct effects on equality of opportunity. Imagine students from disadvantaged backgrounds trying to fulfill the various quantitative reasoning (mathematics) requirements of a bachelor's degree at an elite college or university. They are more likely than the average student to have received low-quality math instruction in high school and less likely to have received compensatory support from parents or personal tutors. Assigning highly skilled and experience instructors, who are invested in student success, to teach them basic math classes has three advantages. They learn more mathematics. They are more likely to pass, and more likely to pass with a better grade, thus affecting success in future competitions within and beyond the university (for example, the competitions to become a business or nursing major, which are substantially influenced by GPA). They are less likely to drop out of college.[12] Now imagine that, instead, the college assigns teachers who are not skilled in teaching math and who have either little investment in student success or limited opportunities for self-improvement through professional development (or both). Perhaps, for example, the instructor is a graduate student who struggles to speak nontechnical English, was selected for graduate school because of research potential rather than teaching skills, and has strong incentives to focus on research rather than improving as a teacher. Such an instructor will probably result in a lower grade, less learning, and higher attrition for such a student.

Now suppose that one of these students wants to become a nurse, and a B or C or above in a specific chemistry course is a prerequisite for admission to the major. An unskilled teacher tilts the playing field to those who have enjoyed better science instruction in high school or have funds and time for private tuition. These resources are not distributed equally across socioeconomic classes. Of course, even those rejected from a nursing program on one campus may still become nurses. But, typically, one's degree (having found some other major) must be completed and additional money and time devoted to school. Lower-income students determined to become nurses must forgo earnings for an extra year and go still further into debt for the want of a skilled teacher in a gatekeeping course. The students more likely to succeed in the face of suboptimal teaching are those whose high school preparation was better and those who have access to private tuition of some sort.

The distribution of the impact of suboptimal instruction thus creates a serious injustice between students on campuses. All students have grounds for reasonable complaint, but the costs are borne disproportionately by first-generation students, students from low-income backgrounds, and racially minoritized students. These increase their probability of academic failure while damaging their professional prospects.

WHAT SHOULD UNIVERSITIES AND COLLEGES DO?

All parties understand the status quo incentives for professors. Tenure, pay raises, outside offers, distinguished professorships, and status among their peers (especially beyond their home institution) are almost exclusively rewards for research excellence and rarely rewards for instructional quality. Teaching undergraduates who struggle—because they are ill-prepared, lack an affinity for the given subject, suffer from emotional or psychological problems, or are just lazy—takes time and expertise better spent, given the incentive structure, elsewhere. How should college and university leaders change the incentive structure? I explore here some proposals for improvement.[13]

The proposals are modest and modular. Improving teaching and learning competes with numerous other demands on leaders. Faculty do not agitate for measures that will improve teaching and learning. They are more interested in improved research support, pay, and course releases. The nonacademic side of the university does not see teaching and learning as within its remit. Alumni do not press for improvements. Conversations with senior administrators at numerous institutions and with students about why they encounter so much suboptimal teaching have the same upshot: neither the students nor their parents complain to administrators. And legislators, even those who enjoy criticizing higher education, do not seem to understand the business model well enough to press for valuable change. If leaders could transform a campus overnight, then a set of interconnected mutually reinforcing reforms might make sense. But few leaders have that sort of power, because faculty have considerable power of veto over curricular and instructional issues and departments have considerable de facto power over issues of teaching and learning. Reforms should not be mutually antagonistic, but leaders need individual reforms that can make a significant difference at varying levels of scale even if others get blocked.

A final prefatory comment. Roughly speaking, four kinds of agents can make a difference to teaching and learning. External agents (legislatures, funders, boards of trustees) can earmark funds and/or create regulatory frameworks. Senior administrators (presidents, provosts, deans) can earmark funds and instigate reforms. Campus units (in particular, departments) can introduce policies and practices, and create programs.[14] And individual instructors can invest in improving their instruction. I'm going to focus entirely on the intermediate agencies: senior administration and departments.[15]

The PhD Program

Most faculty on most campuses trained initially in PhD programs. A small number of universities account for a very large proportion of the faculty in American colleges and universities. Most PhDs who become professors will devote the vast majority of their career to teaching, yet programs rarely provide pedagogical training. Early training, and enculturation into the practice of taking teaching seriously as a complex practice focused on inducing student learning, are essential. Departments can implement and require ongoing training in pedagogy. Requiring students to take just four 1-credit semester-long courses during their first two years of teaching does not seem excessive. Some departments are already well-equipped to implement such a program, while others that are less so may need sensitive and well-targeted support and encouragement from campus and college leadership.

Department Reviews

Accreditation requires periodic reviews of each program on campus. College guidelines can shape expectations for departments to give appropriate focus to the undergraduate programs and, for example, provide (and review committees to scrutinize) evidence of the *quality of learning* rather than evidence merely about *outcomes*. Colleges can, and should, provide advance warning of these expectations. Most departments need lead time, as well as infrastructural support, to create systems that measure learning. Colleges can also clearly signal that frankness in departmental self-reports about deficiencies in teaching and learning will be rewarded, not penalized, and they can select review committee personnel for their interest and competence in evaluating teaching and learning.

Tenure

At research institutions, tenure is largely decided on the grounds of the quality and promise of the candidate's research. At teaching institutions, the quality of teaching is given more weight, but the measures of such are typically poor. I'm skeptical that research institutions can do a great deal to rebalance the significance of teaching and research in the tenure process. Suppose that a campus promised to give as much weight to teaching as to research in tenure decisions. It would be hard for candidates to believe this was happening, partly because the process is somewhat opaque, and partly because they know that the main inputs into the decision come from senior faculty who value research over teaching. And they also know that they might not get tenure anyway, so they have to make themselves competitive for positions on other campuses, which means they have to focus on research. And everyone involved would understand this.

Although they can't do *much* to rebalance teaching and learning in tenure decisions, leaders could do *something*. Exactly what might vary from campus to campus, but one measure would be to insist that departments systematically consider, and report, levels of participation in instruction-oriented professional development. The tenure "moment" can be valuable in other ways. It is a rare occasion on which a range of outsiders can scrutinize a department's practices. Divisional committees are well placed to provide feedback to both departments and deans on the quality of the processes that departments use to evaluate teaching: Are student surveys well constructed? Is there evidence that teachers and departments attend to the qualitative data student evaluations provide? How well do peer observations match up with student evaluations? Are peer observations haphazard or systematic, and do the peer observers use good protocols?

A Parallel Track

As teaching loads for regular tenure-line faculty have declined, non-tenure-line instructors with lower status, less job security, and weaker governance rights have filled the gap. Universities could establish a formal status for instructors with no research responsibilities but with higher teaching loads, a clear career ladder, and, importantly, parity of status with what are currently tenure-line faculty. Of course, the informal status order cannot be controlled directly through institutional rules. But "parity of status" here could be understood to include various benefits. Dedicated funds available for professional development, similar salary progression, parallel tenure and promotion procedures, and, importantly, equal governance rights would allow employees on this track to participate as fully in decision-making at all levels as employees currently in tenure-line positions. This would militate against the tendency of departments to treat teaching staff as second-class citizens and would enable them to elevate the importance of instruction in departmental, college-level, and campus-wide decision-making. Essentially it would create a cohesive group with long time-horizons and an ongoing interest in putting instruction closer to the center of the actual mission.

Teaching and Learning Centers

Think about how someone learns to become, and becomes better at being, a researcher. They take classes, do research, get feedback on the research from their expert teachers, submit to journals where they get feedback from anonymous experts, go to conferences where they get more feedback from nonanonymous experts, participate in labs and reading groups, and continually consume the research of other experts. They're embedded in an infrastructure designed to improve the quality of research. Instructors also need an infrastructure that supports continuous improvement. Many universities have Centers of Teaching and Learning whose mission is maintaining and extending such an infrastructure. Leaders of campuses without these centers can create them. Leaders of campuses *with* such centers can provide others with necessary resources and political backing. They can highlight their work, indicate to faculty that they expect high levels of engagement with the center, and provide incentives for individuals to engage. Centers themselves, if sufficiently supported by leadership, can take a proactive stance, seeking to partner with departments that have weak—or even strong—cultures regarding instruction.

Departments

Judith Warren Little says this about a good school:

> Teachers engage in frequent, continuous and increasingly concrete and precise talk about teaching practice (as distinct from teacher characteristics and failings, the social lives of teachers, the foibles and failures of students and their families, and the unfortunate demands of society on the school). By such talk, teachers build up a shared language adequate to the complexity of teaching, capable of distinguishing one practice and its virtue from another.[16]

That's what a department that takes teaching and learning seriously would look like. How can departments make that happen? They can ensure that all junior faculty are regularly observed by, and regularly observe, senior faculty. They can organize the same practices among tenure faculty. They can introduce regular colloquia on specific problems of instructional practice and earmark funds to support colleagues attending targeted instruction-oriented events from which they can bring back valuable information to their colleagues. Department meetings can include short presentations about instruction.

CONCLUDING COMMENT

Suppose that more money is spent on training and providing professional development to support high-quality instruction, or a budget is dedicated to the development of a teaching-focused career track, or individual professors in regular tenure-line appointments simply spend more time, effort, and energy on improving their instruction. What is the opportunity cost? At research institutions, it is liable to come from research. Any move to elevate the importance of instruction may be perceived, especially by faculty, as threatening the importance of research. But does elevating the importance of instruction risk damaging the research enterprise *unacceptably*?

I doubt it. In research universities the superior position of research is so entrenched that it would take far more extensive changes than I believe are feasible to knock it off its perch. Consider professional development—the amount of time typical tenure-line professors spend at research conferences, colloquia, and symposia dwarfs the amount they spend on professional development on instruction, even if their contract makes teaching and research coequal.

More controversially, I'd conjecture that for most faculty, switching 3% or 5% or even 10% of the time we do research, which we do very well, to improving their instruction, which we do less well, would enhance, rather than diminish, their contribution to overall social value.

Finally, I am not arguing for measures that would require immense time commitment. I have argued for investing in training teachers in graduate school by devoting about 10% of PhD credits to that end. Requiring faculty members to engage as little as 36 hours/year in professional development to improve instruction would yield large benefits. A campus that induced faculty to engage for an additional 18 hours/year throughout the rest of their career in observing colleagues, debriefing after being observed, collaborative reflection on their practice, and learning and refining new techniques would soon improve student learning dramatically. Anybody who knows the profession would regard an administrator who achieved those modest numbers as a genius. The research enterprise is safe.

Chapter 28

Assessing Faculty Unions

Judith Wagner DeCew

Emerging as early as 1910 and the 1930s, faculty unions became more prominent from the mid-to-late 1960s onward. One of the multiple factors contributing to their rise was social, based on critiques of the status quo accompanied by skepticism that student protests promoted regarding the ability to solve social problems. The difficult national economic climate was another major factor as the movement to unionize faculty grew dramatically in the 1970s, slowed somewhat in the 1980s, and reemerged during subsequent years through today, even as more traditional labor unions in America have lost resources and much of their influence. Increasingly, government at all levels has attempted to control higher education to improve its economic efficiency, enhance delivery of education, and reduce faculty's role in institutional governance. Politically, efforts of public officials to restructure and reorganize universities, to impose new tenure policies, and to prioritize teaching over research affect public institutions where faculty seek to retain power and status as well as private institutions where faculty and students benefit from federal grants. Thus, social, economic, and political forces all contribute to feelings of uncertainty and the proliferation of academic unions.

The American Association of University Professors (AAUP) believes unions can protect individual rights, shared institutional governance, tenure, and academic freedom while safeguarding teaching and working conditions by pooling faculty strengths. The AAUP also argues that "academic senates and academic unions can effectively coexist, with clearly defined responsibilities,"[1] although leadership and a cooperative environment are still needed. According to the AAUP and other sources, 21% of all universities have faculty unions, and among public universities, 35% have unions. Some believe these estimates are low, and some argue that the numbers of faculty unions are still growing despite the fact that many states still do not allow collective bargaining in the public sector. Whatever their exact numbers, academic unions help shape American higher education by exerting a considerable impact on campus culture, its values, priorities, and distribution of power.

Unionization for faculty is more complex than that for industry, not only because of political and economic forces but also because of issues and values peculiar to the profession. The breadth of items that faculty unions often see as within their scope and thus subject to collective bargaining is remarkable. Some issues are generally nonacademic and more clearly economic, including salary, merit pay, and compensation for additional activities, as well as other benefits such as life and disability insurance, moving expenses, tuition waivers for dependents, sabbatical leave, leaves of absence, and maternity and sick leave. Other issues fall under the category of working conditions, including reappointment, tenure and promotion policies, grievance procedures, course load, number of students, the college calendar, office space, administrative assistant and research staff, committee work, and so on. But collective bargaining often covers more obviously academic issues as well, including admissions, educational policy, curriculum, program development, nominations and selections for administrators, searches for presidents, naming of endowed chairs and distinguished professorships, to name a few.

Debates about unions have featured heated political rhetoric from the outset. Despite the significant percentage of faculty working under unions, most of the literature on higher education has either ignored, overlooked, or disparaged unions. Although a union can provide legal protections for faculty, joining one is often stigmatized. This paper offers a balanced account of faculty unions: their many and varied strengths and weaknesses, and multiple arguments in favor of and against them. These considerations can be grouped under four headings: collegiality, effectiveness, institutional structure, and academic values. Let us consider them in turn.

COLLEGIALITY

Debate endures about whether faculty unions promote collegiality or adversity. Those favoring unions insist that faculty should have the freedom to decide for themselves whether unions will benefit their particular campus. Advocates claim that unionization can enhance collegiality, respecting the values of freedom of choice and association. Rather than creating adversity, unions help ameliorate it by improving communication between faculty and administrators or a governing board. Supporters believe unionization improves faculty's working relationship with the administration and helps them present a united voice on issues of salary, personnel practices, and grievance procedures. When legislators weigh in on how state-supported schools should be run and endorse an anti-intellectual perspective, unionization can even unite faculty and administrators. Indeed, many point to its moral and psychological benefits of community, a view expressed by philosopher Richard Rorty that unions can provide excellent examples of comradeship and loyalty.[2]

Advocates also contend that unions do not undermine but rather support and enhance traditional forms of shared governance such as academic senates. Because they provide written policies and procedures, already agreed to by faculty and administration, unions can help ensure clear guidelines for mutual decision-making. According to the AAUP, "Essentially a collective bargaining agreement puts the legal force of a contract behind the principles of shared governance and due process. It obliges the university to negotiate . . . and it gives the faculty a vehicle for enforcing the policies articulated in faculty handbooks."[3]

These advocates of collective bargaining, who believe unions can facilitate communication and cooperation with administrators and managers, steadfastly support this vision. They argue that most faculty have little voice in university governance as few campuses give them genuine authority. Ideally, collective bargaining promotes discussion and compromise, providing a system of self-governance between management and the faculty union.

Those who oppose unions claim they do increase adversity, tension, and division between faculty and administrators as well as among faculty members who disagree about whether to unionize and who may remain bitter even after a successful union vote. In their view, the mere presence of a union on campus fosters antagonism in part because the union model from industry, which treats its members as laborers and not professionals, is inflexible and bureaucratic rather than collegial.

Administrators claim that unions tie their hands and restrict them from making decisions in the best interests of faculty. Some argue that this adversarial model alienates administrators and changes their role. After all, faculty senates and committees allow their members a strong say in university governance, and many even believe the faculty run the show. Opponents of unions believe faculty governance works well enough in its role negotiating for faculty interests. Faculty unions therefore only diminish and weaken faculty governance; their very existence makes spending time on committees perceived as ineffectual far less appealing.

Defenders of faculty governance prefer keeping these voices within the university management team rather than polarizing faculty and losing them to a union. Given their positive assessment of faculty governance, these faculty and administrators argue that unions merely add another layer of administration and bureaucracy that increases the time involved bargaining over every term and condition.

An additional argument is that unions create adversity between faculty members. Many votes for unionization have been close, and bad feelings between proponents and opponents often linger and even fester. Moreover, a union majority that proceeds with collective bargaining and ignores the concerns of minorities may generate even more tension among the faculty.

EFFECTIVENESS

Another set of arguments examines unions' effectiveness as a political force for achieving faculty goals. Defenders assert that unions, most importantly, have given faculty a governing role at certain universities. Contracts can be as flexible or detailed as negotiating parties determine. Unions, for example, can improve faculty salaries by establishing salary pools, minimum salaries at each rank and for years of service, and so on, as well as benefits such as health insurance and professional and family leave. Advocates believe unions improve working conditions, workloads, and grievance procedures to protect faculty autonomy and ensure fair treatment.

Unions are crucial for job security. Legally strong contracts for tenure are critical in an age where advancing technology may threaten faculty appointments and when many in the public and even in the administration of higher education question the value of tenure. Unions often secure advantages for the lowest paid and most vulnerable faculty, and they enhance equity in salary and parity in work conditions, addressing private deals certain faculty strike with administrators that generate wide discrepancies in treatment.

Union advocates stress that public institutions and even small private colleges are again cutting budgets, freezing hiring, and offering minimal salary increases. In this view, faculty no longer have much control over budgets. Financial woes also reduce the number of full-time faculty. In such times of fiscal austerity, unions are the most effective way to maintain faculty compensation and benefits while enhancing faculty autonomy. Contracts can also help guarantee faculty a role in the appointment of instructional staff.

Those opposed claim that unions have a negative effect or no influence at all on compensation. Many who concede unions make occasional gains for faculty may still see unions as largely self-interested or out of touch with changing times. They also view unions as coercive by nature, entities that tend to violate rights and freedoms. They worry that unions protect unproductive faculty and prolong the already costly and lengthy process of collective bargaining. Unions slow down decision-making that is easier to complete in a collegial and consensus-oriented atmosphere while harming the effectiveness of administrators and faculty to enhance life on campus. At their worst, faculty unions shift decision-making on crucial academic issues such as personnel evaluations and decisions to nonacademics.

Opponents of unions also claim that their collective bargaining agreements leave less flexibility for policy changes that affect faculty and less leeway for pay raises and recognition for outstanding work. Without merit pay raises, the quality of an institution's faculty declines as the best faculty leave and incentives that encourage intellectual creativity and achievement are stifled. In addition, detractors believe that unions on campus pose liabilities. Because administrators and management usually insist on no-strike clauses in academic union contracts, they happen less frequently than with other unions, but a strike or other controversy that does occur can tarnish the campus image and university reputation, affecting undergraduate admissions and the ability to appoint the best faculty.

Another concern is the decreased intellectual productivity of faculty who find themselves focusing on union activity and outside influences on their educational institutions. Furthermore, critics believe that far from enhancing faculty autonomy, unions, particularly at state-supported universities, may lead to the end of autonomy when faculty bypass administrators and negotiate through unions directly with legislators. At such institutions, legislators achieve possibly more power over tenure and even curricular matters.

INSTITUTIONAL STRUCTURE

A third concern involves the advantages and disadvantages of faculty unions for the nature and structure of universities and unions. Those supporting faculty unionization argue that many universities are big businesses that need unions to represent and protect faculty, employees in a corporate environment who are insufficiently valued and seen as replaceable. Unions can also serve as watchdogs to monitor administrators and managers, ensuring ethical behavior and decision-making. Defenders see unions as positive organizations promoting the interests and values of the faculty as well as the institutions of higher education they serve. Advocates believe that collective bargaining is one way to maintain the traditional values of the academy, and the only effective way at some institutions.

Some even approve of unions becoming more militant as collective bargaining becomes more prominent. In this view, a union is an independent institution to which faculty members, who are less powerful than administrators, can appeal in defense of their rights. These include due process and fair treatment, an argument that suggests unions are compatible with personal liberty.

In contrast, others emphasize the solitary nature of many a professor's work, an ideal that appears to conflict with the collectivism of unionization. Critics of faculty unions also counter that colleges and universities are very different in structure and goals than businesses, so the industry model dictating a need for unions does not apply. They worry, in addition, that the rise of unions tends to make universities function more like corporations whose standardization and inflexibility should be avoided, not embraced. Opponents also point out that faculty unions do not represent all faculty members as only a majority vote is needed to introduce a union, and often a split vote occurs between different groups of faculty members. Despite this split, those who do not wish to be members of the union cannot opt out. Furthermore, the union majority need not heed minority interests. Detractors also worry that unionization outsiders unfamiliar with academia may end up controlling the campus.

ACADEMIC VALUES

A fourth issue focuses on the academic values of a university. When an ideal collegial atmosphere exists and the administration ensures faculty autonomy and roles in university governance, harmony is likely, rendering a union unnecessary. When an administration breaches these principles, unions can intervene through moral persuasion, appeals to the media, and legal action. In a less-than-ideal collegial atmosphere, a union can be of enormous benefit to faculty defending their rights.

The freedom to determine the content of their teaching, their research, and their academic programs is one of the values most cherished by faculty members. Indeed, a view of freedom and self-reliance as foundational values that allow scholarly creativity and intellectual productivity to thrive may promote distrust of unions. When administrators, trustees, and others overseeing colleges and universities have the vision to understand and respect academic freedom, faculty members feel understood and respected. Faculty who believe their managers are acting in the best interests of the faculty and their institutions are unlikely to seek unionization. But when academic freedom is jeopardized, faculty can be highly motivated to protect this value, and many believe unions are the most effective way of doing so.

Finally, a crucial value to institutions of higher learning is what may be described in the tradition of John Stuart Mill as the search for the truth. Devotion to truth and understanding, to teaching and research, to seeking knowledge and following one's imagination, and to intellectual striving and vigorous open debate are all at the heart of the meaning and quest of a college or university. They signify the essence and importance of institutions of higher learning. When these values are alive and vigorous on campus, unionization seems incompatible with their further promotion. When they are neither encouraged nor protected, institutions of higher learning may find union organizers on their doorsteps.

If faculty members are beleaguered, disrespected, powerless, and treated as expendable by an administration, trustees, or legislators, they are more likely to share common values and visions for their institutions. In the face of grossly unfair treatment, they are more likely to unite around issues of job security and community, fairness and justice through equitable pay, autonomy that preserves dignity, and empowerment through enhanced participation in faculty governance. In such cases, faculty unions are more likely to succeed in gaining both pragmatic and moral legitimacy. Pragmatic legitimacy is achieved by clarifying the benefits a union can provide to its members and demonstrating their delivery as promised. Moral legitimacy is achieved when a union moves past pragmatic concerns to foster larger social improvement valued by those inside and outside the union. If, however, faculty members feel well-compensated, highly valued and respected, included in institutional governance, and secure in their positions through tenure and the academic freedom it brings, then worries about unions and their legitimacy will be few.

CONCLUSION

In conclusion, the balanced arguments for and against faculty unions may often reflect how greatly unions in academia vary. Some take a more "industrial" form, with management and workers cast as adversaries, and others share an approach of cooperation and collegiality between administration and faculty. Competing arguments can also be attributed to the wide range of academic institutions with varying levels of managerial power, varying levels of agreement on values, different constituencies with different priorities, and so on. All these factors help explain the complexity of and controversy surrounding faculty unions, why some educational institutions become unionized and others do not, and why some unions succeed while others fail.

Faculty without unions and those who oppose them should nevertheless consider their influence on academia, often to the benefit of nonunionized schools. In essence, those on unionized campuses usually do the hard work, but in the end, faculty at colleges and universities without unions often benefit from their work. This process can be subtle and take time, but as unions gain better salaries and benefits for professors, for example, other institutions need to match or increase theirs to attract the best candidates. Whatever one's particular views, faculty unionization can provide broad benefits within the academic profession. Still, supporters of academic unions should take careful note of its many potential deleterious effects. Increased adversity on campus, decreased effectiveness of faculty and administrators, compromised institutional structure, and eroded academic values are all serious drawbacks to consider.[4]

Chapter 29

Friendraising

Deni Elliott

> Those who are friends because of what is useful dissolve their friendship as soon as it ceases to be of advantage to them; for it was not each other they loved, but what profited them.
>
> Aristotle, *Nicomachean Ethics*, Book VIII, 1157a15

> Most people delight in being honored by those in positions of power because of the hopes it raises—they think that, if they need something, they will get it from them, and so delight in the honor they receive as an indication of good things to come.
>
> Aristotle, *Nicomachean Ethics*, Book VIII, 1159a20

Aristotle may have been the first philosopher to elucidate the moral failings of friendships based on utility. Perhaps he was musing about the donors to the Lyceum, his school for scholarly and public study, or maybe he first confronted the odd relationship fostered between institution and donor when he was still a student studying at Plato's Academy. Reciprocal relationships between organizations and philanthropists have existed since antiquity. Ancient Hebrew text chiseled into a temple wall thanking donors has been found at Israeli archaeological sites that predate the Common Era.

Institutions of higher education (IHE) bestow recognition on and offer funding opportunities to individuals and organizations. Institutional leaders reach out to those included in the school census as students, staff, administrators, or faculty, and to a larger pool of "friends." Some external friends have earned institutional recognition through service that represents the mission, vision, and values by which the school defines itself. Other people have received recognition, such as honorary degrees, simply because the decision-maker at a college or university decided that linking the individual with the institution might assist in launching an upcoming capital campaign or other major fundraising initiative. While donors were traditionally connected to the school in some way—most usually as wealthy alumni—and honorees might be invited for recognition from anywhere in the world, those groups have merged. Corporate wealth has added an additional wrinkle to those honored and solicited, as some businesses and entrepreneurs have recognized that they can further their own goals by providing funds that position them as connected to particular IHE.

Some individual-institutional relationships are intended to confer glory on the individual. Others are intended to enhance the institution's importance. The relationship can backfire for both. If agreements are not carefully written and aligned with institutional messaging, an identified booster may become an albatross for the school as the donor's bad behavior becomes publicly known. If agreements fail to meet specific criteria important to donors, they may find their philanthropic intent perverted and funds used to support programs or projects that are anathema to them.

Here I examine donations to institutions of higher education and institutional recognition as instructive examples of how institutional-individual relationships can fail. I conclude with guidelines for how to protect all parties in these peculiar, utility-based "friendships."

Let's start with an examination of the institutional role and its related responsibilities. Institutions of higher education can be uniquely identified by one characteristic—advancing knowledge through teaching and research. These entwined prongs require mission-driven faculty who can advance knowledge through critical inquiry, creativity, vision, and experimentation, and who can teach postsecondary-school students the skills and insight to become the next generation of researchers, effective leaders, and educated citizens. Almost every college or university displays a mission statement on its public website. Some statements are succinct, others all-encompassing. In each case, the mission statement describes how the particular institution interprets its unique IHE role. Few schools explicitly state the obvious—that the organization itself is a moral agent. Through its leadership it makes institutional choices that affect students and employees as well as the community in which the school and its citizens live.

In a well-run IHE, activities not directly connected to teaching or research can either be shown to support the "advancing knowledge" responsibility or can be demonstrated as secondary, but not contradictory, to the school's mission. But many IHE are not so well-aligned. Too often, the school's mission is fenced off to address the Academic Affairs side of the house while other school choices and activities are siloed by a focus on meeting financial goals. This creates dissonance between messaging and action.

It is not unusual for advancement professionals—the marketing and communication specialists, recruitment and enrollment officers, and those who develop and maintain relationships with alumni and other donors—to have their achievement assessed by the school's media presence, student applications and enrollment, and donated dollars. All those outcomes are arguably in service to the school's role-related responsibilities, but ethical concerns emerge when advancement staff members are encouraged to prioritize bottom-line performance over working in concordance with the institution's stated mission.

One easy test of how closely an institution has aligned its business productivity with its mission is to examine the list of the college or university's preferred vendors. Most schools present themselves as committed to overcoming racial inequity and promoting social justice. However, if messaging and action that demonstrate these values are limited to faculty hires, student cohorts, and course curricula while leadership choose suppliers based on the lowest bid from a national purveyor, dissonance is created. Addressing racial inequality and promoting social justice should be campus-wide. An institution with message alignment seeks diverse students and faculty and curriculum but also populates preferred purveyors lists with vendors and suppliers that represent local small businesses owned by people of color, women, LGBTQ+ populations, people with disabilities, and veterans. These schools practice what they teach. The IHE can also be perceived as hypocritical if leaders subsume institutional values under donor desires.

THE UNIVERSITY OF NORTH DAKOTA AND AN EVERLASTING LEGACY

Consider the case of Ralph Engelstad, a hockey player and a 1954 graduate of the University of North Dakota, who continues to have posthumous influence on UND to this day. By 1959 Engelstad had become a millionaire, and that was only the beginning of his impressive entrepreneurial life. He built on his success through ownership of a series of casinos on the Las Vegas strip. At the time of his death in 2002, his last venture, the Imperial Palace Hotel and Casino, was the sixteenth largest hotel in the world.

The University of North Dakota recognized Engelstad's accomplishments, as well as his capacity to give back to the institution. In 1981 the UND Alumni Association honored him with the Sioux Award, named after the school's then-mascot, The Fighting Sioux. Six years later, Englestad was inducted into the Fighting Sioux Hall of Fame. Englestad endowed the hockey program with a $5 million donation in 1988, for which UND renamed the sports center the Ralph Engelstad Arena. Before and following Englestad's death, the family foundation had donated more than $124 million to UND.[1] But the gifts came with conditions and controversy.

The University of North Dakota's mission is "to provide transformative learning, discovery and community engagement opportunities for developing tomorrow's leaders." The school identifies six core values: community, discovery, diversity, inclusivity, liberal arts, and lifelong learning.[2] The school describes "diversity" as an understanding and appreciation of diverse people, experiences, and ideas; UND describes "inclusivity" as a welcoming, inclusive, and supportive environment for all. While there are few potential African American or Latinx students in North Dakota, Native Americans make up almost 5% of the state's population. The Sioux people, which belong to thirty distinctive tribes in the United States and Canada, number approximately 150,000. The longstanding UND nickname, The Fighting Sioux, was first adopted in 1930. By the 1970s activists argued for the removal of the mascot and logo based on exploitation and stereotyping of Native Americans. The Fighting Sioux logo features a male Indian head with face painted for battle. At games, tom-tom drums accompanied ritual chants of "Sioux, yeah, yeah." Rival teams answered by chanting, "Sioux suck shit."

In the 1980s, the decade in which UND was recognizing Engelstad for his accomplishments, unique characteristics of the alumnus came to light. In 1988, the year that the sports arena was named for Ralph Engelstad, he was investigated by the Nevada Gaming Commission for his seeming obsession with Adolf Hitler. Details of Engelstad's extensive collection of Nazi memorabilia became public. A delegation from UND flew to Las Vegas to meet with Engelstad at his hotel, view his private collection of Nazi memorabilia, and discuss with him the parties he had thrown in 1986 and 1988 to celebrate the birthday of Adolph Hitler. The UND delegation decided that Engelstad was "unthinking," but that his attention to Hitler was meant "as a joke."

Publicly apologizing for his "bad judgment," Engelstad said that he "despises Hitler and everything he stood for." However, he reportedly handed out T-shirts depicting Nazi battle scenes as party favors.[3] The Gaming Commission also found that Engelstad had 500 bumper stickers proclaiming "Hitler was Right" produced at the hotel's print shop. His car collection included Hitler's staff cars.

UND might have been convinced that Engelstad was sorry for his oversight in proclaiming Hitler as "right," but the Nevada Gaming Commission was not. The Commission determined that Engelstad had damaged the state's image by "glorifying Hitler and the Third Reich."[4] It collected $1.5 million in fines and damages from Englestad along with a promise that he would not hold any more Hitler-themed birthday parties.

The UND delegation continued to accept donations from this wealthy alum, who became even more engaged with university affairs. Engelstad said that he would no longer donate to the school unless the athletic director he didn't like was removed. His donations paused. Four years later, after this athletic director left UND, Engelstad pledged more than $100 million to build a new 400,000-square-foot hockey arena.[5] The arena was fashioned to be the envy of every athletic department in the country and the natural home for postseason NCAA games.

Engelstad was proud of his record when he played for The Fighting Sioux hockey team and wanted the team and his name to be linked in perpetuity. He wanted the nickname, mascot, and traditions to continue regardless of the effect of the name on those offended by the dismissive use of their heritage. In the late 1990s, while Engelstad was negotiating details of the sports facility he would build, the North Dakota House of Representatives failed in its attempt to force UND to retire the Fighting Sioux nomenclature. When Engelstad added the condition to his donation that the Fighting Sioux nickname and logo remain indefinitely in his new arena, University leaders agreed.

To ensure that The Fighting Sioux could never be removed from the arena, Engelstad directed that more than 3,500 images of the logo be embedded in the chairs and floors and walls and windows throughout the stadium. A life-sized statue of Englestad dominates the front hall of the Ralph Englestad Arena, which opened in 2001. His dedication is etched in the wall and includes: "The Fighting Sioux logo, the Fighting Sioux uniforms, the aura of the Fighting Sioux tradition and the spirt of being a Fighting Sioux are of lasting value and immeasurable significance to our past, present, and future." In public areas of the arena, spectators cannot help but see multiple Fighting Sioux logos.

In 2005 the NCAA sanctioned IHE, including UND for "hostile and abusive" college athletic representations. The Fighting Sioux name and logo could not be used in any postseason play games, and UND was not allowed to host any postseason playoffs. The Fighting Sioux name was finally retired in 2012, after 67% of North Dakota voters chose to do away with the controversial reference, although there is some question of whether confusing language in the ballot initiative resulted in citizens voting against their intent. Three years later, the UND athletic teams were named "The Fighting Hawks."

Ralph Engelstad died the year after his arena opened. Ever the businessman, rather than give UND control of the arena or its full profits, he had created RE Arena Inc. to own and operate the facility. Ticket and advertising revenues are divided between UND and RE Arena Inc., with Engelstad's business venture, controlled by his family, receiving the larger amount of proceeds. Issues of control between UND and the Engelstad family have continued. On March 1, 2019, the local newspaper, *Grand Forks Herald,* reported, "The Engelstad family plans to pull donations from UND until President Mark Kennedy is removed from office." According to Engelstad's daughter, he "didn't like the structure of the original gift from my dad and thought it . . . wasn't fair to the university." Kennedy, who had been looking for work elsewhere, resigned the following month.

Four months after his departure, Kris Engelstad McGarry signed a commitment to fund the Ralph Engelstad Arena through September 2030 and expressed her appreciation of interim president Joshua Wynne. Although UND athletes are now known as The Fighting Hawks, spectators and visitors confront a Ralph Engelstad Arena full of The Fighting Sioux logos. Fighting Sioux trademarked items continue to be available for purchase at The Sioux Shop, located in the arena. Diehard fans wear "Sioux" clothing and paraphernalia to games.

The moral of the story is that the more a school allows a donor to push boundaries, the harder regaining control and changing culture becomes for the institution. Boundary violations evolve. No institution starts a relationship with a donor with the intent of allowing the donor to make decisions that are appropriate for IHE leadership. The time to prevent confrontations between donors and institutions is prior to the school accepting or returning any gifts that can leverage influence.

PHILANTHROPIC ISSUES IN TWENTY-FIRST CENTURY HIGHER EDUCATION

Gone are the days when donors and institutions automatically knew that donor control ended once the institution fulfilled donor intent or chiseled a name into a building or other campus property. Donor understanding that it is the school's business to decide who to hire to fill an endowed named chair and to make any other personnel or programming decisions can no longer be assumed.

Givers in the twenty-first century are as likely to describe themselves as venture capitalists as they are to call themselves donors or "friends" of the institution. Unlike traditional donors that may wish to fund a scholarship or contribute toward the building of a concert hall, venture capitalists bring ideas for programs and curriculum that may be larger than their donations. They present the school with assessment criteria rather than donor intent. They want to create change rather than have mere public testaments to their generosity. The venture capitalist approach recognizes IHE as the transformative organizations that colleges and universities should be. However, leadership at the school should be independently interested in seeking the change proposed, as these donors may expect the school to use their donation as seed funding and include an exit strategy as part of the donation agreement. The IHE–venture capitalist relationship allows for clarity of expectations and contractual agreements not possible if one or both parties is hiding behind the façade of friendship.

When philanthropists become party to decisions traditionally made in-house, however, what may be considered expected reciprocity to the donor may feel like bribery to a university officer. For example, a classic case of misguided donor recognition arises in conflict between the development and admissions offices. The development office might ask the admissions office to include the daughter of a wealthy alumna in the incoming class, contrary to published admissions standards. The 2019 Department of Justice charges against fifty-three people involved in a criminal conspiracy to bribe school officials and use fraudulent practices to gain college admissions showed only the illegal tip of the iceberg. Parental use of wealth to weight the scales in favor of their child's admission has a long history.⁶ Rather than reject parental wealth as admissions criteria, some institutions have become transparent about the practice, acknowledging that they give preference or "points" to children of alumni in "order to strengthen family ties to the institution and to encourage traditions of financial support among generations."⁷ Other schools, including Harvard, have determined that gifts should not be solicited from a person whose family member has applied for admission and that unsolicited gifts at that time will not be accepted.⁸

IHE fundraising initiatives have moved far beyond soliciting annual gifts from alumni, with schools and corporations finding ways to provide financial benefit to one another. Colleges and universities let corporations name sports arenas, privatize the sales of books and merchandise through for-profit suppliers, and fill their campuses with vending machines. The agreement reached between RE Arena Inc. and UND, with the corporation receiving most of the profits, has become the norm for schools that offer corporate branding opportunities or allow other corporate access to students. The Week of Welcome that greets students on most campuses is likely to have booths that encourage student applications for credit cards and purchases of school spirit paraphernalia that benefit corporations more than the school. Industry-supported majors, an easy channel for students to move from classroom to worksite upon graduation, may skew curriculum. As students serve as fodder for profits for both institutions and corporations, it is up to the IHE to resist having both powerful parties view students simply as consumers. If school leadership is going to expose students to corporate "opportunities," it incurs an obligation to make students educated consumers of those opportunities.

Universities and colleges single out individuals for honors and awards, including those who are already in the school's census and those who have gained fame or fortune completely independent of the school. Some individuals are honored as they are thought to embody the school's core values. Sometimes these individuals are already donors. Sometimes leaders seek to publicly entwine celebrities with the school in hopes that the association will further support. If the honoree is a public figure who has an equally public fall from grace, the honor may be revoked as easily as bestowed. For example, a favorite commencement speaker, Bill Cosby, received more than seventy honorary doctorates,⁹ with many of those rescinded after his conviction for aggravated indecent assault. It is not known how many of those were reinstated when the Supreme Court of Pennsylvania in 2021 vacated the charges against Cosby. Middlebury College rescinded an honorary degree given to presidential attorney Rudolph Giuliani for his role preceding the January 6, 2021, raid on the U.S. Capitol,¹⁰ while the St. John Fisher College Board of Trustees voted to allow Giuliani to keep his honorary degree. Wagner College, Lehigh University, and others that had awarded honorary degrees to Donald Trump also rescinded those awards following the January raid. It is unusual, but not unheard of, for someone who has had an honorary degree revoked to claim injuries based on the institution's change of heart. Recipients may claim defamation if an award is withdrawn for a claimed discretion before a public charge is proven.

Naming opportunities that are withdrawn or retired more often result in pushback from designees or heirs. Prestigious schools including Harvard, Stanford, and MIT took money from wealthy financier Jeffrey Epstein, even after he had been convicted of trafficking and sexual acts with underaged girls. Yale, Columbia, and Cornell accepted donations from the Sackler family even as family members were facing civil suits because of their drug company's role in the U.S. opioid crisis. Most schools attempt to at least remove the name that damages the interests or credibility of the school. Some seek to redirect the gift to fund research related to the donor's conviction or misbehavior. But none of that is within the school's control unless the gift agreement includes acknowledgment from the donor under what conditions these actions might take place.

THE POWER OF TRANSPARENCY

Institutions of higher education serve a unique need in society and should preserve the boundaries that support academic freedom and unquestioned commitment to knowledge and free expression. The power of the university incurs ethical obligations to students and employees affected by leadership choices.

Institute gift policies should be transparent and available for review by every campus member as well as potential donors. A committee representative of administration, faculty, staff, and students as well as the advancement team should make final determinations on a questionable gift as everyone on campus is affected by the negative publicity that follows a former institutional friend turned felon. Criteria that send a potential gift for review to the committee should be standardized before a question arises. For example, Harvard's gift policy identifies "triggering criteria" which includes the gift's size, a donor's lack of connection to Harvard. The policy also details "known concerns" regarding a potential donor's actions.[11]

Honorary degrees and other recognitions should be saved for those who make a difference regardless of giving capacity. For example, Emory & Henry College's longtime chef was awarded the Honorary Doctor of Culinary Arts for nearly sixty years of service to the school. In the newly recognized spirit of social justice, African American and Native American individuals are more likely than ever to be included as honorary degree recipients.

The ethical ideal for colleges and universities is to find ways to make the school's business interests, including solicitation, acceptance, and use of external funds, the topic for campus community discussion. Students rarely know how little their tuition truly funds. Their recognition of where the rest of the money comes from and how that can create conflicts of commitment for their educational experience turns such dilemmas into teachable moments.

Part XIV

SPORTS

Chapter 30

Intercollegiate Athletics as Entertainment

Peter A. French

Harold W. Stoke (1903–1982), former president of the University of New Hampshire, Louisiana State University, and Queens College, CUNY, was one of the first to write a provocative article on the relationship between university missions and their athletic programs. Since the *Atlantic Monthly*'s publication of "College Athletics: Education or Show Business?" in 1954, other reform-minded critics of intercollegiate athletics have echoed Stoke, though without citing this work they were unlikely to have been seen.

Stoke begins his piece by claiming that many American universities are discovering their "latest and growing responsibility—namely to provide public entertainment."[1] In our society the need for entertainment is "an inevitable consequence of the changing conditions of our lives" as Americans are living longer, working shorter hours during the week, and enjoying greater mobility and prosperity than they had prior to World War II. Those changes have created a social emptiness, and for "filling social vacuums the American system of education—and particularly higher education—is one of the most efficient devices ever invented." Universities have the ability to provide compelling and engrossing entertainment for public consumption in many different formats, including theater, music, and art. But Stoke specifies that "of all the instrumentalities which universities have for entertaining the public, the most effective is athletics."

Stoke's undisguised point is that viewing all the potential pursuits available to students in higher education as merely variations on a foundational academic function that require only one style of management and a single corridor of success would be to make what Gilbert Ryle calls a "category mistake."[2] If intercollegiate athletics are lumped in as an element of advanced education, what actually happens within such athletic programs would have to be understood as "inexplicable, corrupting, and uncontrollable." If, however, intercollegiate athletics are conceived of as purely a form of public entertainment, football and basketball within the organizational and governance structure of a university become activities distinctly unlike the academic fields populated and controlled by those in the professorial ranks with doctoral degrees. The failure to come to grips with such an alternative conception of athletics has provoked serious management and funding issues in some intercollegiate programs, along with bewilderedness and resentment among some professors in the school's academic programs and, in certain cases, scandals that besmirch the university's reputation.

Typically, supporters and funders of intercollegiate athletics in universities spend much of their energy and cash trying to obscure the distinction between the actual primary function of such programs and the educational function of much of the rest of the university. They often conjure up a seemingly endless parade of defenses of sport as a form of character education. Intercollegiate athletics, however, is much more than sport and only incidentally character building, if at all. If the only defense of intercollegiate athletics is the character education gambit, then such an argument really supports only a vigorous intramural program. The honest and potentially successful defense of intercollegiate athletics, especially those elite sports of football and basketball, is that they are the way, or at least one way and probably the most visible and successful way, to satisfy the university's public service obligation by providing public entertainment. In fact, intercollegiate athletic events more effectively touch the lives of more people than any other service or program the university may make available to the broader public in their communities.

Stoke notes that a university's real interest in its athletes is not at all the same as its interest in its academic students, a clue to the different functions that the university at least de facto recognizes. The academic departments of universities recruit students to "teach them what they do not already know." Athletes are recruited because they are already beyond proficient in the basic skills desired by the coaches of a given sport and have shown themselves to be so on their high school playing fields and courts. Academic students are educated by professors who expect to some degree that those students, or at least some of them, will devote part of their lives to noteworthy occupations or professions after graduation; athletes are required by their coaches to spend the majority of their time on campus participating in activities whose usefulness or value often disappears upon graduation or dissipates soon thereafter. Hours spent bashing into tackling dummies in the heat of August football practices are not likely to have much enduring value to a player who proves not good enough to make a professional team, as is annually the case for the vast majority of collegiate footballers and basketballers.

The spectacle that is a college football game, Stoke argues, has no conceivable educational purpose. The marching bands, the baton twirlers, the dance lines, and all the other accoutrements are entertainment and identity aids for the spectators, nothing more. But there is nothing wrong with "the show" as long as the institution's leadership admits that entertaining the public and the collegiate community is one of the university's functions, perhaps even one of its top responsibilities. Stoke urged that universities take seriously the differences between education and entertainment by managing their academic and athletic enterprises differently and consistent with the roles each performs. This should include tailoring admissions, course completion requirements, and grades to the athletes. Time spent in practice, travel, and performance should not be allowed to undermine progress toward graduation should the athlete intend to actually graduate, although many of the better athletes are unlikely to focus on that direction.

According to Stoke, "No matter what the [academic] regulation, if it prevents athletes from supplying the public entertainment for which [the sport] exists, a way around must be found." The bald fact is that "athletics requires an atmosphere of academic accommodation to its necessities." Academics in a university may not like to hear such a statement, and administrators may feel the pressure from both sides that athlete accommodations impose on them. The tension that sets the academic and the athletic sides of the campus at odds, however, is often primarily caused by a general failure of academic personnel and faculty to appreciate the multiple, rather than single and strictly educational, missions of a contemporary university.

On first reading, especially by an academic, Stoke appears ironic, even facetious. He could not really have meant it. After all, he was a college president. But Stoke was deadly serious, though not taken as seriously as he should have been by collegiate institutions. His article concludes with a number of recommendations that he admitted his academic colleagues and even those in athletic departments under the mythological spell of amateurism and character education will scorn and disregard. His first and clearly central recommendation is that universities and the NCAA must admit that intercollegiate athletics operate primarily for public entertainment and fundraising and that universities, especially if state supported, have a responsibility to provide such entertainment even if funding endeavors of their sports fall somewhat short of expectations. Once universities openly acknowledge that at least some of their intercollegiate sports are purely in the entertainment business, then, regardless of the academic successes or failures of its athletes, producing winning athletic teams becomes a legitimate university operation because only winning teams provide adequate entertainment and monetary value to the school.

The most proficient and therefore most desirable athletes, according to Stoke, should be paid whatever it takes to get them to play on a university team. That only the more prosperous institutions will be able to attract the best athletes is of no concern because the same sort of thing happens in most every department of a university. General competitive equity ought not to be a goal. If Princeton thinks there is nothing unethical about outbidding the University of California, Riverside, for a philosophy student, why should we look askance at the University of Michigan for outbidding the University of Idaho for a top linebacker?

In a paragraph guaranteed to raise the hackles of some academics, Stokes writes:

> Why should there be concern about the academic record of a young [person] who comes to a university primarily to play on a team and whom the university has brought for exactly that purpose? I submit that nothing is lost by relieving all athletes of the obligation to meet academic requirements if they cannot or do not wish to do so. Let us be courageous enough to admit that the university's interest in them is that they be good athletes, not that they be good students.

Stoke also champions the construction of a "firewall" between academic and athletic functions with respect to managerial and financial matters; no university's general academic budget should have to support the entertainment operations of the athletic department, and intercollegiate athletics that are not self-supporting should be terminated.

Forty-seven years after Stoke published his paper, Robert H. Atwell, former president of Pitzer College and president emeritus of the American Council on Education, supported virtually everything Stoke had recommended. In an essay in the *Chronicle of Higher Education*, Atwell urges universities to acknowledge professionalism in their elite sports and hire their athletes in what he calls the "entertainment wing of the university."[3] Football and basketball should exist separately from the other sports. And, like Stoke, Atwell proposes that they "could hire football and basketball players who would be students only if they wished to be; there would be no special admissions requirements or arrangements."

Stoke and Atwell affirm that universities have an obligation to the general public to provide entertainment and that football and basketball are doing so. A justification for professionalizing those sports in the university, this approach has the virtue of honesty and avoids the hypocrisy of the current system and the baseless rhetoric of the NCAA and many athletic departments. Nonetheless, some will dispute the premise that universities have an obligation to provide entertainment for the general public. For example, James J. Duderstadt, president of the University of Michigan, argues that universities have no responsibility whatsoever to provide entertainment for the public and programming for the commercial radio and television networks: "We have no business being in the entertainment business. We must either reform and restructure intercollegiate athletics on terms congruent with the educational purpose of our institutions, or spin big-time football and basketball off as independent, professional, and commercial enterprises no longer related to higher education."[4]

Of course, for many decades now, universities have provided such entertainment opportunities. As Stoke mentions, they sponsor theatrical performances, concerts, art shows, and the like. Admittedly, there is a significant, perhaps fundamental, difference between the entertainment that the public may garner from a play put on by the university's theater department or a recital sponsored by the music department and an intercollegiate football game or basketball game. The former cases provide public entertainment that derives and emerges directly from subjects in the university's standard curriculum in those fields. Intercollegiate athletics have no such direct link to the academic programs that make universities institutions of higher learning. To Stoke, that is an important difference, while Duderstadt would argue that even if sports such as football and basketball are morally desirable, that would be insufficient cause to justify their inclusion within the university absent a direct link to the academic enterprise that justifies its very existence. Stoke, of course, would counter that a university is not a single-function entity; it has multiple missions.

Stoke seems to have a far better grasp of intercollegiate athletics and the functions of the university (or multiversity) in contemporary American society than many who have participated in debates on the subject. Perhaps it is worth noting that though despite denouncing the commercialization of collegiate sports, Duderstadt made no noticeable dent in the University of Michigan's athletic intercollegiate programs while president.

Imagine the following situation. A major state-supported university has one of the country's best football teams annually rated in the top five in the national polls. The enormous fan base for its games regularly rewards the television networks with high ratings, allowing them to command top dollar for advertising minutes. The state, however, is experiencing a major recession. A legislator, an alumnus and former star player on its football team, proposes that the state close most of the academic programs but continue supporting the football team and just enough academic programs to keep the players eligible according to conference and NCAA rules. The legislator claims that in tough economic times the diversion a first-class football team provides is crucial to maintaining the morale of the people of the state, whereas programs, especially research programs in the standard academic disciplines, provide no such communal relief.

I strongly suspect that, if made in the legislature, such a proposal to gut the academic enterprise of the university and save the football team would cause the faculty to rise up in arms. Sports are not fundamental to the university, they would argue. Football should go before the traditional disciplines are devastated or demolished. Perhaps sports were not thought to be essential elements in the ancient universities of Europe or of some of the most prestigious technological institutions today, but the question of what is fundamental to the multiversities, today's major state institutions of higher education, is not a settled matter regardless of how absurd the imagined legislator's proposal might seem. The fact that university mission statements explicitly refer to serving the needs of the general public of their states and regions suggests that not all their rudiments reside in the traditional academic disciplines or even in teaching and "pure" research.

Embracing the entertainment function of intercollegiate athletics, especially with regard to the elite sports, has occurred in many if not all Division I universities in practice though not in principle. What the universities neither do nor the conferences permit, primarily because it is not in their financial interests, is to carry the entertainment mission model to its proper conclusions about students who perform on the field or the court. That many star athletes who hope to attract the attention of professional teams will continue to play for a university without being offered its financial support is not an ethically acceptable argument.

When I first started to think about the intercollegiate athletics situation as it has evolved since Stoke wrote in the *Atlantic Monthly*, I must confess my inclination was to side with those like Duderstadt who believe that collegiate sports have veered wildly off the track from what a collegiate institution is meant to be and do. No longer am I sure, however, that at least intercollegiate football and basketball are not fulfilling an important obligation of state-financed universities to serve the real needs and desires of those who support the university—the general public. Many of us in academia, including myself, should consider that commitment far more earnestly.

But an issue remains: Who gets to define and determine what the public needs from its universities? The challenge is to confront that question without presuming that academics can answer it better than the folks in the community who watch those games on television or who venture on campus only to attend a Saturday football game or an evening basketball game. Academic arrogance, while offensive to nonacademics who have a stake in the matter, can also be a moral defect that blinds academics to the full spectrum of responsibilities that their institutions have to their various constituencies.[5]

Chapter 31

Intercollegiate Athletics and Educational Values

Robert Simon

Many critics of intercollegiate athletics lead with the surely acceptable premise that a primary mission of the university is academic and intellectual and then jump to the conclusion that the *only* major or fundamental missions of the university are academic and intellectual.

This inferential leap is questionable, however. Surely other concerns must at times supersede the academic and intellectual goals of the university. Consider, for example, the postponement of a controversial speech due to security concerns, or budget allocations to preserve the aesthetic beauty of the campus rather than strengthen an academic department, or support for schools devoted to purely professional training rather than the humanities, arts, or sciences. That the merit of such compromises remains debatable reflects the ethically controversial nature of the university's fundamental mission(s) and function(s).

Why wouldn't the mission of the university, if conceived more broadly than purely academic and intellectual, be plausibly extended to cover the provision of public service, including the entertainment that intercollegiate athletics can offer the student body and wider community? Proponents of this view argue that the university provides entertainment for the community in a variety of areas such as theater, music, dance, and other performing arts, as well as programming on college-sponsored radio and television stations. Intercollegiate athletics is another way in which academic institutions extend this good to their students and staff and to the population at large.

Indeed, these advocates claim the university may even have a duty to do so. Peter French points out that the mission statements of many universities, especially large state institutions, often explicitly mention service to the community and to the economic and cultural needs of the population. Similarly, some mission statements of athletic departments, sanctioned by their universities, include entertainment among the specific functions of their programs.

Accordingly, once we abandon the assumption that the fundamental mission of the university should be solely and purely academic, encompassing teaching and scholarship in recognized academic disciplines, the sponsorship of intercollegiate athletics can be defended as fulfilling other legitimate functions. We should also challenge the assumption, relied on by both French and his critics, that athletics and academics are two sharply distinct kinds of activities.

I propose that a theory or model focused on sport as a mutual quest for excellence through competition is highly relevant to our inquiry into the relation of academics and athletics. This approach not only helps explain the enduring mass appeal of competitive sport but also provides an ethically defensible account of it as well.

In an important analysis of the nature of sports, philosopher Bernard Suits identifies these activities as a subclass of games. A game, in turn, is defined by rules that seemingly attempt to thwart its primary goals by creating obstacles that may seem unnecessary to an outsider. In one of Suits' examples, a bystander can't understand why a person who wants to get from point A to point B as quickly as possible doesn't just drive there. However, the person in question is a marathon runner who obeys race rules such as starting at a certain time and running the course rather than taking shortcuts or using alternate forms of transportation. Similarly, the rules of checkers prohibit simply knocking an opponent's pieces to the floor as a method of removing them from the board. Suits suggests that overcoming unnecessary obstacles produced by constitutive rules makes games, including all or most sports, inherently interesting because these activities feature participants who test themselves against artificial but demanding barriers to success. More specifically, participants in competitive sports attempt to jump sport-specific hurdles while besting opponents' moves and strategies.[1]

Let me turn to how this account might apply to our inquiry. First, although not most important for our purposes, this account explains much of what makes competitive sport so fascinating for participants and spectators alike: meeting challenges designed to bring out the best in us and seeing others attempt to do the same. A full season or athletic career generates a narrative with high and low spots, with chances for improvement, failures, and successes. Tiger Woods' lifetime quest to surpass Jack Nicklaus' record for the most major golf championships is one such story. Another is that of the basketball team starting its season with a string of losses but managing to turn things around to win the rest of its games. Or conversely, how many talented teams designated the best preseason go on to lose a series of games, even to inferior opponents, due to their inability to overcome differences and work together? Failures, and what can be learned from them, are just as much part of such narratives as are successes. Even if the losing team does not learn from their experience, observers may draw meaningful conclusions about the need to cooperate and surmount differences in pursuing common goals. Clearly, these insights can be important outside as well as inside the world of competitive athletics.

Second, as the last example suggests, athletic contests also have a normative dimension. One level of this normative structure is the identification and cultivation of personal virtues that promote success in a sport. This can include the familiar requirements of dedication and commitment but might also involve honesty about one's abilities and those of opponents, willingness to accept criticism and overcome weaknesses, and respect for the challenges set by the constitutive rules of the contest. What is not always noted, however, is that the good athletic performances reveal and convey to a wider audience the virtues of skilled athletes, which fans not only appreciate but may also hope to emulate in their own lives. Finally, such norms may also provide grounds for criticism, as when athletes fail to show respect for the deeper values of their sport or when they avoid playing worthy opponents to deliberately rack up win after win against inferior competitors.

Athletes are often called upon to make moral choices about fairness, sportsmanship, and other values implicit in the traditions and structure of their sport. Indeed, the model of the athletic contest as a mutual quest for excellence suggests that opponents not be regarded as mere things, obstacles standing in the way of one's own victory, but as facilitators who make the good contest possible.

Indeed, such a view of the athletic contest shows why winning is a significant but nevertheless imperfect indicator of athletic success. A winning record is a sign of excellence only if attained (at least for the most part) against worthy opponents. Right now, I happen to be the best basketball player on my block, which considering my age and declining skills might be surprising. Of course, the next best player is four years old and cannot shoot the ball high enough to reach the basket. My string of victories against her unfortunately lacks significance, since the element of challenge is missing.

In fact, athletic competition has many parallels with dialogue in critical inquiry. In sports, each opponent reacts to the choices and skills of the other, tries to anticipate and respond to strategies, and over time overcome weaknesses to become more formidable competition in the future. Similarly, in critical inquiry we respond to the criticism of intellectual detractors, try to anticipate their strategies, and consider how best to overcome weaknesses in our own position. Subjecting ourselves to both intellectual and sporting challenges can enhance the process of self-examination and moral growth. Participants in critical dialogue should want to address the strongest version of alternate positions rather than formulations made of straw.

Of course, we need to be careful about reducing competitive sport to an alternate form of inquiry or assigning it a monolithic function or goal. Competitive sport can be played or observed purely as a form of amusement or entertainment, or pursued for reasons of health or friendship, or engaged in to achieve external rewards like fame and fortune with little regard for the internal values of the practice. These other objectives may, however, compromise the idea of pursuing excellence through challenge. Those interested only in health could simply exercise and not play sports competitively or even watch them. Moreover, much of what audiences find entertaining about sport is precisely the pursuit of excellence in the face of obstacles.

What all this suggests is that competitive intercollegiate athletics can and often does enjoy a relationship of mutual reinforcement with academics. This is most likely to occur and be readily fostered in the atmosphere of the NCAA Division III and in Division I conferences such as the Ivy League, which at least attempt to integrate athletics and academics (although even they may improve their efforts in these areas). Perhaps with some modifications, this can be a feature of intercollegiate athletics elsewhere as well. In particular, if many values of intercollegiate athletics, conceived of along the lines of the mutual quest for excellence, have parallels in intellectual inquiry, emphasis on commonality of virtues necessary for success in one area can help promote development in the other.

This discussion suggests that regarding academics and intercollegiate athletics as independent practices often in conflict is a mistake. Rather, these practices, when properly conceived of and conducted, can be mutually reinforcing. Let me briefly suggest some approaches that may aid such a process.

One is to more explicitly examine issues about athletics within the normal curriculum, or to provide special extracurricular programs for athletes that discuss the ethical and educational issues that may arise in intercollegiate athletics. For example, athletes, as well as students at large, might be encouraged to enroll in courses that discuss ethical, psychological, and sociological issues in sports. As prominent features of our culture, sports, including intercollegiate athletics, should be subjected to critical scrutiny as are medicine, law, and business. If courses are not available, informal discussion groups for athletes, including coaches perhaps and moderated by parties independent of athletic departments, can examine ethical issues in sports, such as the pursuit of victory, coaching philosophies, and the values that should be promoted in intercollegiate athletics. Of course, these formal occasions should be designed to pursue genuine reasoned inquiry rather than instill a favored philosophy of athletics; different points of view should be presented and engaged.

Less formally, avenues for interaction between faculty and coaches should be developed and utilized. I can attest that even in small institutions, faculty misunderstandings and misperceptions of coaches and vice versa develop simply because of lack of contact. Miscommunication, and sometimes unfair stereotyping, can hardly be good for student athletes who may get caught in the middle. Good communications and personal relationships can go a long way toward alleviating problems. Moreover, mutual understanding of the problems facing both coaches and faculty can often lead to accommodation, as when a scheduled contest conflicts with an examination or review session.

In addition, if one accepts the idea of athletics as a quest for excellence through challenge, the role of coach as educator needs more emphasis. After all, the coach is teaching student athletes how to meet certain kinds of challenges and learn from both successes and failures. While winning is surely important and often signifies success at meeting the demands of a sport, it is not everything and not always within the control of the coach. Although their record of wins and losses should not be ignored, coaches should be evaluated on more than that. One way of doing this is including faculty on committees who make recommendations on the reappointment of coaches, something already done at many institutions.

Finally, setting reasonable limits on the time participants must devote to athletics is crucial. In particular, even at the Division III level, off-season activities such as strength training, summer camps, and unofficial scrimmages among players are encouraged. I do not think all of this is wrong or undesirable: competitive athletes want to train hard to improve in the off-season. The trick is to reconcile the understandable and even admirable desire of athletes to improve and be ready for next season with the demands of a rigorous academic schedule, all without unduly limiting their freedom to determine their own priorities.

I hope to have shown that an important case can be made for the compatibility of and even mutual support of principles implicit in academic and athletic practice. Athletics need not be regarded as hostile to academic inquiry but can and frequently does enhance the educational experience of athletes, express and celebrate important values, and enrich the academic community itself.[2]

Notes

CHAPTER 1. RACISM, NAMING RACISM, AND ACADEMIC FREEDOM

1. Classics professor Joshua Katz published "A Declaration of Independence by a Princeton Professor" in *Quillette* on July 8, 2020.
2. Christopher Eisgruber, "Why Mutual Respect Makes Free Speech Better," *Daily Princetonian*, July 20, 2020.
3. Is the topic of the value and significance of gay and lesbian relationships still a politically live issue? Yes. While there is now a right to same-sex marriage throughout the United States, that right has not been secured in all other countries, and freedom from discrimination more broadly for gay, lesbian, and bisexual people has not been secured within the United States nor in many other countries.
4. One contribution to Princeton's summer 2020 campus discussions of racism and academic freedom argued along these lines, Princeton English professor Andrew Cole's essay "What Is Academic? What Is Freedom?," *Daily Princetonian*, July 15, 2020.
5. Beacon Press, 2018.
6. John McWhorter, "The Dehumanizing Condescension of *White Fragility*," *Atlantic*, July 15, 2020.
7. Sally Haslanger, "Gender and Race: (What) Are They? (What) Do We Want Them to Be?," *Noûs* 34, no. 1 (2000): 31–55.
8. Katharine Jenkins, "Amelioration and Inclusion: Gender Identity and the Concept of *Woman*," *Ethics* 126, no. 2 (2016). In response to this objection, Haslanger emphasized the historical context in which she published the paper (Sally Haslanger, "Going On, Not in the Same Way," in *Conceptual Engineering and Conceptual Ethics*, ed. Alexis Burgess, Herman Cappelen, and David Plunkett (Oxford University Press, 2020)), and she agreed with the objector that our central use of "woman" should not exclude any transgender women (see Haslanger's lengthy comment on the Pea Soup blog post discussion of the Jenkins paper, at https://peasoup.princeton.edu/2016/01/ethics-discussions-at-pea-soup-katharine-jenkins-amelioration-and-inclusion-gender-identity-and-the/).

9. Sherif Girgis, Robert P. George, and Ryan T. Anderson, "What Is Marriage?," *Harvard Journal of Law and Public Policy* 34, no. 1 (2010): 245–87.

10. Thanks to Gideon Rosen for conversation on this point.

11. I first offered this view in "Racist Research Must Be Named, But Often Allowed," *Daily Princetonian*, July 27, 2020.

12. A fourth view is what we might call "the anti-woke view"; it agrees with the woke view that there is racist academic work being done and that it needs to be found and squashed; but it holds that it's the "woke" ideas such as Critical Race Theory that are racist (against white people) and need to be outlawed. (While 2021 has seen a surge of anti-Critical-Race-Theory legislation, Republican politicians' attacks on the academic freedom of leftist professors has a long history.) My attitude to this fourth view is that it is wrong on both counts: its categorizations of certain views as racist are incorrect, and its view that we should censor racist views is also incorrect.

13. Girgis, George, and Anderson, "What Is Marriage?"

14. For helpful comments on drafts of this essay, I thank Elizabeth Barnes, Tyler Doggett, Lidal Dror, Kyla Ebels-Duggan, Alex Guerrero, Harvey Lederman, Gideon Rosen, Elliot Salinger, Rosa Terlazzo, and audiences at Clemson University and Princeton University.

CHAPTER 2. FREE SPEECH VIOLATIONS AND CAMPUS POLITICS

1. For background on a free speech principle, see Frederick Schauer, *Free Speech: A Philosophical Enquiry* (Cambridge: Cambridge University Press, 1992); and "Introduction and Overview" in *Speech and Harm: Controversies Over Free Speech*, ed. Ishani Maitra and Mary Kate McGowan (Oxford: Oxford University Press, 2012), 1–23.

2. Perhaps nothing else is required for something to be a free speech violation and the further conditions identified (i.e., systematicity and harmfulness) are necessary for a free speech violation to warrant our collective concern. This difference (between a free speech violation and free speech violation that warrants our concern) is henceforth ignored.

3. For more on self-silencing, see Kristie Dotson, "Tracking Epistemic Violence, Tracking Practices of Silencing," *Hypatia* 26, no. 2 (2011): 236–57; and Mary Kate McGowan, "On Multiple Types of Silencing," in *Beyond Speech: Pornography and Analytic Feminist Philosophy,* ed. Mari Mikkola (Oxford: Oxford University Press, 2017), 39–58.

4. For a survey of options, see Schauer 1982, note 1.

5. Fellow students might understand what Sarah literally says but misunderstand what she means to get across in saying it; communication is highly inferential in this way. See H. P. Grice, *Studies in the Way of Words* (Cambridge, MA: Harvard University Press, 1989).

6. Another possibility is that Sarah self-silences out of fear that her liberal professor will grade her coursework more harshly. This raises separate issues about professional misconduct and overlooks the practice of anonymous grading.

CHAPTER 3. IN DEFENSE OF ACADEMIC TENURE

Adapted by the author from Richard T. De George, *Academic Freedom and Tenure: Ethical Issues* (Rowman & Littlefield, 1997).

CHAPTER 4. WHAT SHOULD COUNT FOR TENURE AND PROMOTION?

Adapted by the author from David Shatz, *Peer Review: A Critical Inquiry* (Rowman & Littlefield, 2004).

CHAPTER 5. ACADEMIC CAREER SUCCESS

1. Judith Jarvis Thomson, "A Defense of Abortion," *Philosophy and Public Affairs* 1, no. 1 (1971): 47–66.
2. Peter Singer, "Famine, Affluence, and Morality," *Philosophy and Public Affairs* 1, no. 3 (1972): 229–43.

CHAPTER 6. CONFIDENTIALITY AND PROFESSIONAL PRACTICE

1. I owe this suggestion to Steven Cahn.
2. Assistant Vice President for Communications Julie Green Bataille, as quoted in the *Georgetown Voice*, https://georgetownvoice.com/2002/11/21/shick-family-reveals-sanctions-in-dead-sons-case/.

CHAPTER 7. BIG DATA AND ARTIFICIAL INTELLIGENCE

1. Kate Crawford, *Atlas of AI: Power, Politics, and the Planetary Costs of Artificial Intelligence* (New Haven: Yale University Press, 2021).
2. Samuel D. Warren and Louis D. Brandeis, "The Right to Privacy," *Harvard Law Review* 4, no. 5 (1890): 193.
3. Charles Fried, "Privacy," *Yale Law Journal* 77, no. 3 (1968).
4. I gratefully acknowledge inspiration for the theme "AI.Humanity" in the emerging strategic framework of my new colleague at Emory University, provost Ravi Bellamkonda. At the time of my writing this chapter, the reference was notional, so responsibility for the way I give it flesh here—for better or worse—is my own.
5. Wolter Pieters, "Beyond Individual-Centric Privacy: Information Technology in Social Systems," *Information Society* 33, no. 5 (2017).
6. Klaus Schwab, "The Fourth Industrial Revolution," *Foreign Affairs*, December 12, 2015. Reprint: https://www.weforum.org/about/the-fourth-industrial-revolution-by-klaus-schwab.
7. Luciano Floridi, *The Fourth Revolution: How the Infosphere is Reshaping Human Reality* (London: Oxford University Press, 2014), 3.
8. BioIntelliSense website, accessed September 22, 2021: https://biointellisense.com/. Oakland University initially required student athletes and dormitory residents to wear the BioButtons; later, it made them optional.
9. Adam D. I. Kramer, Jamie E. Guillory, and Jeffrey T. Hancock, "Experimental Evidence of Massive-Scale Emotional Contagion through Social Network," *Proceedings of the National Academic of Sciences of the United States of America*, June 2, 2014.

10. Brian Burke, ed., *Top Strategic Technology Trends for 2021* (Gartner) p. 4, emphasis mine. https://www.gartner.com/en/publications/top-tech-trends-2021.

11. Some large-scale potential impacts are charted in Elana Zeide, "The Structural Consequences of Big Data-Driven Education," *Big Data* 5, no. 2 (2017): 164–72, doi: 10.1089/big.2016.0061.

12. See Katherine Mangan, "Dartmouth Dropped a Shaky Cheating Investigation, but Concerns Over Digital Surveillance Remain," *Chronicle of Higher Education*, June 14, 2021. Critiques of uses of AI in proctoring include: Daniel Woldeab and Thomas Brothen, "21st Century Assessment: Online Proctoring, Test Anxiety, and Student Performance," *International Journal of E-Learning and Distance Education* 34, no. 1 (2019); D. Christopher Brooks, *Student Experiences Learning with Technology in the Pandemic*, research report (Boulder, CO: EDUCAUSE, April 2021); Shea Swauger, "Software That Monitors Students During Tests Perpetuates Inequality and Violates Their Privacy," *MIT Technology Review*, August 7, 2020; and Todd Feathers, "Proctorio Is Using Racist Algorithms to Detect Faces," *VICE*, April 8, 2021. These sources are drawn from "EDUCAUSE QuickPoll Results: Artificial Intelligence Use in Higher Education," D. Christopher Brooks, June 11, 2021, https://er.educause.edu/articles/2021/6/educause-quickpoll-results-artificial-intelligence-use-in-higher-education#fnr8. Accessed August 29, 2021.

13. See a Brookings Institute report: Alex Engler, "Enrollment Algorithms Are Contributing to the Crises of Higher Education," September 14, 2021, https://www.brookings.edu/research/enrollment-algorithms-are-contributing-to-the-crises-of-higher-education/. Accessed September 27, 2021.

14. Dawn Papandrea, "The Data Pitch: Playing with Big-League Data to Approach and Attract Students," *University Business*, March 2018, 39.

15. See Cathy O'Neil, *Weapons of Math Destruction: How Big Data Increases Inequality and Threatens Democracy* (New York: Crown, 2016).

16. For example, see Joy Buolamwini and Timnit Gebru, "Gender Shades: Intersectional Accuracy Disparities in Commercial Gender Classification," *Proceedings of Machine Learning Research* 81 (2018): 77–91.

17. The GDPR includes a section on profiling. In the main, it is a refusal of automated decision-making in higher-stakes areas of life (e.g., credit applications), asserting a right to appeal to a human being. https://gdpr.eu/Recital-71-Profiling/.

18. See "AI in My Life' project," an effort to develop awareness, understanding, and critical thinking about current uses of artificial intelligence among fifteen- to sixteen-year-olds in Dublin, Ireland. The program is designed specifically for students from underrepresented and lower-resourced communities. A curriculum overview is provided in "AI in My Life: AI, Ethics & Privacy Workshops for 15-16-Year-Olds," https://dl.acm.org/doi/fullHtml/10.1145/3462741.3466664; doi: https://doi.org/10.1145/3462741.3466664. Organizations supporting greater AI education, literacy, ethics, and a more just AI ecosystem include the Algorithmic Justice League, founded by Joy Buolamwi (https://www.ajl.org/) and the "AI Now Institute." See also Jordan Harrod, "We're Talking About AI Wrong," in *The Black Agenda: Bold Solutions for a Broken System*, ed. Anna Gifty Opoku-Agyeman (New York: St. Martin's, 2022). Harrod highlights challenges with the very ways in which we frame and discuss artificial intelligence, what she describes as "language underspecification," particularly with respect to how bias, fairness, and automation are taken up in discussions of AI in the multiple disciplines engaged in the development and analysis of artificial intelligence.

19. For more on the opportunities and risks, including elaboration of the risks named in this conclusion, see Luciano Floridi et al., "AI4People—An Ethical Framework for a Good AI Society: Opportunities, Risks, Principles, and Recommendations," *Mind and Machines* 28, no. 4 (2018): 689–707.

CHAPTER 8. MISOGYNY, "HIMPATHY," AND SEXUAL HARASSMENT

1. See Nancy Chi Cantalupo and William C. Kidder, "A Systematic Look at a Serial Problem: Sexual Harassment of Students by University Faculty," *Utah Law Review* 671 (2018), for data regarding student allegations of unwelcome physical contact perpetrated by faculty.

2. This summary draws upon Catharine MacKinnon, "In Their Hands: Restoring Institutional Liability for Sexual Harassment in Education," *Yale Law Journal* 125, no. 7 (2016): 2038.

3. Kate Manne, *Down Girl: The Logic of Misogyny* (New York: Oxford University Press, 2018), 63.

4. This section draws upon Anita M. Moorman, "An Examination of the Legal Framework Between Title VII and Title IX Sexual Harassment Claims in Athletics and Sport Settings: Emerging Challenges for Athletics Personnel and Sport Managers," *Journal of the Legal Aspects of Sport* 18, no. 1 (2008); and Sandra J. Perry and Tanya M. Marcum, "Liability for School Sexual Harassment Under Title IX: How the Courts Are Failing Our Children," *University of La Verne Law Review* 30, no. 1 (2008): 3.

5. Catharine MacKinnon, *Sexual Harassment of Working Women: A Case of Sex Discrimination* (New Haven: Yale University Press, 1979).

6. Stephen Henrick, "A Hostile Environment for Student Defendants: Title IX and Sexual Assault on College Campuses," *Northern Kentucky Law Review* 40 (2013): 49.

7. Vicki Schultz, "Reconceptualizing Sexual Harassment, Again," *Yale Law Journal Forum* 128, no. 22 (2018): 29, note 19. Prior to the Department of Education's release of a Dear Colleague Letter in 2010, behavior actionable under Title IX was limited to unwelcome conduct of a sexual nature, including sexual advances, requests for sexual favors, or other verbal or nonverbal conduct of a sexual nature. Title IX now covers gender-based harassment, unwelcome conduct based upon a student's sex or their failure to conform to sex stereotypes. Generally, both sexualized harassment and sex-based harassment are referred to as "sexual harassment" (even though "sexual" has the sense of "sexualized"). This essay follows that practice.

8. This section draws upon Vicki Schultz, "Reconceptualizing Sexual Harassment," *Yale Law Journal* 107, no. 6 (1998): 1683.

9. Following Schultz, ibid.

10. I say "anti-masculine" here instead of "feminine" because the competence approach is able (unlike the desire-dominance approach) to explain male-on-male harassment (so-called "horseplay") and the harassment of gender-nonconforming individuals as part of the effort to maintain a traditionally masculine work environment. See Chris Diffee, "Going Offshore: Horseplay, Normalization, and Sexual Harassment," *Columbia Journal of Gender and Law* 24, no. 32 (2013).

11. Schultz (1998), 1765.

12. Schultz (2018), 47.

13. Ibid., 2.

14. Manne (2018), 33.
15. Ibid., 66.
16. Ibid., 61.
17. Ibid., 109–14.
18. Ibid., 47, 76.
19. This section draws upon Perry and Marcum (2008) and MacKinnon (2016).
20. I assume in this section that the deliberate indifference rule includes the requirement that an appropriate person received actual notice of the harassment.
21. I am determining that a certain factor is implicit in Title IX's objective by appeal to the OCR's guidelines for funding recipients' administrative enforcement of Title IX outlined earlier.
22. Manne, 196–97.
23. Ibid., 40–45.

CHAPTER 9. INSTITUTIONAL INEQUALITY

1. Raj Chetty, John Friedman, Emmanuel Saez, Nicholas Turner, and Danny Yagan, "Mobility Report Cards: The Role of Colleges in Intergenerational Mobility," NBER Working Paper No. 23618, 2017.
2. Sara Goldrick-Rab, *Paying the Price* (University of Chicago Press, 2021).
3. An argument I make in Jennifer Morton, *Moving Up Without Losing Your Way* (Princeton University Press, 2019).
4. William G. Bowen, Matthew M. Chingos, and Michael S. McPherson, *Crossing the Finish Line* (Princeton University Press, 2009).
5. Andrew H. Nichols and Jose L. Santos, "A Glimpse Inside the Coffers: Endowment Spending at Wealthy Colleges and Universities," Education Trust, 2016, https://edtrust.org/resource/a-glimpse-inside-the-coffersendowment-spending-at-wealthy-colleges-and-universities/.
6. Rick Seltzer, "How Much Are Most Colleges Paying in Endowment Tax?," *Inside Higher Ed*, February 18, 2020, https://www.insidehighered.com/news/2020/02/18/wealthiest-universities-are-paying-big-endowment-tax-bills-how-much-are-others-who.
7. National Center for Education Statistics, "Young Adult Educational and Employment Outcomes by Family Socioeconomic Status," The Condition of Education 2019, https://nces.ed.gov/programs/coe/pdf/coe_tbe.pdf.
8. Anthony P. Carnevale and Jeff Strohl, "Separate & Unequal: How Higher Education Reinforces the Intergenerational Reproduction of White Racial Privilege," Georgetown University, McCourt School of Public Policy, Center on Education and the Workforce, 2013.
9. John Bound, Michael F. Lovenheim, and Sarah Turner, "Why Have College Completion Rates Declined? An Analysis of Changing Student Preparation and Collegiate Resources," *American Economic Journal: Applied Economics* 2, no. 3 (2010), 156.
10. Larua T. Hamilton and Kelly Nielsen, *Broke: The Racial Consequences of Underfunding Public Universities* (University of Chicago Press, 2021).
11. For an argument that makes this case, see Christopher Martin, *The Right To Higher Education* (Oxford University Press, 2022).
12. Though there are some reasons to be skeptical about this often-cited data point. See Peter Cappelli, *Will College Pay Off?: A Guide to the Most Important Financial Decision You'll Ever Make* (Public Affairs, 2015).

13. Amy Gutmann, *Democratic Education*, revised ed. (Princeton University Press, 1999), 174.
14. I develop this argument in Jennifer M. Morton, "The Miseducation of the Elite," *Journal of Political Philosophy* 29, no. 1 (2021): 3–24.

CHAPTER 10. RECKONING WITH PAST INJUSTICE

1. The line here is not absolutely clear, as murky or ineffective institutional processes and policies can make these kinds of wrongs more difficult to uncover and confront.
2. Two important sources for understanding the early history of American academic institutions' involvement and benefit from slavery and slaveholding are "Slavery and Justice: Report of the Brown University Steering Committee on Slavery and Justice," 2006, https://www.brown.edu/Research/Slavery_Justice/documents/SlaveryAndJustice.pdf; and Craig Steven Wilder, *Ebony and Ivy: Race, Slavery, and the Troubled History of America's Universities* (New York: Bloomsbury, 2013).
3. The story of Georgetown's reckoning with this past event was reported by Rachel L. Swarns, "272 Slaves Were Sold to Save Georgetown. What Does It Owe Their Descendants?," *New York Times*, April 16, 2016, https://www.nytimes.com/2016/04/17/us/georgetown-university-search-for-slave-descendants.html.
4. The Morrill Act of 1862 provided land to found Land Grant Universities, in some cases by locating the university on the land and in others by gifting land for the university's endowments. These were native lands ceded to the federal government in treaties that were coercively negotiated and sometimes not even subsequently ratified. See Robert Lee and Tristan Ahtone, "Land-Grab Universities," *High Country News*, March 30, 2020, https://www.hcn.org/issues/52.4/indigenous-affairs-education-land-grab-universities.
5. The University of Texas at Austin engaged in "urban renewal" projects that displaced Black residents from East Austin to expand the campus on land they were able to acquire cheaply, in large part due to the forced segregation of an earlier era. See Mia Taylor, "The Expansion of the University of Texas: Urban Renewal, 'N–ro Removal'," on the University of Texas Division of Diversity and Community Engagement website: https://diversity.utexas.edu/integration/2019/01/the-expansion-of-the-university-of-texas-urban-renewal-n-ro-removal/.
6. See Wilder (2013) for numerous examples of enslaved workers who built universities.
7. Poor women, who long served as maids taking care of young men at elite colleges and universities, were grossly underpaid and exploited.
8. "Haskell opened its doors in 1884 as the United States Industrial Training School to 22 elementary school students. Children as young as 4 years old were separated from their families for months at a time as they attended the school, which focused its training on domestic arts. In keeping with the thinking of the day, Indian culture and language were seen as the culprits that kept American Indians from becoming American citizens. Children were routinely punished for speaking their language or disobeying the military-style rules of the school. Punishment included incarceration in a jail on campus." Quoted from Mary Annette Pember, "Haskell Indian Nations University Commemorates 125th Anniversary, Recognizes Painful History," *Diverse Issues in Higher Education*, May 31, 2009, https://www.diverseeducation.com/leadership-policy/article/15088572/haskell-indian-nations-university-commemorates-125th-anniversary-recognizes-painful-history.
9. A case that resurfaced at my university early in my tenure as provost is an honorary degree presented to General Rafael L. Trujillo Molina, the notorious dictator of the Dominican

Republic and mass murderer of at least 17,000 Haitians. Presented at a time when the heinous actions of Trujillo were well known, the degree has now been revoked by the university.

10. William Faulkner, *Requiem for a Nun* (New York: Random House, 1951), p.92. Then-senator Barack Obama famously used this quote in his "A More Perfect Union" speech when speaking about race relations.

11. Of course, there was nothing primitive about the cultures of Africa or Native America that existed contemporaneous with colonial America—they had complex languages, sciences, medicine, arts, music, family structures, religions, and governing systems.

12. The University of Pittsburgh removed Thomas Parran's name from its Graduate School of Public Health building in 2018.

CHAPTER 11. SHOULD UNIVERSITIES PAY REPARATIONS?

1. For a full discussion of the differences between German reparations and proposals for our government's paying reparations to African Americans, see Stuart E. Eizenstat, "What Holocaust Restitution Taught Me About Slavery Reparations," *Politico*, October 27, 2019.

CHAPTER 12. RETHINKING AFFIRMATIVE ACTION

1. John Kekes, "The Injustice of Strong Affirmative Action," in *Affirmative Action and the University: A Philosophical Inquiry*, ed. Steven M. Cahn (Philadelphia: Temple University Press, 1993), 151.

2. Celia Wolf-Devine, "Proportional Representation of Women and Minorities," in Cahn, *Affirmative Action*, 230.

CHAPTER 13. ACHIEVING DISABILITY INCLUSION

1. For example, a group at Michigan State University has been using tracking software to observe the impact of in-class laptop use on performance. One of their recent studies found that students who use their laptops for class-related activities, particularly viewing slides, tend to perform better on exams, while students who engage in nonclass-related activity such as social media do worse. Alison J. Day, Kimberly M. Fenn, and Susan M. Ravizza, "Is It Worth It? The Costs and Benefits of Bringing a Laptop to a University Class," *PLoS One* 16, no. 5 (2021): e0251792, https://doi.org/10.1371/journal.pone.0251792.

2. ADA Best Practices Tool Kit for State and Local Governments, Chapter 6, "Curb Ramps and Pedestrian Crossings Under Title II of the ADA," https://www.ada.gov/pcatoolkit/chap6 toolkit.htm.

3. *Southeastern Community College v. Davis*, 442 U.S. 397 (1979).

4. The confusion was not entirely the Court's fault but also involved some complex aspects of the timing of the case—it began before the § 504 regulations were issued and only reached the Court afterward—and the issues presented by the plaintiff both at the lower court and on appeal. I have discussed this decision and its impact in far more detail in "Debilitating *Southeastern Community College v. Davis*: Achieving The Promise Of Disability Civil Rights," *University of the District of Columbia Law Review* 23: (2020).

5. *Olmstead v. LC*, 527 U.S. 581 (1999).
6. Or so I have argued in detail in "Debilitating *Southeastern Community College v. Davis*."
7. *Rawdin v. American Board of Pediatrics*, 582 Fed. Appx. 114 (3d Cir. 2014) (unreported).
8. Scott Jaschik, "No More LSAT 'Flagging'," *Inside Higher Ed*, May 21, 2014, www.insidehighered.com/news/2014/05/21/law-school-group-agrees-stop-flagging-scores-students-who-get-extra-time-due.
9. Law School Admission Council, "LSAT Fairness Procedures," https://www.lsac.org/about/lsac-policies/lsat-fairness-procedures.
10. Martha Minow made this point powerfully in *Making All the Difference: Inclusion, Exclusion, and American Law* (Ithaca, NY: Cornell University Press, 1990).

CHAPTER 14. DISCONTENT WITH DISABILITY ACCOMMODATIONS

1. My focus here is on the policies of some liberal arts colleges. Though I have taught at several large universities, I have been teaching at a liberal arts college for twenty-plus years. My college is part of a consortium, and I have thus had students from these other affiliated colleges in my classes. Each individual college's disability policies and practices differ in their details but not in their substance. The student complaints I discuss are ones that have come from people enrolled at (all of) the different colleges.
2. Keith Wailoo, *Pain: A Political History* (Baltimore: John Hopkins University Press, 2014).
3. PTSD had not yet been identified as such. But—then, as now—it clearly affected the health and well-being of returning veterans in deep and important ways.
4. I follow Wailoo in describing those with opposing political views about disability as "conservatives" and "liberals."
5. This was a view explicitly articulated by veterans' groups which insisted that "disability benefits were not 'welfare' payments but justly earned compensation based on a contractual relationship." Wailoo, *Pain*, 25.
6. Ibid., 40–41.
7. I am not intending here to present a comprehensive map of these changes, of course, nor do I suppose that there is a clear, univocal, unalterable metric that can be invoked to distinguish medical problems from problems that are not medical or are better described as "problems in living" than as indications of health. Rather, my purpose is to offer a guide to some points of interest we will find on the journey.
8. Ray Moynihan and Alan Cassels, *Selling Sickness: How the World's Biggest Pharmaceutical Companies Are Turning Us All into Patients* (New York: Nation, 2005), xvi.

CHAPTER 15. OVERLOOKING COMMUNITY COLLEGES AND THE WORKING CLASS

1. For a more detailed essay on this topic see, Keenan, "The Community Colleges: Giving Them the Ethical Recognition They Deserve," *Journal of Moral Theology* 9, no. 2 (2020) 143–64 https://jmt.scholasticahq.com/article/18040-the-community-colleges-giving-them-the-ethical-recognition-they-deserve; also, Matthew J. Gaudet and James F. Keenan, eds.,

"Contingent Faculty," *Journal of Moral Theology* 8, no. 1 (Spring 2019). https://msmary.edu/academics/schools-divisions/college-of-liberal-arts/documents-images/jmt-spring-vol.8-no.1-2019.pdf.

2. Philo A. Hutcheson, "Reconsidering the Community College," *History of Education Quarterly* 39, no. 3 (Autumn 1999): 307–20.

3. James L. Morrison, "The Community College and the Disadvantaged," *Research in Higher Education* 1 (1973) 401–15.

4. American Association of Community Colleges 2019 fact sheet, www.aacc.nche.edu/wp-content/uploads/2019/05/AACC2019FactSheet_rev.pdf.

5. Ibid.

6. "Community Colleges vs. Universities," Education Corner, www.educationcorner.com/community-college-vs-university.html.

7. Jeffrey J. Selingo, "What's Wrong with Going to a Community College? How Two-Year Colleges Can Be Better than Four-Year Universities," *Washington Post*, June 29, 2015, www.washingtonpost.com/news/grade-point/wp/2015/06/29/whats-wrong-with-going-to-a-community-college-how-two-year-colleges-can-be-better-than-four-year-universities/.

8. American Association of Community Colleges, "Community College Enrollment Crisis? Historical Trends in Community College Enrollment," August 7, 2019, 1, www.aacc.nche.edu/wp-content/uploads/2019/08/Crisis-in-Enrollment-2019.pdf.

9. American Association of Community Colleges, 3.

10. Lauren Stanforth, "Community Colleges Grapple with Enrollment Crash," *Times Union*, January 13, 2020, https://www.timesunion.com/news/article/Community-colleges-grapple-with-enrollment-crash-14971707.php; and "Enrollment Declines Seen at Community Colleges Nationwide," Community College Review (blog), www.communitycollegereview.com/blog/enrollment-declines-seen-at-community-colleges-nationwide.

11. "Community Colleges FAQs," Community College Research Center, Teachers College, Columbia University, ccrc.tc.columbia.edu/Community-College-FAQs.html.

12. Charles T. Clotfelter, Helen F. Ladd, Clara G. Muschkin, and Jacob L. Vigdor, "Success in Community College: Do Institutions Differ?," *Research in Higher Education* 54, no. 7 (2013): 805–24, doi 10.1007/s11162-013-9295-6.

13. "How Low Graduation Rates Camouflage Student Success at Community Colleges," *Chronicle of Higher Education*, January 5, 2020, www.chronicle.com/article/How-Low-Graduation-Rates/247802. *The Chronicle* argues that notwithstanding the rates, a variety of modest successes are achieved by very specific schools.

14. National Student Clearinghouse Research Center, "Completing College: A National View of Student Completion Rates—Fall 2012 Cohort," Signature Report no. 16 (Herndon, VA: NSCRC, 2018), 6, nscresearchcenter.org/wp-content/uploads/SignatureReport16.pdf.

15. James E. Rosenbaum, Julie Redline, and Jennifer L. Stephan, "Community College: The Unfinished Revolution," *Issues in Science and Technology* 23, no. 4 (Summer 2007), 49–56.

16. Sara Goldrick-Rab, "Challenges and Opportunities for Improving Community College Student Success," *Review of Educational Research* 80, no. 3 (September 2010): 437–69.

17. Ibid., 453.

18. David B. Monaghan and Paul Attewell, "The Community College Route to the Bachelor's Degree," *Educational Evaluation and Policy Analysis* 37, no. 1 (2015), 70–91, doi.org/10.3102/0162373714521865.

19. Mikhail Zinshteyn,"Making the Jump to a Four-Year Degree Difficult for Community College Students," *Education Writers Association*, March 21, 2014, www.ewa.org/blog-educated-reporter/making-jump-four-year-degree-difficult-community-college-students.

20. Allie Bidwell, "Report: 1 in 10 Community College Transfers Lose Nearly All Course Credits," *U.S. News and World Report*, March 19, 2014, www.usnews.com/news/articles/2014/03/19/report-1-in-10-community-college-transfers-lose-nearly-all-course-credits.

21. Derek Bok, *Higher Education in America* (Princeton: Princeton University Press, 2013), 187.

22. Center for Community College Student Engagement, "Contingent Commitments: Bringing Part-Time Faculty Into Focus," A Special Report from the Center for Community College Student Engagement (Austin, TX: University of Texas, 2014), 3, www.ccsse.org/docs/PTF_Special_Report.pdf.

23. Paul Fain, "Low Expectations, High Stakes: New Report Sheds Light on the Oft-Ignored Adjunctification of Community Colleges, Which May Be a Barrier to College Completion," *Inside Higher Ed*, April 7, 2014, www.insidehighered.com/news/2014/04/07/part-time-professors-teach-most-community-college-students-report-finds.

24. Ryan Craig, "America's Community Colleges Should Become Placement Colleges," *Forbes*, January 11, 2017, www.forbes.com/sites/ryancraig/2017/01/11/americas-community-colleges-should-become-placement-colleges/#3d0532d82a51.

25. Special thanks to Gabriela Prostko and Kelli Rodrigues for their research assistance and counsel in writing this essay.

CHAPTER 16. THE CRUELTY OF THE ADJUNCT SYSTEM

1. "National Trends for Faculty Composition Over Time," Delphi Project on the Changing Faculty and Student Success, Pullias Center for Higher Education, University of Southern California, 2019, https://pullias.usc.edu/download/national-trends-faculty-composition.

2. "Digest of Education Statistics," Table 316.8, National Center for Education Statistics, 2019, https://nces.ed.gov/programs/digest/d19/tables/dt19_316.80.asp?current=yes.

3. "A Portrait of Part-Time Faculty Members: A Summary of Findings on Part-Time Faculty Respondents to the Coalition on the Academic Workforce Survey of Contingent Faculty Members and Instructors," Coalition on the Academic Workforce, June 2012, http://www.academicworkforce.org/survey.html.

4. "Selected Research on Connections Between Non-Tenure-Track Faculty and Student Learning," Delphi Project, May 2020, https://pullias.usc.edu/download/selected-research-on-connections-between-non-tenure-track-faculty-and-student-learning-2020-2/?wpdmdl=20785&ind=1593023311823; and Adrianna Kezar, Daniel Maxey, and Lara Badke, "The Imperative for Change: Fostering Understanding of the Necessity of Changing Non-Tenure-Track Faculty Policies and Practices," Delphi Project, 2014, https://pullias.usc.edu/wp-content/uploads/2014/01/IMPERATIVE-FOR-CHANGE_WEB-2014.pdf.

5. We could reconceive the professor's career as less akin to that of a professional—like a doctor or lawyer—and more akin to that of an artist—project-based with an ever-present side hustle. But that would only be acceptable if all professors were in the same boat.

6. Adrianna Kezar and Daniel Maxey, "Dispelling the Myths: Locating the Resources Needed to Support Non-Tenure-Track Faculty," Delphi Project, 2013, https://pullias.usc

.edu/download/dispelling-myths-locating-resources-needed-support-non-tenure-track-faculty/?wpdm dl=13895&refresh=611213c8b22eb1628574664.

CHAPTER 17. PRUDENT RESERVE IN ACADEMIC ADMINISTRATION

1. There is also the practical danger that the kind of damage to faculty morale that can result from uncoupling budget priorities from academic priorities will lead to departures of the best faculty from the highly ranked but unprioritized department. If an administrator doesn't consider and think through this possibility, that would be careless, a failure of stewardship. But the point here is that, even if the administrator does weigh this possibility, and correctly estimates its likelihood, the fact that her funding request is determinatively shaped by some strictly political considerations suggests that actual academic priorities are, for now, judged less weighty.

2. See Immanuel Kant's *Lectures on Ethics* ("Ethical Duties Towards Others: Truthfulness"), where he muses on the limits of candor and, with the notion of "prudent reserve," justifies our concealing truths from one another. The defender of the idea that we have a categorical imperative to "act only according to that maxim whereby you can at the same time will that it should become a universal law," to "act in such a way that you treat humanity, whether in your own person or in the person of any other, never merely as a means, but always at the same time as an end," explains in detail why he still does not believe we are always obliged to speak our minds or tell the whole truth. (See Kant's *Groundwork of the Metaphysic of Morals* for a discussion of the categorical imperative.)

3. The philosophical problem of "dirty hands" centers on the question of whether someone can be morally justified in committing a bad act for the sake of a very great good.

4. Tenure was developed to ensure academic freedom for faculty. There is a good reason the job protections it provides for the professoriate do not extend to any faculty member's occupation of an administrative post.

CHAPTER 18. THE DISCRETION OF ACADEMIC ADMINISTRATORS

1. See H. L. A. Hart, "Discretion" (November 9, 1956), reprinted, *Harvard Law Review* 127, no. 2 (2013): 652–65.

2. See Kenneth C. Davis, *Discretionary Justice: A Preliminary Inquiry* (Baton Rouge, LA: Louisiana State University Press, 1969), p. V.

3. Ibid.

4. See, e.g., Jennifer L. O'Donnell and Stephen T. Sadlier, "University as Secret Society: Becoming Faculty Through Discretion," *Society* (May 2021): 1–8. These authors view discretion-as-virtue as prudent secrecy in opposition to transparency.

5. Ronald Dworkin, *Taking Rights Seriously* (Cambridge, MA: Harvard University Press, 1977), 31–33, 38. (Recognizing a sense of discretion as final authority, as requiring interpretative judgment and a "strong" sense of discretion where choice is not controlled or bound by a prescribed rule or standard.)

6. Henry M. Hart, Jr. and Albert M. Sacks, *The Legal Process: Basic Problems in the Making and Application of Law*, ed. William N. Eskridge Jr. and Philip P. Frickey (University Casebook Series: Foundation, 1994).

7. The American Association of University Administrators, "Ethical Principles for College and University Administrators," https://aaua.org/administrator-ethics/. The list of principles, clusters of hortatory values and aspirational commitments, includes: (1) integrity (honesty, conflict of interest avoidance and taking responsibility for actions); (2) fairness and equity; (3) accuracy and transparency (sharing complete, truthful information and complying with federal, state, and local governments and agency rules and regulations); (4) confidentiality and privacy; (5) respect for institutional mission and reasonable interests; (6) consultation for support and expertise; and (7) speaking out when professional ethics are not followed.

CHAPTER 19. ETHICAL ONLINE UNIVERSITY INSTRUCTION

1. Susan Meisenhelder, "MOOC Mania," *Thought & Action* 29 (Fall 2013): 12, https://eric.ed.gov/?id=EJ1017285.

2. Ibid., 13.

3. Ibid.

4. Ibid., 14.

5. Justin Reich, *Failure to Disrupt: Why Technology Alone Can't Transform Education* (Cambridge, MA: Harvard University Press, 2020), 34–37.

6. Robert Paul Churchill, "The Ethics of Teaching and the Emergence of MOOCs: Should Philosophers Support the MOOC?," *Philosophy in the Contemporary World* 21, no. 1 (Spring 2014): 26–40. https://doi.org/10.5840/pcw20142113; San José Philosophy Department, "An Open Letter to Professor Michael Sandel from the Philosophy Department at San José State University," April 29, 2013, accessed August 6, 2021, https://www.documentcloud.org/documents/695716-an-open-letter-to-professor-michael-sandel-from.html. (Originally published in the *Chronicle of Higher Education*, May 2, 2013. https://www.chronicle.com/article/an-open-letter-to-professor-michael-sandel-from-the-philosophy-department-at-san-jose-state-u/.); and San José Philosophy Department, "The Open Letter to Michael Sandel and Some Thoughts About Outsourced Online Teaching," in *MOOCs and Their Afterlives: Experiments in Scale and Access in Higher Education*, ed. Elizabeth Losh (Chicago: University of Chicago Press, 2017), 255–70.

7. San José Philosophy Department, "The Open Letter to Michael Sandel and Some Thoughts About Outsourced Online Teaching," 257.

8. Ibid.

9. Churchill, "The Ethics of Teaching and the Emergence of MOOCs: Should Philosophers Support the MOOC?"

10. San José Philosophy Department, "An Open Letter to Professor Michael Sandel," 2.

11. Ralph Lamar Turner and Carol Gassaway, "Between Kudzu and Killer Apps: Finding Human Ground Between the Monoculture of MOOCs and Online Mechanisms for Learning," *Educational Philosophy and Theory* 51, no. 4 (2019), https://doi.org/10.1080/00131857.2018.1465816.

12. Digital Promise, "Suddenly Online: A National Survey of Undergraduates During the COVID-19 Pandemic" 8–9, 12–14, accessed August 20, 2021, https:/digitalpromise.org/suddenlyonline.

13. Ibid., 12, 20.

14. Frank R. Castelli and Mark A. Sarvary, "Why Students Do Not Turn on Their Video Cameras During Online Classes and an Equitable and Inclusive Plan to Encourage Them to Do So," *Ecology and Evolution* 11, no. 8 (2021): 3566–67, https://doi.org/10.1002/ece3.71233566-67.

15. Digital Promise, "Suddenly Online," 13.

16. Jeffrey Martin, "Building Relationships and Increasing Engagement in the Virtual Classroom: Practical Tools for the Online Instructor," *Journal of Educators Online* 16, no. 1 (January 2019): 2, https://eric.ed.gov/?id=EJ1204379.

17. Cameron Sublett, "Distant Equity: The Promise and Pitfalls of Online Learning for Students of Color in Higher Education" (Washington, DC: American Council on Education, 2020), https://www.equityinhighered.org/resources/ideas-and-insights/distant-equity-the-promise-and-pitfalls-of-online-learning-for-students-of-color-in-higher-education/.

18. Churchill, "The Ethics of Teaching and the Emergence of MOOCs," 37–39.

19. Digital Promise, "Suddenly Online."

20. National Student Clearinghouse Research Center, "Fall 2021 Current Term Enrollment Estimates," accessed August 17, 2021, https://nscresearchcenter.org/current-term-enrollment-estimates/.

21. Shannon D. M. Moore, B. D. Jayme, and J. Black, "Disaster Capitalism, Rampant EdTech Opportunism, and the Advancement of Online Learning in the Era of COVID19," *Critical Education* 12, no. 2 (2021), https://ices.library.ubc.ca/index.php/criticaled/article/view/186587.

CHAPTER 20. IMPROVING FULLY ONLINE INSTRUCTION

1. "List of Accredited Online Degree Programs," OnlineU, https://www.onlineu.com/degrees.

2. "Undergraduate Enrollment," Institute of Education Sciences, National Center for Education Statistics, https://nces.ed.gov/programs/coe/indicator/cha.

3. Karen Costa, "Cameras Be Damned," LinkedIn, https://www.linkedin.com/pulse/cameras-damned-karen-costa/.

4. Live chat with Provost Liesl Folks, University of Arizona, March 23, 2021. "Lessons Learned from a Year of Remote Teaching." Faculty/Instructor COVID-19 Survey Fall 2020. Presented by Andrea Romero and Lisa Elfring. For the full report and slides go to https://facultyaffairs.arizona.edu/faculty-reports-and-data.

CHAPTER 21. MERIT, WEALTH, AND THE ETHICS OF COLLEGE ADMISSIONS

1. I am grateful to Ellis Reid, Nithyani Anandakugan, and Sara Nichols for doing significant intellectual and written work on a set of webpages for justiceinschools.org about the ethics of college admission in light of the Varsity Blues scandal. I have borrowed a few sentences from the web page, and I have learned a lot from them during our collective discussions about these issues over a period of years. I am also grateful to Ellis Reid and to Steven Cahn for feedback on earlier drafts.

2. Laura Smith, Special Agent, FBI, "Affidavit in Support of Criminal Complaint," https://www.justice.gov/file/1142876/download.

3. Charlie Curnin, Julia Ingram, Elena Shao, and Holden Foreman, "Expelled Student's Family Paid $6.5 Million in Scandal to Secure Her Admission to Stanford," *Stanford Daily*, May 1, 2019, https://www.stanforddaily.com/2019/05/01/expelled-students-family-paid-6-5-million-in-scandal-to-secure-her-admission-to-stanford/.

4. Daniel Golden, "The Story Behind Jared Kushner's Curious Acceptance into Harvard," *ProPublica*, November 18, 2016, https://www.propublica.org/article/the-story-behind-jared-kushners-curious-acceptance-into-harvard.

5. Jennifer Levitz and Melissa Korn, "'Father Is Surgeon,' '1 Mil Pledge': The Role of Money in USC Admissions," *Wall Street Journal*, September 3, 2019, https://www.wsj.com/articles/father-is-surgeon-1-mil-pledge-the-role-of-money-in-usc-admissions-11567548124.

6. "Defense Attorneys Say 'Varsity Blues' Parents Were Victims of a Fraudster," Litigation: Editor's Picks, Law.com, September 13, 2021, https://www.law.com/2021/09/13/defense-attorneys-say-varsity-blues-parents-were-victims-of-a-fraudster/.

7. Josh Moody, "What to Look for When Hiring a College Consultant," *USNews*, April 4, 2019, https://www.usnews.com/education/best-colleges/articles/2019-04-04/what-to-look-for-when-hiring-a-college-consultant.

8. All of the figures in this paragraph are derived from The Upshot, "Some Colleges Have More Students from the Top 1 Percent than the Bottom 60. Find Yours.," *New York Times*, January 18, 2017, https://www.nytimes.com/interactive/2017/01/18/upshot/some-colleges-have-more-students-from-the-top-1-percent-than-the-bottom-60.html.

9. See Joseph Fishkin, *Bottlenecks: A New Theory of Equal Opportunity* (Oxford University Press, 2013).

10. Neeraj Kaushal, Katherine Magnuson, and Jane Waldfogel, "How Is Family Income Related to Investments in Children's Learning?" in *Whither Opportunity? Rising Inequality, Schools, and Children's Life Chances*, ed. Greg J. Duncan and Richard J. Murnane (New York: Russell Sage, 2011), 187–206.

11. Raj Chetty, John N. Friedman, Emmanuel Saez, Nicholas Turner, and Danny Yagan, "The Determinants of Income Segregation and Intergenerational Mobility Using Test Scores to Measure Undermatching," NBER paper, February 2020, https://opportunityinsights.org/wp-content/uploads/2020/02/coll_mrc_NBER_paper.pdf.

12. My calculations using Table III (p. 42) of https://opportunityinsights.org/wp-content/uploads/2020/02/coll_mrc_NBER_paper.pdf.

13. "Athletics and Recreation: Overview," Stanford Undergraduate Admission, https://admission.stanford.edu/student/athletics/index.html.

14. Kate Chesley, "Faculty Senate Approves Early Admission Pilot for Student-Athletes," *Stanford Report*, June 11, 2021, https://news.stanford.edu/report/2021/06/11/faculty-senate-approves-early-admission-pilot-for-student-athletes/.

15. Scott Jaschik, "A Little More Information on Legacy Applicants," *Inside Higher Ed*, July 2, 2020, https://www.insidehighered.com/admissions/article/2020/07/06/california-law-sheds-light-how-private-colleges-handle-applications.

16. "Admissions Considerations for Children of Alumni or Donors," Stanford: Office of the Provost, https://provost.stanford.edu/2020/06/26/admissions-considerations/.

17. Ibid.

18. Anemona Hartocollis, Amy Harmon, and Mitch Smith, "'Lopping,' 'Tips,' and the 'Z-List': Bias Lawsuit Explores Harvard's Admissions Secrets," *New York Times*, July 29, 2018, https://www.nytimes.com/2018/07/29/us/harvard-admissions-asian-americans.html.

19. Jaschik, "A Little More Information."

20. Hartocollis et al., "'Lopping,' 'Tips,' and the 'Z-List'."

21. See Robert Samuelson, "How to Fix the College Admissions Scandal (Warning: You May Hate It)," RealClear Politics, March 20, 2019, https://www.realclearpolitics.com/articles/2019/03/20/how_to_fix_the_college_admissions_scandal_warning_you_may_hate_it_139794.html for similar arguments.

22. Caroline M. Hoxby and Christopher Avery, "The Missing 'One-Offs': The Hidden Supply of High-Achieving, Low Income Students," NBER working paper, December 2012, https://www.nber.org/system/files/working_papers/w18586/w18586.pdf.

23. Susan Dynarski, "Breaking Barriers to College for High-Achieving, Low-Income Students," EconoFact: Higher Education, March 17, 2019, https://econofact.org/breaking-barriers-to-college-for-high-achieving-low-income-students.

24. See, e.g., Susan Dynarski, C. J. Libassi, Katherine Michelmore, and Stephanie Owen, "Closing the Gap: The Effect of a Targeted, Tuition-Free Promise on College Choices of High-Achieving, Low-Income Students," NBER paper, https://www.nber.org/papers/w25349.

25. The Upshot, "How Much Does Getting into an Elite College Actually Matter?," *New York Times*, March 15, 2019, https://www.nytimes.com/2019/03/15/upshot/elite-colleges-actual-value.html

26. Stacy Dale and Alan B. Krueger, "Estimating the Return to College Selectivity over the Career Using Administrative Earnings Data," NBER working paper, June 2011, https://www.nber.org/papers/w17159.

CHAPTER 22. THE ETHICS OF DOCTORAL ADMISSIONS

1. "The Disposable Academic: Why Doing a PhD Is Often a Waste of Time," *Economist* 397, no. 8713 (December 18, 2010), http://www.economist.com/node/17723223.

2. Quoted in William G. Bowen and Michael S. McPherson, *Lesson Plan: An Agenda for Change in American Higher Education* (Princeton, NJ: Princeton University Press, 2016), 111.

3. "The Disposable Academic."

4. Thomas H. Benton, "Graduate School in the Humanities: Just Don't Go," *Chronicle of Higher Education* 55, no. 21 (2009): 21.

5. Bowen and McPherson, *Lesson Plan*, 115.

6. Eric P. Bettinger, Bridget Terry Long, and Eric S. Taylor, "When Inputs Are Outputs: The Case of Graduate Student Instructors," *Economics of Education Review* 52 (2016): 63–76.

7. See Julie R. Posselt, *Inside Graduate Admissions: Merit, Diversity, and Faculty Gatekeeping* (Cambridge, MA: Harvard University Press, 2016).

8. Onora O'Neill, *Autonomy and Trust in Bioethics* (Cambridge: Cambridge University Press, 2002).

9. The Nuremburg Code, U.S. Department of Health and Human Services, National Institutes of Health (NIH), https://history.nih.gov/research/downloads/nuremberg.pdf

10. Ruth Faden, Tom L. Beauchamp, and Nancy M. P. King. *A History and Theory of Informed Consent* (New York: Oxford University Press, 1986).

11. Ibid., 302.
12. Ibid., 308.
13. Ibid., 307.
14. Leonard Cassuto, *The Graduate School Mess: What Caused It and How We Can Fix It* (Cambridge, MA: Harvard University Press, 2015), 8.

CHAPTER 23. THE GOALS OF CAMPUS DISCIPLINE

Adapted from David Hoekema, *Campus Rules and Moral Community: In Place of* In Loco Parentis (Rowman & Littlefield, 1994).

1. In June 2021 Education Secretary Miguel Cardona announced a "sweeping rewrite" of Title IX rules ("Education Department Begins Sweeping Rewrite of Title IX Sexual Misconduct Rules," *USNews,* June 7, 2021, https://www.usnews.com/news/education-news/articles/2021-06-07/education-department-begins-sweeping-rewrite-of-title-ix-sexual-misconduct-rules), and in August 2021, the U.S. Department of Education revoked the requirement for live hearings with cross-examination of witnesses ("Update on Court Ruling about the Department of Education's Title IX Regulations," August 24, 2021, https://content.govdelivery.com/accounts/USED/bulletins/2ee0a5d). A helpful overview can be found in the Department of Education publication, "Questions and Answers on the Title IX Regulations on Sexual Harassment (July 2021)," https://www2.ed.gov/about/offices/list/ocr/docs/202107-qa-titleix.pdf.
2. Neil Gross and Solon Simmons, "The Social and Political Views of American College and University Professors," in *Professors and Their Politics*, ed. Neil Gross and Solon Simmons (Baltimore, MD: Johns Hopkins University Press, 2014).
3. For the most recent results and some chronological comparisons, see Ellen Bara Stolzenberg et al., "Undergraduate Teaching Faculty: The HERI Faculty Survey 2016–2017," Higher Education Research Institute, Graduate School of Education and Information Studies, University of California, Los Angeles, 2019.
4. Jeffrey Adam Sachs, "The 'Campus Free Speech Crisis' Ended Last Year," report published by the Niskanen Center, January 25, 2019, https://www.niskanencenter.org/the-campus-free-speech-crisis-ended-last-year/.

CHAPTER 24. THE SOCIAL COSTS OF A COLLEGE EDUCATION

1. Tara Westover, *Educated: A Memoir* (New York: Random House, 2018), ch. 27.
2. William, a white, "doubly disadvantaged" student quoted in Anthony Abraham Jack, *The Privileged Poor: How Elite Colleges Are Failing Disadvantaged Students* (Harvard University Press, 2019). "Renowned" is the pseudonym Jack gave to the elite college where he conducted his research.
3. Todd, quoted in Jennifer Morton, *Moving Up Without Losing Your Way: The Ethical Costs of Upward Mobility* (Princeton University Press, 2019), 29.
4. C. Thi Nguyen, "Trust as an Unquestioning Attitude," in *Oxford Studies in Epistemology*, vol. 7 (Oxford University Press, forthcoming).

5. Thank you to Harry Brighouse, Michael McPherson, Steven Cahn, Gina Schouten, James Tully, Jennifer Morton, Sarah Stitzlein, Sam Fleischacker, Anne Eaton, and the members of the Center for Ethics and Education Graduate Summer Institute (2020) for helpful feedback on earlier versions.

CHAPTER 25. WHY COLLEGE? AN EDUCATION FOR FREEDOM

1. We include universities under this designation, although they are more than undergraduate institutions.
2. W. E. B. Du Bois, *The Souls of Black Folk* (Gramercy Books, 1994), 80.
3. See Emily Levine, *Allies and Rivals: German-American Exchange and the Rise of the Modern Research University* (Chicago: University of Chicago Press, 2021).
4. On this debate, see Bliss Carnochan, *The Battleground of the Curriculum* (Stanford: Stanford University Press, 1994), ch. 2. See also Andrew Delbanco, *College: What It Was, Is, and Should Be* (Princeton: Princeton University Press, 2014).
5. See Louis Menand, *The Marketplace of Ideas: Reform and Resistance in the American University* (New York: Norton, 2010).
6. The Chicago core curriculum includes the natural and social sciences as well: see John Boyer, *The University of Chicago: A History* (Chicago: University of Chicago Press, 2015).
7. See Gilbert Allardyce, "The Rise and Fall of the Western Civilization Course," *American Historical Review* 87, no. 3 (1982): 695–725.
8. See Daniel Bell, "Reforming General Education," *Columbia Daily Spectator* (February 28, 1966), S1–4 (emphasis added). Available online at https://www.college.columbia.edu/core/content/daniel-bell-report.
9. For more details on this initiative, see https://college.stanford.edu/. During an implementation period, students will only be required to take courses in two out of the three quarters.

CHAPTER 26. ETHICS REQUIREMENTS IN THE LIBERAL ARTS CURRICULUM

1. Joe Pinsker, "The Yale Happiness Class, Distilled," *Atlantic*, June 25, 2019, https://www.theatlantic.com/family/archive/2019/06/yale-happiness-class/592477/.
2. Compare Bernard Williams, *Utilitarianism: For and Against* (Cambridge: Cambridge University Press, 1973), 91–92.
3. Compare Elizabeth Anscombe, "Modern Moral Philosophy," *Philosophy: The Journal of the Royal Institute of Philosophy* 33, no. 124 (January 1958): 1–19.

CHAPTER 27. TAKING UNDERGRADUATE TEACHING AND LEARNING SERIOUSLY

1. Steven M. Cahn, *Navigating Academic Life: How the System Works* (Routledge, 2021).
2. Derek Bok, *The Struggle to Reform Our Colleges* (Princeton University Press, 2016).

3. Ernest T. Pascarella and Patrick T. Terenzini, *How College Affects Students: A Third Decade of Research*, vol. 2 (Jossey-Bass, 2005).

4. Richard Arum and Josipa Roksa, *Academically Adrift: Limited Learning on College Campuses* (Chicago: University of Chicago Press, 2011).

5. For a simple explanation see Bok, *The Struggle to Reform*, 30.

6. Philip Babcock and Mindy Marks, "The Falling Time Cost of College: Evidence from Half a Century of Time Use Data," *Review of Economics and Statistics* 93, no. 2 (2011): 468–78.

7. Bok, *The Struggle to Reform*, 35.

8. David W. Concepción, Melinda Messineo, Sarah Wieten, and Catherine Homan, "The State of Teacher Training in Philosophy," *Teaching Philosophy* 39, no. 1 (2016): 1–24.

9. "Graduate Funding: Financial Support," Harvard University, Department of Philosophy, retrieved March 19, 2019, https://philosophy.fas.harvard.edu/funding-graduate.

10. See John Rawls, *A Theory of Justice* (Cambridge, MA: Harvard University Press, 1970).

11. Rebecca D. Robbins et al., "The Class of 2014 by the Numbers," *Harvard Crimson*, June 2014, https://features.thecrimson.com/2014/senior-survey/.

12. Mathematics requirements are heavily implicated in the high rates of attrition at open access institutions, and may well be related to attrition at more selective public institutions. See William G. Bowen and Michael S. McPherson, *Lesson Plan: An Agenda for Change in American Higher Education* (Princeton University Press, 2016).

13. Little of what I say in this section is original. The suggestions are largely drawn from recommendations made, variously, in the following:

Derek Bok, *Our Underachieving Colleges: A Candid Look at How Much Students Learn and Why They Should Be Learning More* (Princeton University Press, 2009).

———. *The Struggle to Reform Our Colleges* (Princeton University Press, 2016).

William G. Bowen and Michael S. McPherson, *Lesson Plan: An Agenda for Change in American Higher Education* (Princeton University Press, 2016).

Project: Commission on the Future of Undergraduate Education, American Academy of Arts & Sciences, https://www.amacad.org/project/future-undergraduate-education.

Aaron M. Pallas, Anna Neumann, and Corbin M. Campbell, "Policies and Practices to Support Undergraduate Teaching Improvement," *Higher Education* 27, no. 3 (2004): 365–84.

Carl Wieman, *Improving How Universities Teach Science* (Harvard University Press, 2017).

14. Wieman (2017) in particular emphasizes the role of departments.

15. For thoughts about what individual instructors can do, see: Harry Brighouse, "Becoming a Better College Teacher (If You're Lucky)," *Daedalus* 148, no. 4 (2019): 14–28, https://doi.org/10.1162/daed_a_01758.

16. Judith Warren Little, *The Power of Organizational Setting: School Norms and Staff Development* (Washington, DC: U.S. Department of Education, 1981), 12–13.

CHAPTER 28. ASSESSING FACULTY UNIONS

1. "Academic Unionism Statement," November 2005, and AAUP Updates: "Faculty Unions and Governance," March 25, 2010, Washington, DC: American Association of University

Professors (AAUP); Mary Ellen Benedict and Lewis Benedict, "What Faculty Unions Can Learn from Workload Policy in Ohio," *Academe* 100, no. 2 (March–April, 2014). See also https://www.aaup.org.

2. Cited in Peter Levine, "The Libertarian Critique of Labor Unions," *Philosophy and Public Affairs Quarterly* 21, no. 4 (Fall 2001): 22.

3. Estelle S. Gellman, "Collective Bargaining and the AAUP," *Academe* 84, no. 6 (1998).

4. Adapted from my *Unionization in the Academy: Visions and Realties* (Lanham, MD: Rowman and Littlefield, 2003).

CHAPTER 29. FRIENDRAISING

1. "University of North Dakota Receives $20 Million," *Philanthropy News Digest*, May 9, 2009, accessed August 20, 2021, https://philanthropynewsdigest.org/news/university-of-north-dakota-receives-20-million.

2. "Mission Statement," University of North Dakota, accessed August 20, 2021, https://und.edu/about/mission/index.html.

3. "University of North Dakota Accepts Money from Man Who Threw Hitler Parties," *AP News*, October 12, 1988, accessed 08 15, 2021, https://apnews.com/article/e86084a125a17c5042f2573ca5bf23ff.

4. Robert Reinhold, "Las Vegas Journal; Nevada Draws the Line: No Hitler in Casinos," *New York Times*, April 3, 1989, accessed August 15, 2021, https://www.nytimes.com/1989/04/03/us/las-vegas-journal-nevada-draws-the-line-no-hitler-in-the-casinos.html.

5. "Ralph Engelstad Papers, 1988–2004: Collection Overview," UND Department of Special Collections, dated acquired August 26, 2002, accessed August 15, 2021, https://apps.library.und.edu/archon/?p=collections/findingaid&id=413&q=&rootcontentid=54174.

6. Patty Morales, "How Some Wealthy Parents Game the College Admissions Process," PBS *News Hour*, March 18, 2019, accessed August 21, 2021, https://www.pbs.org/newshour/education/how-some-wealthy-parents-game-the-college-admissions-process.

7. Holly Smith and Marilyn Batt Dunn, "Gifts and Donors' Expectations," in *The Ethics of Asking: Dilemmas in Higher Education Fund Raising*, ed. Deni Elliott (Baltimore: John Hopkins University Press, 1995), 107.

8. Camille G. Caldera and Michelle Kurilla, "Harvard Releases Gift Policy Guide, Outlines Considerations for Philanthropic Gifts," *Harvard Crimson*, July 1, 2020.

9. Katja Lee and P. David Marshall, "Honorary Degrees for Celebrities: Persona, Scandal, and the Case of Bill Cosby," *Celebrity Studies* 12, no. 1 (April 15, 2019): 102–18.

10. Janet Lorin, "Middlebury College Will Revoke Giuliani's 2005 Honorary Degree," *BloombergQuint*, January 12, 2021.

11. Caldera and Kurilla, "Harvard Releases Gift Policy Guide."

CHAPTER 30. INTERCOLLEGIATE ATHLETICS AS ENTERTAINMENT

1. Harold W. Stoke, "College Athletics: Education or Show Business," *Atlantic Monthly* 193 (March 1954): 46–50.

2. Gilbert Ryle, *The Concept of Mind* (London: Hutchinson, 1949).

3. Robert H. Atwell, "The Only Way to Reform College Sports Is to Embrace Commercialization," *Chronicle of Higher Education*, July 13, 2001, B20.

4. James J. Duderstadt, *Intercollegiate Athletics and the American University: A University President's Perspective* (Ann Arbor: University of Michigan Press, 2003).

5. This brief essay is adapted from my *Ethics and College Sports: Ethics, Sports, and the University* (Lanham, MD: Rowman & Littlefield, 2004).

CHAPTER 31. INTERCOLLEGIATE ATHLETICS AND EDUCATIONAL VALUES

1. Bernard Suits, "The Elements of Sport," in *The Philosophy of Sport: A Collection of Essays*, ed. Robert Osterhoudt (Springfield, IL: Charles C. Thomas, 1973), 48–64.

2. This essay is adapted by the editor from Robert Simon, "Intercollegiate Athletics and Educational Values: A Case for Compatibility," in *A Teacher's Life: Essays for Steven M. Cahn*, ed. Robert B. Talisse and Maureen Eckert (Lanham, MD: Lexington Books, 2009); reprint Eugene, OR: Wipf and Stock, 2021), 113–42.

Index

AAUP. *See* American Association of University Professors
abortion, ethics of, 4–5
academic administration: compromises in, 165; confrontation of, 162–63; decision-making in, 160–62, 167; digital culture and, 174–75; dirty hands problem for, 164; discretion used by, 168–69, 172–73; diversity funds and, 173–74; ethical obligations of, 172–73; faculty tracks and, 175–76; on faculty unions, 275; institutional capital and, 160–61; moral hazards in, 159–60; prudent reserve in, 162, 164; public relations and, 162, 165–66; as rules-bound, 168, 175–76; rulings with no exceptions, 171–72; secrecy of, 165–66; shared governance in, 159
academic birth control, 210–11
academic freedom: academic tenure and, 25–26, 30, 32; Climate Objection to views on, 11; conservatism on, 225; conservative view on, 4; Defense Mistake, 12; Ending Debate Objection to views on, 13–14; Harm Objection to views on, 11; in liberal arts education, 246; Moral Peril Objection to views on, 14; protection of, 10–11; Psychological Naïveté Objection to views on, 12; racism and, 4; Third Person Objection to views on, 13; for undergraduates, 7–8; views of, 10–11; wokeness and, 10
academic integrity, in online learning, 193–94
academic quality: academic standards and, 44; improvement of, 268; in online instruction, 185–87
academic standards: academic quality and, 44; at community colleges, 137; competitiveness and, 44–45; Minimally Decent Samaritan moral obligation and, 46–47
academic tenure, 314n4; academic freedom and, 25–26, 30, 32; attacks on, 26, 30–31; competitiveness and, 27–28; confidentiality and, 53; deadwood argument against, 26, 30–31; defining, 25; economic arguments against, 29–30; envy of, 29–30; inefficiency as argument against, 27–28; justification of, 25–26; Minimally Decent Samaritan moral obligation and, 46; obligations of, 30; politicization attack on, 32; postmodern attack on, 31–32; review of, 53; rights of, 30; salaries and, 28; six-year conformity training argument against, 31; teaching and learning in, 269; wisdom in, 28
Academos, xiii
accessibility, 114–15

accrediting commissions, 189
acquaintance rape, 223
actual notice standard, for sexual harassment, 77–78
ADA. *See* Americans with Disabilities Act
ADHD, 128, 129–30
adjunct teachers: at community colleges, 142–43; cruelty of adjunct system, 149–54; negative consequences of adjunct system, 148–49; permanent, 47; poverty of, 149–50. *See also* non-tenure-track professors
admissions: bidding for, 206, 208; bribery and, 199–200; to elite universities, 201, 203; to Harvard University, 199, 200–201, 206; for high-achieving students, 202, 207; inequality and, 200–201, 205–6; merit and, 207; middlemen in, 200; need-blind, 202, 207; philanthropy and, 205; SAT scores and, 200; standards, 207–8; to Stanford, 199; transparency in, 208; in United States, 203–4
advertising: of Big Pharma, 127–28; DTC, 127–28
affirmative action: candidates, 108–9; contractors and, 106; defining, 106–7; goals of, 109; Johnson, L. B., on, 105–6; Kekes on, 108; preferential, 106–7; procedural, 106–7; Supreme Court on, 107
agora, xiv
AI/ML. *See* artificial intelligence and machine learning
Akadēmeia, xiii–xiv; intellectual freedom at, xiv; of Plato, xiv, xvii
alcohol abuse, campus discipline for, 223
alumni, 267
American Association of University Professors (AAUP): on faculty unions, 273–74; principles of, 315n7; Statement of Principles on Academic Freedom and Tenure, 25
American Council on Education, 294
American Philosophical Association, 261
Americans with Disabilities Act (ADA), 113, 123
anthologized articles, 36
anti-Black racism, 3

anticipation of harm, free speech and, 19–21
anti-intellectualism, 149, 274–75
anti-masculinity, 73, 307n10
anti-woke view, 304n12
Apology (Plato), xiv
Archytas of Tarentum, xv
Aristotle, xiii–xiv, 221; on friendship, 281; *Nicomachean Ethics*, 281
artificial intelligence and machine learning (AI/ML), 306n18; applications of, 60; bias in algorithms of, 67; humanity and, 63–67; integration of, 63
Arum, Richard, 262
athletic programs: critical inquiry parallels with, 299; education programs distinguished from, 292–93; as entertainment, 291–92; faculty and coach interactions, 300–301; mission statements of, 297–98; within normal curriculum, 300; normative dimension of contests, 299; professionalism in, 294; Stoke on, 291–94, 296; success in, 299
athletic recruits, at Stanford, 204
Atlantic Monthly, 296
Attewell, Paul, 140
Atwell, Robert H., 294
autocracy, 168–69
autonomy, 221; of universities, 26
Axiothea of Philius, xiii

Babcock, Philip, 262
background, diversity of, 239–40
Bakke decision, 107
behaviors without subjects, 65
Bell, Daniel, 248
Benton, Thomas H., 209
Biden, Joe, 223
bigotry: defining, 9–10; naming, 9–10; views of, 10–11
Big Pharma, advertising of, 127–28
BioButtons, 64
Black Americans, 82–83, 99, 103–4, 184; burden of lowered expectations, 245; categorical exclusion of, 91, 94; representation of, in academia, 94
Black Justice League, 3
Black Lives Matter, 3, 10

Bok, Derek, 142, 262
Boston University, 207, 208
Bound, John, 83
bribery: admissions and, 199–200; donations and, 200, 286–87; ethics of, 208

Cahn, Steven M., 261
California, 83
Calvinism, 245–46
Cambridge, 203
campus: conservatism on, 15–16; free speech on, 15; leadership, 270; on-campus housing, 226
campus discipline: atmosphere of dialogue and debate promoted by, 224–27; for drug and alcohol abuse, 223; for exploitation prevention, 221–24; for harm prevention, 221–24; for plagiarism, 223; sense of community and, 227–30; for sexual harassment, 223
campus police force, 163–64
capital: human, 265–66; institutional, 160–61; moral, 63; social, 265–66; university planning, 160–61
capitalism, 266
careerism, 228
career success: externalities and, 43–44, 47–48; moral value of, 45; parenthood and, 44
category mistakes, 291–92
Center for Community College Student Engagement, 142
chains of trust, 232–33; dysfunctional topographies and, 235–37; improvement of, 238
character, formation of, 227
chatbots, 65–66; data from, 60–61
cheating, 23, 66. *See also* plagiarism
Chetty, Raj, 200
children, inequality and education of, 201–2
Chronicle of Higher Education, 139, 294
Churchill, Robert Paul, 182, 186–87
Civil Rights Act: Title IX, 54, 62–63, 71, 72, 78; Title VI, 105; Title VII, 72, 75
Civil War, xvi, 244; academic institutions founded before, 95–96

CLA. *See* Collegiate Learning Assessment
classroom: laptops in, 113, 121; webinars compared with, 193
Clotfelter, Charles T., 139
Coalition and the Academic Workforce, 146
COBRA, 150
collective bargaining: advocates for, 275; of faculty unions, 274; opposition to, 277
collectivism, 277–78
college education, goals of, 233–35
College Parallel program, 116
collegiality, faculty unions and, 274–76
Collegiate Learning Assessment (CLA), 262
Columbia Core, 248
Columbia University, 288
Committee on Equal Employment Opportunity, 105–6
common law traditions, 62
communication skills, 192–93
community, campus discipline and, 227–30
community colleges, 135; academic standards at, 137; adjuncts at, 142–43; completion rates at, 138–40; credibility of, 141–42; dismissal of, 136; diversity at, 139; enrollment decline in, 138; failure to recognize, 136; Federal Work-Study aid at, 139; selling of, 136–38; transferring to four-year colleges from, 140–42
compensation. *See* principle of compensation
competence-centered approach, to sexual harassment, 73–74
competitiveness, 124; academic standards and, 44–45; academic tenure and, 27–28; externalities and, 44–45; peer review and, 41
completion rates, 83
Confederacy, 91
confidentiality: academic tenure and, 53; defining, 54–55; department rules and problems of, 54–55; duties of, 51–52; at Georgetown University, 56; letters of recommendation and, 54; limits of, 53–54; promotion and, 57; of student information, 54–55; trust-based duties of, 52–57; violation of, 51

conservatism: on academic freedom, 225; on campus, 15–16
conservative watchdog groups, 225
conspiracy theories, 236
Constitution, US, First Amendment, 16, 175
contingent faculty, at community colleges, 142–43
contractors, affirmative action and, 106
contracts, faculty, 276
copyright laws, 223
core disclosure, 214–15
Cornell, 288
corporations: CEOs of, 29; hierarchy of, 29; universities as, 28–29
Cosby, Bill, 287
course management systems, 186
Coursera, 180
COVID-19 pandemic, 48, 188; data from, 60; MOOCs in, 179, 184
Craig, Ryan, 143
crime prevention, 222
criminal code, 222
criminal law, students and, 222
Critical Race Theory, 304n12
critical thinking, as education goal, 234
cults, 236
culture of substance, 212
CUNY, 291
curb cuts, 114–15

Dangaremba, Tsitsi, 248
Dartmouth, 66
data: brokerage, 67; from chatbots, 60–61; collection policies, 67–68; from COVID-19 pandemic, 60; interpretation costs, 61; from IoB, 64–65; from IoT, 64; on NTT professors, 146; retention, 67; types of, 59
Davis, Frances, 117–18
Davis v. Monroe County Board of Education, 73
dead dogmas, 243
deadwood argument, against academic tenure, 26, 30–31
debt, from student loans, 202
decision-making, in academic administration, 160–62, 167

deliberate indifference standard: himpathy and, 78–79; for sexual harassment, 77–78, 80
Delphi Project, 148
democracy, xiv; institutional inequality and, 85; participatory, 246
Democratic Education (Gutman), 84
Department of Justice, 120, 286–87
Department of Labor, 106
department reviews, 268–69
depression, 128, 129–30
desire-dominant approach, to sexual harassment, 73–74
dialogue, campus discipline promoting, 224–27
difficult tasks, 262–63
digital culture, academic administration and, 174–75
digital footprint, 190
Diogenes Laertius, xiii
direct-to-consumer (DTC) advertising, 127–28
dirty hands problem, 164, 314n3
disability, 113; accommodations and modifications for, 114–15; benefits, 126–28; cultural views on, 125–27, 130–31; examination accommodations for, 118–19; inclusion and accommodations for, 118–19; policies on, 124–25, 131; of veterans, 125–26; WWII and policy on, 125–26
disciplinary fluency, 234
discipline. *See* campus discipline
disclosure: core, 214–15; subjective, 214–15
discretion: academic administration using, 168–69, 172–73; ethics and, 168–69
distraction factor, in FOI, 190
distributive justice, online instruction and, 187
diversity funds, academic administration and, 173–74
diversity of background, 239–40
dogmatism, 254–55
donations, bribery and, 200, 286–87
downsizing, 27, 29
drug use, campus discipline for, 223
DTC advertising. *See* direct-to-consumer advertising

Du Bois, W. E. B., xvi; at Harvard, 245; on liberal arts education, 244–45
Duderstadt, James J., on entertainment, 294–95
due diligence standard, for sexual harassment, 80
Dumont University, 33–35
duties: of confidentiality, 51–52; gaining of, 52; tacit, 52; trust-based, 52–57
dysfunctional topographies: chains of trust and, 235–37; echo chambers, 236; epistemic nests, 236–37; epistemic valleys, 235; filter bubbles, 236

echo chambers, 236
economics courses, 254–55
Education Amendments. *See* Title IX
Education Trust, 83
edX, 180
Eisgruber, Christopher, 3–4
elective system, 245
Eliot, Charles William, 244; on freedom, 246–47; on liberal arts education, 245–46
elite universities: admissions to, 201, 203; high-income student body at, 200–201; philanthropy at, 204–5
Ellipsis Health, 64–65
The Emergence of the American University (Veysey), 136
Emory College, 288
emotional harms, 256–57
Employee Retirement Income Security Act of 1974 (ERISA), 171
Engelstad, Ralph, 283–85
entertainment: athletic programs as, 291–92; Duderstadt on, 294–95; education distinguished from, 292–93
epistemic nests, 236–37; social costs of leaving, 237
epistemic valleys, 235
Epstein, Jeffrey, 288
equity, 169–70; in online instruction, 184–85
ERISA. *See* Employee Retirement Income Security Act of 1974
Eudoxus of Cnidus, xiii

Executive Order 11246, 106
exploitation prevention, campus discipline for, 221–24
external goods, 182
externalities: career success and, 43–44, 47–48; combating, 48; competitiveness and, 44–45; defining, 43–44; faculty and, 43–44; identification of, 48; negative, 43–44

Facebook, 64, 174–75; filter bubbles on, 236
faculty: coach interactions with, 300–301; contracts, 276; externalities and, 43–44; FOI impact on, 194–95; haughtiness of, 239; morale of, 314n1; tracks, 175–76. *See also specific topics*
faculty unions: AAUP on, 273–74; academic administration on, 275; academic values and, 278–79; collective bargaining of, 274; collegiality and, 274–76; effectiveness of, 276–77; history of, 273; institutional structure and, 277–78; job security and, 276; militancy of, 277–78; moral legitimacy of, 279; opposition to, 275, 277, 279; productivity and, 277; Rorty on, 275; stigmatization of, 274; unionization process, 274; as watchdogs, 277; on working conditions, 274
fairness, 105–6, 169–70; of tests, 119–20
Family Educational Rights and Privacy Act (FERPA), 51, 61; educational resources about, 55–56; rules for honoring, 54–55
FATE standards, 67
Faulkner, William, 92
FDA, 129
Federal Work-Study aid, at community colleges, 139
femininity, 73–75
FERPA. *See* Family Educational Rights and Privacy Act
Fighting Sioux, 283, 285–86
filter bubbles, on Facebook and Google, 236
financial aid, need-based, 202
First Amendment, Constitution, 16, 175
first-year retention rates, 66–67
fixed curriculum, 246

FOI. *See* fully online instruction
Forbes, 143
foreign aid, 101
Foucault, Michel, 225
Frain, Paul, 142
Franklin v. Gwinett County Public Schools, 72
freedom: of association, 230; Eliot on, 246–47; of expression, 230; intellectual, xiv; McCosh on, 246–47. *See also* academic freedom
free speech: anticipation of harm and, 19–21; on campus, 15; defining, 16–17; as legal right, 16; mere disagreement and, 18–19; Noisy Truck case, 16–17; nonlegal rights to, 16; Political Conservative Student case, 15–20; Unconstitutional Treason Law case, 18, 20, 21; violation of, 16–17, 304n2
French, Peter A.: on mission statements, 297
Friedman, Milton, 225
friendship: Aristotle on, 281; funding and, 281–82; IHEs and, 281–82; invited work and, 36–37
From Plato's Academy To Ours (Goldstein), xii–xvii
fully online instruction (FOI): distraction factor in, 190; emotional appeal against, 192; faculty impacted by, 194–95; instructor burden in, 194–95; learning outcomes in, 189–92; mitigation of negative effects of, 195–96; prevalence of, 189; syllabus in, 190; teaching aids in, 191; technology in, 191–92; webcams in, 191
funding, 264; friendship and, 281–82
fundraising, of IHEs, 287

gap year, 201
General Data Protection Regulation (GDPR), 61
George, Robert, 9–10
Georgetown University, 95, 204; confidentiality at, 56; historic injustices of, 90; slavery and, 90
gift policies, 288
gig economy, 147
Gini index, 203

Giuliani, Rudolph, 287
goals, college education, 233–35; critical thinking as, 234; disciplinary fluency, 234; new social ties, 234
Goldrick-Rab, Sara, 140
Goldstein, Rebecca Newberger, xii–xvii
Good Samaritan moral obligation, 45
Google, 190; filter bubbles on, 236
Great Recession, 266
Gutman, Amy, 84

harm, anticipation of, free speech and, 19–21
harm prevention: campus discipline for, 221–24; moral ground for, 221–22; paternalism of, 223–24
Harvard University, 142, 180, 228, 288; admissions to, 199, 200–201, 206; Du Bois at, 245; Philosophy Department at, 263; women at, 91; Z list at, 201
Haslanger, Sally, 9
Hayek, Friedrich, 225
Helsinki, 46–47
hetairos (companions), xiii
high-achieving students, admissions for, 202, 207
Higher Education Act, 223
Higher Education Research Institute, 225
higher education sector, institutional inequality in, 83–85
himpathy: defining, 71–72; deliberate indifference standard and, 78–79
historic injustices: of academic institutions, 90–91; accountability for, 102; categorical exclusion as, 90–91; curricular exclusion as, 91; descendants of, 92; of Georgetown University, 90; harms caused by, 92; institutional responsibility for, 93–94; norms perpetuated by, 92–93; principles for reckoning with, 95–97; reckoning with, 92–93; reparations for, 100–101, 102–3; slavery as, 95–96; symbolic and cultural, 91; systemic epistemic, 93, 94, 96–97
A History and Theory of Informed Consent, 213
Hitler, Adolf, 284

Hobbes, Thomas, 248
Holocaust, reparations for, 101
homophobia, 5
honorary degrees, 287–88
hostile environments, sexual harassment and, 75–77
House Committee on Education and the Workforce, 146
housing: on-campus, 226; substance-free, 227
Huffman, Felicity, 199
human capital, 265–66
humanity, AI/ML and, 63–67
Hutcheson, Paul, 136

IDEA. *See* Individuals with Disabilities Education Act
IEPs. *See* Individualized Education Plans
IHE. *See* institutions of higher education
immoral research, 5; permission of, 6–8
individual-institutional relationships, 282
individualism, 228
Individualized Education Plans (IEPs), 201
Individuals with Disabilities Education Act (IDEA), 61
indoctrination, 254–55
inequality: admissions and, 200–201, 205–6; aspects of, 81; child education and, 201–2; Ivy Leagues perpetuating, 103; online instruction and, 187–88; tuition and, 206. *See also* institutional inequality
informed consent, for PhD admissions, 213–15
injustice: of MOOCs, 182–83; towards NTT professors, 146–48; racial, 256. *See also* historic injustices
in loco avi, 224
in loco avunculi, 224, 227
Inside Higher Ed, 142
Instagram, 174–75
institutional capital, 160–61
institutional inequality: addressing, 85; defining, 81–82; democracy and, 85; in higher education sector, 83–85; state interference aggravating, 84–85; tax exemptions and, 84
institutional structure, faculty unions and, 277–78

institutions of higher education (IHE): characteristics of, 282; friendship and, 281–82; fundraising of, 287; gift policies at, 288; philanthropic issues in, 286–88; transparency at, 288; venture capitalists and, 286
Integrated Postsecondary Education Data System, 146
intellectual freedom, xiv
Internet of Behaviors (IoB), data from, 64–65
Internet of Things (IoT): data from, 64; privacy and, 63–64
interpersonal communication skills, in online learning, 192–93
interracial marriage, 10
invited work: friendship and, 36–37; T&P and, 35–39
IoB. *See* Internet of Behaviors
IoT. *See* Internet of Things
IP addresses, 59
Israel, 101
Ivy Leagues, inequality perpetuated by, 103

January 6, 2021 Capitol Hill raid, 287
Jim Crow, 91
job security, faculty unions and, 276
Johnson, Lyndon B., on affirmative action, 105–6

Kant, Immanuel, 221–22, 314n2
Kaplan, David, 40
Kekes, John, on affirmative action, 108
Kennedy, John F., 91, 105
Kezar, Adrianna, 146
knowledge, wisdom contrasted with, 28
Kushner, Jared, 199

Land Grant Universities, 309n4
laptops, in classroom, 113, 121, 310n1
Lastheneia of Mantinea, xiii
Latinx Americans, 82–83, 184
Law School Admission Council (LSAC), 119–20
leadership, campus, 270
learning: centers, 270; improvement of, 267–68; outcomes, 268; problems with

suboptimal, 264–67; quality of, 268; suboptimal, 261–64; in tenure, 269. *See also* artificial intelligence and machine learning
learning management systems (LMS), 59, 66
learning outcomes, in FOI, 189–92
Lehrfreiheit, 246, 247, 249
Lernfreiheit, 246, 247
letters of recommendation, 39; confidentiality and, 54
Leviathan, of Hobbes, 248
LGBTQ+ students, 229, 303n3
liberal arts education, 182, 311n1; academic freedom in, 246; debates on, 243–49; defining, 251; Du Bois on, 244–45; Eliot on, 245–46; history of, 243–49; McCosh on, 245–46; normative questions in, 252; pedagogy of, 246; as social surgery, 244; at Stanford, 248–49; value of, 243; Washington, B. T., on, 244–45
liberal bias allegations, 225
libertarianism, 226
lip-reading, 117
Little, Judith Warren, 270–71
LMS. *See* learning management systems
Louisiana State University, 291
Lowell, A. Lawrence, 246
lowered expectations, burden of, 245
LSAC. *See* Law School Admission Council
LSAT, 119–20
Lyceum, xiv; donors to, 281

machine learning. *See* artificial intelligence and machine learning
MacKinnon, Catharine, 80
Manne, Kate, 75, 78
Marks, Mindy, 262
marriage: interracial, 10; same-sex, 5, 303n3
Marx, Karl, 225
Marxism, 226
masculinity, 73–76
massive open online courses (MOOCs): in COVID-19 pandemic, 179, 184; criticism of, 179–83; ethics and, 183–88; faulty pedagogies of, 181–82; injustice of, 182–83; national prominence of, 180;

neoliberalism and, 183, 187; student success rates in, 180–81
Mayer, J. R., 38
McCosh, James, 244; on freedom, 246–47; on liberal arts education, 245–46
McGarry, Kris Engelstad, 285–86
medicalization, 127–29
mental health: crisis, 64–65; moral stances on, 256–57
mere disagreement, free speech and, 18–19
Meredith, James, 91
Michigan State University, 310n1
middlemen, in admissions, 200
Mill, John Stuart, 243, 278
Minimally Decent Samaritan moral obligation, 43; academic standards and, 46–47; academic tenure and, 46; Singer, P., on, 45–46; Thompson on, 45
minority groups, defining, 106
misogyny, 5; defining, 71–72, 75; sexual harassment and, 75–77
mission statements, 282; of athletic programs, 297–98; French on, 297–98
MIT, 180, 288
Modern Language Association, 210
Monaghan, David B., 140
MOOCs. *See* massive open online courses
moral capital, privacy as, 63
moral hazards, in academic administration, 159–60
morality: of faculty unions, 279; harm prevention and, 221–22; mental health and, 256–57; in modern society, 229; philosophy and, xvi
moral philosophy, role of, 4–5
moral value, of career success, 45
Morrill Act of 1862, 309n4
multitasking, 262

Nasser, Larry, 90
National Center for Education Statistics, 83, 146, 243
Native Americans, 93, 99, 103–4, 309n8
Nazis, 284
NCAA, 293, 295, 300
need-based financial aid, 202
need-blind admissions, 202, 207

negative, externalities, 43–44
neoliberalism, MOOCs and, 183, 187
neural networks, 65
Nevada Gaming Commission, 284
New Deal, 126
The New York Times, 236
Nguyen, C. Thi, 232
Nicklaus, Jack, 298
Nicomachean Ethics (Aristotle), 281
Nixon, Richard, 106
Nobel Prize, 169
Noisy Truck case, 16–17
nondisclosure agreements, 56
non-tenure-track (NTT) professors, 145; advocating for, 155; contracts of, 150; data on, 146; families of, 151–52; feelings of failure of, 152–53; injustice and, 146–48; job openings for, 150; sadness of, 153; salaries of, 150; students taught by, 153–54
nonverbal cues, 185
normative questions, 258; in ethics courses, 253–54; in liberal arts education, 252
Notre Dame, 204
Nozick, Robert, 148
NTT professors. See non-tenure-track professors
Nuremburg Code, 213
nurses, 266–67

Obama, Barack, 223
Office of Civil Rights (OCR), 72, 80
on-campus housing, 226
online instruction: academic excellence in, 185–87; academic integrity in, 193–94; distributive justice and, 187; equity in, 184–85; ethical, 183–88; inequality and, 187–88; interpersonal communication skills in, 192–93. See also fully online instruction; massive open online courses
open dialogue, fostering, 229–30
Oxford, 203

parallel track, 269–70
parenthood, career success and, 44
parity of status, 269
parking, 114

Parran, Thomas, 94
parrhesia, xiv
participatory democracy, 246
paternalism: of harm prevention, 223–24; of PhD students, 211
Paxil, 128
pedagogical training: demands of, 271; of graduate students, 263, 268
pedagogy: of liberal arts education, 246; of MOOCs, 181–82
peer review: competitiveness and, 41; forgoing, 47; T&P and, 36–37
Peloponnesian War, xiv
personalized learning environments, 65
personhood, privacy and, 62–63
personnel committees, 37–38
Phaedrus (Plato), xv
PhD students: advanced academic study as public good, 211–12; core and subjective disclosure, 214–15; ethics of admissions, 209–10; flexible futures of, 215–17; funding for, 210; informed consent in admissions for, 213–15; nonvocational, 212–13; paternalism of, 211; pedagogical training of, 263, 268; program completion times for, 210; program costs for, 209–10; program improvement, 268; self-enrichment of, 211; social and institutional value of programs for, 217; social justification for, 212–13; soft skills in programs for, 216
philanthropy: admissions and, 205; at elite universities, 204–5; in IHEs, 286–88; USC and, 205
Philip of Opus, xiii
philos (friends), xiii–xiv
philosophy: morality and, xvi; in Western academic tradition, xiii
Pitzer College, 294
plagiarism, 160; campus discipline for, 223
Plato, 162–63, 168, 248; *Akadēmeia* of, xiii–xiv, xvii; *Apology*, xiv; *Phaedrus*, xv; *Republic*, xvi
Political Conservative Student case, 15–20
politicization, of academic tenure, 32
postmodernism, academic tenure and, 31–32
poverty, of adjunct teachers, 149–50

Powell, Lewis, 107
Pregnancy Discrimination Act, 121
prescription drugs, 128–29
Princeton University, 3, 180
principle of compensation, reparations and, 101
privacy: data and, 61–62; defining, 62; IoT and, 63–64; legal and regulatory infrastructure, 61–62; as moral capital, 63; personhood and, 62–63; safeguarding, 61–62
privatization, 187
professionalism, in athletics, 294
professional socialization, 216–17
promotion: confidentiality and, 57. *See also* tenure and promotion
Protagoras, xiv
The Protocols of the Elders of Zion, 231
provincialism, 248
psychology classes, 255
public good: advanced study as, 211–12; defining, 264; social and human capital and, 265–66; undergraduate programs contributing to, 264
public relations, academic administration and, 162, 165–66
punishment: of racist research, 3, 5–6; of unpopular views, 20
Pythagoreans, xv

Queens College, 291
quid pro quo sexual harassment, 74

racial injustice, 256
racism: academic freedom and, 4; in academic work, 3–4; anti-Black, 3; conservative view on, 4; debates on defining, 9–10; naming, 9–10; wokeness and, 4
racist research: permission of, 6–8; punishment of, 3, 5–6
rape: acquaintance, 223; shield laws, 62–63
rational choice theory, 255
Rawls, John, 148
reckoning, with historic injustices, 92–93
Reconstruction, xvi, 244
redistribution, 85
Rehabilitation Act, Supreme Court on, 117

relativism, xiv, 255–56
religious authorities, 237
Renowned, 231
reparations: for historic injustices, 100–101, 102–3; for Holocaust, 101; principle of compensation and, 101
Republic (Plato), xvi
research: immoral, 5–6; misconduct, 5–6; racist, 3, 5–8
responsibility, for historic injustices, 93–94
rest rooms, 115
résumés, 216
Revised Order No. 4, 106
Ritalin, 128
Rorty, Richard, on faculty unions, 275
Rosenbaum, James E., 139
Roska, Josipa, 262
Ryle, Gilbert, 291

Sackler family, 288
salaries, academic tenure and, 28
same-sex marriage, 5, 303n3
Sandusky, Jerry, 90
San José State University Philosophy Department, 181
SAT, 119; admissions and scores on, 200
scholarships, 100
Schultz, Vicki, 73
self-enrichment, 211
self-government, 248
self-knowledge, 216
self-silencing, 18–21, 304n6
Selingo, Jeffrey, 137–38
sex, ethics of, 4–5
sex discrimination, sexual harassment as, 72–73
sexual harassment, 54; actual notice standard for, 77–78; campus discipline for, 223; competence-centered approach to, 73–74; conceptions of, 73–75; defining, 71, 307n7; deliberate indifference standard for, 77–78, 80; desire-dominant approach to, 73–74; due diligence standard for, 80; elimination of, 79–80; hostile environments and, 75–77; misogyny and, 75–77; quid pro quo, 74; as sex discrimination, 72–73

shared governance, in academic administration, 159
Shelley, Mary, 248
Shick, David, 56
silencing, 19–21
Singer, Peter, 45–46
Singer, William, 204
Sioux Award, 283
six-year conformity training argument, 31
slavery, xvi, 94, 102–3; Georgetown University and, 90; as historic injustice, 95–96
social anxiety, 128, 129–30
social capital, 265–66
social costs, 231–32; confronting, 237–40; education goals and, 233–35; of epistemic nests, 237; transparency of, 239
social justice, 288
social media, 64, 174–75
social sciences, ethics and, 252–53
social ties, new, 234
social welfare, 125–26
sociology, 252
Socrates, xiv
soft skills, in PhD programs, 216
Southeastern Community College v. Davis, 116–18, 120, 121
Spartans, xiv
speakers, controversial, 225
specialization, in US, 243
standardization, 278
Stanford, 180, 288; admissions to, 199; athletic recruits at, 204; first-year requirements at, 248; liberal arts education at, 248–49
Statement of Principles on Academic Freedom and Tenure, AAUP, 25
State University of New York (SUNY), 138
stereotyping, 108, 300–301
stipends, 195–96
St. John Fisher College Board of Trustees, 287
Stoics, 246
Stoke, Harold W., on athletic programs, 291–94, 296
student conduct codes, 228
student loans, 207; debt from, 202

students: behavior of, 228; conceptual tools of, 256–57; confidentiality of information of, 54–55; criminal law and, 222; high-achieving, 202, 207; NTT teaching, 153–54; success rates of, in MOOCs, 180–81; teachers distinguished from, xiii. *See also specific topics*
studying, average hours spent, 262
subjective disclosure, 214–15
subjectivity, 213–14
suboptimality thesis, 261–62
substance-free housing, 227
substantial understanding, 213–14
Suits, Bernard, 298
sunēthēs (associates), xiii
SUNY. *See* State University of New York
Supreme Court, US: on affirmative action, 107; on Rehabilitation Act, 117; on Title IX, 72–73
syllabus, in FOI, 190
systemic epistemic injustice, 93, 94; addressing, 96–97

Tagore, Rabindranath, 248
TAs. *See* teacher's assistants
tax exemptions, institutional inequality and, 84
teachers and teaching: centers, 270; improvement of, 267–68; problems with suboptimal, 264–67; students distinguished from, xiii; suboptimal, 261–64; in tenure, 269; training of, 263–64. *See also specific topics*
teacher's assistants (TAs), 151
teaching aids, 191
technology: access to, 185; in FOI, 191–92
tenure and promotion (T&P), 33; invited work and, 35–39; peer review and, 36–37; unpublished work and, 39–40. *See also* academic tenure
terrorism, 3–4
test-taking, 118–20
Thatcher, Margaret, 231
Theaetetus of Athens, xiii
thermodynamics, 38
Thirty Tyrants, xiv
Thompson, Judith Jarvis, on Minimally Decent Samaritan moral obligation, 45

3D models, 192
TIAA-CREF, 146
Title IX, Education Amendments, 54, 62–63, 71, 307n7, 319n1; establishment of, 72; objectives of, 78; Supreme Court on, 72–73
Title VI, Civil Rights Act, 105
Title VII, Civil Rights Act, 72, 75
T&P. *See* tenure and promotion
transcripts, 53–54
transgender students, 9, 229–30, 303n8
transparency: in admissions, 208; at IHEs, 288; of social costs, 239
trauma, 256–57
Trujillo Molina, Rafael L., 309n9
Trump, Donald, 82, 287–88
trust. *See* chains of trust
trust-based duties, of confidentiality, 52–57
truth, 278
tuition: inequality and, 206; lowering, 206
Turner, Brock, 78
Tuskegee Institute, 244
Tuskegee Syphilis Study, 5–6, 94
Twitter, 174–75

UCLA, 225
Udacity, 180
Unconstitutional Treason Law case, 18, 20–21
undergraduates, academic freedom for, 7–8
undermatching, 202–3, 206
unions. *See* faculty unions
Unitarianism, 245–46
United Kingdom, universities in, 203
United States: admissions in, 203–4; higher education history in, 243–49; specialization in, 243
universalizability, 221
universities: autonomy of, 26; as businesses, 165–66; capital planning, 160–61; as corporations, 28–29; in eighteenth and nineteenth century, 228; epistemological foundation of, 165; idealization of, 165–66; in United Kingdom, 203. *See also specific topics*
University of Idaho, 294
University of Michigan, 294
University of North Dakota: legacy of, 283–86; values at, 284
University of Southern California (USC), 200, 204; philanthropy and, 205
University of Texas, 142, 309n5
unpopular views, punishment of, 20
unpublished work, T&P and, 39–40
unrefereed work, 37
up-or-out rules, 170
urban renewal, 309n5
USC. *See* University of Southern California
U.S. News and World Report, 141–42

values, 253
Varsity Blues cases, 90, 199
veterans, disabled, 125–27
Veysey, Laurence, 136
victimization, 101
virtuous habits, 221

Wailoo, Keith, 125, 127
Wall Street, 266
Washington, Booker T., xvi; on liberal arts education, 244–45
Washington, George, 96
Washington Post, 137
water polo, 200
webcams, 191
webinars, classrooms compared with, 193
Weiss, Paul, 91
Western Civ, 248
wisdom: in academic tenure, 28; knowledge contrasted with, 28
wokeness: academic freedom and, 10; racism and, 4
Wolf-Devine, Celia, 108–9
women, at Yale College, 91
Woodrow Wilson School of Public and International Affairs, 3
Woods, Tiger, 298
World War II, disability policy after, 125–26
Wynne, Joshua, 285

Yale College, 204, 288; women at, 91
Yalow, Rosalyn, 38

Zinshteyn, Mikhail, 141
Z list, Harvard, 201
Zoom, 184, 185, 186, 193

About the Authors

Christa Davis Acampora is Professor of Philosophy and Deputy Provost for Academic Affairs at Emory University.

Anita L. Allen is the Henry R. Silverman Professor of Law and Professor of Philosophy at the University of Pennsylvania, where she served as Vice Provost for Faculty and is a faculty affiliate in Africana Studies.

Alexandra Bradner is Visiting Assistant Professor of Philosophy at Kenyon College and Instructor in Philosophy at Capital University.

Harry Brighouse is Mildred Fish Harnack Professor of Philosophy and Carol Dickson Bascom Professor of the Humanities at the University of Wisconsin–Madison, and Director of the Center for Ethics and Education.

Steven M. Cahn is Professor Emeritus of Philosophy at the Graduate Center of the City University of New York, where he served as Provost and Vice President for Academic Affairs, then as Acting President.

Ann E. Cudd is Professor of Philosophy and Provost and Senior Vice Chancellor at the University of Pittsburgh.

N. Ann Davis is Professor Emerita of Philosophy at Pomona College, and former McConnell Professor of Human Relations.

Judith Wagner DeCew is Professor Emerita of Philosophy and Senior Research Scholar at Clark University, where she was Chair of the Philosophy Department and served as Associate Dean of the College.

Richard T. De George is Distinguished Professor Emeritus of Philosophy at the University of Kansas.

Kyla Ebels-Duggan is Associate Professor of Philosophy at Northwestern University.

Dan Edelstein is William H. Bonsail Professor of French and History at Stanford University, where he is Faculty Director of Stanford Introductory Studies and W. Warren Sheldon University Fellow in Undergraduate Education.

Deni Elliott holds the Eleanor Poynter Jamison Chair in Media Ethics and Press Policy and is Professor of Journalism and Digital Communication at the University of South Florida, where she is Interim Regional Vice Chancellor of Academic Affairs for the University's St. Petersburg Campus.

Keota Fields is Associate Professor of Philosophy at the University of Massachusetts Dartmouth.

Leslie P. Francis is Distinguished Professor of Philosophy and Distinguished Professor of Law at the University of Utah, where she is Director of the Center for Law and Biomedical Sciences.

Peter A. French is Professor Emeritus of Philosophy at Arizona State University and former Director of the Ethics Center and Chair of the Department of Philosophy at the University of South Florida.

Alan H. Goldman, who was Chair of the Department of Philosophy at the University of Miami, is Professor Emeritus of Philosophy at the College of William and Mary, where he served as William R. Kenan Jr. Professor of Humanities.

Karen Hanson is Rudy Professor Emerita of Philosophy and former Executive Vice President and Provost at both Indiana University and the University of Minnesota.

Elizabeth Harman is Laurence S. Rockefeller Professor of Philosophy and Human Values at Princeton University.

David A. Hoekema is Professor Emeritus of Philosophy at Calvin College, where he served as Chair of the Department of Philosophy, Academic Dean, and Vice President for Student Services.

Laura M. Howard is Associate Professor and Director of Undergraduate Studies in the Department of Philosophy at the University of Arizona.

James F. Keenan, SJ, is Canisius Professor of Theology and Vice Provost for Global Engagement at Boston College.

Anthony Simon Laden is Professor of Philosophy and former Chair of the Department at the University of Illinois at Chicago, and Associate Director of the Center for Ethics and Education.

Meira Levinson is Professor of Education and Society at the Harvard Graduate School of Education and Director of the Design Studio at Harvard's Edmond J. Safra Center for Ethics.

Peter Markie is Curators' Distinguished Teaching Professor of Philosophy Emeritus at the University of Missouri, Columbia, where he served as Department Chair and Vice Provost of Undergraduate Education.

Mary Kate McGowan is the Margaret Clapp '30 Distinguished Alumna Professor of Philosophy at Wellesley College.

Jennifer M. Morton is Presidential Penn Compact Associate Professor of Philosophy at the University of Pennsylvania.

Debra Satz is Vernon R. & Lysbeth Warren Anderson Dean of the School of Humanities and Sciences at Stanford University, where she is the Marta Sutton Weeks Professor of Ethics in Society, Professor of Philosophy, and Professor of Political Science.

David Shatz is the Ronald P. Stanton University Professor of Philosophy, Ethics, and Religious Thought at Yeshiva University.

Robert Simon (1941–2018) was Professor of Philosophy at Hamilton College and served as President of the International Association for the Philosophy of Sport.

Cynthia A. Stark is Professor of Philosophy at the University of Utah.

Bryan Warnick is Associate Professor of Philosophy of Education and former Associate Dean in the College of Education and Human Ecology at The Ohio State University.

Shelley Wilcox is Professor of Philosophy at San Francisco State University.

www.ingramcontent.com/pod-product-compliance
Lightning Source LLC
Chambersburg PA
CBHW050855300426
44111CB00010B/1265